Western Media System

MW00905083

Western Media Systems offers a concise, authoritative and critical introduction to media systems in North America and Western Europe. It explains how media systems developed historically and how mass media sectors, especially broadcasting and the press, are being transformed today. The book offers a wide-ranging survey and an original contribution to comparative media analysis, addressing the economic, social, political, regulatory and cultural aspects of Western media systems.

Are Western media systems converging? Against smooth narratives of media globalisation, this book argues for an appreciation of the continuing significance of nationally organised media and nation-state influence for understanding changes in media systems and continuing differences between them. It assesses the extent of convergence taking place and examines TV, newspapers, new media markets, production and consumption, journalism, political communication, media policies and regulations, and media transnationalism.

Jonathan Hardy takes a thematic approach, guiding the reader through critical issues and debates, introducing key concepts and specialist literature in an accessible style. *Western Media Systems* will be essential reading for undergraduate and postgraduate students studying comparative and global media.

Jonathan Hardy is Senior Lecturer in Media Studies at the University of East London, and teaches political economy of media at Goldsmiths College London. He is secretary of the Campaign for Press and Broadcasting Freedom (UK).

Communication and Society
Series Editor: James Curran

Western Media Systems

Jonathan Hardy

Routledge
Taylor & Francis Group

LONDON AND NEW YORK

First published 2008
by Routledge
2 Park Square, Milton Park, Abingdon, Oxon, OX14 4RN

Simultaneously published in the USA and Canada
by Routledge
270 Madison Ave, New York, NY 10016

Routledge is an imprint of the Taylor & Francis Group, an informa business

© 2008 Jonathan Hardy

Typeset in Baskerville by
Bookcraft Ltd, Stroud, Gloucestershire
Printed and bound in Great Britain by
CPI Antony Rowe, Chippenham, Wiltshire

British Library Cataloguing in Publication Data
A catalogue record for this book is available from the British Library

Library of Congress Cataloging in Publication Data
Hardy, Jonathan.
Western media systems / Jonathan Hardy.
    p. cm. — (Communication and society)
    1. Mass media—European Union countries. 2. Mass media—United States.
    3. Mass media—Ownership. 4. Mass media policy. 5. Mass media—Social aspects.
    6. Convergence (Telecommunication) I. Title.
P96.E252E8514 2008
302.23094—dc22   2008003876

ISBN10: 0-415-39691-3 (hbk)
ISBN10: 0-415-39692-1 (pbk)

ISBN13: 978-0-415-39691-2 (hbk)
ISBN13: 978-0-415-39692-9 (pbk)

To my parents, Joy and Richard

Contents

Abbreviations

ADSL	asymmetric digital subscriber line
API	application programming interface
BBC	British Broadcasting Corporation
BSkyB	British Sky Broadcasting
CBC	Canadian Broadcasting Corporation
CoE	Council of Europe
CPE	critical political economy
CSA	Conseil Supérieur de l'Audiovisuel
CUSFTA	Canada–US Free Trade Agreement
DBS	direct broadcast satellite
DCMS	Department for Culture, Media and Sport (UK)
DG	Directorate General
DSL	Digital subscriber line
DTH	direct-to-home
DTT	digital terrestrial television
DTV	digital television
EBU	European Broadcasting Union
EC	European Community; also European Commission
ECHR	European Convention on Human Rights
ECJ	European Court of Justice
ECU	European currency unit
EEC	European Economic Community
EP	European Parliament
EPG	electronic programme guide
EU	European Union
FCC	Federal Communications Commission
FTP	*Four Theories of the Press*
GATS	General Agreement on Trade in Services
GATT	General Agreement on Tariffs and Trade
IBA	Independent Broadcasting Authority (UK)
ICANN	Internet Corporation for Assigned Names and Numbers
ICC	International Chamber of Commerce
ICRT	International Communications Round Table
ICT	Information and Communication Technologies
IPR	intellectual property rights
IPTV	internet protocol television
IS	information society
ISP	internet service provider
ITA	Independent Television Authority (UK)

ITC	Independent Television Commission (UK)
ITU	International Telecommunication Union
ITV	Independent Television
MEP	Member of the European Parliament
MM-CM	Committee of Experts on Media Concentration, Council of Europe
NAFTA	North American Free Trade Agreement
NBC	National Broadcasting Company (US)
NCER	National Committee on Education by Radio
NGO	non-governmental organisation
NOS	Dutch Broadcasting Foundation
NRA	National Regulatory Authority
NVOD	near video-on-demand
NWICO	New World Information and Communication Order
OECD	Organisation for Economic Cooperation and Development
OFCOM	Office of Communications (UK)
PBS	Public Broadcasting System (US)
PCI	Partido Communista Italiana
PETV	pan-European TV
PP	Partido Popular
PPV	pay-per-view
PSB	public service broadcasting/broadcaster
PSOE	Partido Socialista Obrero Español
RAI	Radiotelevisione Italiana
RTF	Radio Télévision Française
SAGIT	Cultural Industries Sectoral Advisory Group on International Trade
STB	set-top box
TRIPS	trade-related intellectual property rights
UNESCO	United Nations Educational, Scientific and Cultural Organisation
USG	user-generated content
VJ	video jockey
VOD	video-on-demand
VoIP	voice over internet protocol
WIPO	World Intellectual Property Organization
WMS	Western media systems
WSIS	World Summit on the Information Society
WST	world-systems theory
WTO	World Trade Organisation

Acknowledgements

This book draws on the work of many scholars. I am indebted to them all, for their insights in print and for the ideas, encouragement and generosity of those I have met. I wish to thank my colleagues at UEL, Ashwani Sharma, Kathy Walker, Jane Stokes and Terri Senft and all of my students with whom I have tested ideas and arguments, principally at UEL and Goldsmiths College, London. I thank the University of East London for granting me sabbatical leave in 2007, enabling me to complete this work, and the many other colleagues there who have aided or encouraged this project. The idea for this book came originally from Professor Roger Silverstone, whom I knew all too briefly, both professionally and personally. We never discussed this book before his untimely death but I cherish his lively intelligence and spirit, and hope that this work may contribute in its own way to the encouragement of scholarship that was his own generous gift to so many. I wish to thank James Curran, from whom I have learnt so much, Rebecca Barden, whose early support for this project was immensely valuable, and Aileen Story and Charlie Wood at Routledge, who have guided me to completion. Finally, having enjoyed reading so many guilty, revelatory acknowledgements by men to their 'without whom…' partners I add my own, with deepest gratitude, to Gill.

Permissions

I am grateful to the following authors and publishers for permission to use their work in this book:

Table 2.1 World Press Association, 2007, *World Press Trends*, pp. 67–9.

Table 3.1 Sage Publications, 1998, published in D. McQuail and K. Siune (eds) *Media Policy*, p. 27.

Table 3.2 Manchester University Press, 1996, published in P. Humphreys *Mass Media and Media Policy in Western Europe*, p. 176.

Table 4.1 Polity Press and Stanford University Press, 1995, published in John B. Thompson *The Media and Modernity*, p. 17.

Table 8.1 Sage Publications, 2001, published in E. de Bens and H. de Smaele 'The Inflow of American Television Fiction on European Broadcasting Channels Revisited', *European Journal of Communication* 16 (1), p. 56.

Table 8.2 European Audiovisual Observatory, 2006, published in *Yearbook 2006: Film, Television and Video in Europe*, vol. 2, p. 18.

Introduction

This book offers a critical introduction to characteristics and differences in Western media systems. It also explores the implications of transformations shaping contemporary mass media systems. The book compares media in 18 countries across North America and Western Europe. It focuses on the mass media of print and broadcasting, especially television, as they emerged and developed into discrete forms and as they now converge and interconnect with contemporary media technologies.

Is there a need for (another) book on Western media? The tendency to extrapolate and 'universalise' media theory based on narrow perspectives and on evidence from a handful of Western societies has been powerfully condemned (Curran and Park 2000b; Downing 1996; Sparks 1998a). The field of media studies has been dominated by 'Anglo-American' research and theory, and marked by 'Western parochialism'. One response to such limitations has been to develop comparative studies of media systems, and this book seeks, above all, to draw upon and contribute to such endeavours. Comparative studies enable us to assess the similarities and differences between media systems; they can help us understand what is going on, how and why arrangements and experiences differ. They can also help to illuminate other possible media arrangements from those that exist in any one place or time.

But another challenge comes to the principal basis for comparing 'media systems': its 'nation'-based conception and orientation. Whether nation-states remain central to media cultures and policy has been a key issue in recent debates (see Robins and Aksoy 2005; Morris and Waisbord 2001). Are media best understood, asks Flew (2007: 26) 'as operating on a global scale, constituting a qualitative break with the recent past where media were primarily local or national in their scope and operations?' Such arguments have been driven, in part, by attention to transnational, supranational and subnational media developments, and by claims that new analytical frames are necessary to address the implications of globalisation, including the perceived reconfigurations of media in recent decades. Even among those most suspicious of 'globalisation theory' it has been argued that to understand contemporary media we must examine the global and then factor in national differences (McChesney 2002: 150).

This book shares a profound scepticism that nations can or should be displaced so readily in understanding contemporary Western media (Curran and Park

2000b). There has been intensifying internationalisation of media, especially over the last three decades. New media technologies realise as never before the inherent transnationalism of media forms such as broadcasting. Yet, communication systems remain, to a significant degree, national in organisation and orientation. Nationally produced television programmes dominate prime-time schedules on mass channels. Nation-states retain important powers, both formal and informal, that shape how media services are provided and received, affecting much of the news, information and entertainment that circulates. National cultural differences and traditions, differences of language, geography, political systems and power structures, economies, international relationships and histories have shaped and continue to influence media systems. It follows that we need to examine and to assess the characteristics and structures of old media *and* their reconfiguration, the local and national *and* the transverse and transnational, the persistence of 'old' mass media features as they appear *within* rapidly changing media environments. Mass, publicly mediated communication, still exists and still matters. By examining how different media systems have been shaped we can better appreciate and interrogate how they are being transformed.

Rationale and focus

This book aims to provide an introduction to the characteristics of Western media systems. The study of media is grouped into three main areas that can be summarised as production, content and audience (Thompson 1995). This book examines all three but focuses on the production and organisation of media, providing little detailed consideration of specific media texts or the psycho-cognitive aspects of reception. Its main focus is on the political, economic and cultural contexts in which mass media institutions have been shaped and organised.

Are Western media systems (WMS) converging and, if so, in what ways? That is the principal question that underlies this study. European media systems are shifting, according to Hallin and Mancini (2004a) towards a 'Liberal' or Anglo-American model whose features include a strong role for markets, limited government intervention, weak ties between media and political groups, and a 'neutral', fact-based conception of journalistic professionalism. This book takes as its main focus a review of the extent to which these features are shaping different media systems, and assesses the contemporary evidence of the forces and limits of convergence. In doing so this book also seeks to address the following questions:

- How have the mass media been organised in WMS?
- What have been the principal differences and similarities in such organisation across WMS?
- What forces (political, economic, technological, cultural and social) have shaped mass media production and performance?
- How have these forces varied in extent and influence?

Outline of the book

Chapter 1 introduces the comparative study of media systems. Chapters 2 and 3 offer a short, selective and mainly chronological account of the emergence and development of press and broadcasting systems, comparing their patterns of organisation across Western media systems (WMS). This aims to introduce and connect together, in a broadly chronological analysis, aspects of change which are subsequently examined in greater detail, but also greater separation, in subsequent thematic chapters. Chapter 4 outlines frameworks of analysis, media theory and normative, political–philosophical divisions concerning media performance which are drawn upon in the chapters that follow. Chapters 5, 6 and 7 are organised thematically around politics, policy and media markets and consider whether media systems are converging. Chapter 8 further pursues questions of media transnationalisation by addressing cultural dimensions and critical debates. Chapter 9 draws together the spectrum of analysis to evaluate evidence and arguments about the convergence and 'homogenisation' of media systems.

This book lifts many stones, each of which is teeming underneath with microcosmic life. It provides neither microscopic analysis of each nor a single, macroscopic analytical framework. Its aim, rather, is to offer an introduction, a guide and a critical assessment of salient aspects of 'Western media systems'. It reviews both recent literature and accumulated scholarship on media systems in Western Europe and North America. This study bears the inevitable particularisms, partiality and prejudice that accompany any act of selection and compilation. Moreover, it pursues and espouses concerns from a critical political economy perspective, although it is not restricted to this approach. One such theme, throughout the book, concerns the nature and influence of ownership of the media. Another closely related theme concerns the scale and quality of content diversity and plurality in 'media systems'. This is, then, a partisan text that nevertheless seeks to offer readers a reliable guide along some stepping-stones, if not to the microcosmic worlds that lie beneath each one.

1 Explaining Western media systems

This study examines the media systems of sixteen Western European countries (excluding some very small countries), together with the United States of America (hereafter 'US') and Canada. These all are developed countries, with capitalist market economies and formally democratic political structures. Our focus is on the shared characteristics and variations in their media systems. These systems are comparable in their overall patterns of economic development, and in their political history. We might go further and speak of common cultural attributes, but here the historical and the mythic can become dangerously fused. In order to understand what is meant by 'Western media systems' (WMS) we need to examine how the relevant ideas and concepts have been developed and disputed. This chapter begins by introducing some key terms and then examines how media systems have been characterised and compared.

PART 1: MEANINGS

West and Western

The classification 'Western' has deep historical roots and provenance but its various dimensions and patterns of inclusion and exclusion are complex, deeply contested, dynamic and changing. 'Western' is a historically sedimented term (Williams 1983) which has accumulated a complex range of meanings and associations over centuries. Divisions between Western and Eastern can be traced back to the expansion of the Roman Empire, while the post-1945 division of Europe into a capitalist West and communist East added further layers of sedimentation to the term. Its most straightforward meaning appears to be geographic, but the location of 'the West' is ambiguous, changeable and a matter of 'imaginary' as well as real geography. Even in geographic terms the boundaries are ambiguous and changing, as Central and Eastern Europe joins the political, economic and, to a lesser degree, cultural association of the European Union. Israel is, for some, considered a Western country, while Turkey is Eastern. Latin America, in the Western hemisphere, has historically been excluded from the 'West'.

The 'West' argues Stuart Hall (1992: 277) is a 'historical, not a geographical, construct': 'By "western" we mean [a] type of society ... that is developed, industrialized, urbanized, capitalist, secular, and modern.' This type of society began to emerge in Western Europe in the sixteenth century, but the term 'Western' now generally denotes all such developed societies, including predominantly white, English-speaking Australia and New Zealand, and even economically advanced 'Eastern' countries such as Japan. For Hall (1992) the concept of the West has served to classify societies into different categories used to explain difference and to support ideological constructions that have historically served to contrast the qualities and achievements of the West with 'the rest', the non-West.

The formation of the modern West can be traced to a period of European expansion that occurred, unevenly, between the late Middle Ages and the period known as the Renaissance which saw rapid changes in social and economic life, scientific knowledge and invention. Through this European expansion the centres of regional power gradually shifted towards Western Europe from its Byzantine centre at the eastern end of the Mediterranean basin (Amin 1988: 10–11). During the Middle Ages, the countries of Western Europe, despite internal differences, 'began to conceive of themselves as part of a single family or civilization' (Hall 1992: 289). An important factor here was the constitution of a Judeo-Christian culture and self-identity in the West, later distinguished in the nineteenth century from an East, an 'Orient', made up of Muslims, Hindus and Buddhists. From the nineteenth century European culture was (self-)conceived as a community of nations with an 'inherited civilization whose important sources are: The Judao-Christian religion; the Greek-Hellenistic ideas in the field of Government, philosophy, art and science and finally the Roman views concerning law' (Pieterse 1991: 3 cited in Williams 2005). These attributes form part of what Pieterse describes as 'mythic Europeanism'.

Cultural theorists (Said 1978, 1993; Amin 1988; Shohat and Stam 1994) have examined how a Western-centred, or Eurocentric, discourse of 'the west and the rest' (Hall 1992) came to be constituted historically and how it continues to influence perceptions and attitudes in the present. Such a discourse tends to represent the West as unified and homogeneous in its characteristics and establishes a bi-polar view generally based on simplistic distinctions and binary oppositions. The West is associated with science, technology, rationalism, secularism, individualism, development and progress. Through such terms and values the West is privileged against its 'others', the 'rest' associated with spiritualism (and primitivism). Drawing on concepts of ideology, discourse and psychoanalysis, Hall argues the 'other' is the repressed and denied 'dark' side of the discourse of 'civilization, refinement, modernity and development in the West'. Amin (1988: 10) traces Eurocentrism to the cultural reconstruction of Europe around a mythic opposition between 'an alleged European geographical continuity and the world to the south of the Mediterranean, which forms the new center/periphery boundary'. This Eurocentric vision produced a well-established version of Western history as one of progression from ancient Greece to Rome, to feudal Christian Europe, to capitalist Europe, based on arbitrary selection (annexing Christianity to Europe), exclusions (removing ancient Greece from the Orient in which it developed) and retaining the marks of racism, for Amin the fundamental basis on which European cultural unity was erected. The divisions on which Eurocentrism is constructed are essentialist, binary oppositions. But these reduce or ignore the complex patterns of interaction, fusions and formation with non-Western societies. Cultural theorists usefully highlight the discursive constructions through which global cultures are mapped, the ideological ordering of values and the investments, psychic and political in the constitution of difference. The selection and analysis of Western media systems cannot be pursued without regard to these insights.

The 'West' generally refers to the nation-states of North America and Western Europe. These are advanced, industrialised capitalist economies. All these states currently have parliamentary systems based on representative democracy and the rule of law. The nature of the political system in which they operate fundamentally shapes the operation of media firms. Historically and ideologically, these range from systems exercising tight government control over the media (forms of authoritarianism and totalitarianism) to 'laissez-faire' capitalist systems espousing no government interference. All WMS today fall between these extremes. All are 'mixed' capitalist political economies, 'in which both private individuals and government exercise their economic influence in the marketplace' (Albarran and Chan-Olmsted 1998: 5).

Europe

Europe comprises a huge range of historical, political, social, cultural, linguistic and geographical differences. Geographically, Europe is a diverse collection of 'nations, sub-nations, regions and cities' with diverse political and cultural influences and affiliations. In common is a history of 'conflict, competition and dislike' (Williams 2005: 2). The European continent stretches from the Atlantic coast to the Urals with various islands, several of which are very small states but two of which are large – the United Kingdom (comprising England, Wales, Scotland and Northern Ireland) and the Republic of Ireland. The territorial shape of the 16 has remained relatively stable since the Second World War, but there have been radical changes in some political systems, notably from authoritarianism towards multi-party democracy. Culturally, there is ongoing dynamic change, in particular as old cultural minorities and 'nations without states' (such as the Catalans, Scots and Bretons) have re-emerged to challenge European nation-states. The migration of peoples into Europe, notably from former colonies of now defunct empires of France, Britain, the Netherlands, Portugal and other powers, has also increased cultural and political diversity.

Nation

There is a complex range of terms and meanings clustered around 'nation' and 'state'. A state is a self-governing political entity. For US writers 'nation-state' is generally preferred, since its helps to distinguish the United States of America from states such as Texas, which are divisions of the federal state. However, in Europe 'state' is preferred, since nation and state do not easily coexist. There are nations without states (such as Scotland and Catalonia) and states such as the United Kingdom of Great Britain and Northern Ireland that contain more than one nation. There are also states that do not contain within their borders the whole nation (such as the Republic of Ireland). We are concerned with both legal-jurisdictional meanings of states, tracing the powers and capacity of states to influence media, and with questions of culture, and so will touch on the increasingly complex issues of the interrelationships between nations, media systems, media cultures and cultural identities.

Media and mass communications

Communications media have played a major role in the development of modern societies, in the formation of nation-states and cultural identities. People have studied communication since at least the birth of writing in 5000 BC. But it was only in the 1920s that people began to talk about 'the media', during the period when mass-circulation newspapers, films, and radio broadcasting were becoming established in their recognisably modern forms. The term 'media' came into common use when television broadcasting became commonly available in the West in the 1950s. It came to refer to technical forms of communication that provide a link between many people, in particular the 'mass media' of print (newspapers and magazines) and broadcasting (radio and television). Mass media has recently been defined as media 'intended for reception by, and which could have a clear impact on, a significant proportion of the general public' (European Commission 2007a: 6).

There are three main connected meanings of media (Williams 1983). The term refers to the *technological means of communication*, the technical 'medium' through which a message is sent and received. Media can thus refer to print, recorded sound, broadcasting, photography and film. A medium can be distinguished from delivery technologies, not least in becoming an established and enduring part of media ecosystems (Jenkins 2001: 93), even though delivery technologies may and do change rapidly. 'Media' is used in a second sense to refer to the institutional and organisational forms through which media content is produced and distributed. This refers, at its simplest, to media industries. The third main sense of 'media' is 'the informational and symbolic content that is received and consumed by readers, audiences, users' (Flew 2007: 3). John B. Thompson (1990: 219; see also 1995: 18–31) defines mass communication as: 'the institutionalized production and generalized diffusion of symbolic goods via the transmission and storage of information/communication'.

The early study of mass communication focused on the public, mass-produced media of print (especially newspapers) and electronic media, in particular radio and television broadcasting, but also encompassed the wider cultural industries of film, publishing, music, advertising and public relations. Processes of technological development and convergence of media forms, firms and markets have greatly expanded the range and rapid transformations of contemporary media.

The ongoing convergence of broadcasting, telecommunications, computing and the wider entertainment/leisure sectors has generated new media forms and integration of formerly distinct forms. In addition, the claims for what constitutes media or indeed warrants study as forms of mediated communications also lead to a lengthening, and contested, list. Today, such a list would include radio, television (analogue and digital; terrestrial, satellite, cable and other distribution systems); practices of journalism and content production for print (newspapers, magazines and other forms), electronic and internet; publishing; film and allied industries. It would include telecommunications and computing, including mobile telephony and wireless technologies, computer games and consumer media electronics, marketing communications, public relations and aspects of corporate communications and lobbying. All these may be said to constitute 'the media' today. Any omission has implications if we are to understand and appreciate the transformation of media. No media form can be properly understood in isolation, since everything from its production to consumption is affected by the influence and availability of other media. However, that does not mean that we cannot justify exclusions, but rather that the consequences of omission should be reflected upon and incorporated into analysis.

This book focuses on the public media of press and broadcasting. It seeks to follow the development paths of these media and the transformation of the markets and environments in which they operate. To this end it examines the transformation of these old media, their changing forms and patterns of production, diffusion and consumption and their relationship, including integration, with other media. It follows these media in order to trace as well a series of arguments and analyses predicated on their influence and importance for societies.

Media system

What is meant by a 'media system'? In general usage, a media system comprises all mass media organised or operating within a given social and political system (usually a state). McQuail (1992) situates media systems within different levels of media structure that may be selected for study. He differentiates a micro-level, referring to a single media channel such as a newspaper title or television station; a meso-level, referring to a particular industry 'sector' such as local radio or daily newspapers; and a macro-level. The latter refers to 'an entire (usually national) media system (or simply all relevant media)' (1992: 96). McQuail notes that macro-level analysis is an 'unusual choice', given the size and complexity of most media systems, but that such analysis can be adopted to make comparisons between national systems or within different time periods within a national system.

The concept of a 'media system' became widely used in the post-Second World War period, when states regulated nationally based broadcasting services. Historically, 'media system' was used to refer to the major mass media organised at national level, namely print media (newspapers mainly), broadcasting (radio and television), in some cases film, and occasionally allied media/industries, including advertising. In this period there was a dominant set of relationships that enhanced the heuristic value of the concept. In all Western states there were clear 'vertical' links between national governments and the organisation and regulation of the major media of public communication. Second, there were clearly dominant national media produced by large national firms in most Western states. Third, the major public media, whether national, regional or local, were predominantly organised and oriented within the boundaries of the nation-state.

The term 'methodological nationalism' is used to describe the use of concepts and tools of analysis that are bounded by a nation-state framework and to critique the ways in which social sciences remain caught up in power relations and traditions that are confined by national boundaries (Beck 2003; see also Livingstone 2003). Is it any longer appropriate to discuss media systems in terms of nation-states? This book examines that question throughout, but it also argues that the concept of national media systems retains its value as an analytical construct, as defining an object of investigation. How mass media are shaped and changed within, as well as across nation-states, remains a central question for analysis. These media systems have undergone considerable transformation. The assumptions that informed the concept of media systems must all be questioned. We need to keep open what explanations, what conceptions, are illuminating and helpful. But, this book will argue, the concepts of media systems and, indeed, of national media systems, remain indispensable, if also problematic, analytical constructs.

The concept of media system is generally used, as I will use it, for the purposes of describing features in order to go on to analyse and question how they may interconnect and relate to one another. However, the concept of system has its origins in the belief that there are necessary and dependent relationships between the parts that make up a system. This book does not pursue such a 'systems theory' approach, but the concept of system, adopted in various strands of thinking and application, needs some brief explanation. The term 'system' was first used in reference to Copernican cosmology in the seventeenth century. For Diderot (1713–84) 'a system is nothing more than the arrangement of the different elements of an art or a science in an order that makes them mutually dependent' (cited in Mattelart 1996). A system comprises primary elements (principles) that explain the other elements of the system. As Mattelart (1996: 3–25), following Foucault and others, reminds us, the concept originates in the life sciences. A system is made up of interconnecting and interdependent parts. System would later become associated with the concept of function. Ludwig von Bertalanffy first developed systems theory in the early twentieth century, conceiving of systems as a 'set of elements in interaction, oriented toward the realization of objectives'.

Systems theory is concerned with the organisation and interdependence of parts that together form a whole. This theory has its roots in structural functionalism, which draws on Durkheim and was developed by Talcott Parsons (1902–79). Functionalism proposes that human activities in societies or cultures can best be understood as complex, internally interdependent functioning systems, whose each part 'functions' by serving the successful working of the whole. Classic Parsonian fuctionalism has an inherent conservative political orientation, providing an account of the integration of social functions to produce a relatively stable social 'order'. Functionalism presupposes that there are such totalities as 'societies' and 'cultures' that function as working systems, and which are conceived of as self-sufficient. Functionalism informed sociology and anthropology in the 1940s and 1950s, especially in the US, but is no longer influential in either field. It has, however, had a more lingering influence within media theory (see Curran 2002b). Liberal media scholars developed functionalist accounts of the ways in which media serve to integrate society, while radical functionalist accounts, such as Herman and Chomsky's (1994), focused on the implication of media in the management of society on behalf of elites (see Chapter 4). According to both, the media perform determinate social functions, which are in turn assessed positively or negatively. Of more immediate concern here are functionalist conceptions of 'media systems'. In a thoroughly functionalist account, each part functions and is articulated in relation to a presupposed totality. Such analysis presupposes too much that needs to be examined and offers a highly deterministic account of the relationship between parts.

Presupposing that elements with a system are in relationships of dependency may be applicable to simple systems, or appropriate where such a level of abstraction assists analysis. In the case of complex, changing media systems these conditions do not apply. Systems theory deals poorly with the contingent, the accidental. Hafez (2007), in a recent attempt to develop a systems theory approach to media globalisation, nevertheless acknowledges that chaos theory may be a more appropriate tool, an approach developed by McNair (2006). Gurevitch and Blumler (1977) propose a systems approach to political communication (based on the assumption that features of the political communication process may be regarded as though they form a system such that variation in one of its components would be associated with variation in the behaviour of its other components). Their later work seeks to incorporate greater appreciation of diversification at all levels but argues for retaining a modified 'systems' perspective that focuses on the interaction of key types of actors (political advocates, mediators and audiences) within an 'environmental field' in order to 'specify possible influences on their mutual relations' and 'identify overall patterns that may be resulting from their interaction' (Blumler and Gurevitch 2005: 118).[1] An approach that posits functionally integrated systems seems especially inappropriate when among the central questions are what constitutes a media system, what are the units, the 'containers' and the appropriate scope for analysis of twenty-first-century media. However, examining how far and in what ways mutual relations and influences do shape communications remains central to the examination of media systems.

There is another variant, World-Systems Theory (WST), associated especially with Immanuel Wallerstein (2006; 1974, 1980, 1989). Wallerstein argues that the 'modern world-system' (not a system of the entire world but a system that is a world) had its origins in the sixteenth century and is located primarily in parts of Europe and the Americas. It is a capitalist world-economy, an interstate system of loosely bound political units and involves common cultural patterns, a geoculture. Derived from Marxism, although opposing traditional tenets, WST argues that 'world-system should be substituted for national state as the standard unit of analysis' (Wallerstein 2006: 16). World-Systems Theory has been challenged for its neglect of cultural autonomy. We will consider it further in relation to globalisation, but despite efforts by media (McPhail 2006; Gunaratne 2001) and cultural scholars (Amin 1988), WST has had little influence within comparative studies of media systems.

Media systems: approaches

There have been three main areas of focus for media system analysts. The first has been to examine how media have been produced, circulated and received and to consider the various forces influencing these processes. Such analysis has focused on media institutions and on the political and economic organisation ('political economy') of media. There have been important differences in conceiving and assessing political economy between liberal pluralist approaches and those of 'critical political economy', which are examined further (Chapter 4). But both have tended to focus on the organisation of media production and the relationships between media and other institutions. A 'media economic systems' analysis has also been pursued (Albarran and Chan-Olmsted 1998), but this may be regarded as a specialist subset of what is a broad, interdisciplinary 'media'-focused field of study.

A second approach has developed from within political science and has been primarily concerned with the relationships between media and politics within nation-states and increasingly in comparative studies. Both of these approaches have undergone important changes in response to the criticisms and insights of a third approach drawn from the heterogeneous field of cultural studies. Cultural studies approaches rejected a perceived productionist bias within social science approaches to media systems and drew on the arts and humanities to focus on processes of meaning making, the formation of cultural meanings and values, and on media consumption, use and appropriation.

Adapting Hafez (2007: 8) we can begin by identifying different implications for communication derived from a focus on 'state' or 'culture', each of which has its own justification and validity. For our study, a 'state' focus would refer to the importance of the communications space made available through the interaction of different actors and structures. This has traditionally focused on vertical sets of relationships, between government and states agencies, media institutions and audiences/publics.

A 'culture' approach focuses on 'exchanges between subjects and groups in their capacity as bearers of linguistically and historically imbued norms, ways of life and traditions' (Hafez 2007: 8). This is not limited to, but foregrounds, more horizontal relationships. This range of focus is relevant to national communication and also to the transnational, where 'state' and 'culture' map out different kinds of foci regarding international and intercultural communications (and where vertical and horizontal relationships become pressing considerations).

Within media studies there have been deep divisions between cultural studies and political economy approaches, especially during the 1980s and 1990s, and these continue to structure ongoing debates and approaches. These divisions have also been 'played out' in many senses and there are now plenty of compilations and (re)assessments available (Mosco 1996, Hesmondhalgh 2007) and collections (Ferguson and Golding 1997). We will draw on relevant aspects of these as we progress, but this book also seeks to contribute to efforts if not to integrate, at least to bring different approaches and perspectives into relationship with one another. In particular, there have been convincing calls to adopt more integrated and holistic approaches to the study of production and consumption of media (Deacon 2003, Hesmondhalgh 2007).

Culture

Media systems approaches direct our attention to apparatuses of cultural production and to the conditions and contexts within which texts are made and circulate. There has always been a cultural dimension to such studies, most obviously in consideration of cultural variations and interaction between systems and cultural consumption. Some analysts have also examined cultures of production across the media and cultures of politics and systems, for example (see Beck 2003; du Gay 1997). The vertical focus has tended to be combined with a focus on the contribution of media in fostering national cultural integration and identity. But close attention to state policies and to the range of media-producing institutions has also resulted in detailed analysis of 'minority' media. Another shared concern has been to evaluate, not merely describe, media systems in terms of their capacity to produce and serve cultural diversity.

Cultural studies approaches have drawn more heavily on anthropology and its 'long history of studying people and places in a cross-cultural and comparative manner' (Gillespie 2000: 169). The cultural turn in anthropology, influenced by post-structuralism and postmodernism (Clifford and Marcus 1986), challenged conventional conceptions of cultures as immutable and unchanging and emphasised instead that all cultures are hybrid, compounds of cultural influence and interaction, not single essences, and constantly changing. Anthropology challenged its own troubled history of collusion with the violence and cultural myths of colonialism and imperialism.

From cultural studies and cultural globalisation approaches have come important reflections on the relationship of culture, identity and place that challenge an assumed homology between nations and culture. Culture is a notoriously difficult word to seek to define (Williams 1976: 87). Its meaning has been restricted to 'great works of art' and so-called 'high' culture, or broadened to its anthropological sense to mean all the practices and distinctions that constitute a 'way of life'. For Raymond Williams, a founding figure in British cultural studies, culture was both, and he insisted on the 'significance of their conjunction' (Williams 1989: 4). 'Cultural texts should never be seen as isolated entities but always as part of a shared practice of making meanings involving everyone in a particular culture' (Couldry 2000b: 24). Williams's call to see 'culture as ordinary' was to reject bracketing culture off as a privileged and exclusionary practice. It meant attending to cultural production in terms of the 'contributions and reflections of all members of a culture', an approach which also stressed 'the political implications of how culture is organised, its material basis' (Couldry 2000b: 26).

But what is a culture? The notion of distinctive, shared culture bounded by territory has been an integral feature of nationalism. For some writers, the notion of a shared national 'culture' is always the projection of a mythic unity, inherently exclusionary and pathological (Bhabha 1994). Williams's work was a sustained exploration of the qualities and conditions for a 'common culture' whereby culture was associated with democratic expression from the people, from below as well as from above. Yet, Gilroy (1992: 3), for instance, criticises the 'cultural insiderism' of writers such as Raymond Williams for its 'absolute sense of ethnic difference' underpinning the idea that cultural differences correspond to ethnic differences and differences of 'race'. There is a 'dangerous link between essentializing notions of "culture" and essentializing notions of "race" and ethnicity; if cultures really are naturally separate and spatially discrete, that is the perfect alibi for other forms of separation (that is, exclusion and discrimination)' (Couldry 2000b: 96–7).

The classical anthropological model of culture powerfully connected the notion of a homogeneous culture to 'place'. As we shall see, another key contribution of cultural theorists has been to problematise the mapping of culture to 'place' and nation that arises in constructions of national media systems and media cultures. This spatially rooted understanding of 'culture' is being increasingly challenged (Chapter 8). This cultural model has been challenged by changes not the least of which has been the increasingly transnational, intercultural flows of people, cultural goods, movements, ideas and activities: processes of 'globalisation'. But people and cultural identities have always been more mobile, more intercon-nected and syncretic than the static typologies established by nineteenth-century anthropology would suggest (Gupta and Ferguson 1992; Couldry 2000b: 95). To examine these issues we shall explore different articulations of 'national media systems' and different understandings of the relationship between media systems, nations and cultures. In particular, having examined the formation of national media systems we shall consider different ways of analysing and evaluating their transformation. The 'new model' of culture(s), argues Couldry (2000b: 110),

> regards cultural space not as a group of separate, coherent entities called 'cultures', but as a vast space of flows whose order and coherence cannot be assumed. The role of cultural analysis, is to understand the structural forces which generate such order and regularity as exists, without assuming that order is 'natural' or 'built into' cultural space.

This approach proposes analysing the structural forces shaping cultural space without assuming and reproducing essentialist notions of culture (or function). That is the task, too, for analysis of media systems which can draw on the insights of cultural analysis to move beyond the sometimes narrow framework in which system 'order' has been conceived.

PART 2: MAPPING MEDIA SYSTEMS

Media studies has wrestled with a tradition of mapping national media characteristics that emerged in the 1950s and was influential over the next 40 years but
was also strongly criticised and increasingly discredited. Its assumptions have been
also challenged, notably by the nature and pace of 'globalisation'. Nevertheless,
there has been renewed interest in comparing media systems in recent years. This
section explores this apparent paradox and considers how – but also why – this
has occurred.

Four Theories of the Press tradition

A short, American book, *Four Theories of the Press*, marks the origins of debate on
comparing and classifying media systems. Published in 1956, the book was a
collaborative effort by three scholars at the University of Illinois. The authors,
Siebert, Peterson and Schramm, classified different media systems according to
normative concepts of what media, in particular 'the press', should do. Written at
the height of the Cold War, the book analysed media systems as emanations from
contrasting liberal democratic, communist and authoritarian political systems. The
book outlined four 'theories' or models 'which have largely determined what kind
of press the Western world has had' (Siebert *et al.*1963: 6). These are Authoritarian
and Libertarian, and twentieth-century derivatives Soviet Communism, a variant
of authoritarianism, and Social Responsibility, a variant of libertarianism.

Four Theories of the Press (hereafter *FTP*) describes how the libertarian theory of
press freedom challenged an authoritarian tradition of censorship and government control in Britain, and became enshrined in the First Amendment of the
US constitution. According to the authors, authoritarian theory has been the
most pervasive, both historically and geographically (Siebert *et al.*1963: 9), encompassing fascist and pre-democratic Europe, Asia, Africa and Latin America.

A central problem for authoritarian states has been maintaining control over
privately operated media (1963: 19). This marks a key distinction from the soviet-
communist model, in which the state holds monopoly control over all avenues of
reaching the masses (28). Libertarianism is defined as the (negative) freedom of a
privately owned press against interference by the state. The other theory, social
responsibility, draws on criticism of private media performance such as that articulated in the United States by the influential Hutchins Commission in 1947. It
marks efforts within liberalism to address perceived problems of media performance without sacrificing core libertarian principles of a privately owned press, free
from undue state control. The world could be classified into three main camps: a
liberal democratic free world in 'the West', typified by the US and UK (with internally competing tendencies towards libertarian and social responsibility models);
a soviet-communist sphere; and authoritarian states (most others, including most
developing countries and parts of Europe). This offered a simple, persuasive schema
that matched the main categories of political systems (as seen by authors) and was
intelligible within the broader division into First, Second and Third worlds.

Approach and critiques

FTP's approach has numerous, connected deficiencies. As one writer puts it (Merrill 2002: 133) there has been '[no] lack of criticism for its ethnocentric perspectives, its inconsistent structure, its questionable typology and its problematic assumptions' (see McQuail 1987; Nerone 1995, 2002; Curran and Park 2000b). Reviewing these helps us appreciate the challenges and choices made in contemporary efforts at comparative media analysis. The central question its authors pose is: why does the press 'apparently serve different purposes and appear in widely different forms in different countries?' (1963: 1). They identify several factors which may explain these differences: the level of economic and technological resources in a country, the degree of urbanisation, and broader social-cultural dispositions. But a 'more basic reason' and the book's central organising claim is that 'the press always takes on the form and coloration of the social and political structures within which it operates' (1963: 1).

Explaining media and political systems

Examining relationships (correlation) between media and political structures continued to be a central task for researchers. However, *FTP* articulates this relationship as one of correspondence between functionally integrated parts. Its argument is 'idealist' (Curran and Park 2000b: 4), since it proposes that media systems reflect the prevailing philosophy and political system of the society in which they operate. Ironically for such an avowedly anti-Marxist account, it shares features of a crude materialism in which the media (superstructure) can be 'read off' from a determining base – here comprising ruling 'ideas' and political philosophy.

To understand how the political and social system relates to the press, the authors argue, one must examine 'certain basic beliefs and assumptions which the society holds' (Siebert *et al.* 1963: 2). However, this justifies reading off both press and social system from analysis of governing beliefs (political, ideological, state). It also presumes that these beliefs hold for society as a whole – society (and indeed the corresponding media system) is conceived as unified and homogeneous in this structural-functionalist account. Consequently, there is no need to examine the complexity and contradictions within social systems, and the way these relate to specific structures, content and performance of the press. The media are conceived of as a dependent variable (Hallin and Mancini 2004a: 8–10). Changes in the media are determined by the presence of independent variables, namely the system of social control – influence, accordingly, flows in one direction. This fails to acknowledge how media may themselves impact on social structures and influence political institutions (Gunther and Mughan 2000).

Media system coherence

A key failing, then, is that *FTP* did not empirically analyse relationship between actual media structures and social systems – it examined only the 'rationales or theories' by which those systems legitimated themselves, ignoring the material heterogeneity of media. *FTP* assumes media systems are bounded, coherent and homogeneous.

Limited scope of 'media' examined

'By press', the authors state, 'we mean all the media of mass communication.' They justify their focus on newspapers on the grounds that print media are 'older' and have 'gathered about them more of the theory and philosophy of mass communication' (Siebert *et al.* 1963: 1). However, problems are compounded as the press stands as a synecdoche for media. And theirs is a narrow and now outdated notion of 'the press', one which provides (mainly political) news and information within the boundaries of the nation-state. As McQuail (1992: 66) writes: 'There is, for instance, little of relevance in any of the variants of theory to the cinema, or the music industry, or the video market, or even a good deal of sport, fiction and entertainment on television, thus to much of what the media are doing most of the time.' Focusing on a normative model of a private press, free from government interference, the book fails most obviously in providing an adequate account of Western European media, which have tended to combine a private 'free press' with state-supported public service broadcasting (McQuail 1994: 133).

Normative over empirical

The fundamental, conceptual problem with *FTP* is that 'it defines the four theories from within one of the four theories – classical liberalism ... it is specifically in classical liberalism that the political world is divided into individual versus society or the state' (Nerone 1995: 21). The book is firmly rooted in Western liberal thinking and the bi-polarism and ideological ferment of the Cold War, and the 'global promotion of the US model of privately owned for-profit media' (Nerone 1995: 7). The book exemplifies Western hubris, Eurocentrism and a modernisation perspective then dominant in mass communication research in the US and to which Schramm was a key contributor (Schramm 1964). *FTP* offers a sweeping, confident account of Western achievement and a frequently dismissive mapping of less developed systems. The book characteristically argues that many 'underdeveloped areas ... found it particularly difficult to transplant the western ideals of a free press' (57; 67).

The book's subtitle, 'concepts of what the press should be and do', highlights its normative, functionalist focus. In spite of its global claim, the book provides scant empirical comparative analysis. Only the United States, Britain, France, Germany and the Soviet Union (Russia) are examined in any detail, while other Western countries, such as Canada and Australia, are barely mentioned. So while the authors acknowledge variations within their typology, the classification deals poorly with differences in national media systems across media sectors. The influence and longevity of the four theories model has generated fierce debate. It has been an influential classroom tool, especially in the US. Numerous works have adopted the *FTP* schema and approach, whether acknowledged (Picard 1985) or not (Head 1985).

Less influential in Europe and long overdue for burial according to many critics, notably the scholars at Illinois who co-wrote *Last Rights* (Nerone 1995), it remains an important text for understanding how media and political system relationships were framed in Western media theory between the 1950s and the 1990s.

Developing the *FTP* model

The most explicit *development* of the *FTP* model has been in efforts to develop historical-normative accounts of state–press relationships and in further efforts to produce typologies of media systems (see McQuail 1992, 2005; Ostini and Fung 2002). Developments along these two paths have operated within the original schema, providing various incremental modifications. McQuail (1983) introduced two new categories: 'development theory' for developing countries whose systems had been largely ignored in the original schema, and 'democratic-participant' theory (reflecting stronger models of democracy). Picard (1985) added a 'social democratic' model (distinct from social responsibility) – one that legitimised public intervention (and emphasised media autonomy from economic as well as political power) and was based on recognition of the 'social welfare' traditions in Western Europe. Picard thus proposed three distinct models within the general category of 'Western' press. As well as the social responsibility model, there was a libertarian (free market) model and a 'social democratic' version. The social responsibility model combines a traditional liberal democratic view of press freedom with a 'capitalist, free-enterprise economic philosophy' (Picard 1985: 66). In contrast, the social democratic version 'views the private control of an institution vital to society as potentially damaging. The state must ameliorate this danger by instituting new forms of ownership, operation and management of the media, as well as by intervening in the economics of the press' (67). This interventionist view emerged from what Picard calls 'democratic socialist ideology' (67) and shaped the policies of Social Democratic and Socialist parties in Western Europe, especially after 1945.

There have also been alternative schemas which have moved further away from *FTP*, such as Altschull (1984/1995) who rejected strict categorisation but identified three broad models: market, communitarian, and advancing media systems – corresponding to Western liberal democratic; communist and reformist socialist; and developing world political systems. Many other scholars have tried to build in other ways on the deficiencies of the original schema. Ostini and Fung (2002) seek to redress the structural-functionalist focus (on state and institutional forces) by incorporating individual journalists' autonomy, professional culture and values. However, their effort to include micro-level analysis fails to avoid problems of undue generalisation, and they provide little evidence or support for their mapping.

Normative models

Can we sustain classifications of media systems? I shall examine the most recent major effort to provide such a classification, but first it is useful to identify three key criticisms that can be made of such efforts.

The narrow scope and focus of classifications

The *FTP* tradition has focused on mass media, namely broadcasting and print, but in particular on newspapers. The press oscillates here between standing synecdochically for media as a whole or being described according to particular, privileged features of press history and ideology. There is, more broadly, a strong focus on state–media (press) relationships. The result is that very many features of the media and their social, political and cultural relationships are ignored or poorly addressed. In particular, economic influences on media and the complex interaction between media power and political and economic power are neglected.

Oversimplification of media systems

Any classification system involves trading off the actual complexity within designated 'systems' for the benefits of an ordering of characteristics and their relationship. Here, classification of media systems can be related to broader issues in any comparative analysis concerning the appropriate levels of abstraction, generality and specificity. To classify media systems may require such a level of abstraction and generalisation that the results may be inherently misleading. 'In most countries', writes McQuail (1994: 133) 'the media do not constitute a single "system", with a single purpose of philosophy, but are composed of many separate, overlapping, often inconsistent elements, with appropriate differences of normative expectation and actual regulation.' McLeod and Blumler (1989: 302) introduce the term 'global typologizing' for approaches (such as *FTP*) which ignore important variations among the many press systems of the world. As well as the complexity and contradictions within 'systems', the complexity of changes over time is also poorly captured by such classification. This makes it impossible to succeed in matching a press theory with a type of society.

The fusion, and confusion, of normative and empirical

A *third* critique is that such models are invariably normative and fuse the normative and empirical in ways that hinder analysis of actual media processes. For McQuail (1992: 66), they 'involve an almost inextricable confusion between actual working principles of a given media system; the theoretical ideals of the system, and the dominant ideology of the society'. The principal charge here is that normative values overwhelm empirical observation. As we shall see, there have been great advances in empirical research, but we will also encounter arguments that comparative media analysis cannot be value-free and arguments that normative values should rightly form the framework for investigation.

Further challenges

FTP's Cold War mapping became redundant in explaining more recent changes affecting media structures – notably, geopolitical, economic, technological as well as social and cultural changes. The effort to define national media systems has been deeply challenged conceptually and in relation to material changes reshaping media, social life and political systems. For Stevenson (1999: 3), 'Arguably then, if the communications media at the beginning of the century were specifically national, at the end they have a more hybrid and global orientation.' Such key changes include:

1   Media proliferation, which defies attempts to grapple with it in a comprehensive way (McQuail 2005a)
2   Media convergence and digitalisation
3   Transnationalisation of media; the growing reach and influence of transnational media corporations, transnational media and cultural flows.

These trends have often been accompanied by the loss of any clear national consensus as to what to expect from the media in performing their public roles.

Alternative approaches

What, then, are current approaches that seek to address these challenges? We can distinguish two main ones, although these are not mutually exclusive.

Classifications which reject any built-in correspondence between political, economic and media system features

In the main, such classifications map the political and economic structures of states but leave open the relationship or correspondence with media system characteristics. Cunningham and Flew (2000: 244) propose a classification of the West, the post-colonial, the communist, and the post-communist. Curran and Park (2000b) offer two axes – political and economic – and then divide the world into authoritarian and democratic political systems, and neoliberal or regulated economic systems. They also add a useful fifth category of 'transitional or mixed societies' for 'countries' being transformed or regions with mixed regimes' (13). This approach is most evident in national, cross-national studies.

Comparative analysis of media systems

The main alternative has been efforts to develop classifications derived from comparative analysis. Rooted in social-scientific approaches, comparative researchers have sought to examine the interrelationship of variables shaping media systems, thus shifting from normative classification to empirical study of variables. This work has thus been empirically based but, on the whole, rejects empiricism and is theory focused, particularly in challenging theories of media derived from the experience of 'a few untypical countries' (Curran and Park 2000b: 15).

The comparative method has two basic functions, it serves in the formation and clarification of concepts and it has a role in causal inference and analysis (Hallin and Mancini 2005). A good example is Humphreys' *Mass Media and Media Policy in Western Europe* (1996). His book explores the relationship between the economic, technological and political factors that have shaped European media systems and examines similarities and the differences between them. These are highly comparable systems, all modern capitalist liberal democracies with many common historical and cultural attributes. But Humphreys' central premise is that:

> while economic laws and technological developments point generally towards historically convergent outcomes, nationally specific political and cultural factors will explain much of the divergence ... Put simply, media systems can be expected to vary significantly across countries because politics and policy have made a difference.
>
> (Humphreys 1996: 2)

Hallin and Mancini's *Comparing Media Systems*

A major, recent contribution to the comparative research tradition has been Hallin and Mancini's *Comparing Media Systems* (2004a), an analysis of 18 Western democracies: the US, Canada and most of Western Europe. It is based, like Humphreys, on 'most similar systems' design, which for Lijphart (1971) is a means of reducing the number of relevant variables by focusing on a set of relatively comparable cases. Hallin and Mancini (hereafter H&M) aim to assess whether 'systematic connections between political and mass media structures' (xiii) can be identified. But they emphasise that their study is necessarily exploratory. With comparative research at a 'relatively primitive' stage, their stated aim is to enable the formation of concepts and hypotheses about the interrelationships, or co-presence, of key variables in media and political systems, arguing that causal inference (seeking to determine causal relationships between variables) belongs to a more advanced stage of analysis (H&M 2004a: 5).

Based on this study, they propose three 'models of media and politics'. These are the Mediterranean or 'Polarized Pluralist' model; the North/Central European or 'Democratic Corporatist' model; and the North Atlantic or 'Liberal' model. As these titles indicate, each model predominates in different countries and regions but is also centrally defined by political system characteristics. The Mediterranean or polarised pluralist model (Italy, Spain, Portugal and Greece) is characterised by the relatively late development of capitalism, industrialisation and democratic traditions. In these largely agrarian societies, feudal relations persisted and the landed aristocracy remained key sources of power into the twentieth century. In the North and Central European model (Germany, Austria, Switzerland, Scandinavia, and the Benelux ['Low Countries'] countries: Belgium, Netherlands and Luxembourg), the power centres of the *ancien régime* were weakened earlier in the nineteenth century. In this 'Democratic Corporatist' model, traditions of power sharing among groups representing different political and cultural interests became more formalised, along with the development of a welfare state in the mid twentieth century. In the North Atlantic or liberal model (USA, Canada, UK and Ireland) there was a stronger influence of classical liberalism, favouring a more restricted role for the state, checks on governmental power and greater freedom for capital.

They identify four key dimensions that characterise (and influence) national media systems:

1   *Development of the media market.* The degree and shape of development of media markets, with particular emphasis on newspapers and the mass circulation press.
2   *Political parallelism.* Political parallelism refers to the character of links between political parties and the media and more generally the extent to which media reflect political divisions.
3   *Journalistic professionalism.* The degree (and direction) of development of journalistic professionalism (associated with formal professional bodies and 'differentiation' of the field of journalism).
4   *The role of the state.* The degree and form of state intervention in the media.

Hallin and Mancini identify a series of five political system variables. We shall examine these in Chapter 5, but to summarise, these are:

1   The role of the state (including policy and regulation).
2   The nature of formal political systems and democratic rule.
3   The role of interest groups and their incorporation into political structures.
4   Rational-legal authority and clientalism. This addresses whether the rule of law (rational-legal authority) prevails over other means of allocating resources. Clientalism refers to a pattern of social organisation in which access to social resources is controlled by patrons and delivered to clients in exchange for deference and various kinds of support (H&M 2004a: 58). One form this takes is a media owner using their media to bargain with political elites.
5   Moderate *vs* polarised pluralism. This distinguishes the depth of 'system' agreement between political parties, an example of a 'polarised' system being post-war Italy with anti-system communist and fascist parties.

Using these sets of variables, H&M explore relationships between political system characteristics and media structures. Unlike the *FTP* tradition, however, they argue that such connections rarely take the form of one-to-one correspondences. Rather, factors of political structure interact with other factors (technological, economic, social, cultural) as well as specific features of media industries and market structure.

One of the main differences between the three models concerns 'political parallelism' – that is, how far the media are integrated into factional politics. In 'Polarized Pluralist' countries, they argue the newspaper press historically served elites. A mass press developed comparatively late, if at all. Weak media markets prevented a strong press emerging and, without a strong civil society, the press remained tied to political loyalties under state influence. In 'Democratic Corporatist' countries, strong media markets with professionally autonomous journalists developed, but were heavily influenced by civil society organisations. In the early twentieth-century 'pillarisation' in Dutch society, for example, broadcasting was organised under separate associations rooted in subcommunities – Protestant (Calvinists), Catholic, socialist, liberal. In 'Liberal' countries strong media markets developed earliest of all and there was the strongest development of a non-partisan view of journalistic 'objectivity'.

H&M's study both extends and repudiates the *FTP* tradition. The authors are critical, above all, of the failure to analyse empirically the relationship of media systems and social systems. They seek out connections between patterns of development of media systems and key characteristics of political systems. But they reject crude causal accounts, instead emphasising the 'co-evolution' of media with other social structures and the 'co-presence' of particular variables. Theirs is a highly reflexive account, undertaken with explicit awareness of ethnocentrism and Western hubris even while acknowledging that it cannot evade such deeply imbued patterns of thought. It seeks to decentre rather than privilege any particular model and eschews efforts to project Western models onto a global classification of media systems.

Comparing Media Systems is a major achievement and advance. Stimulated by a need to challenge and correct deficiencies in *FTP*, in many respects it completes the burial of that tradition. Yet it also shares some of the limitations of the *FTP* tradition. First, problems of classification remain. The authors emphasise the considerable imprecision in allocating countries to what they accept to be 'ideal types'. For instance Britain, the United States, Canada and Ireland are all grouped under the 'Liberal' model. These countries may be inevitably linked ('Anglo-American' media), but they are heterogeneous. Britain has more in common with the North European model, not least because of a strong public broadcasting system. This begs important questions. Is the liberal norm the US (low 'political parallelism', minimal public broadcasting) or Britain (partisan press, strong public broadcasting)? Neither France nor Germany, among the largest European states, fits easily into their respective 'Polarized Pluralist' or 'Democratic Corporatist' boxes. H&M do offer lots of careful caveats on applying their classification within WMS and strongly reject the imposition of their categories onto other systems, as *FTP* did. In a later essay (H&M 2005: 232) they go further: 'We hope that our research will serve as an example of how to do comparative analysis, how to think about media systems and their relation to political history, structure and culture, rather than as a set of categories for classifying media systems.' This book will draw upon but also re-evaluate their framework and assess its adequacy.

Second, there is an underlying indeterminacy concerning the temporal dimension of the three ideal types. The authors argue that they were most distinguishable up to the 1970s but are now converging towards the liberal model. Close attention to historical development and change is also in tension with the fixity of 'ideal type' classification.

The third area concerns the explanatory range and scope of media systems. Scholars have highlighted Hallin and Mancini's neglect of some system-differentiating factors, including country size and regionalism (McQuail 2005b; Remington 2006). More significantly, their account is focused on news media, on the way in which news and information is organised and how this serves political opinion formation. Defending this focus on 'news media and media regulation', they write: 'A comparative analysis of media systems could certainly include much more about cultural industries – film, music, television and other entertainment; telecommunication; public relations; and a number of other areas. But this would involve other literatures and require very different sets of concepts' (2004: 7). From the perspective of efforts to develop a conceptual framework, this focus may be amply justified. However, it is an unavoidable challenge if our aim is to describe and analyse the characteristics of contemporary media systems. Even on its own terms, news media and broadcasting cannot be adequately understood if entertainment (what media do most of the time) is neglected. In order to compare mass media systems we must incorporate entertainment and examine broader dimensions of media production and cultural exchange. We need a wider mapping of media than is offered in the *FTP* tradition and sustained by H&M's focus on political communication. The relationship between popular culture and official/elite culture (Martin-Barbero 1993) is one relatively neglected area. Another is that of media that crosses, or lies outside the frame of, national media, including transnational media, ethnic minority, diasporic, radical and alternative media. H&M offer rich empirical material and sophisticated theorisation of media systems in formation, but this needs to be built upon and broadened. As they highlight, however, the scope of cultural industries is very large. My study does not purport to overcome the deficiencies of selecting a partial focus. It aims rather to contribute by offering a shifted focus, brought into relationship with the ground covered in greater depth by Hallin and Mancini. To this end it focuses more heavily on broadcasting, and in the later chapters on developments since 1970.

Conclusion

Recent research has answered the need to move away from normative, ethnocentric models towards properly comparative studies combining empirical analysis and theoretical consideration of differences between media systems. This resurgence has occurred in the context of new challenges to the value and validity of comparing national media systems. Various globalisation theorists propose that a post-national analysis is more appropriate and highlight the erosion of nation-state powers across politics, the economy, culture and media. As Chapter 8 examines, some otherwise radically opposed perspectives agree that global forces are eroding national particularities. However, as Chadha and Kavoori note (2005: 86) 'what is often overlooked in ... analyses of globalization ... is the structural and institutional transformation of media systems that has occurred in the context of the phenomenon at the *national* level'. Further, as Straubhaar (2002: 203) affirms, while 'cultural production boundaries are being most powerfully changed by the expansion of capitalist market economy forms into almost all nations', 'nation-states still have the power to define crucial structures for media production'. The political economy, cultural and communications policies of nation-states still play a very important role in determining how media industries and markets are organised.

There is a need, argue Chadha and Kavoori (2005: 100), 'to develop a model of media globalization that recognises the continuing role of the national and conceptualizes the phenomenon in terms of a convergence of policy orientations, market developments and programming trends within countries'. Here comparative analysis of media systems can make a significant contribution, investigating how the national is being transformed and rearticulated, while attendant to the complexity and unevenness of globalisation processes. H&M's analysis offers qualified support for the thesis of global convergence in Western media systems. Differences between the models that were 'quite dramatic' in the 1970s, they argue, 'have eroded to the point that it is reasonable to ask whether a single, global media model is displacing the national variation of the past ...'. But, deferring consideration of answers, this approach also offers a necessary corrective to the neglect of the state and of the national level within theories of globalisation (and localisation). In focusing on the nature and problem of media systems, comparative analysis can offer an important bridge between traditional studies of (national) media, which are no longer sufficient, and new media and globalisation perspectives, which have tended to neglect nationally based media, even though this forms a crucial part of their smooth and frequently overstated narratives of transformation. As the authors of an important earlier work in comparative media scholarship, *Comparatively Speaking*, put it (Rosengren, McLeod and Blumler 1992: 286):

> even if and when a world symbol system should be common to all of us, we would no doubt keep the regional, national, and local symbol systems of our own for a very long time to come. The interplay between the common world system and those spatially more restricted systems would actually offer fertile ground for a large number of comparative studies ...

2 Media system evolution

This chapter provides a brief comparative history of Western media systems. It illustrates how different histories and political, economic, social, cultural and religious as well as geographic factors help to explain the different characteristics of media systems. It begins by focusing on the historical evolution of systems of mass media and the patterns of development across Western systems. Here, it describes the relationship of media and political systems and the development of the mass media of newspapers and broadcasting.

On media history

Media historians have made three claims that this chapter (and book) seeks to illustrate and confirm. First, media systems are shaped by different histories. The shape of individual media systems reflects the histories of different peoples, regions and nations (Williams 2005: 3). Second, in order to fully understand media systems today it is essential to understand the early development of the press (H&M 2004a). Third, how media systems developed continues to influence and help explain aspects of their current form and the differences between them. Such historical patterns of development are also important in understanding international communications (Thussu 2006: xvii).

If formative history is important, so too is the way in which that history is conceived and constructed. The history of media and communications systems has been a specialist and often neglected aspect of broader historical research. But selecting media as the focus runs risks of mediacentrism, of privileging media in ways that fail to assess the relationship of media with broader political, economic and cultural processes. In particular, there are dangers in basing an account of changes in media systems on the identification of media forms and tracing their 'history' of technological development and diffusion. Mediacentric perspectives tend to bracket off modern (mass) media from the long history of multiple forms and ideas of communication (Mattelart 1996).

One of the central arguments in media history concerns ways of understanding innovation and change. What Raymond Williams and others identify as technological determinism is the tendency to conceive of technology as a self-acting force whereby change arises from media technologies themselves (Williams 1974: 13–14). As Anthony Smith (1993: 4) elegantly puts it:

> we remain prisoners still of an essentially Victorian idea of the requisite constituents of social change, in the sense that we tend to predicate the transformation upon the technology. We relate and chart development according to a measure of machinery, alongside the evolution of inventions.

Another tradition, popularised in the work of McLuhan (1994 [1964]) but developed in more thoughtful ways by historians such as Harold Innis (1991 [1951]), has examined the influence of media technological development on cultures. McLuhan asserted the centrality of media forms and their self-acting influence, tracing their characteristics, 'irrespective of the people who use them, the organisational structures within which their providers operate and the purposes for which they are used' (Briggs and Burke 2002: 12). This debate, then, concerns how we assess the medium of communication in relation to its context of production and in relation to uses of systems of communications.

There are many common features in the development of media in the West from around 1500. Similar forces of technological and economic development, of the growth of markets with rising literacy, for example, are evident and help explain some common patterns of development of mass media. However, there are also marked differences in the ways media systems developed. If economic forces and technology tended to produce similar development paths, other factors including politics, policy and culture shaped variations. Press systems all evolved largely along free market lines, and economic dynamics and technological developments tended to generate similar development paths, but the political-economic, policy and cultural environment (including readership, market size and characteristics) gave rise to variations (Humphreys 1996: 2). How newspapers developed, in particular mass-circulation papers, marks one of the most obvious differences in Western media systems. Hallin and Mancini (2004a) offer the most ambitious and comprehensive effort to trace these different patterns of development. Some countries such as the United States, Britain and most of Northern Europe had developed a mass-circulation newspaper industry by the late nineteenth century, with highly industrialised production and a mass consumer market expanding in the early twentieth century. Elsewhere, notably in Southern Europe, circulation remained low and a mass press did not emerge until into the twentieth century, if at all, with broadcasting becoming the first mass medium. Those countries that did not establish a mass press by the early 1900s never did so fully, subsequently, and so historical differences help to explain the sharp variation in patterns in contemporary newspaper circulation (see Table 2.1). The differential development of newspapers influenced in turn the different roles the print and electronic media played in media systems in the twentieth century (H&M 2004a: 22–3).

PART 1: PRINT MEDIA

Printing spread rapidly though Europe following the invention of the movable letter press using metal type by Johann Gutenberg around 1450. Printing had been practised in China and Japan since the eighth century and Western invention may have been influenced by developments in Korea, but it took off in Europe, paving the way for the production of books, pamphlets, 'chap books' (booklets sold by 'chapmen' or pedlars) and later newspapers. The needs of a growing class of merchants and traders were served by the circulation of printed information and the development of postal systems for communication. Early printed materials were a mixture of official and semi-official notices of government decrees, political and religious tracts and speeches, descriptions of noteworthy or sensational happenings, actual or fictitious. Most material was one-off rather than serial or periodical and was sold by street hawkers, especially in growing urban areas. The invention of the printing press, introduced to England in 1477 by William Caxton, marked the beginning of a transformation in the capacity of books, pamphlets and print reproduction to reach people.

In their social history of media, Briggs and Burke (2002) emphasise the importance of understanding media in relation to the wider range of available resources for communications among social groups in any given historical period. 'To think in terms of a media system means emphasizing the division of labour between the different means of communication available in a given place and at a given time, without forgetting that old and new media can and do coexist and that different media may compete with or echo one another as well as complement one another' (Briggs and Burke 2002: 22–3).

To understand the development of newspapers we must understand their formation within media systems – within the range of communications media used in particular societies. Oral culture, coterminous with human civilisation, and reaching highly sophisticated form in the ancient world, remained a principal means of dissemination and exchange, interacting with print reproduction which allowed stories, songs and 'news' to circulate more rapidly and extensively. The earliest European news organs were hand-written official news bulletins in ancient Rome (Barker and Burrows 2002: 5). Painting and visual representations (with their attendant and diverse structures of production and patronage systems for religious and secular works) remained highly influential. Gutenberg's alphabetic type circulated alongside printed images, particularly important in cultures with very low literacy rates. Other forms of communication, including music and spectacle as well as increasing adoption of vernacular languages, amply justify Briggs and Burke's (2002: 40) provocative claim for the presence of rich 'multimedia communication' in early modern Europe. Then, as now, old media forms coexisted with and interacted with 'new' media. Manuscripts survived as major channels for the public circulation of messages into the early modern period (44–6).

Europe and 'print capitalism'

In the sixteenth century the pre-eminence of Latin (the language of the religious and political elites, scholarship and education) was rapidly supplanted (Anderson 1991: 18). More and more books were published in vernacular languages. The movement known as the Reformation challenged clerical mediation and emphasised direct access to the divine. Martin Luther, a German pastor and university professor, encouraged reading of the Bible in the vernacular. Only a minority of the population in Western Europe could read, but print forms, including printed ballads, enabled wider circulation within oral cultures. What Anderson calls 'print capitalism' marks the interaction of early forms of capitalist production by printing businesses and the growth of linguistic diversity. Once the elite Latin market for print was saturated, the potentially huge markets represented by monoglot masses were opened up for capitalist development. For Anderson, print capitalism made it possible for rapidly growing numbers of people to think about themselves and to relate to others in profoundly new ways (36), marking the early formation of national consciousness and identity. His main argument is that the possibility of imagining the nation only arose when three fundamental cultural conceptions (all of great antiquity) lost their ideational influence:

1   the idea that particular script language offered privileged access to ontological truth (religious community)
2   the belief that societies were naturally organised around high centres of authority (dynastic realms)
3   a conception of temporality in which cosmology and history were indistinguishable.

The slow decline over centuries of these interlinked certainties occurred first in 'Western Europe' under the impact of economic change, the 'discoveries' arising from trade and travel, navigation to the 'new' world, science and arts, and the development of increasingly rapid communications. One of the important resources for this new consciousness was printed information. Through reading vernacular texts, individuals became aware that they belonged to a corpus of readers, virtual in the sense that they would never meet more than a fraction of the larger community, but all connected through the medium of print. Thompson (1995) highlights weaknesses in Anderson's account: the precise nature of the link between the development of printing and the rise of nationalism is not spelled out in detail. Anderson's compelling theory focuses on explaining the phenomenon of nationalism, offering a very limited account of the nature and impact of communication media as such (Thompson 1995: 63). In his efforts to remedy this deficiency, Thompson focuses on early periodical literature to argue that its emergence marked a transformation in patterns of communication in early modern Europe. Print made it easier to accumulate and circulate data about the natural and social worlds as well as to stimulate and meet renewed interest in the classical texts of antiquity. The church, an important network of communication, began to lose its monopoly over religious authority as print contributed to the diffusion of Protestantism from Northern Europe. Above all, it was the growing class of commercial traders whose information needs were served by print capitalism, and it was the commercial bourgeoisie who played a key role in the development of newspapers, as success in market economies depended on a steady flow of reliable information about prices and conditions for trade.

Early newspapers and public spheres

The development of the newspaper press arose through a mixture of political, economic and cultural conditions which varied across countries and regions. In some cases market capitalism, in others political and religious struggles, were key stimulants. In Britain, a combination of commercial expansion, the influence of Protestantism, and the struggle against absolutist monarchy and towards parliamentary democracy influenced the comparatively early development of newspapers. More generally, newspaper growth was associated with rising forces of capitalism and of political liberalism challenging systems of absolutist, monarchical rule and feudalism, and growth depended upon the expansion of a literate middle class. How the press developed also depended on the nature of political authority and controls. The early response by political and religious authorities to print, to the production and circulation of political and religious ideas and arguments, was censorship and authoritarian control (Thompson 1995: 56–58; Siebert *et al.* 1963). However, during periods of intense political and religious conflict, such as the wars of religion in France (1560s–1590s) and the Eighty Years' War in the Netherlands (1568–1648), pamphleteering flourished (Briggs and Burke 2002: 85–7). In 1607 corantos ('currents' of news), short newsletters, began to appear in Holland, and by the 1620s Amsterdam was the centre of an expanding trade in news. The first regular newsletters were produced in 1609 with *Aviso* in Wolfenbüttel and *Relation* in Strasbourg (H&M 2004a: 148). Periodicals or *Messrelationen* appeared in Germany in the sixteenth century. Rapidly, early weekly journals emerged along the major trade routes in several European cities in Germany and the Netherlands. The first newsletters or early newspapers began circulating in Britain around 1620. In France the first official newspaper, *Gazette*, was founded in 1631. In Germany, the first daily newspaper was *Einkommende Zeitung*, published in Leipzig in 1650. London did not have a daily paper until 1702, France 1777 and America 1783. A weekly provincial press developed in England from 1701 and in France from the 1750s (Barker and Burrows 2002: 6).

According to Hallin and Mancini (2004a), the development of a mass press depended on several structural elements that distinguished most of Northern from Southern Europe. Newspaper growth depended on the expansion of a literate middle class. The early growth of mass literacy was closely connected with the spreading influence of the Protestant Reformation. Early industrialisation and the growth of market institutions contributed to growth of a mass-circulation press, while the demands of local bourgeoisie for particular local news and information, what has been called 'local patriotism' (Anderson 1991), stimulated the creation of papers serving growing urban communities.

In Germany and the Austro-Hungarian empire, aristocratic and absolutist rule remained strong and the transition to a liberal order took place later than elsewhere. Nevertheless the development of a large commercial and industrial middle class was sufficient to support many of the institutions of the emerging social order, including a strong mass-circulation press (H&M 2004a: 146; Humphreys 1996). In parts of Northern Europe, in the Netherlands, Switzerland and Belgium, feudalism was weaker and a class of merchants had dominated society from the early seventeenth century. Even where, as in Scandinavia, industrialisation developed late, ascendant mercantilism stimulated early newspaper growth. Commercial centres where news was both available and of greatest value became the most significant and innovative journalistic centres: Venice in the mid sixteenth century, Amsterdam in the seventeenth and London in the eighteenth century. The first newspapers evolved from handwritten Venetian gazettes, which pioneered the publication of diverse sets of reports in a single, dated issue, a format which became highly influential and remained commonplace for over two centuries. Venice was a major centre for printing and early journalism (Chalaby 1996, Barker and Burrows 2002), but the expansion of printing was undermined by the Counter-reformation led by the church in Rome. In 1501 Pope Alexander VI sought to establish a more comprehensive system of censorship permitting only books approved by ecclesiastical powers to be printed, and from 1559 the church established an *Index librorum prohibitorum* of banned books, a system maintained for four hundred years (Thompson 1995: 56–7).

It is argued that the print culture of Protestantism challenged an image culture of Catholicism, which promoted icons, images and the rituals of the Latin mass to a largely illiterate populace, although it would be misleading to substitute a stark opposition here in place of the actual interweaving of text and image in both cultures (Briggs and Burke 2002). Nevertheless, most Mediterranean countries underwent very different patterns of newspaper development, and religion was an important factor. Catholicism dominated in France, Italy, Spain and Portugal. In most of Southern Europe the bourgeoisie was smaller and weaker than in Northern Europe and feudalism was more deeply rooted, enduring into the early twentieth century. In the early medieval period the Mediterranean was the centre of power in Europe and the heart of expansion in trade, innovation and culture that gave rise to powerful military empires as well as to the development of humanist, artistic and scientific thought in the Renaissance. It was Southern European traders, notably the Phoenicians, whose quest to expand trading with the East led to the 'discoveries' of the New World. But in the seventeenth and eighteenth centuries, during which newspapers developed, most Mediterranean countries did not develop the urban capitalist middle class or the industrial productive sectors found in Northern Europe. Early newspapers were tied more closely to the aristocracy, whose wealth depended largely on landownership and agriculture rather than on trade (H&M 2004a: 91).

In Britain newspapers developed during a period of political upheaval that challenged absolutism. Publication of domestic news was forbidden until 1641, the eve of the English Civil War when conflict between the monarch, Charles I, and the Long

Parliament gathered pace. Star Chamber, the system of strict government licensing of printing and censorship established under the Tudors, was abolished in July 1641, after which corantos began to devote more attention to domestic news and political and religious opinion. Stricter controls were reimposed after the Civil War and strengthened by Charles II, until the Glorious Revolution (1688) put an end to absolutism and the Licensing Act lapsed in 1695, bringing to an end the elaborate system of state censorship and control of printing through the Stationers' Company that had existed since 1557 (Briggs and Burke 2002: 94; Humphreys 1996: 19). The ending of direct state censorship was a turning point in the development of the British press (Williams 1998). Soon, tri-weekly papers emerged such as the *Flying Post*, the *Post Boy*, *Post Man*, whose titles attest to the importance of postal communications. Alongside the twice-weekly official paper, the *London Gazette* (circulation 6,000), unofficial papers such as the *Post Man* achieved circulations of 4,000. The first daily paper, the *Daily Courant* (1702–35), established by Samuel Buckley, was financed by the government and established during a period in which both political parties and the parliamentary division between government and opposition were being formed. During the reign of Queen Anne, politicians and parties owned or financed papers to mobilise opinion and factional support and to compete in an environment of intense political argument and propaganda. New literary journals were also formed, circulating a mix of social and political comment including Jonathan Steele and Joseph Addison's *Tatler* (1709–10) and *Spectator*, Daniel Defoe's *Review* and Jonathan Swift's *Examiner*.

The modern press emerged over a period of 300 years from 1600 to the early 1900s. During that time most Western states moved from trying to control printing presses (licensing) and content (what was said and who could speak) to new forms of legal and economic controls. In Britain, political elites opposed the unchecked expansion of the press, fearing rebellion by the poor against the propertied classes. Efforts to re-establish licensing were unsuccessful, but in 1712 the Stamp Act was introduced which taxed newspaper publishers one penny for each printed sheet and one shilling for every advertisement. The aim of this and subsequent Acts was to restrict the production and circulation of newspapers among the poorer, labouring classes. Economic measures were accompanied by frequently brutal enforcement, leading to the imprisonment, sometimes execution, of publishers and editors. Yet, repressive measure did not prevent the development of a radical press in the eighteenth century, comprising unstamped, unauthorised papers and later successful stamped papers such as *Reynolds News*. The various Acts, which taxed newsprint, paper and paid advertising, the so-called 'taxes on knowledge', delayed the development of a commercial mass press until the later nineteenth century (O'Malley 2000). Britain did, however, establish a thriving newspaper industry earlier than most European nations (Chapman 2005: 22). Annual consumption of newspapers rose from 7.3 million in 1750 to 12.6 million in 1775. In 1785 the *Daily Universal Register* was founded, which became *The Times* on 1 January 1788, Britain's oldest surviving daily newspaper with (near) continuous publication. Launched as a government-subsidised news-sheet, from 1803 *The Times* began to develop its own newsgathering capacity and built its reputation as a powerful and influential authority on news and political affairs ('the Thunderer').

One of the principal theorists of the early public sphere is Jürgen Habermas (1989). In *The Structural Transformation of the Public Sphere* (1989) Habermas attributes a pivotal role to the periodical press, which provided a new forum for public debate and contributed to the formation of public opinion. With the exception of the Dutch Republic, the development of a permanent bourgeois public sphere in Europe lagged behind Britain, where conditions were most favourable (Briggs and Burke 2002; Thompson 1995: 69–75). Historians have criticised Habermas's neglect of the earlier political press from the Civil War period (Thompson 1995: 72), of the plebeian press that emerged in part as a counter public sphere (Negt and Kluge 1993), and for inattention to 'national or other cultural specificity' (Calhoun 1992b: 34). Nevertheless, Habermas's historical account, while imperfect, has considerable merit and his normative model of the public sphere, an idealisation of actual historical processes, continues to inspire critical assessments of media systems (Chapter 4).

The press in Western Europe

In France, the press was subject to censorship and control during the long reign of Louis XIV; minimal public criticism of the regime was permitted. Before the French Revolution there was only one official daily paper, *Journal de Paris*, and newspaper publishing became an underground industry, production largely being undertaken abroad (Chapman 2005: 15). In the eighteenth century, absolutism was challenged by a rising movement of Enlightenment thinkers (Voltaire, Diderot) advocating greater social justice and freedom, and the exercise of reason to govern the conduct of states and individuals. Radical ideas stimulated the growth of a more challenging and outspoken press and calls for press freedom. In the first year of revolution, there was an explosion of new publications, with some 250 founded in the last six months of 1798. By the mid 1820s Paris was the centre of a mass-circulation press, with more papers sold than in London. *Le Petit Journal*, selling 250,000 copies in 1863, had, arguably, the largest circulation in the world (Briggs and Burke 2002: 194) and in 1890, after repeal of the last French newspaper tax, it was the first newspaper to sell one million copies (Tunstall 2008: 337). The press in France, however, was subject to massive swings between repressive control and freedom during the eighteenth and nineteenth centuries, at the end of which the modern press in the twentieth century was markedly smaller than in most Northern European countries.

The institutional structure of the British press, its journalistic practices and legal framework, was exported to Britain's colonies. Stamp duty, extended to the North American colonies in 1765, became one of the principal points of conflict in the lead-up to the War of Independence. Within a decade American newspapers 'changed sides' and began opposing the British empire (Tunstall 2008: 333). By 1775 there were some 42 different newspapers in the American colonies, and these 'assisted the emergence of a new imagined community, defined against the British' (Briggs and Burke 2002: 98). By 1800 in the United States there were 178 weeklies and 24 dailies.

If newspapers tended to serve geographically defined communities, their information sources were nevertheless international. Early newspapers relied heavily on foreign papers and handwritten newsletters, which they 'recycled shamelessly' (Barker and Burrows 2002: 7). For Tunstall (2008: 332), the newspaper was initially an international medium through which foreign news circulated around Europe. Foreign news was generally safer to print, as governments censored domestic news. By the mid eighteenth century newspapers could draw on official publications such as government gazettes. But increasingly, if often under extremely repressive state measures, journalists found an editorial voice.

Press freedom and regulation

Governments and political elites could use a variety of means to restrict the content and circulation of the press, chiefly licensing, taxes and legal measures. In addition, patronage, political subsidies and bribery were common. In pre-revolutionary France only news reproduced from the official *Gazette de France* was permitted. Journalists could be imprisoned at the sovereign's pleasure, a fate bestowed on over 800 publishers and writers. In the Netherlands papers required special privileges in order to publish, and domestic public affairs news was heavily restricted. Despite such draconian powers, *ancien régime* governments tended to lack the machinery to monitor the press effectively. As the eighteenth century progressed, governments recognised their dependence on the press, for instance recognising its strategic importance in influencing policy circles in foreign states (Barker and Burrows 2002: 8), and began a gradual shift from reliance on suppressing information towards news management techniques.

Freedom of the press emerged as the guarantor of freedom of expression, within liberal democratic theory. As McQuail (1987: 123) states:

> From the seventeenth century onwards, in Europe and its colonies, the newspaper (or similar print publications) was widely seen as either a tool for political liberation and social/economic progress, or a legitimate means of opposition to established orders of power (often both at the same time).

Freedom of expression was first legally established in Western Europe in the latter part of the eighteenth century. The 1789 Declaration of the Rights of Man and Citizens in France and the First Amendment of the US Constitution 1791, both influenced by the radical English emigré Tom Paine, produced foundational statements of press freedom. Two decades earlier, in 1766, Sweden's parliament adopted a Freedom of the Press Act (Humphreys 1996: 19). The post-revolutionary French constitutions of 1791 and 1793, building on the 1789 Declaration, explicitly protected freedom of expression. However, the brief period of press freedom was successively diminished by the Directory, the Consulate, Napoleon and monarchist Restoration (Humphreys 1996: 20; Chapman 2005: 25). It was not until the Third Republic that measures were reintroduced in 1881 to protect the press from a priori administrative action (in Britain termed 'prior restraint').

Significantly too, the political and legal framework which defined the parameters and possibilities of the press, as well as the broad contours of societies and economies, were to a high degree co-extensive with national borders, even in *ancien régime* Europe (Barker and Burrows 2002: 1).

According to liberal theory, the 'free press' arose from the struggle to remove state controls and restrictions imposed by licensing or censorship. Here, press freedom is premised on the importance and implications arising from the press's role as 'watchdog'. Prefiguring such articulations, Matthew Tindal, in *Reasons Against Restraining the Press* (1704), likens a free press to 'a faithful centinel [who] prevents all surprize, and gives timely warning of any approaching danger' (cited in Keane 1991: 14). The protection of the press's right to criticise the state acts in turn as insurance against despotism, either through alerting citizens about threats to their liberties, according to the notion of natural rights, or by circulating ideas which, according to Enlightenment belief in the efficacy of rational thought, ought finally to prevail against falsehood or tyranny. The utilitarian case for liberty of the press put forward in the nineteenth century by Jeremy Bentham, and developed and modified by J. S. Mill in *On Liberty*, is that it acts as a counterweight to despotic government or more pervasive, uncontested belief systems. The press is also conceived as a conduit for 'public opinion' to government, providing a vehicle for the circulation of ideas and opinion vital to ensuring an informed citizenry.

Immensely important for comparative analysis is the First Amendment of the American Constitution (1791), which has continued to influence policy and media not only in the US but internationally: 'Congress shall make no law… abridging the freedom of speech, or of the press …'. In James Madison's original draft: 'the people shall not be deprived or abridged of their Right to speak, to write, or to publish their Sentiments; and the Freedom of the Press, as one of the great Bulwarks of Liberty, shall be inviolable'. In a period of numerous, intensely political and partisan newspapers, the drafters were concerned that the dominant party or faction in power might outlaw opposition newspapers, as happened in much of Europe, unless they were explicitly prohibited from doing so.

While the First Amendment asserts an absolutist claim, what followed was a complex history of judicial interpretation about the scope and application of constitutional protection for 'speech' and expression. In the years after its drafting the First Amendment was often interpreted narrowly as leaving regulation of the press to the states rather than the federal government. Then, under the Federal Alien and Sedition Act 1798, press freedom was curtailed. It was fierce controversy over this Act (allowed to lapse in 1800) which contributed to the emergence of more libertarian interpretation of press freedom, upholding the right of the press to criticise government. Rulings of the Supreme Court on a spate of cases dating from first years after the First World War entrenched the more modern, libertarian interpretation of press freedom as a 'negative' right to freedom from state interference, although, in practice, US supreme court judges have upheld various legal 'restrictions', including state regulation of broadcasting.

In Europe, press freedom was formally established in several countries by the early nineteenth century. Norway established laws protecting press freedom in

1814, the Netherlands in 1815, Denmark in 1848 (H&M 2004a: 147). Belgium recognised press freedom in the Constitution of 1831 and abolished its taxes on knowledge in 1848. Following abortive revolutions across Europe in 1848, press freedom was introduced into Denmark (Constitution of 1849) and Switzerland, in both indicating the strength of bourgeois liberalism against comparatively weak feudalism. Even where absolutism was stronger, such as in Germany and Austria, press laws were partly relaxed. Pre-publication censorship was abolished in Austria (1862) and Germany (1874), although post-publication censorship and interference was actively maintained (Humphreys 1996: 21), and in 1878 (until 1888) the powerful Chancellor Bismarck outlawed the publication of socialist opinion. As the bourgeoisie grew stronger in the latter half of the century, press laws were liberalised even in countries that remained authoritarian. By the early 1900s the concept of press freedom had widely taken root across Western Europe.

Towards a mass-circulation press

The 'taxes on knowledge' created by the British state in response to the expansion of the press in the early eighteenth century created a 'new system of regulation' (Williams 1998: 25). The clamour for press freedom grew, with popular champions such as John Wilkes, and celebrated cases where juries threw out efforts to apply draconian laws against publishers for criminal or seditious libel. The Chartist reform movement of the 1830s, involving an alliance of middle- and working-class action, was partly built through radical communication networks in which illegal, unstamped papers played a key role in circulating information and ideas about resistance to 'old corruption'.

　After the threat of revolution had receded in Britain with the demise of Chartism, stamp duty was abolished in 1855, and other taxes were repealed in the period from 1853 to 1861. The state moved to a position whereby, formally at least, 'it claimed no power to interfere significantly in the content of the press' (Ward 1989: 39)

　In what was, and in general terms remains, the orthodox account, press freedom was achieved through progressive liberalisation of newspaper publishers from state control and interference. Repeal of taxes opened the way for the creation of cheap, mass-circulation newspapers. However, Curran examines how 'market censorship' supplanted state controls as what remained of a working-class political press was largely defeated by the new market conditions that required increased capitalisation and a readership attractive to advertisers in order for papers to remain competitive (Curran and Seaton 2003: 24–37). According to O'Malley (2000: 18), while most pre-publication censorship ended:

> Other kinds of relationship that involved devices for controlling and manipulating press content remained after the 1860s and formed part of a wider set of tools which successive governments used to influence the development and content of other forms of mass communication like radio and film.

New legal restrictions were imposed through the Obscene Publications Act (1857) and first Official Secrets Act (1889). The position is summed up by Robertson and Nicol (2002: 2): 'no generalised right of free expression, however common in rhetoric, entrenched itself in law'. But as well as highlighting the persistence and modification of state controls, critics highlight the impact of market controls and what Curran calls the 'licensing' power of advertising. According to this argument, market controls were more effective than the state in suppressing the radical, alternative press, and so in limiting the range of political expression available in the media.

The journalism of the French Revolution was innovative in political expression but was produced using technology that had barely changed since the sixteenth century. In the nineteenth century, especially from the 1830s, the pace of technological development was rapid in the US and the advanced economies of Europe. The American press in the early nineteenth century comprised a number of papers that were small-scale and undercapitalised and whose contents tended to reflect the personal or political predilections of owners, many of whom also edited their papers. The business prospects in America, though, were promising, with greater peace and political stability than in Europe. The vast distances between cities and communities gave newspapers a key role in communications, alongside and aided by the telegraph. Distance also prevented the establishment of a 'national' daily newspaper press. Rather, geography and market conditions allowed small, community papers to survive. The most commonly found newspaper in the early 1900s was a weekly serving dispersed rural communities and this provision persisted well into the twentieth century, alongside city papers and the growth of chain-owned newspapers.

Before the technological advances of the late eighteenth century printers gained no significant savings from increasing capacity (no 'economies of scale'). Increasing capacity by means of a second press required the hiring of additional printers and compositors. An important breakthrough was the König steam press first used to print *The Times* of 29 November 1814. In place of older presses capable of printing some 250 impressions per hour, König's machine impressed 1,100 per hour, and by 1830 steam presses could produce 4,000 impressions per hour. The steam press required huge initial investment and accelerated the transformation of newspaper production into a large-scale, capital-intensive industry, although that transition was already under way in Britain by 1800 (Barker and Burrows 2002). By the end of the eighteenth century most London papers were large-scale businesses with several shareholders, a salaried editor and a small staff of journalists. In the 1830s increasing investment in more efficient mass production, advertising finance and cultivation of a mass audience through cheaper and more popular papers emerged. This phenomenon, known as the 'penny press', occurred first in the US with the daily *New York Sun*, established by Benjamin Day in 1833 and selling 34,000 copies by 1838. Reaching sales of 5,000 within four months, the paper's success confirmed Day's conviction that there was a market for a paper that did not support any political party (Ward 1989: 27). By no means all US papers followed these trends; the model that persisted in most small towns in America was the newspaper run by a single printer-editor. Many newspapers continued their traditional role as channels of commercial intelligence or (party) political opinion and a significantly diverse diasporic press also emerged (see below). Yet, henceforth, journalism in the US developed predominantly along commercial lines.

Industrialisation and concentration of ownership

When and how an industrialised mass press was established marks out formative difference in media systems. The forms of newspapers that emerged also varied considerably in terms of journalistic cultures and styles, production and organisation, the status and reflexive image of 'journalists', newspaper content, audience and orientation. Among the conditions which gave rise to a commercial mass press was growing demand and capability to supply. Industrialisation and slowly rising prosperity among the working classes brought increased purchasing power and access to sufficient leisure to purchase and read newspapers. The growth of literacy was essential here, with markedly different rates of literacy, in general low in Southern Europe and relatively high in Northern Europe and America. Literacy rates were highest in North-Western Europe, where, by 1800, over half of adults could sign their name (see Barker and Burrows 2002: 9). In Britain the expansion of mass education after the 1870 Education Act was pivotal, although literacy was already spreading beforehand. Market expansion depended on improvements in the economics and supply of newspapers, such as improvements in paper production (shifting from cloth to wood pulp), printing technology, but also distribution (railways) and the collection and circulation of news (telegraph). The popular newspapers that reached their developed form in the 1890s were, argues Tunstall (1977), the first major mass media form pioneered in the US and then copied around world.

In Britain the birth of an industrialised press is associated with the so-called 'Northcliffe revolution'. Alfred Harmsworth (later Lord Northcliffe) graduated from publishing small magazines to purchasing and developing the *London Evening News*, 'a paper that exemplified the new popular style of journalism of the 1890s, with concise and lively stories, simplified news reporting, greater use of illustrations and more varied typography, and a women's column to enhance the paper's appeal to a wider audience' (Gorman and McLean 2003: 10). Harmsworth went on to establish the *Daily Mail* in 1896, a national morning newspaper which achieved a circulation of around one million by 1899. Populist papers such as the *Daily Mail* and *Daily Express* were strongly jingoistic, reflecting and promoting the British empire in an era of strongly nationalistic and imperialist newspapers from the 1870s into the 1940s and beyond. The significance of the 'Northcliffe revolution' also lay in the economic reorganisation of the newspaper industry, which became intensely capitalised and more dependent on advertising finance. Northcliffe's *Daily Mail*, aimed at a 'mass' but relatively affluent readership, was attractive to advertisers and was the first British newspaper to accept display advertising, including whole-page adverts. Instead of charging advertisers for space, Northcliffe charged per 1,000 readers and established circulation figures which eventually led to other publishers agreeing to the establishment of an Audited Bureau of Circulation (ABC) in 1931.

From the 1880s there was increasing reliance on advertising revenue to keep pace with rising costs of production and distribution and keep cover prices low. The *Daily Mail* became the first halfpenny paper, with the masthead slogan 'The penny paper for half penny' (Williams 1998: 59). The increased importance of advertising changed not only the structure of the British press but also newspaper content. The 'Northcliffe revolution' marked the emergence of an enduring feature of the British press, the polarisation between mass-circulation tabloids ('down-market' and 'populist') and up-market, elite broadsheets with small circulations (see Williams 1998; Sparks 1999). Quality papers were under economic pressure to concentrate on readers with high purchasing potential. The increasing acknowledgement of the growth and importance of women as consumers, confirmed by early market research in the 1920s and 1930s, led newspapers to try to offer more content that was appealing to women readers. Finally, in Britain but especially in the United States, the economics of advertising, with its demands to reach a consumer mass audience that cut across political and class divides, reinforced pressures for greater objectivity and 'neutrality' in news reporting (Baker 1994; Schiller 1981). In the US advertising expenditure rose from $40 million in 1881 to over $140 million by 1904 and a billion dollars in 1916 (Briggs and Burke 2002: 207).

The industrialisation of the press ushered in changes in newspaper ownership, which became increasingly concentrated. In the United States the press continued to serve local markets but 'chain ownership' grew in the late nineteenth century. By the 1870s big newspaper companies were among the largest manufacturing firms in the US (H&M 2004a: 203). One new entrepreneur, E. W. Scripps (1854–1926), owned the largest chain of papers, while another, William Randolph Hearst (1863–1951), established a cross-media empire, by 1918 owning 31 newspapers and six magazines as well as interests in cinema and telegraphic services. In Britain, Northcliffe had amassed a large press empire by 1921 and, together with his brother Lord Rothermere, owned three national dailies (Northcliffe's *The Times*, *Daily Mail* and Rothermere's *Daily Mirror*) and Sunday and regional newspapers.

In Canada there were imitators of the US penny press in the 1830s, but the commercial press took off in the 1880s. In Ireland the first penny paper was established in 1859, shortly after the Great Famine (1845–51). Ireland was then part of the United Kingdom of Great Britain and Ireland, following the 1800 Act of Union, repeal of which was the central demand of a growing nationalist movement. Most newspapers supported the union with Britain, while the *Freeman's Journal* (1763–1924), the oldest nationalist paper in Ireland, represented the Irish Parliamentary Party in the 1880s and the movement for 'Home Rule' (Horgan 2001: 6). The first commercially successful modern newspaper was the *Irish Independent*, launched in 1905, into which the *Freeman's Journal* was incorporated in 1924.

The market forces that shaped the commercial press in Britain and America developed more slowly in continental Europe, notably advertising revenue. In

Germany strict advertising controls held back the development of a commercial press (H&M 2004: 158), but by 1914 there were over 4,200 titles: nearly half were 'non-political' newspapers called 'General Anzeiger', heavily dependent on advertising. Few sold more than 15,000 copies, with the exception of the *Berliner Morgenpost* selling nearly 400,000 copies as the First World War began. Whereas in Britain and America commercialism supplanted party political ties, in Germany half the German press remained politically aligned on social class and ideological lines. Liberal and radical papers had emerged from the Revolution of 1848, including the *Neue Rheinische Zeitung*, which Karl Marx, among others, founded. In France, during its 'golden age' for newspapers (1881–1914, see H&M 2004a: 92), *Le Petit Parisien* reached a circulation of over 2 million, the largest in the world. However, the industry was never as profitable as its US and UK counterparts, drawing smaller advertising revenue. By the 1930s the French press was in decline and cartels, corruption and collaboration under Nazi occupation all damaged its post-war development.

The press in Southern Europe

In Southern Europe there were commercial newspapers in the 1880s, at the same time as a mass-circulation press was developing in Northern Europe, North America and East Asia, but 'a true mass-circulation press never fully emerged in any of the Mediterranean countries' (H&M 2004a: 91). The economic and political conditions for a mass press were not present until the mid twentieth century, by which time radio was already an important medium and television was beginning to emerge. Hallin and Mancini qualify their argument by highlighting the growth of a mass newspaper market in post-dictatorship Spain and Portugal in the 1970s and 1980s. The process of industrialisation went furthest in France but, despite a large population, the press industry remained weak in both France and Italy (Humphreys 1996: 36). Table 2.1 shows daily paid sales per thousand and also paid and free paper circulation in 2006. While the figures largely confirm Hallin and Mancini's account, the increasing readership in Greece marks an important shift; Ireland's recent readership growth and the expansion of free papers, while uneven, indicates resilience in the medium.

In Southern Europe newspapers (whether commercially owned or linked to parties or the church) have been directed, for most part, to an educated elite interested in the political world (H&M 2004a: 95). In contrast to the stratified market that emerged in Britain, tabloid or sensationalist popular papers did not emerge and remain virtually absent from the Mediterranean region, with the exception of *France Soir*. In Southern Europe the roots of journalism lay more strongly in a literary public sphere, dominated by aristocratic interests, rather that the bourgeoisie. In Italy the clergy, closely associated with landowning aristocrats, made up an estimated 50 per cent of Italian journalists in the nineteenth century. Historians highlight a journalism of ideas and opinion: intellectual, literary and political, that developed across the Mediterranean (Chalaby 1996, 1998). Another marked difference was the economic and professional status of journalists. In Southern

Table 2.1   Daily newspaper sales per 1,000 adult population (2006)

	Paid sales 2006	Paid sales % change from 2002	Paid and free newspapers 2006
Norway	601.2	−10.06	601.2
Finland	514.7	−0.74	561.0
Sweden	466.2	11.06	624.1
Switzerland	370.5	4.34	554.9
United Kingdom	335.4	−3.87	385.3
Austria	340.7	10.25	435.9
Germany	297.9	−9.35	300.2
Denmark	287.3	−11.51	766.1
Netherlands	287.0	−11.13	357.2
Greece	282.0	−2.79	334.8
Ireland	245.2	35.36	295.7
United States	241.2	−5.18	259.4
Canada	169.5	−8.63	232.8
Belgium	163.4	−3.46	189.3
France	155.8	−5.7	198.7
Italy	115.9	−4.49	214.8
Spain	109.8	−1.13	242.3
Portugal	74.7	12.7	113.9

Source: World Association of Newspapers, World Press Trends 2007.

Europe and France 'the failure of the press to attain a sufficient level of financial independence made it more difficult for journalism to develop as a profession and establish its autonomy from the state and political groupings' (Williams 2005: 66). In much of Northern Europe, Britain and North America forms of professionalism became institutionalised; salaried journalists and trade unions developed codes of ethics early in the twentieth century, principles of autonomy and editorial independence were emphasised and schools for journalistic training were established. What constitutes 'professionalism', however, is complex and contested, as the privileging of 'Anglo-American' models of journalism is challenged by appreciation of the conditions in which different journalisms developed (Chapter 5).

Market differences

Markets vary considerably in the balance between national, regional and local papers. In some countries (Britain, Austria, Spain, Italy) national or large-regional papers predominate, in others local papers serving cities or smaller regional areas predominate (US, Canada, Switzerland) while others have a greater mixture (Germany, France, Scandinavia). It was a technical and economic challenge to print and physically distribute the same product over a large area, particularly for daily newspapers and for the highly 'perishable' commodity of news. In Britain a stratified national press emerged in which papers competed fiercely in their respective markets (elite broadsheet, mid market and tabloid). A key factor was the availability of a railway network enabling speedy distribution across a relatively small land mass. In Britain, the national press was heavily concentrated in a single city, the capital, London. The railways meant London newspapers could reach most of the country and compete with provincial dailies, 78 of which were established between 1855 and 1870 (Chapman 2005: 56). There were, additionally, large circulation newspapers in Scotland and cities in England and Wales and a thriving local press, until paid papers went into decline in the twentieth century.

In the vast United States, newspapers remained local, serving geographically distinct markets, with some 1,500 papers remaining today. Advances in technology (low-powered satellites and computing) enabled the *Wall Street Journal* and later *USA Today* to become the only properly national papers, printed and distributed from multiple sites across the country. *USA Today*, launched in 1982, was simultaneously printed in 17 cities. In most of continental Europe a substantial local press grew alongside a very small number of titles with a wider remit (Sparks 2000a). For instance, today the largest-selling paper in France is a provincial daily, *Ouest France* (781,668 in 2006). In Europe and in small communities in the US a decentralised, local and regional press, facing less intense competition, survived into the twentieth century and local papers, under increasingly consolidated ownership, remain very important aspects of national media systems today.

The press and political parallelism

Commercialisation transformed newspapers from small-scale enterprises into highly capitalised and often highly profitable businesses. In 'liberal' systems there was a shift from an older patronage model in which papers were dependent on subsidies and on support from 'wealthy individuals, communities of readers, political parties or the state' (H&M 2004a: 203). In general, growing financial independence, through sales and advertising revenue, allowed increasing independence from organised political, interests. However, the political links and affiliations of the press took very different forms in different system and in different periods.

The changes that took place in US journalism are especially associated with the movement from political partisan journalism towards journalistic objectivity, detachment and neutrality in recording news (the objectivity norm). According to Schudson (1978, 2003) the ideal of objective journalism was born in the US. For Williams (2005: 63),

> The emphasis on facts and objectivity accorded with the commercial needs of the Anglo-American press. By presenting the facts and allowing readers to draw their own opinion of them, newspapers were able to sell to more people, across a broad range of political views and attitudes.

From the 1830s publishers began to loosen ties to political figures, parties and interest groups and to cultivate selling news to audiences. Papers such as the *New York Times* (launched 1851) professed to adopt a balanced line, (in the twentieth century explicitly separating 'news' and 'views' (Briggs and Burke 2002: 193). Objectivity and political de-alignment served the interests of advertisers seeking to reach an aggregated consumer audience that was not fractured along political lines. Commercialism thus 'entailed a political secularisation process' (Humphreys 1996: 29). Another important factor was concentration of ownership. The economic dynamics of advertising encouraged monopolisation, as advertisers' decisions tended to favour the larger and more cost-effective papers, driving out competitors. This structural outcome (of the many decisions of advertisers about where to place their adverts) needs to be distinguished from intentionality, not least because the resulting monopoly of supply was an often adverse and unintentional outcome of these cumulative decisions (see Baker 1994: 101–3; Curran 1978). Daily newspaper competition began to decline around 1890, shortly after the role and extent of advertising in the print media began a long-term expansion (Baker 1994: 14).

Overall, the economic rationale was that, with less bias, more readers would be attracted to a paper. According to Donsbach (1995: 19), by the beginning of the twentieth century the main traits of American news media were established, and comprised 'press freedom and commercialism, a relatively rigid system of job specialisation and management organisation, a recognised role as a common carrier that required journalists to cater to a mass audience, and a core work ethic consisting mainly of objectivity, fairness and detachment'.

In liberal systems, as Hallin and Mancini emphasise (2004a: 203), '[c]ommercialization did not mean that the press lost all ties to political parties, nor that it ceased to play a political role; instead, it meant that the press, its editors, and its owners became independent political players as time went on'. This was especially the case in Britain in the era of the 'press barons' (1910s–1930s), such as Lord Northcliffe, who 'saw newspaper ownership as a means by which to impress their views on politicians and political parties as well as shape the pressing issues of the day' (Williams 1998: 63). Northcliffe claimed a new kind of legitimacy for his newspapers as 'representative' of their readers in the same way that politicians represented voters. The expansion of advertising had created a more 'independent' national press, freed from dependence on political parties, but one whose economic framework limited the range of voices that could be heard. Proprietorial intervention was certainly not new, and indeed Curran argues that pressures to maximise audiences led to a downgrading of political coverage. Curran's principal critique is that the press controlled by the barons 'helped to sustain the social order by stigmatizing its radical opponents', and reinforcing their middle-class readers' opposition to progressive change, until a new social democratic press emerged in the 1930s and 1940s (Curran and Seaton 2003: 49).

The period between the First and Second World Wars was a 'golden age' for the political press. Sharp ideological divides and strong political polarisation enhanced demand for overtly political papers. However, the range of political papers was greater in continental Europe. In Britain the party-aligned political press was small, except for the communist *Daily Worker* ranged against a right-wing tending mass press. In the US and Canada the commercial press was already well established before significant labour movements had emerged, and the movements' papers achieved only small circulation; the largest, *Appeal to Reason*, had a circulation of 760,000 in 1912 (H&M 2004a: 206).

In the so-called 'Democratic Corporatist' countries, the patronage model associated with particular powerful individuals declined with industrialisation of the press. Newspapers either became profitable commercial businesses or continued with the support of representative institutions such as political parties, churches and trade unions. In contrast to liberal countries, a strong political press tied to organised social-political institutions was a major feature well into the 1970s. Principles of publicity developed early and strongly, characterising both political systems of parliamentary democracy and the press as a social institution. In 'pillarised' Dutch society almost two-thirds of the press was aligned to Calvinist, Catholic, Liberal or Labour social groupings. In Southern Europe newspapers were often not profitable, and so tended to have greater dependence on subsidy from political actors. A political press emerged in the nineteenth century, with fluid lines between the spheres of journalism and politics, which played a key role in the national development in Italy and Spain. In Greece newspapers developed mostly as small-circulation political papers aimed at elites.

Hallin and Mancini's North Atlantic model is characterised by the early development of a mass-circulation press based on private ownership under conditions of relatively high 'press freedom'. Commercial newspapers came to dominate and political parallelism was low, with the important exception of the politically partisan press in Britain. The North Central European model also features early, and high, newspaper circulation and early development of press freedom, but is characterised, they argue, by the coexistence of features that are seen to be incompatible within 'Anglo American' media theory (2004a: 144–5; 195–6; see Chapter 5):

- the simultaneous development of a strong, mass-circulation commercial media and of media tied to political and civil groups
- the coexistence of political parallelism and journalistic professionalism
- the coexistence of liberal traditions of press freedom with traditions of strong state intervention in the media (seen as social institution not a purely private enterprise).

A history of strong party papers coexisting with a commercially oriented press continued well into the twentieth century until it faded in the 1970s.

News agencies and internationalisation

Newspapers have remained a predominantly national or subnational medium. Complex flows and dependencies structure newsgathering, but the production and consumption of newspapers and television news remains overwhelmingly national and local (Chapter 8). However, there has always been an important transnational dimension, from the early circulation of foreign news to the use of technologies such as the telegraph to enhance the gathering and circulation of news in the nineteenth century. News agencies, established by or allied to imperial powers, were the first global media organisations (Herman and McChesney 1997; Thompson 1995). Three Western powers, Britain, France and Germany, dominated, together with

Russia. After the Second World War, the US emerged as an 'information super-power' (Thussu 2006: xvi) and key agenda setter in international communications. American news agencies Associated Press (AP) and United Press Association (UPA) came to dominate world news media in the 1950s (Tunstall 2008: 345). During this period the empires of the old European powers were being transformed by decoloni-sation and by struggles for independence in their former dominion territories.

The other presses

Our account has highlighted different patterns in the development of a mass press in Western media systems, but this developed in complex relation to 'other' presses. All systems have also included a radical or 'alternative' press, whose size, form and influence has varied with political and social conditions. The religious press has often been influential, with papers such as Bayard's *La Croix* (France) achieving a circula-tion of over 105,000 in 2006, mostly to subscribers by post. Minority ethnic groups established newspapers where political and economic conditions allowed, while settle-ments and movements of people created additional markets for foreign newspaper sales. The United States in 1914 had 160 foreign-language daily newspapers, the majority in European languages: 55 German, 12 each in French, Italian and Polish, 10 in Yiddish, 8 in Spanish and 8 'bohemian' Czech (Emery and Edwin 1996: 9, cited in Tunstall 2008: 342). US immigrants came especially from Central, Eastern and Southern Europe, where newspapers tended to be heavily censored. Papers were carriers of 'old country' sentiment and some battled on behalf of independence move-ments in 'home' states, but these papers also served as an 'Americanizing agency', mediating American ways of behaviour for their readers. Well-established German-language papers that had reluctantly switched from German nationalism to American nationalism during the First World War went into steep decline after 1918 (Tunstall 2008: 343). Newspapers served other immigrant communities with ten Japanese and five Chinese dailies by 1914, and by 1920 five Arabic-American dailies.

By the time radio emerged in the 1920s there was growing talk of crisis in the newspaper press. Critics on the left condemned the increasing concentration of ownership and the monopoly of voice in right-wing dominated press systems such as Britain and America (see McChesney and Scott 2004). Liberals criticised the perceived falling quality of journalism that accompanied commercial expansion and popularisation. Whatever it was doing, the press was not serving as the basis for the free exchange of different views on matters of public concern. The aspira-tions for broadcasting must be assessed in this context.

PART 2: BROADCASTING

Newspapers have overwhelmingly belonged to the private sector in modern liberal democracies. The requirement that states organise the allocation of scarce wave-lengths placed radio, then television, in the public domain. The 'free' press was subject to limited prior interference in editorial content; by contrast, radio and television were subjected to close supervision. Governments had no choice but to act to resolve the problem of wavelength scarcity and determine the criteria for awarding broadcast licences. But broadcasting regulation was never merely a technical matter. All governments, democratic or otherwise, took a keen interest in a medium through which messages entered directly into private homes.

Telegraphy had been quickly established on a transnational basis, connecting empires and trading partners and necessitating international agreement between states on interoperability (Mattelart 1994; Ó Siocrú *et al.* 2002). Radio and television were developed largely in a national mould. All WMS exercised sovereignty over the licensing and regulation of national broadcasting in the post-war period and, although under different and greater pressures, retain these powers today (Chapter 6).

Models of broadcasting

Three main models of broadcasting emerged in Western media: state, commercial and public service. In the state model, which existed in Austria, in Fascist Italy and in Germany in the 1930s, and in Greece, Portugal and Spain under authoritarian regimes, the state organises and controls the monopoly provision of broadcasting. In the public service system, established in Britain, post-war Germany, Italy and most Western European states, broadcasting services are provided by organisations formally independent of the state but subject to regulation and insulated from commercial pressures – which dominate the third, commercial model. However, in some democratic states such as France (until 1982) and Denmark, public service broadcasting (PSB) was established under direct state control.

By the early 1930s US broadcasting was firmly established as a commercial system. Broadcasting would be privately owned and operated, funded by advertising, and free at the point of use once you had bought a radio set. America was the only broadcasting system to develop in this way. The different ways in which broadcasting has been organised and developed mark the most profound differences between the United States and post-war Europe. These systems have interlocked materially and symbolically, through the flow of programmes, formats, talent, business practices and ideas, but also through mutual hostility and reaction. The spectre of American commercialism haunted European policy makers and cultural elites while US policy and governing opinion rejected 'state' directed provision and its perceived lack of responsiveness to consumers. Both North American and Western European broadcasters (except in Luxembourg) were subject to public regulation, with services licensed by either the state or appointed public authorities. Yet broadcasting has been the most decisive marker of difference between the US and European media systems, especially when PSB dominated in Western Europe between 1945 and 1980. And even in a post-broadcasting era, debates about the convergence of media systems remain largely based on consideration of the qualities and characteristics of the US broadcasting model introduced in the 1930s.

US broadcasting

In the United States radio was allowed to be built and operated by private firms, but with certain regulatory parameters designed to safeguard the public interest. As Comstock observes (1989: 16) 'the federal government aligned itself with the values of private enterprise in devising a system of broadcasting, and then, in accord with the deep-rooted American distrust of those same values, established a means to temper the outcome'. Broadcasting developed in keeping with the country's traditional liberalism, distrust of government ownership and promotion of 'free enterprise'. The fundamental principles and the institutional structures established in the 1920s persisted over several decades (Galperin 2004). But the establishment of a commercial system was not automatic; it arose from protracted struggles between different interests during the first decades of the 1900s. Aside from military use, early radio adopters were mainly amateur enthusiasts accessing distant radio signals. Commercial broadcasting (one-to-many transmission) began in 1920 and expanded quickly (Smulyan 2001). Under the Radio Act of 1912 the federal government had issued licences and allocated station frequency, power and time periods in an effort to minimise signal interference. But radio proved popular, commercial interests jumped in to take up frequencies, and the allocation was soon exhausted. Commercial licence holders established the National Association of Broadcasters (NAB) and sought government action to protect their incumbency rights. However, in 1926 a US district court ruled that the Department of Commerce did not have the power to prevent the Zenith Corporation using another frequency from the one assigned; a free-for-all ensued, bringing 'chaos' to the airways. That same year, RCA (Radio Corporation of America) created the first radio network, really an amalgamation of several national companies involved in radio manufacture that by then dominated radio. The court ruling also provided impetus for the creation of a government radio regulatory body. The 1927 Radio Act re-established control with the creation of the Federal Radio Commission.

Radio manufacturers had initially proposed that national network programming should be paid for out of sales of radio sets. However, programme costs increased. For instance, early programming relied on amateur musicians, then professionals persuaded to play for free, but who soon began to organise and to demand fees. The payment of royalties was the principal demand of the American Society of Composers, Authors and Publishers (ASCAP) formed in 1922. Increasingly radio production costs were met by sponsorship from commercial advertisers. This led to a shift towards programming that would attract larger national advertisers to sponsor radio programmes (Smulyan 2001).

The battle for control of radio broadcasting

The orthodox version of US broadcasting history describes the establishment of rapid support for a commercial system. In fact, there were a small but significant number of non-profit radio stations created, and there was a struggle, particularly in the period 1928–35, to shape the development of the US system (McChesney

1993). One coalition, the National Committee for Education by Radio (NECR), sought unsuccessfully to ensure that dominant portions of US broadcasting would be non-profit and non-commercial. The NECR preferred the newly created British Broadcasting Corporation (BBC), established as a public corporation, considering this arrangement 'ideal' in many respects, although politically impossible to establish in the US. Some campaigners placed hopes in the inauguration in 1933 of a reforming Democrat President, Franklin D. Roosevelt, whose New Deal sought to ameliorate the excesses of monopoly capitalism. But Roosevelt backed the agenda of commercial radio. Significantly, Roosevelt had access to the nation via radio, and through his innovative 'fireside chats' could bypass the strong ideological opposition he faced from a largely Republican-supporting newspaper industry. The 1934 Communications Act supported the demands of incumbent national broadcasters. Calls for 25 per cent of channels to be reserved for non-profit broadcasters were defeated in the US Senate. The 1934 Act established a new regulator, the Federal Communications Commission (FCC), which henceforth regarded commercial broadcasting as the legally authorised system. The FCC was an administrative agency, a unique model for regulation until Great Britain and Japan adopted it for commercial broadcasting in the 1950s.

How should radio broadcasting be organised and regulated? The US solution was that, in return for the exclusive use of a portion of radio spectrum, broadcasters would be regulated as trustees of the public airways. They would be required to act, as the 1927 Radio Act put it, 'in the public convenience, interest or necessity'. Borrowing from telecommunications (utilities) regulation, these were vague but important guiding principles, defended and contested in ensuing debates. This solution characterised the American regime of broadcast regulation until the 1980s. The resulting 'deal' was a compromise that benefited the two main parties: government and incumbent industry. Licensees were given 'free' spectrum; this was formally held in trust and subject to licence renewal, but effectively it conferred property rights that could be bought and sold. Against the assumptions or rhetoric of 'free markets', licensees were granted protection from competition. The initial justification for regulating broadcasting had been mainly technical: 'spectrum scarcity'. However, when technical capabilities changed, so too did the justification. Backing established incumbents was now defended on the grounds that it was protecting those charged to act in the public interest. Selling spectrum would have established a market mechanism in place of government regulation, but Congress's decision to retain spectrum as a public resource required a licensing system to be established, with rights to use a frequency conferred and renewed for specified, usually three-year, periods, until these were extended in 1981 (to seven years for radio licences and five for television). US broadcasting was thus founded on two opposing principles (Boddy 1998). A federal licence conferred a limited privilege on broadcasters required to operate in the public interest (the so-called 'public trustee' model). On the other hand, licences established and protected de facto property rights and private operators could run radio, and later television, stations under limited regulatory oversight of network operations and programme content. The licensing deal protected broadcasters from direct government censorship but it also meant that legislators could 'leverage' public-interest obligations through the mechanism of periodic licence renewal.

The US broadcasting system is characterised by very little regulation of content. An important exception was the Fairness Doctrine passed in 1949, an outgrowth of the 1934 Communications Act, whereby broadcasters were required to be non-partisan, to give airtime to news and public affairs programmes and to balance their representation of controversial views with reasonable opportunity for representation from all sides (Lichtenberg 1990: 252). The doctrine grew out of concerns that radio stations should not become advocates for singular perspectives. Broadcasters were required to 'afford reasonable opportunity for the discussion of conflicting views of public importance'. It was also a measure of content regulation close to politicians' concerns about their own access to the airways. The Fairness Doctrine was subsequently removed in 1987 as part of the 'deregulation' of broadcasting by the FCC under Ronald Reagan's presidency (Chapter 3); broadcasters would no longer have the formal obligation to report information without bias.[1]

By the end of the 1930s commercial broadcasting was consolidated ideologically as well as economically and institutionally (Brown 1998) and organised opposition had diminished (Smulyan 2001: 167). CBS President William Paley declared: 'He who attacks the American system [of broadcasting] attacks democracy itself,' while David Sarnoff (founder and President of NBC) pronounced: 'It is a free system because this is a free country' (cited in Brown 1998). The system that ensued has been aptly described as 'corporate liberalism' (Streeter 1996), whereby belief in individual rights in a free market has been balanced with the evident dominance of the market by a few large corporations. No special provision was made for non-commercial educational stations; of the 600 educational stations that reached 40 per cent of US homes, most collapsed under the combined impact of the 1930s 'Great Depression' and the consolidation and networking of popular commercial stations (Katz 1989). A key, enduring characteristic of the US system was localism. Licences were awarded to serve cities and communities in every corner of the United States. However, the system rapidly became network centred. Rising programme costs and the cost efficiencies for large networks, including lower transaction costs in dealing with advertisers, created powerful economic incentives for a network-based system. RCA owned the National Broadcasting Corporation (NBC), which operated two national radio networks and competed with Columbia Broadcasting System (CBS). Local stations broadcast network programmes especially in prime time, profiting from the sale of local advertising.

US television

Television developed along the same regulatory and institutional path as radio. By the 1950s the US had created 'a commercial oligopoly by a handful of national networks protected by spectrum and licensing rules that artificially restricted entry, with the commission unable to extract any significant content obligation from its licensees' (Galperin 2004: 60–61). RCA had experimented with television broadcasting in the 1930s. Industry disagreements over technical standards led the FCC

to call on the industry to agree a single standard, achieved by the National Television Systems Committee (NTSC). The FCC ratified the NTSC recommendations
and began issuing licences in 1941, but developments were soon interrupted by
US entry into the Second World War. After the war CBS proposed revision of
the NTSC standard and transmission using the UHF (ultra-high frequency) band,
which would have allowed many more service licences than the VHF (very high
frequency) band would permit. The FCC, which had resumed allocating licences
on a prewar basis, rejected CBS's proposals, but intense demand for frequencies and signal interference soon led it to impose a freeze on new licence allocations, which lasted from 30 September 1948 to July 1952. The FCC subsequently
rejected proposals by the small fourth network, Du Mont, for each station to cover
a larger geographic area, which would have resulted in more stations per market.
Du Mont struggled to achieve national coverage, as local licensees preferred to
affiliate to the larger networks, and ceased broadcasting in 1955. As this illustrates,
television in America was far from a simple story of the triumph of free-market
competition. The FCC made key decisions on technology and licensing that established barriers to market entry, although it would also act later to curb network
power.

Television became a mass medium across the West, but the American television market was established earlier and grew more rapidly than that of Western
Europe, where economies were slowly rebuilding after the Second World War. In
the US the proportion of households with TV sets went from 9 per cent in 1950
to 78 per cent in 1955. Within a decade the television audience had grown from
a small, affluent, urban elite to a mass audience watching predominantly network
TV in prime time. Across Europe, television only became widespread in the late
1950s and early 1960s. As late as 1954 there were only 125,000 sets in France and
fewer than 90,000 in Germany, although there were nearly 3 million in the UK
(UNESCO 1963: 81).[2] When TV arrived in America there was a significant shift
of advertising towards the new medium, but while TV programmes were aimed
at a largely white, middle-class audience (sought by advertisers), commercial radio
began to specialise and diversify. From the late 1940s many African-Americans,
uninterested in television's portrayal of a 'lily white nation'(Brown 1998: 156), and
often unable to afford sets, turned to radio stations that broadcast rhythm and
blues, jazz, gospel and, in the 1950s, rock 'n' roll.

Europe and public service broadcasting

The public service model of broadcasting became most established in Western
Europe. Radio broadcasting grew rapidly as a mass medium after the First World
War (1914–18). Broadcasting was allowed to be developed initially by private
firms in some countries, notably Britain, Belgium, Norway and Denmark. Elsewhere, states established public corporations. In Switzerland various broadcasting
corporations were established to serve different regions ('cantons') under a federal
system, while Sweden created an exclusive monopoly, the Swedish Broadcasting
Corporation (SBC), as a private, non-profit organisation. The SBC's stock belonged

to electronics manufacturers, publishers and 'national popular movements' (non-state organisations). Today, the government elects the chairman and some board members, but the majority are non-government appointments. The government has power over funding, but programming and production decisions are made by the SBC with little political interference (Head 1985: 84–5; Humphreys 1996: 56). In Germany, radio developed under tight state control (Humphreys 1996: 112), while in France, alongside state-controlled radio, an unofficial private sector was tolerated into the post-war period. A common characteristic was that broadcasting was regulated by state-owned postal, telegraph and telephone authorities (PTTs), since radio, as an electronic technology, grew out of telephony and telegraphy (Humphreys 1996: 112). European states, drawing their own lessons from the 'chaos of the airways' in the United States, either controlled broadcasting outright or exercised control though licensing.

Broadcasting in Britain

In Britain, as in the US, the same institutions that developed mass radio broadcasting were also responsible for ushering in the age of television (see Briggs and Burke 2002: 216). The British Broadcasting Company, formed in 1922 as a joint venture of various radio manufacturers, was granted a licence to broadcast by the Post Office, a state-owned PTT service. Broadcasting was financed by an annual licence fee, charged on all households with a radio set (wireless), and by an additional tax on sales of radios. In Britain, technical considerations – the available spectrum could only support a limited number of services – were enhanced by consideration of radio wavebands as a 'public utility' (Sykes Committee 1923; see Scannell 1990). The 'mission' of public service broadcasting was developed, above all, by the managing director of the company, John Reith (1889–1971) (Scannell and Cardiff 1991: 3–19). Reith argued for the creation of a public corporation and went on to become the first Director General of the British Broadcasting Corporation (BBC), established in 1927 by Royal Charter (powers of the monarch vested in executive government). If 'spectrum scarcity' required controlled access, the vision of public services involved a more substantive, positive claim for monopoly provision based on a 'public interest' rationale. Reith's vision was based on four main principles (Negrine 1994: 84):

1   assured sources of funds
2   brute force of monopoly
3   public service motive
4   a sense of moral obligation.

Broadcasting was regarded as a public utility that the state ought to control in the public interest but, at same time, liberal traditions in Britain favoured independence from government. The Crawford Committee (1926) recommended that broadcasting be established as a public service delivered by a public corporation, incorporating the nine regional operations of the company. Direct state control was rejected by the government, which nevertheless retained indirect control through its powers to set the licence fee. The government would not interfere with the BBC's editorial independence but the BBC would be obliged to remain impartial in coverage of political affairs. This endorsement of independence drew upon liberal principles as well as concepts of utility and public service derived from government administration; it also arose from the cultural cohesiveness of elite power in Britain (Michael 1990: 53; Curran and Seaton 2003).

Radio was established on what would later be identified as principles of public service. There would be universal availability and access: radio transmission would be established wherever technically feasible. Listeners had a choice of national and local/ regional services. A policy of 'mixed' programming ensued, comprising news, talks, drama, sport, religion, music (mainly classical), variety and light entertainment.

Taken together, the service was designed to cater for different needs (education, information, entertainment) and for different sectional interests, providing 'something for everyone' and 'everything for someone'. In cultural terms, actual provision was narrow and restricted, with comparatively little of the popular, entertainment programming found on US radio. Reith's BBC is associated with values of paternalism and cultural elitism, values fiercely challenged by cultural studies in the 1970s and 1980s (Curran 2002c). However, we need to qualify this critical assessment. Broadcasting emerged in an era of democratic advances in many Western states, the extension of the male franchise and implementation of the demands of suffragists and campaigners for greater political representation and votes for women. Radio was seen as having great potential to create the educated and enlightened electorate seen as necessary for a well-functioning democracy (Scannell 1990). In *Broadcast Over Britain* (1924) Reith argued:

> Till the advent of this universal and extraordinary cheap medium of communication a very large proportion of the people were shut off from firsthand knowledge of the events that make history. They did not share in the interests and diversions of those with fortune's twin gifts – leisure and money. They could not gain access to the great men of the day, and these men could deliver their messages to the limited number only. Today all this has changed.
>
> (cited in Briggs and Burke 2002: 221)

These words capture the tensions and contradictions of early British broadcasting as it developed in a new era of mass democracy. A mission to democratise, that draws on Enlightenment confidence in knowledge as empowerment, is nevertheless framed in terms of widening access to cultural goods whose values are unquestioned. The call for inclusion is based on an assured sense of cultural hierarchy as well as an assumption of national cultural homogeneity. Reith seemed authoritarian to his contemporary critics, his stand against pandering to 'the lowest common denominator' appearing with time 'rigid and ultimately obsolete' (Briggs and Burke 2002: 221). Yet, Reith's argument for monopoly supply as the mission of broadcasting won official, and broader, support.

During the Second World War, radio underwent significant changes which saw an early form of audience segmentation. In 1939 the National Service was replaced by a Home Service and Forces Service, the latter aimed at working-class audiences and introducing entertainment, comedy, popular music styles which had previously been neglected in favour of classical music and opera. After the war, the Forces Service became the Light Programme, intended to offer 'easy listening', popular music and serials, the Home Service became a news and current affairs network and a new service, the Third Programme, offered a more Reithian, high cultural diet of intellectual discussion, drama and classical music that secured a meagre audience share of 1–2 per cent (Curran and Seaton 1997: 159). The BBC, with a monopoly on radio broadcasting, continued these services unchanged until 1967.

European public service broadcasting

The period from 1945 to the early 1980s saw the establishment and dominance of public service broadcasting in Western Europe. This occurred in the context of post-war reconstruction following the defeat of the Axis powers. The fascist media of Germany and Italy and the collaborationist press in occupied France were purged and reconstructed. Fascists had demonstrated the power of communications such as radio to serve totalitarian and anti-democratic ends, and the Allied powers sought to establish structures that would ensure pluralism and prevent the capture of media by a central, state power (H&M 2004a: 156).

Post-war broadcasting also emerged in the context of popular pressure for a more egalitarian economic and social order and for greater democracy. Capitalist crises in the 1930s, and the ensuing world war, sharpened pressure for a new settlement. A new international order was created with the setting up of the United Nations and new arrangements for regulating capital (the so-called 'Bretton Woods' system). In Europe, where post-war reconstruction was under way with US aid (from the Marshall Plan), social welfare states were created based on a 'consensus that society had responsibility to guarantee a minimum level of well-being for its citizens, in terms of health services, social security, education, environment, and so on' (Dahlgren 2000: 25). States undertook to provide directly, or through authorised providers, basic levels of social and economic welfare, including unemployment benefit and pensions, and access to services including health and social amenities. They (re-)established public, state-run industries and regulated private markets to serve economic and social objectives from job creation to macro-economic policy. European welfare states grew as economies expanded from the 1950s to the 1970s and broadcasting was incorporated into the welfare model and its apparatuses.

Organisation and finance

The BBC, admired across liberated Europe for its wartime performance, became an influential model for the public service systems established elsewhere in Europe as well as for the Canadian Broadcasting Corporation (CBC). Across Western Europe either the state directly or a public body provided radio and television services, mostly as a monopoly but sometimes within systems of limited and controlled competition. Only in Luxembourg was broadcasting organised as a private monopoly financed by advertising. In all others, television was established initially as a public (or state) monopoly. Between 1945 and 1970 three main variants emerged: 'pure' public monopolies funded solely by licence fee; 'mixed revenue' public monopolies financed by a mixture of licence fees and advertising; and 'dual' systems where public broadcasters coexisted with commercial ones (Brants and Siune 1992). The licence fee particularly suited an era in which access to broadcasting was limited in society – paid by the corpus of users (public good) but not by those without receiving equipment.

Advertising finance was very controversial because of fears of advertiser influence on editorial content and commercialisation, but, partly under pressure from the growing advertising lobby, several countries introduced advertising as a supplementary source of funding for PSBs (Humphreys 1996: 126–8; Sepstrup 1989). In Germany and the Netherlands advertising revenue supplemented licence fee income while monopoly supply of broadcasting was maintained. The 'invisible' burden of advertising costs on viewers became an increasingly attractive option politically to meet the rising costs of television in the 1960s and 1970s. However, advertising was subject to regulatory constraints designed to ensure that commercial interests did not distort programme agendas and services. Rules on the amount, scheduling and content of advertising were common to PSBs. Into the 1980s, reliance on advertising was not allowed to 'marketise' the public broadcasting system (Humphreys 1996: 120).

While broadcasting systems largely corresponded to the three main types outlined, there was considerable variety (Humphreys 1996: 122–30). In Spain under the authoritarian rule of Franco, broadcasting, which began in 1956, was funded by direct state subsidy (and advertising), with no licence fee. This was the only case of direct subsidy and in the 1980s it was reduced considerably as a share of revenue. Commercial television was introduced in Britain much earlier than in the rest of Europe. The Television Act (1954) paved the way for Independent Television (ITV) to begin broadcasting in 1955. Created by a Conservative government that was characteristically more innovatory than its Labour counterpart in the post-war period, the Act was a triumph of lobbying by a coalition of backbench Conservative MPs, commercial firms and advertisers (Wilson 1961). It introduced commercially funded broadcasting, and a broadcasting 'duopoly' that lasted 35 years, yet the new ITV was established within the public service system, not in competition to it. ITV was made up of 15 franchises, required to provide 'regional' as well as 'network' programmes. The ITV companies had detailed obligations to provide impartial news, current affairs, religious, children's and other programme requirements and a high proportion of domestic over acquired (mainly US) programmes. The regulatory structure and precise requirements changed many times over the years but the 'deal' by which monopoly rents from advertising were granted to companies in exchange for public service obligations survived into the period of digital competition, where a new settlement is required if commercial PSB is to continue. The so-called 'duopoly' was designed to stimulate 'competition for quality' but not for revenues. Conflicts with the regulator ensued, but this system of managed competition was successful, stimulating the BBC to connect with popular audiences and win back audiences lost to ITV in its early years. In contrast to the increasingly staid output from some PSBs, competition from ITV forced a shift in BBC output to more popular programming and a 'golden age' in the 1960s and 1970s cultivating large audiences for socially relevant dramas. It was during the 1960s that television became the principal source of news.

Public service principles and features

Public broadcasting was justified as the best means to guarantee that radio spectrum would be put to use to promote social objectives. How those objectives should be identified and evaluated has been hotly debated since, as conditions changed in each decade. While structures and performance varied considerably, the main characteristics of PSB are providing diversity of content catering to all tastes and interests, quality and universal access to services. Broadcasting should provide 'public goods' available to all at a price shared by all and the provision of such services should be guaranteed by the state and overseen and controlled in the public interest (Brants and de Bens 2000).

Various attempts have been made to identify the key purposes and goals for PSB, particularly, as we shall see, in response to growing threats to these systems during the 1970s and from more recent requirements to distinguish public service from market provision. Efforts include the Council of Europe (1994, cited in Brants and De Bens 2000; Brants and Siune 1992: 99–104; Tracey 1998: 26–9; Hesmondhalgh 2007: 119). Blumler (1992) summed up PSB as embracing a comprehensive remit; generalised mandates; diversity, pluralism and range; cultural roles; a place in politics; non-commercialism. Another account from Britain in the 1980s (BRU 1985) identified core principles as:

- geographic universality – everyone should have access to the same services
- catering for all interests and tastes
- catering for minorities
- catering for 'national identity and community'
- detachment from vested interests and government
- one broadcasting system to be funded directly from the corpus of users
- competition in good programming rather than for numbers; and
- guidelines to liberate programme makers and not to restrict them.

The UK Communications Act 2003, s264 defines the purposes of public service television broadcasting in the UK and provides a list of criteria by which these may be fulfilled, including:

[ensuring] that cultural activity in the United Kingdom, and its diversity, are reflected, supported and stimulated ... facilitating civic understanding and

fair and well-informed debate on news and current affairs ... a wide range
of different sporting and other leisure interests ... a suitable quantity and
range of programmes on educational matters, of programmes of an educational nature and of other programmes of educative value ... programmes
dealing with ... matters of international significance or interest and matters
of specialist interest ... a suitable quantity and range of high quality and original programmes for children and young people; ... a sufficient quantity of
programmes that reflect the lives and concerns of different communities and
cultural interests and traditions within the United Kingdom, and locally in
different parts of the United Kingdom ...

For Blumler (1992b: 12) PSBs 'assumed some responsibility for the health of
the political process and for the quality of public discourse generated within it'.
Audiences were addressed as citizens. In Italy the public broadcaster RAI had
what Mazzoleni (1992: 80–1) describes as an 'intentional pedagogic function'.
The role of broadcasting was conceived as one of entrenching democracy but also
of fostering national consciousness and integration (Weymouth 1996).

Regulation and political control

Authority to broadcast was determined by each nation state. Licensing regimes
regulated market access and provision of broadcast services. Together with
regulation of technical standards and access, PSB regimes were characterised
by strong content regulation, both 'negative' (concerning taste and decency) and
'positive' obligations, for new regional, religious and children's programmes,
for instance. PSB involved a close relationship between broadcasters and state
but the strength of ties and nature of that relationship varied between states.
Kelly (1983: 73) classifies three forms of linkage to politics that prevailed (see
also H&M 2004a: 30–1; Humphreys 1996: 155–8; Blumler 1992b: 13). The
first is formally *autonomous systems* involving mechanisms to distance political
factions from broadcaster operations and decision making, such as prevailed
in Britain, Iceland and Sweden. Second are *politics-in-broadcasting systems*, those
where the governing bodies include representatives of the countries' main
political parties (and social groups), which prevailed in Germany, Denmark
and Belgium. In Austria, for example, governors of public broadcasters were
appointed in proportion to the strength of political parties as measured by
voting share. Third, there are *politics-over-broadcasting systems*, where state organs
intervene directly in broadcaster decisions, a model which prevailed in Greece,
Italy and France (before 1982).

In France (before 1982), Denmark (1926–64), Greece and Austria there was
direct state control of the broadcasting organisation. The capture of broadcasting under de Gaulle in France represents a strong instance of centralised state
control of public broadcasting (Kuhn 1995). By the 1980s the majority of PSBs
involved clear principles of independence from government along the lines of the
public corporation model in Britain, or systems in which social groups played a

more inclusive, organised role as in Sweden, the Netherlands and Germany. In Britain, the BBC was defended as an independent institution at 'arm's length' from government, although government pressure could be unrelenting, especially during periods of civil unrest or foreign wars. The security services vetted programmes on politically sensitive issues and the BBC's Board of Governors often bowed to pressure to censor output, even sacking Directors Generals at the behest of government.

From a US libertarian perspective, European broadcasting has often been equated with 'state broadcasting', its supposed autonomy from the ruling parties being viewed with suspicion. Certainly, the organisation of PSB has always been a highly political issue, and states, in certain periods, have exercised considerable political control. States have all, to varying degrees, been a repressive force, politically and culturally, acting in the interests of elites. But, to appreciate the achievements of PSB we need to adopt a more complex understanding of the state, beyond the merely negative assessment provided by a foundational libertarian critique. PSB has also involved states acting as a positive force, enabling the enhancement of democratic cultural space that the market alone would not or could not provide. As an ideal, PSB systems are accountable to the public they serve, unlike commercial organisations, which are ultimately accountable to their shareholders. In reality, accountability in PSB systems has always been more complex, and broadcasters have varied in their responsiveness to publics or their political representatives. The main structures for accountability were regulatory bodies and legislatures. In most systems, enforcement and supervision were entrusted to governing bodies built into the organisations they oversaw. Variants reflected wider political system differences and influence. In Northern Europe, structures of accountability involving 'socially relevant groups' reflected social democratic and corporatist traditions. In the UK there was the paradox of the 'public interest' being upheld by boards of governors selected by government from narrow elites – 'the great and the good' – although regional broadcasting councils, with limited advisory powers, added a modest level of decentralisation (Michael 1990).

In Germany, during the post-war occupation by Allied forces, broadcasting was established on an entirely regional basis to entrench a democratic and pluralistic system that would not be susceptible to efforts to reassert central state control. Broadcasting was integrated into the new political-legal structure of the Federal Republic. The 1949 Constitution (called 'Basic Law') gave jurisdiction of broadcasting (except its telecommunication aspects) to the regional government structures, the Länder, which enacted their own broadcasting laws. Although partly modelled on the BBC, the German system deviated by including representatives of organised interest groups (gesellschaftlich relevante Gruppen) in governance structures to provide greater safeguards against any resurgent autocracy, in place of Britain's reliance on a more culturally cohesive elite. In most other countries, regional or local broadcasting was limited and subsidiary to 'national' broadcasting. Some countries, including Britain and Sweden, established bodies to deal with complaints or alleged remit violations. However, as PSB became institutionalised, accountability to viewers was margin-

alised, according to Mitchell *et al.* (1994), a factor in the 'crisis' for PSB in the late
1970s, examined in the next chapter.

European broadcasting cultures (1950s to 1970s)

In 1945 Europe was still governed by social and moral values that had characterised the prewar order of highly stratified societies, with defined class hierarchies and cultures. For most Europeans, social class and religious affiliation were
powerful forces defining identities, and there were strong allegiances to social, religious and political groupings that were relatively clearly defined. These distinctive groupings were served above all by newspapers and the periodical press,
while radio and then television served to promote and foster, over time, stronger
national or collective identifications. After 1945 PSB was charged with the task of
contributing to national reconstruction. PSB was responsible for 'sustaining and
renewing the society's characteristic cultural capital and cement' (Blumler 1992b:
11). Media scholars have shown that public broadcasting was often successful in
fostering national cultural identities and integration, through shared rituals both
in broadcast content and in patterns of access and engagement. But evaluations
often highlight contradictory tendencies and paradoxes as well as wider differences
in assessing state power. PSB has been a mixture of contending forces and values,
argues Blumler (1992b: 14), 'a meeting ground of idealism and realism; of Platonic
high-mindedness and toughly pragmatic power politics'. Into the 1970s PSB was
closely aligned to political establishments, often displayed cultural elitism and paternalism, and gave limited communications space for cultural minorities. PSB also
fostered a national civic sphere, in which news and politics were much more central
than in fully commercial systems, although nationally oriented PSBs were much
less successful in contributing to the creation of a European-wide public sphere.

The impact of television was initially limited by the high cost of sets and the few
hours of transmission each day. By the late 1950s, programming generally began
from mid afternoon and often ended before midnight. In 1964 French television
broadcast 11 hours per day. Prime time comprised a 'mixed schedule' of mass-
and minority-appeal programmes. Within this mix, programme styles varied
considerably from country to country. In contrast to Britain, French television was
heavily factual, and this category (comprising news, current affairs, documentaries
and education, but also sport) constituted 59 per cent of output in 1973 (Tunstall
2008: 252). The 1950s and 1960s were a period of expansion for television.
Numbers of households with television sets increased across Europe (UNESCO
1963). The introduction of colour television and, with it, more expensive licence
fees meant revenues grew steadily, outstripping for a time rising production costs.
Some television broadcasters had always served regions, linguistic or cultural
segments since 1945, others opened up more diversified services from the 1960s.
In Belgium there were separate broadcasting services for the two main linguistic
groups, French and Flemish (Dutch speakers) (with a broadcasting organisation
to serve the German-speaking minority established in 1997). In Switzerland the
Swiss-German speaking majority effectively cross-subsidised programming for

French- and Italian-speaking minorities. In Britain, national PSBs were required to produce specified programme hours for minority-language cultures, Scots Gaelic and Welsh-language speakers. Following radio, television also underwent modest specialisation as new channels were established to serve varied, special remits (Blumler 1992a: 8). In Britain, BBC2 came out of a process of government-sponsored review of the existing broadcasters BBC and ITV, which found the latter wanting (Pilkington 1962). Such changes in television broadcasting nevertheless took place within enduring monopoly or duopoly structures (Humphreys 1996: 171).

Television overtook the press as the main source of news. This occurred by the late 1950s in Italy, and across Western Europe by the early 1960s. In the late 1960s in Britain ITV led a shift from a news culture of deference towards political elites to more critical and independent perspectives, influenced by satire and wider social changes, including the growing influence of feminism, youth culture and political radicalism amongst labour and 'new social movements'. From the late 1960s British television was gradually 'opened up'. Governing values began to shift, under social pressure, towards catering for a wider range of social groups and interests that traditional PSB had encompassed. Such pressures led to the Annan Committee in 1977 recommending a new model of an 'open broadcasting authority' that would commission programmes from a greater range of sources in society, a vision that led, in modified form, to the launch of Channel 4 in 1982.

A range of factors shaped distinctive broadcasting structures and programme cultures, including country/market size, language community and audience access to other media services from within and beyond nation-state boundaries. Private broadcasting from Luxembourg, a small country bordering France, Belgium and Germany, had a wide reach across Europe. Luxembourg granted its private sector monopoly, CLT (Compagnie luxembourgeoise de télédiffusion), legal rights to collect advertising revenue from other countries where it provided unlicenced 'pirate' radio. Radio Luxembourg soon had large audiences across France and the UK, attracting advertisers able to reach national consumer markets they could not otherwise reach in their own countries. Legal, commercial independent local radio (ILR) did not begin until 1973 in Britain.

By the 1970s, economic growth had flattened, Western states experienced recession and rising inflation throughout the decade. In the audiovisual industry inflation rose even more steeply than in the economy as a whole (Collins *et al.* 1988). This was the beginning of a sustained period of financial and political pressure on PSBs as governments set licence fee increases that did not keep pace with inflation, resulting in restricted growth or in service cuts. In Sweden, the value of licence fee revenue fell by 30 per cent in the ten years from 1973 (Nowak 1991).

Summary

Broadcasting in the US and Europe developed in highly distinctive ways and the underlying differences are vital in understanding and evaluating the content and output of each. In the United States distrust of governmental control is illustrated by the prohibition on government broadcasting to citizens on national territory, except through the private broadcasters (Ó Siocrú *et al.* 2002: 26). The differences between commercial and public service broadcasting were and remain profound. Yet there are also considerable risks in adopting a simplified, smooth account. All broadcasting systems have been internally complex and variegated, dynamic and changing. Systems have also always been interconnected, albeit differentially and in highly unequal ways, with linguistic, cultural, historical and economic/ market factors shaping these interactions (Chapter 7). Nor has the division between systems ever been absolute. In the US alternative structures of broad-casting, notably the Public Broadcasting Service (PBS), later occupied the margins of the commercial system. Although the struggle for community broadcasting in the 1930s was mostly unsuccessful, in later decades the FCC reserved one or two channels for non-commercial broadcasters in most markets but required that they provide 'programming that is of an entirely different character from that available on most commercial stations' (Streeter 1996: 88). The 1967 Public Broadcasting Act established the Corporation for Public Broadcasting (CPB) to oversee some 350 stations that formed the Public Broadcasting Service. This service is partly funded by federal, state and local governments, but relies very heavily on grants from private and corporate sources, as well as from universities and colleges and non-profit foundations (Hoynes 1994). In June 2005 a congressional subcom-mittee voted to sharply reduce and then eliminate federal funding for CPB (OSI 2005: 118). Today US public broadcasting accounts for less than 5 per cent of market share.

Moreover, while the structural arrangements shaped the quality and range of output, it is vital to avoid a reductive approach that would 'read off' the nature of content from a bare account of the structure and organisation of broadcasting. To give one example, the high value placed on news brought US network televi-sion closer to its European counterparts and sustained unprofitable news divisions well into the 1970s and beyond. This valuation arose from changing influences, including the experience of the Second World War on the two powerful founders of television, David Sarnoff of NBC and William Paley head of CBS (Brown 1998), as well as the political, commercial and cultural requirements to demonstrate the responsible use of this powerful new medium, values of journalistic profession-alism, the differential quality of news in other media and the wider social inter-ests in news, particularly in the era of civil rights and Vietnam in the 1960s and 1970s.

The North American and European systems differed considerably in the way broadcasting was organised, financed and regulated. But from the early years of radio, the social power of broadcasting was recognised and intervention on behalf of the public interest was justified in all Western systems. This rationale remains salient today but is best characterised, in Raymond Williams's (1980) terms, as residual, for reasons we will examine in the next chapter.

3 Transformations and continuities in media systems (late 1970s to 2000s)

Introduction

The post-war period was one of enormous social and cultural as well as economic changes, reflected across media output. But media systems had some relatively settled features; media were predominantly national or sub-national and comprised, in different ratios, the mass media of print, analogue terrestrial or cable television, radio, alongside cultural and entertainment industries. From the late 1970s on these media systems have been structurally transformed. This chapter outlines some of the main changes, continuities and variations in Western media systems. It introduces some key terms and processes, and indicates where these are dealt with more fully in later chapters.

The first part of the chapter concentrates on changes in European broadcasting but sets these in the broader context of the processes of re-regulation, transnationalisation and marketisation across WMS. The chapter then outlines more recent changes in broadcasting and print media as these sectors converged. It was public service broadcasting (PSB) above all 'which singled out European media systems from their counterparts elsewhere in the world' (Williams 2005: 7). The weakening of the PSB system is thus an important element in our consideration of growing convergence in media systems. Since the 1980s, a series of developments has radically altered the media structures in all Western European countries. There have been shifts in the organisation and regulation of media, described by key terms such as liberalisation, deregulation and privatisation. The 1980s were marked by the increased influence of processes which earlier regulatory structures, especially in Europe, had sought to control, contain or ameliorate: marketisation, commercialisation, media concentration and transnationalisation.

European broadcasting and the commercial deluge

Broadcasting systems were reorganised under the impact and influence of various forces for change that grew in the 1970s, in particular changes in technology, economics and politics. The most significant change has been the abolition of PSB monopolies and the expansion of commercial television to become an integral and increasingly dominant part of national media systems. At the beginning of the 1980s the public service paradigm was dominant in most Western European

Table 3.1   Typology of national broadcasting systems

System	1980	1990	1997	2007
Public monopoly	Belgium Denmark Norway Sweden			
Public monopoly/ mixed revenue	Austria Finland France Germany Greece Iceland Netherlands Portugal Switzerland	Austria Denmark Iceland Ireland Netherlands Portugal Switzerland	Austria Ireland Switzerland	
Private monopoly/ advertising only	Luxembourg	Luxembourg	Luxembourg	Luxembourg
Dual system (public service; commercial broadcasters)	Italy UK	Belgium Finland France Germany Greece Italy Norway Spain Sweden UK	Belgium Denmark Finland France Germany Greece Italy Netherlands Norway Portugal Spain Sweden UK	Austria Belgium Denmark Finland France Germany Greece Ireland Italy Netherlands Norway Portugal Spain Sweden Switzerland UK

Source: Adapted from Siune and Hultén (1998: 27).

countries. Together they had 41 television and 61 radio channels, predominantly public. State-owned or public service monopolies existed in all systems except the UK, Finland and Italy (dual systems) and Luxembourg (private). By 1990 Western Europe had 36 commercial terrestrial channels as well as new satellite and cable television channels (Brants and Siune 1992: 104).

Weymouth and Lamizet (1996: 211) summarise the main changes in West European media environments in the 1980s and early 1990s:

- emergence of the communications/media sector as a dynamic industry in its own right
- trend towards concentration of media groups and establishing of multi-media conglomerates
- increasing availability of new services through cable and satellite

- reorganisation of broadcasting/communications sectors through deregulation and privatisation
- weakening of public service broadcasting
- fragmentation and differentiation of media markets
- development of common European legislation
- general shortage of programmes and significant increase in production costs.

Forces of change

Technological developments played an important enabling role. Broadcasting was hit by a 'shockwave' of technological changes on several fronts (Dyson *et al.* 1988). The development of new delivery technologies of cable and satellite, offering much greater channel capacity for the transmission of programmes and advertising from sources external to nationally regulated systems, had far-reaching implications.

Satellite technology dates back to the 1950s and was dramatically realised with the launch of Sputnik by the Soviet Union in 1957. In the ensuing super-power race for space, the United States launched Telstar in 1961, with the first experimental telecasts on 11 July 1962 linking live broadcasts from the UK to the US (Briggs and Burke 2002: 291). Satellites were later used in broadcasting international sporting events, but such transmissions were limited and intermittent. The first direct broadcast satellite (DBS) system began transmitting regular programmes in 1975 in America. The first European systems began in 1986, and by the early 1990s DBS systems were operating, or planned, in other parts of the world. From the early 1980s, satellite technology was viewed by the European Community as a means to project European culture within the EC and to aid the integration of European identities (Collins 1994; Schlesinger 1991; Morley and Robins 1995b). The first satellite cable television system, SATV, was operational from 1982 and the European Broadcasting Union, made up of European PSBs, began an experimental service, Eurikon (later renamed Europa), using the European Space Agency's test satellite OTS-2.[1]

As Thompson (1995: 162) writes:

> Part of the significance of DBS is that it creates new distribution systems outside of the established terrestrially based networks of broadcasting – systems which are often privately owned and controlled and in which the large communication conglomerates may have a substantial stake. Moreover, these new distribution systems are inherently transnational since, from a technical point of view, there is no reason why the reception area (or 'footprint') of a DBS satellite should correspond even roughly to the territorial boundaries of a particular nation-state.

The development of alternative, and transnational, distribution technologies – satellite, cable and the VCR/videocassettes – undermined the 'spectrum scarcity' rationale for PSB and reduced the capacity and legitimacy for state regulation. Yet changes in broadcasting were not the inevitable outcome of technological innovation, but were shaped by the willed actions of states under pressure and influence from a variety of actors and interests. Technology was crucial, but by no means the sole cause.

By the 1980s what McQuail calls the public service model of communications regulation was in 'crisis', a term used by many European media scholars. For Blumler (1992a: 2) the crisis was marked not only by the break-up of old public service monopolies, 'but also and more profoundly by a loss of consensus over the purposes that broadcasting should serve and how it should be organised to achieve them'.

As these analysts highlight, then, there was a complex range of forces shaping trends towards a market model in Western European broadcasting. Indeed, it is the sheer density of these pressures that helps to explain their strength and the sense of their 'inevitability'. The phenomena of 'internationalisation' and of 'deregulatory' ideology seem to point to the impact of the American model. Technological change, too, appeared to be acting as an independent force that had been 'hijacked' by market ideologists. At the same time, social changes within Europe were also a powerful factor. They induced policy makers to be more ready to adopt a market model of social communications and gave added justification for liberalisation. There was growing demand for more 'home based' leisure and greater consumer choice to meet the diverse needs of family members as social habits and family structures changed (Dyson *et al.* 1988; Blumler 1992b: 15). There were also various, increasing challenges to the capacity of media to reflect and represent national communities which had defined the mission of public media in the post-war period (Williams 2005: 7).

Different dimensions of change, technological, cultural, political and economic need to be distinguished analytically, 'even if we conclude in the end that these different dimensions are interrelated' (H&M 2004b: 28). A further issue for comparative analysts has been to determine whether specific forces for change were exogenous or endogenous. There were exogenous forces of change, emanating in particular from business, cultural and policy practices in America. But there were also endogenous forces of change in Europe. The changes in media are also best understood when set in the broader context of shifts in governing values towards marketisation.

From social welfarism towards neoliberalism

To understand the policy responses we need to consider the extra-media context, in particular the ascendancy of neoliberalism shaping political and policy responses. Indeed, so-called 'deregulation' cannot be properly understood by examining factors internal to the regulation of television or even communication industries, but only in this broader context. Such an approach underlies Horwitz's (1989) exemplary account of the Reagan-era reforms of broadcasting and telecommunications. For the advanced economies of Western Europe and North America the post-war period from the 1950s to the 1970s was characterised by economic growth, rising living standards and increased consumer spending and consumption. With the exception of Southern Europe, it was also characterised by relatively stable liberal democratic systems of government. However, these economies experienced a 'long downturn' in the 1970s, marked by cycles of severe recessions in 1974–75, 1979–82 and 1991–95 (Hesmondhalgh 2007: 83–7). According to Brenner (1998), the USA experienced a crisis of overproduction in manufacturing in the face of growing competition and as German and Japanese corporations increased their share of manufacturing output following their post-war recovery. This generated a crisis across other economies, made worse by the OPEC decision to raise oil prices in 1973. The two decades from 1973 to 1993 were marked by world instability and crisis (Hobsbawm 1994: 403–32). During the slump of 1974–75, industrial production in developed capitalist economies fell by 10 per cent in one year and international trade by 13 per cent. Growth slowed in the West, while other regions, particularly Africa, Western Asia and Latin America, suffered severe economic crises. The capitalist world economy suffered another economic slump in 1980–82, and again in the late 1980s, the period in which the economies of the Eastern European 'socialist' states collapsed altogether. In the West, mass unemployment and mass poverty, which had been largely eliminated in the post-war years of economic growth and social welfare provision, reappeared. The social welfare systems provided a cushion, and arguably contributed to lowering levels of social unrest, but welfare payments generally climbed faster than state revenues, and governments responded by introducing cuts and austerity measures in the 1980s. Social insecurity increased, feeding into growing feelings of resentment toward governments and political representatives and increasing political alienation.

In most Western systems social democratic parties had dominated during the post-war period and ruled for much of the 1970s, continuing policies of Keynesian economic management that had been successful in previous decades. For Keynes, corrective measures for the economy, including government intervention, were justified in response to market failure and on grounds of socially desirable 'externalities', such as the public policy goal of full employment. Keynes's insistence on tackling the inherent tendencies to disequilibrium in markets and underemployment of resources shaped Western economic policies in the period from 1940 to the early 1970s (see Hutton 1996; Caporaso and Levine 1992; Schiller, H. 1996). The faith of neoclassical economists in free, self-adjusting markets had fallen out of favour after the crises of the 1930s and mounting evidence of 'uncontrolled' monopoly tendencies across capitalist industries. Keynesian economics claimed that full employment, high wages and the welfare state system generated consumer demand that fuelled growth in the economy.

Into the 1970s Keynesian efforts to stimulate demand through state expenditure, to manage mixed economies of private and state-run enterprises, and to achieve full employment were dominant. However, capitalism was becoming far less governable by such means, if not uncontrollable. The Bretton Woods international monetary system broke down, leading to increasing globalisation and liberalisation of financial markets. Transnational corporations were becoming key actors in shaping trade and economic policies, with increasing levels of foreign direct investment (FDI) and cross-border mergers and acquisitions (M&As) (Flew 2007: 68; Held *et al.* 1999: 199–205). As the crisis deepened, a long-isolated minority of free market advocates such as Friedrich von Hayek and Milton Friedman became more influential in the 1970s and then, in the 1980s, dominant forces in the new-right governments of Reagan and Thatcher.

In the 1970s inequality increased and wage rises stalled. Corporatist systems of governance in which government, employers and workers' representatives would seek to manage economies through agreement and consensus began to break down. In Britain, liberal corporatism had provided a 'remarkably stable' system in which the electorate divided its support fairly evenly between two class-based parties which ruled 'on terms more or less agreed between representatives of both labor and capital' (Curran and Leys 2000: 222). The period from the 1970s, however, was marked by growing industrial unrest, with clashes between the trade unions and capital.

This 'crisis' for capitalist growth prompted a reassertion of 'free market' capitalism and the unleashing of market forces. Governments, including social democratic and socialist ones, sought to reduce inflationary pressures through cutbacks in public services and sought to curb wage demands and weaken the power of trade unions. Models of state intervention and Keynesian economic management were delegitimised, most notably in the United States and Britain, by governments of the 'new right'. The Conservatives won the 1979 election under Margaret Thatcher and maintained power until the Labour Party victory in 1997. In the United States, Ronald Reagan was elected president in 1981, serving until 1989, and increased the rate of 'deregulation' that had begun in the second half of the 1970s (Horwitz 1989). From the re-election of Thatcher in 1983 and of Reagan the following year, neoliberal doctrine became more entrenched, spreading first to New Zealand, Canada and Ireland.

The promotion of market forces over state intervention occurred in complex relationship to wider social changes, including shifts towards individualism and away from older forms of collective allegiance. The process has been described, metaphorically, as 'secularisation', since not only religious but also political and social affiliations were seen to be declining in the post-war period (Chapter 5). This involved 'declining loyalty to the institutions that used to structure European social life' (Williams 2005: 10), including state or public broadcasting, and increasing emphasis on consumer choice and individualism. These shifts and the growth in demand for an expanded choice in media services were undoubtedly factors influencing policy changes. However, if marketisation was not merely technology-led it was also not merely consumer-led either.

For Murdock and Golding (1999: 118), marketisation means 'all those policy interventions designed to increase the freedom of action of private corporations and to institute corporate goals and organizational procedures as the yardsticks against which the performance of all forms of cultural enterprise are judged'. Among the main processes of 'marketization' have been privatisation, 'the sale of public communication assets to private investors'. In Europe, this occurred across the telecommunications sector including in broadcasting, for example in the controversial privatisation of the French public channel TF1 following legislation in 1986 (Kuhn 1995: 185–98). The other main process has been liberalisation, the introduction or extension of competition in media markets.

Deregulation in the United States

In 1959 the US Federal Communications Commission (FCC) ruled that since cable was neither broadcasting nor a 'common carrier' telecommunications service it had no jurisdiction over it. The regulator intervened in 1968 to restrict cable stations from importing 'distant signals' from outside designated service areas – and thereby competing with network TV – but it faced fierce criticism from the nascent cable industry, and in 1972 the FCC permitted two distant signals to be included in local cable services. The FCC introduced 'must carry' rules, requiring cable television providers to set aside channels for education, local government and the 'general public', but within four years, after much court action, many of these requirements were removed. In the absence of congressional decision making on how to treat cable – whether like broadcasting, or like the press, protected from interference under the First Amendment – US policy shifted towards liberalisation of broadcasting policy through the limited regulation of cable television.

There was a boom of cable services in the 1970s. Cable households increased from 8.7 per cent in 1970 to 23 per cent in 1980, when 4,300 cable systems served 17.2 million households. Into the mid 1970s cable systems mainly served remote rural areas, small towns or those in mountain valleys, where terrestrial signal reception was difficult (Tunstall 2008: 272); but then new services were launched, using satellites to transmit channels to cable relay stations or via satellite dishes direct-to-home (DTH). In 1972 Washington's deregulation of civilian air space allowed Home Box Office (HBO), launched by the publishing company Time Inc., to deliver DTH programmes. HBO in 1976 achieved nationwide distribution capabilities via RCA's Satcom 1 (at a fraction of the cost of the terrestrial networks' national reach) and by 1977 HBO was available on 350 local cable systems in 45 states. By the mid 1980s almost half of US homes had cable. Cable technology enabled niche content channels to be economically viable for the first time, serving geographically dispersed interest groups whose aggregate size and profile was attractive to advertisers, or otherwise profitable for pay-TV models. New, themed channels such as the History Channel and Discovery were launched, together with teleshopping. The cable industry rapidly consolidated, with the top ten firms serving nearly half the country's subscribers, and by the end of the 1980s several billion-dollar enterprises had been formed.

In 1975 US homes could receive up to eight channels, more than in any country in Europe. By 1985 average American cable-subscribing households could receive around 25 channels, while local system operators could select from around 55 nationally available services, including some 30 'basic' services, four superstations (such as Turner's Atlanta station TCG (later WTBS) available by satellite nationwide to local cable systems), and 11 'pay' services (mainly movies and live sports). In Western Europe in the early 1980s only 10 per cent of homes had cable. By

1995 US cable households could receive around 40 channels. Radio services were also abundant; in 1975 the 40 largest US cities averaged 27 radio stations each.

Cable competition and the prospect of an abundance of channels was viewed as a catalyst and incentive for deregulation, a prospect favoured not only by industry and policy makers but by critics of the mass-market fare served by the US networks. TV commentator Neil Hickey believed that 'The public will be addressed, at last, in all its variety, potentiality and dignity rather than as an immense herd of dim-witted sheep to be delivered to the highest bidder.' Twenty years on, one media historian offered the opposite verdict: 'The cable channels have almost totally failed to alter the established genres and forms of television broadcasting in any significant way, never mind add to them' (both cited in Briggs and Burke 2002: 274).

A change of long-term significance for communications 'deregulation' was the break-up of the telecommunications monopoly AT&T (American Telephone and Telegraph Company) in 1984. AT&T had been allowed to act as a private monopoly supplier, justified on the grounds that the huge costs of installing and maintaining a nationwide telephone infrastructure service represented a 'natural monopoly'. In return for this protected position, AT&T was subject to close regulation of prices and banned from entering the broadcasting content and supply markets. The break up of AT&T followed a Federal Court ruling in 1982 deciding a case first brought by the Justice Department in 1974. The Bell telephone monopoly was broken up and seven local phone companies, 'Baby Bells', were created, with the objective of increasing market competition. In return, AT&T was allowed to enter the information and computer markets from which it had previously been barred and began its expansion of national and international operations.

In broadcasting, with the exception of the 1984 Cable Act, the significant changes did not come about through legislation. Attempts to revise the 1934 Communications Act failed until the far-reaching Telecommunications Act of 1996. Instead, 'deregulation' arose from action and inaction on the part of key regulatory agencies, notably the FCC and the Federal Trade Commission, whose responsibilities included company mergers, competition policy and consumer protection. Already by the 1970s the FCC had acquired a reputation as 'Reluctant Regulators', as one study was titled (Cole and Oettinger 1978). Under Reagan, deregulation was championed by FCC chairmen Mark Fowler (1983–84) and Dennis Patrick. Fowler was appointed with the brief to remove 70 per cent of regulations from the FCC rulebook (Belfield *et al.* 1991: 196; Sterling and Kitross 2002). In particular, the FCC removed numerous controls on media concentration, leading to intensifying merger and acquisition activity across broadcasting (Chapter 6). Fowler rejected the 'trusteeship model' which had provided the rationale for the FCC to impose content regulations, arguing that the regulator should confine itself to assigning property rights over spectrum and sustaining competition. Pro-marketisation interests, including the cable companies and powerful trade associations such as the NAB, gained ground in the 1980s, promoting unregulated private business in 'free markets' as being in the best interests of consumers. Neoliberals promoted market competition, to encourage efficiency and consumer choice, over regulatory intervention. The success of companies and their lobbyists, with the support of conservative politicians, in dismantling broadcasting rules gave encouragement to pro-marketisation interests elsewhere (Hesmondhalgh 2007: 118). In the early 1980s the US cable 'basics' (CNN, ESPN, MTV, USA and Nickelodeon) also looked to Europe to expand their markets – with support from the US government, advocating liberalisation of Western European broadcasting.

Varieties and patterns of change in European broadcasting

During the 1980s the rationale for government intervention in broadcasting was challenged and partially dismantled. As we have seen, radio and television were developed largely in a national mould. All Western states exercised sovereignty over the licensing and regulation of national broadcasting in the post-war period, as they continue to do today. Access to other nations' broadcasting systems depended on geography, technology and politics. During the Cold War, radio and television signals were broadcast, and jammed, between East and West as both sides financed propagandist radio directed at each other's populations. In Western Europe, some countries received non-domestic European TV channels. However, such incursions had been largely contained within the existing system since, with the important exception of commercial radio, there were very few commercial TV channels, and so viewers received mainly PSB from neighbouring states (Humphreys 1996: 167–9).

Into this managed environment, the new distribution technologies of satellite and cable posed a profound set of challenges. An EC report (1983) considered the implications for the future structure and regulation of television, from satellite, cable and the videocassette recorder (VCR). The advent of new delivery technologies – cable and satellite – gained momentum in the second half of 1980s, putting increasing strain on the position of broadcasting monopolies. Public service advocates urged that new services be subject to regulation within the public service framework. Instead, in varying ways, policy makers permitted the prompt expansion of national, private commercial channels (Humphreys 1996: 169; Brants and Siune 1992). In most cases, the new commercial channels were subject to lighter regulation (so-called 'light touch' regulation) than was applied to the existing terrestrial services.

In the late 1980s and early 1990s there was considerable focus on the 'vulnerable values' and 'novel conditions' (Blumler 1992a) in Western public service broadcasting (Dyson *et al.* 1988; Ferguson 1990; Siune and Truetzschler 1992; Petley and Romano 1993). Dyson and Humphreys (1990) identified as key trends in European communications policy the challenges to the legitimacy of 'public service' principles and provision; the displacement of a cultural conception of communication by an economic one; the internationalisation and diversification of business operations; the impact of technological innovation (including undermining of the 'scarcity' rationales for broadcasting regulation); and ideological changes, including political frustration with the performance of public service operators.

Pressure for regulatory change came from various actors and interests. Established and new commercial media interest sought access to media markets. Advertisers sought increased opportunities to reach and target consumers, as well as economic and other benefits arising from increased competition amongst media to secure advertising finance (Tunstall and Palmer 1991). Humphreys (1996) identified the main actors and interest groups in reshaping European broadcasting policies in the 1980s and 1990s (Table 3.2).

Parties of the right, newspaper publishers and the advertising lobby argued that emergent new technologies of cable and satellite made deregulation inevitable (Tunstall 2008: 258). In the early 1980s new governments of the right (Britain, Germany) and left (France) shared a motivation to marketise PSB systems they perceived as biased against their parties in opposition (Humphreys 1996: 174-5). Yet, in Europe pro-market advocates met stronger resistance than in the United States from social democratic parties and PSB supporters. There was resistance to commercialisation in smaller states with historically strong commitments to PSB (Belgium, Austria. Netherlands, Switzerland) as well as in states where PSBs retained high audience share such as Britain. This meant that changes were often protracted and marketisation was constrained by the strength of opposition. Others highlight that deregulation (across all democratic systems) was mainly the result of ideological commitment to free markets by governing elites, and 'not the product of an irresistible groundswell in public demand' (Gunther and Mughan 2000: 444). Nevertheless the defence of traditional public service provision was

Table 3.2   The deregulation of broadcasting: the coalition of actors

Pro-market actors	Their interests
The Electronics Industry	To exploit markets for new TV sets; Pay TV decoders; satellite reception equipment etc.
Cable & Satellite TV lobbies	Freedom to provide commercial services
PTTS	To develop and diffuse new media technologies.
Newspaper publishers	To diversify media operations; to preempt further competition for adv. revenue
Advertisers	To gain outlets and strengthen market position
Governments	To promote the economy; to attract media investors
Parties of the Right	Pursuit of neo-liberal agenda; promotion of business interests
European Commission	To liberalise European markets

Public service supporters	Their interests
Public-service broadcasters	Self-defence; continuance of public resourcing, etc.
Unions	Protection of jobs and employment and conditions of employment
Parties of the Left	Promotion of public-service ethos (and labour interests)

Source: Humphreys (1996: 176)

also facing mounting opposition from a variety of quarters with critics from the left and liberal centre as well as neoliberals (Syvertsen 1991; Blumler 1992b: 15–16).

The gradual removal of technical and regulatory barriers in broadcasting and the privatisation of telecommunications in Europe encouraged new investors to enter these markets (Leys 2001). Some were new entrants to media, others were media companies seeking to diversify into new fields of activity (Humphreys 1996: 202; Chapter 7). Newspaper publishers were among the most important media owners to diversify, both in terms of structural changes and as influential actors shaping government policies towards liberalisation. In the early 1980s mono-media press expansion was limited by regulation of ownership and by both low-growth but fiercely competitive markets. Diversification allowed risks to be spread; it allowed print companies to seek some 'future proofing' by acquiring electronic media interests. Press interests shared a 'defensive–offensive' motivation, fearing the loss of vital advertising revenue to the new media, notably cable and satellite, and of their share of the information market (Dyson and Humphreys 1990: 18; Humphreys 1996). In addition, increased profitability from new technology and greater advertising revenues during the 1980s gave some press groups greater financial capacity to expand.

Italy's was the first European broadcasting system to allow market competition into a formerly monopoly provision, initiating what became known as 'wild' or 'savage' deregulation. After 1945, Italian politics and broadcasting had been dominated by the Christian Democrat party (DCI). Following the party's electoral defeat in 1974, the broadcasting system was reformed, leading to greater pluralism within what remained a highly politicised system in which each major party controlled one of the three public service television channels: the DCI (RAI-1), socialists (RAI-2) and communists (RAI-3) (Humphreys 1996: 154). RAI, challenged by the emergence of local pirate radio stations took legal action. However, a surprise ruling of Italy's Constitutional Court in 1976 declared that the PSB monopoly was only necessary and valid at national level. This 'deregulatory' decision paved the way for the setting up of hundreds of private radio and television channels, 188 by 1977, rising to a peak of 500 in 1980 (Petley and Romano 1993; Marletti and Roncarolo 2000). Some leading publishing groups moved into broadcasting and, in defiance of the court ruling, began to establish de facto national networks, an outcome accepted by a further pro-market ruling by the Constitutional Court in 1981 (Humphreys 1996: 179). During the 1980s, all three main commercial networks, Retequattro, Canale 5 and Italia 1 were acquired by Silvio Berlusconi, leading to a broadcasting environment that was significantly deregulated and highly concentrated. With immobility among politicians, who were unable to reach compromise agreements, economic actors such as Berlusconi were largely free to establish services on their own terms. A belated broadcasting act in 1990 legitimised the market outcome and was dubbed 'Lex Berlusconi'.

Marketisation followed in France and Germany, then in Britain and Spain among the large European states, all of whom created 'mixed' public and private broadcasting systems (Tunstall 2008: 259). Brants and Siune (1992) describe three levels of change in EU countries: minimal, medium and strong. By 1990 there were still no domestic commercial channels in Austria, Denmark, Ireland, the Netherlands or Switzerland. In Austria, some 15 foreign channels (mostly German) were available via cable by 1990, although the two domestic channels of the Austrian broadcasting corporation the ORF (Österreichischer Rundfunk) maintained a combined viewing share of 94 per cent, showing a mixture of 41 per cent own productions, 33 per cent acquired and 25 per cent repeats (Trappel 1992).

Ireland's sole national commercial channel, TV-3, was awarded a licence in 1989 but only began broadcasting in 1998. That year also saw the first commercial radio licences issued for 26 regional stations, and a short-lived national station, Century Radio. Ireland's small population (3.5 million in 1991 but increasing to 4.3 million by 2006), most of whom could access British television, restricted the market for a fourth terrestrial channel to compete with the public service Radio Telefís Éireann (RTE 1, Network 2 and Telefís na Gaeilge (TG-4)), although by 2001 TV-3's audience share had increased to 10.3 per cent. A majority of Irish households subscribe to cable television and Sky Digital, the sole provider of DTV services in Ireland (Truetzschler 2004).[2]

In France, despite statist (*dirigiste*) traditions, there was strong marketisation in the 1980s. State broadcasting had been dominated by the Right, most notably under President de Gaulle. The capture of public broadcasting had helped to discredit French television and increased pressure for liberalisation. The Left gained power in 1981–86 and 1988–93 with a socialist president, Mitterrand, in office from 1981 to 1995. The socialists legalised France's growing pirate radio sector: the country went from no legal commercial radio in 1981 to 1,200 local stations by 1991, most of whom were part of a new national network, NRJ (Tunstall 2008: 253). The socialists introduced the first francophone satellite channel (TV5) in 1983, the first subscription channel (Canal+) in 1984, and licensed two new commercial TV channels (TV6 and Le Cinq) in 1985 – both to 'friends' of the president (Rollet 1997). State broadcasting was modified as a public service system under an independent regulatory authority. The right-wing government of Jacques Chirac (1986–88) went further, privatising one of the main public service channels, TF1, acquired by Bouyges, France's leading construction company and Agence Havas (owner of Canal+). Many socialists had wanted broadcasting to be liberated from state control but maintained through regulation, with production quotas to ensure French industry dominance of output. However, presidential control led to more politically expedient and pro-market outcomes, and the privatisations were not reversed when the socialists resumed power (1988–93).

In West Germany (Federal Republic), commercial services were permitted alongside the public service system and grew rapidly in the 1980s, thanks in part to extensive cabling supported by the government. Private broadcasting was licensed from 1984 (Hoffman-Riem 1992). By contrast, in Germany's smaller neighbour, Austria, the public service ORF (Österreichischer Rundfunk) was the only legal broadcaster until 1995 and national private television services did not begin until 2002 (Trappel 2004: 7–9) making Austria one of the last European countries to introduce a 'dual system'.

Under the Conservative government (1979–97), UK broadcasting policy favoured increasing competition, embracing the new technologies of cable and satellite in the 1980s, and digitalisation of television in the 1990s (Goodwin 1998). The cable television services introduced in the 1980s, following the Cable Act 1984, were relatively insignificant in audience share, but provided investment opportunities for UK and overseas capital, especially from North American cable companies, and were subject to new, 'light touch' regulation.[3] BSkyB's satellite service, also subject to minimal regulation, introduced much more significant competition for the terrestrial broadcasters (Horsman 1998). Audiences for the two main terrestrial channels declined sharply during the 1990s as competition increased from satellite, a revived cable television industry and a strongly performing fifth terrestrial channel, Channel 5, introduced in 1997.

From 1984 especially, Prime Minister Margaret Thatcher, supported by the newspapers of her political ally Rupert Murdoch, led attacks on the content and editorial decisions, on the finances and then on the management of the BBC, and promoted the establishment of a competitive broadcasting market. Throughout this period, up to 1992, broadcasting remained the responsibility of the Home Office. However, this department was perceived by Thatcher and some ministers as being too close to the ethos and interests of the existing public service broadcasters.[4] While Thatcher's first Home Secretary, William Whitelaw, powerfully restrained changes which he perceived might adversely affect the BBC, cable policy was given to the Department of Trade and Industry (DTI) (O'Malley 1994: 6–7), and from the mid 1980s there was inter-departmental rivalry between the Home Office and DTI, with the latter promoting greater commercial media expansion. The success of the commercial television lobby in 1954 (and the commercial radio lobby in 1971) 'produced new apologists for a "market-oriented" conception of broadcasting' (Dyson *et al.* 1988: 74), exemplified in the Peacock Committee's *Report of the Committee on Financing the BBC* (1986). The BBC survived the threats to its institutional survival, but bore the impact of marketisation, one dimension of which Murdock and Golding (1999: 19; see also Murdock 2000) describe as corporatisation 'encouraging or compelling organizations still within the public sector to pursue market opportunities and institute corporate forms of organization'. The BBC retained its licence fee, although with growth restricted until a period of significant increase in 1998–2001, but was required to increase revenues through commercial ventures both internationally and in Britain, to introduce significant cost-cutting measures, to establish an 'internal market' known as 'Producer Choice' and to open up an increasing share of programme output to independent producers (Born 2004). These reforms had their origins in recommendations of the Peacock Committee, set up by government to review the future financing of the BBC, which recommended that the BBC and ITV commission 25 per cent of programmes from independents and introduce greater financial discipline. Led by free-market advocates such as chair Alan Peacock and Samuel Brittan, the committee went beyond its narrow brief, and reconceptualised broadcasting largely as a private commodity, rather than a public good, and advocated a market-led system (O'Malley 1994). Yet the committee found justification for public service to address 'market failure' and provide those socially valued programmes that the market, left to itself, would neglect or undersupply. The goal, according to the report (1986: 133), was a

> sophisticated system based on consumer sovereignty. That is a system which recognises that viewers and listeners are the best ultimate judges of their own interests, which they can satisfy if they have the option of purchasing the broadcasting services they require from as many alternative sources of supply as possible. There will always be a need to supplement the direct consumer market by public finance for programmes of a public service kind ... supported by people in their capacity as citizens and voters but unlikely to be commercially self supporting in the view of broadcasting entrepreneurs.

Broadcasting Acts in 1990 and 1996 had advanced the liberalising re-regulation of the media in favour of market forces. The 1990 Act established a new licensing system for the main commercially funded public service channel, ITV, and relaxed rules on media ownership. ITV licences were awarded through competitive sealed bids (although evaluation of the bids on quality grounds was reimposed after a successful rearguard lobbying effort on behalf of the new regulator, ITC (Goodwin 1998)). ITV went from 14 regional franchises, then dominated by six companies, to effective control by two main companies, Granada Media Group and Carlton, who were permitted to merge in 2004 to form ITV plc.

Telecommunications were privatised and cable and satellite systems were encouraged to expand, with minimal structural or content regulation. British Satellite Broadcasting (BSB), a consortium initially made up of Pearson, Granada and Virgin Group was awarded the first DBS (direct broadcasting satellite) licence by the Independent Broadcasting Authority (IBA) in December 1986, providing monopoly supply of three licensed channels for 15 years. Bypassing this regulatory arrangement, Rupert Murdoch used leased space on the Luxembourg-registered Astra satellite to launch Sky in 1989, transmitting four channels for the UK. Intense competition between BSB (launched in March/April 1990) and Sky proved too costly for both, and in November 1990 the companies merged in what was 'effectively a takeover' by Sky (Horsman 1998: 78, 67–84). By 1996 Sky was in 11 per cent of British TV households. Murdoch had breached rules on cross-media ownership but Sky survived, 'substantially due to the favouritism which successive Thatcher and Major Governments showed to him and his enterprises' (King 1998: 284; Goodwin 1998).

With the expansion of commercial channels, public service television and radio suffered falls in audience share across all systems. Public broadcasters had severe difficulties in holding on to their audiences in some countries, such as Greece, Switzerland and Belgium. In Germany and Sweden, countries with strong PSB systems, PSB viewing declined by nearly half in the early 1990s. However, this fall was greatest up to 1995, slowing since, and with audience share, in some cases, even increasing again in the early 2000s following PSBs' launch of new digital channels (see Chapter 7).

Summary

The PSB model was destabilised by a series of changes in the late 1970s and 1980s. The 'spectrum scarcity' rationale was undermined as new systems for delivery emerged. Spectrum scarcity had never been the only foundation for public broadcasting: securing the quality content and programme diversity that a commercial system could not guarantee were important objectives in the early formulation of PSB. But the end of technical scarcity challenged central tenets of the old system. Why, commercial operators asked, should they be kept out of the provision and development of electronic media to improve consumer choice and market efficiency?

Policy makers also responded to media transnationalisation, which brought greater competition and new ways to circumvent national broadcasting regulation (Chapters 6 and 8). Firms such as BSkyB, using Luxembourg's Astra satellite, could uplink from the least regulated broadcasting system in Europe. Three main changes were indicative of the growing internationalisation of television: the international trade in television, the development of transfrontier television, and increasing supranational regulatory activity. The advent of transfrontier television 'has forced states to act together (or at least try to) so as to guarantee common and acceptable standards and rules' (Negrine and Papathanassopoulos 1991: 3).

European 'deregulation' represented a paradigm shift in values, but in comparison to the largely voluntarist arrangements in the United States, and those created in Italy, most European systems retained substantial controls. In France, commercial broadcasters were required to show particular types of programming and to uphold values that included protecting national cultural heritage. Moreover, supranational regulation, above all the EC 'Television without Frontiers' Directive (1989, amended 1997), faced two ways, promoting free trade in television but setting minimum standards for all television services (Chapter 6). Despite the weakening of the scarcity rationale, democratic and cultural rationales remain powerful and still influential arguments for regulatory intervention in the digital era (Marsden and Ariño 2005: 14, 24)

Commercialisation and content

The expansion of commercial television, and increasing competition among all broadcasters, led to growing evidence of commercialism. Tunstall and Palmer (1991: 43) usefully identified some features of commercially led systems:

> competition for audiences between a substantial number of channels; direct inter-channel competition for advertising; aggressively competitive programming; a sharp decline in serious programming in peak hours; aggressive competition for popular talent, leading to star salary inflation; wholesale resort to imported programming; extension of the broadcasting day to include most of the twenty-four hours; aggressive scheduling of repeat programming (including daily 'stripping' of series originally shown weekly).

Total broadcasting hours increased by 125 per cent between 1980 and 1987 (Petley and Romano 1993: 29). With the expansion of broadcasting hours came growing dependence on imports, on which new commercial services tended to rely more heavily than PSBs (Chapters 7 and 8). Yet Euromedia Group researchers found that no PSB channel broadcast more than 55 per cent of 'serious' programmes in prime time, the highest being Norway (53 per cent), followed by Germany and Switzerland (50) while the UK share was 37, Italy 28, Spain 26 and Finland 24 (De Bens *et al.* 1992: 84).

For public service broadcasters there were three main strategies, described by Hultén and Brants (1992: 118) as adaption, purification or compensation (see also Siune and Hultén 1998). PSBs could seek to compete with commercial stations by offering popular entertainment programmes, a strategy pursued by RAI in Italy. They could withdraw from competition and seek to distinguish themselves by focusing on programmes the market shunned (purification). Alternatively, they could attempt to pursue a middle way, 'avoiding both the logic of commercial television and the role of a marginalised cultural enclave'. The strategies adopted remain relevant when considering the pressures and constraints on PSB today, but the conditions in which such strategies are adopted are radically altered as the era of analogue television gives way to digital.

Digital television

Until the 1990s, America had always been in the lead in television innovation and at any time Americans had more television channels than were available to viewers elsewhere. The US was one decade ahead of Europe in introducing multichannel television. With digital television, however, America was slower than Europe. It had been innovative in 1994 with the first auctioning of electromagnetic spectrum, but this had only released a tiny proportion for wireless telephony. The development of digital television was handed to the broadcasting industry, an indication of its power – especially that of the National Association of Broadcasters (NAB) – over politicians and regulators. Incumbent broadcasters were granted digital frequencies without paying for spectrum. An Advisory Committee (1998) under the authority of Vice President Al Gore proposed that, in return, each local station should broadcast three hours of children's programmes per week and offer free airtime for politicians during elections, but these proved to be vain attempts to revitalise the notion of broadcasters as public trustees (Benton Foundation 2007). Broadcasters reluctantly signed up, but the measures were never implemented. By 2000 political support for serious reform had waned, Gore was fighting for the presidency, and from 2001 the FCC had, in its new chairman Michael Powell, an uncompromising advocate of further deregulation. However, the FCC set February 2009 as the date for analogue switch-off, and while there are few digital-only channels, most broadcasters in 2007 were simulcasting in analogue and digital.

Technologically, the US was highly advanced but the television industry faced costly challenges and lacked the market incentives to adopt digital. Comprising many local markets, it lacked integration, while the low user-base and demand for digital TV created little incentive to invest – take-up was very slow compared to that in the UK. In his thorough comparative analysis Galperin (2004) sums up US policy as involving minimal reforms to the existing regime, a defence of commercial incumbents, fragmented implementation, and policy gridlock. In the UK, digital policy was developed by John Major's Conservative government (1990–97), and implemented largely under the New Labour government from 1997. Digital policy combined a strong promotion of principles of competition with efforts to sustain public service broadcasting. In contrast to the US, digital policy was characterised by extensive reforms to the existing regime, aggressive promotion of competition, and swift implementation (Galperin 2004).

Moving broadcasting from the analogue system to digital would enable more channels to be carried on existing terrestrial frequencies and free up spectrum to be sold for telecommunications, broadcasting and other uses. The 1996 Broadcasting Act established digital multiplexes which firms could bid for, to operate and to offer DTV services over them. Slots for digital versions of their analogue channels (simulcast) were guaranteed to the terrestrial public service channels. The BBC actively embraced digital broadcasting, securing government approval for new public service channels such as BBC Choice in 1998 and digital radio services.

The new digital terrestrial television (DTT) licence was awarded to ONdigital (later ITV Digital), formed by Carlton and Granada ,which launched in November 1998. However, the service faced fierce competition from BSkyB, which launched its digital satellite service on 1 October 1998, as well as from digital cable services from 1999 on. BSkyB, 40 per cent-owned by Rupert Murdoch, had been a partner in the winning consortium for the DTT licence until the television regulator, the ITC, ruled that BSkyB must withdraw as a condition of awarding the licence (see Horsman 1998: 195–206). BSkyB supplied some Sky channels to ONdigital, but the ITC ruling meant BSkyB was a competitor, and many analysts subsequently charted the failure of ONdigital's business model from this decision. Other factors, however, contributed to ONdigital/ITV Digital's demise, including poor programming and lower-than-anticipated consumer demand; signal and other technical problems; piracy; and highly competitive marketing and pricing strategies, especially following BSkyB's decision to give away digital set-top boxes. The ITC invited new bids and awarded the DTT service to Freeview, a consortium of the BBC, BSkyB and Crown Communications, which established a highly successful free service. By June 2007, 84 per cent of UK households received digital TV on their primary TV set. There were 9.1 million DTT-only households, slightly ahead of those with satellite – 9 million homes, of which 8.1 million were BSkyB subscribers (Ofcom 2007).

The first DTV broadcasts in Europe were in 1996 (via satellite), with Canal+ (France), DSTV (Telepiú) in Italy and DF1 in Germany all using different proprietary standards. Digital terrestrial television was first launched in the UK (November 1998, the same month as in the US), followed by Sweden (1999), Spain (2000), Finland (2001) and Germany (2002) (Brown and Picard 2005: 337). DTT had a difficult start in several European countries. In Spain and Greece, as in Britain, the original DTT operator went out of business. In Spain political interference was a contributing factor. Two rival digital platforms were established, allied to the two main political parties, while experts agreed that the market could sustain only one. Canal Satellite Digital (jointly owned by Prisa and Canal Plus) was aligned to the PSOE, while Via Digital was part owned by the state broadcaster TVE and Telefonica, whose management had close ties to both the PP and the old Franco dictatorship (Papatheodorou and Machin 2003).

Digital services have developed rapidly over recent years (Iosifides *et al.* 2005; Brown and Picard 2005). Sweden launched in 1999, initially to poor take-up. By 2002 DTT reached 90 per cent of households, but only 100,000 subscribed to the state-supported DTT platform, Boxer, until free digital boxes were given to all licence-paying households. In October 2007 Sweden completed the switch-off of its analogue terrestrial service. In general, the conversion of satellite and cable services has occurred fastest and has been determined mainly by commercial operators. The transition to digital for terrestrial broadcasting has involved government decisions (Brown and Picard 2005; Chapter 6). DTT has been the 'natural' platform for free-to-air channels (PSB and commercial) (Hujanen 2005) and of political importance and sensitivity for governments in determining when sufficient numbers have access to digital services, so that analogue signals can be switched off and the released spectrum sold or (exceptionally) reappropriated for public use.

The press: continuities and change

In post-war Europe the number of paid newspaper titles continued to decline. The 1980s saw a period of relative stability, but decline continued even more sharply, if unevenly, in the 1990s. Paid daily newspapers, especially, experienced a 'sustained' decline in the 1990s. In France, their number fell from 142 in 1950 to 69 in 1994; the Netherlands experienced a sharp decline from 115 in 1950 to 29 in 1996; while Norway experienced a comparatively small decline from 91 to 85 papers over the same period. Newspaper circulation and readership also fell steadily from the 1960s, leading many to forecast an inexorable decline in the medium. However, while the general trend has been downwards, a more complex pattern has emerged. In Spain, new papers emerged in the 1990s and newspaper reading increased overall. Political changes in Spain and Portugal after long periods of dictatorship have been put forward as explanations for this resurgence (Gustafsson and Weibull 1997), while Williams (2005: 31) identifies socio-economic developments as decisive, in particular the liberation of women from traditional domestic confinement and their increased reading of newspapers and magazines, following their entry into the labour market.

Competition from other media has been a factor in the decline, in particular the expansion of commercial television and radio stations. Yet there is little evidence to support the thesis that television viewing caused newspapers to decline in Western Europe (Gustafsson and Weibull 1997). Newspapers adapted to coexist and to compete with television, and continued to offer more detailed background information than TV news, as well as commentary and features. Social-cultural changes were undoubtedly a factor, and newspapers have struggled to attract and maintain numbers of younger readers. The decline of newspapers has also been largely the result of changing economic conditions, making more and more papers uneconomic. The relaxation of newsprint controls, maintained in many European countries into the 1950s, led to a period of increasing competition. With production costs rising steeply, many smaller papers succumbed. Advertising revenue became even more important, but tended to favour papers with more affluent readerships. In Britain the *Daily Herald* was selling a million copies a day, outselling all other national papers, but its demographic profile, older, more working class, attracted less advertising, a principal reason for the paper's downfall in 1963, although it had also failed to modernise its editorial appeal (Curran and Seaton 2003: 87–90).

The expansion of commercial television in the 1980s brought increasing competition for advertising, but newspapers retained a comparative advantage in job recruitment and classified advertising. Across Europe, paid newspapers still attract the majority share of media advertising. From the 1990s the small share of, but exponential rise in, internet advertising has provided a growing threat, particularly for papers reliant on classified advertisers or sectors such as housing and cars, where advertising is beginning to migrate to online sites (Chapter 7).

The *Wall Street Journal* is the largest-circulation daily in the US. Published by Dow Jones (until Murdoch's News Corporation acquired the paper in 2007), it has a readership of some five million, mostly affluent Americans. It has regional editions in Asia and *WSJ Europe*, which has a circulation of some 300,000. US papers have achieved an important international presence and influence. In global circulation eight of the top ten newspapers and magazines originate in the US (Thussu 2006: 124). The *International Herald Tribune*, originally jointly owned by the *New York Times* and *Washington Post* and bought by *NYT* in 2003, is an English-language paper based in Paris. In 1928 copies were flown to London from Paris each day to reach morning readers. By 2006 the paper was being printed via satellite at more than 30 sites and distributed in 180 countries (Thussu 2006: 123).

In the EU, 46 per cent of the citizens read a newspaper on a daily basis (CoE 2004). In line with the readership patterns outlined in Chapter 2, newspaper audiences are greatest in the north of Europe – in Finland and Sweden (77 per cent) and in Germany and Luxembourg (around 65 per cent) – while the lowest are found in the south – in Greece, Spain and Portugal, where the daily readership is around 20 per cent. According to UNESCO (2003), for every 1,000 inhabitants 261 Europeans read a daily newspaper, as compared to 141 Americans and a world average of 96 (cited in Williams 2005). Newspaper readership in the UK, Norway, Sweden and Finland is double that of the US. Scandinavia retains the highest readerships among Western media systems. In Sweden 80 per cent of adults read newspapers, despite a decline in circulation since the 1970s.

Technology

The newspaper industry was also transformed by waves of technological change and wider restructuring of the industry. Digitalisation impacted on the press earlier than on the broadcasting media, and print industries were the first to convert to digital technology as a means to reduce costs and improve production (Albarran and Chan-Olmsted 1998).

Computerisation was gradually introduced into newspaper production from the 1970s. But management efforts to introduce 'new technology' into production and printing met with resistance where trade unions were strong. In Britain, France, Germany and parts of Northern Europe trade unions had won significant concessions on working practices from newspaper owners in the 1960s. By the 1970s, as costs rose and many papers experienced falling profits, there was growing confrontation between management and print workers, including protracted strikes.

In Britain print workers had established protective 'closed shop' arrangements and initially fought the feminisation of the workforce (Cockburn 1991), as well as opposing the 'de-skilling' and loss of craft union jobs as a result of computerisation. Eddie Shah fought the trade unions, with Thatcher's support, and launched *Today* in 1986, but the paper struggled, was acquired by Murdoch's News International in 1987, and folded in 1995. *The Independent*, also launched in 1986, is the only successful national daily paper established since the tabloid *Daily Star* in 1978. In Britain the battle over new technology culminated in the 'Wapping Dispute' in 1986, the outcome of which was defeat for the print unions, with power shifting decisively to press owners, many of whom soon abandoned their traditional base in Fleet Street, London, for more cost-efficient, technologically advanced facilities.

New technology did not significantly offset the high and rising costs of production and distribution that meant many existing papers struggled to remain economically viable, and few papers were successfully launched into established markets. New technology reduced some costs, enabling some new players to enter the market, but very high barriers to competition in established markets remained. Concentration of newspaper ownership in the hands of a few increased, and today multiple ownership of titles is common in every sector of the newspaper industry. A small alternative press did grow in the 1970s, using low-cost production and reproduction and, later, computing technologies (Atton 2002). Further expansion occurred in the 1990s, with the successful launch and spread of daily free newspapers. The Swedish company Kinnevik introduced the concept of the free newspaper with *Metro*, since established in many European cities. *Metro* was launched in Sweden in 1995 and distributed to commuters in the capital Stockholm. With a skeletal staff and content relying heavily on wire services, the format was profitable, and by 2002 there were 22 editions of the paper in 14 countries (Hultén 2004: 239). Between 1995 and 2005 *Metro* launched free daily newspapers in over 100 cities around the world and in 15 languages (Tunstall 2008: 265). In the1990s the diffusion of the internet brought a further wave of change, transforming the very nature of the medium (Chapter 7).

In Chapter 2 we highlighted some important, enduring differences in market structure and readership levels. There is also significant variation in how and where newspapers are purchased. In the 'liberal' countries of the UK, Ireland, the US and Canada most newspaper are purchased at news-stands or other outlets, although North America has significant self-service kiosk sales which are negligible in the UK and Ireland. Most Northern Europeans subscribe, receiving their paper through the letterbox each morning.

State subsidies and the party press

In parts of Central and Northern Europe, states have intervened in the newspaper market. Even in America, newspaper businesses have benefited from action by the state, with reduced postal rates. However, in parts of Europe state intervention on a scale anathema to American polity was adopted. Some form of direct state aid for the press has featured in every European country, with the exception of Britain, Germany, Ireland and Switzerland (Humphreys 1996: 103). The most enthusiastic adopters were the Nordic countries, but also France, and Italy (see Williams 2005: 40–1), while Portugal also established distribution subsidies (Pinto and Sousa 2004: 182). The most developed and influential model was the Swedish press subsidy system, which originated in 1964 when the Swedish parliament voted to provide ten political parties with funds to assist with the costs of distributing their party newspapers. This failed to stop the decline of party papers, including those of the governing Social Democratic Party. In 1971 a scheme of supporting 'second papers' was introduced, to provide financial support towards the production costs of papers with circulations smaller than those of their competitors in relevant markets. This was funded in part by a tax on newspaper advertising and was administered by an independent agency, the Swedish Press Subsidies Council. According to Hadenius and Weibull (1999), over 57 newspapers received support in 1997 and 'second papers' in metropolitan areas received subsidies accounting for between 5 and 35 per cent of revenue. Norway's system of subsidies was introduced in 1969 and has slowed, but not prevented, monopolisation in local markets (Østbye 2004). All such subsidies were designed to redress monopolistic tendencies in the press and sustain media diversity in the face of commercial threats to the continuation of the once-dominant party-aligned press. In France, direct support (ECU150 million) and 'indirect support' from tax exemption has been calculated to amount to some ECU2 billion (Charon 2004: 71). For some critics, subsidies are seen as embodying state control over the press, interference in the 'free market', or providing indiscriminate subsidy. Spain scrapped its subsidy scheme, in part because it was tending to favour stronger papers with large circulations. Press subsidies in Austria were cut back by a new conservative-nationalist coalition government elected in 2000, falling to ECU7 million in 2001 from a peak of ECU15 million in 1990 (Trappel 2004: 11). However, the systems in Sweden and Norway developed strict economic criteria to ensure the 'politically neutral allocation of subsidies' (Murshetz 1998: 303 cited in Williams 2005: 42), controls lacking elsewhere. There is little doubt that subsidies have enabled a more diverse press to remain viable than under regulation by market forces alone. Strong critics of the government, such as Norway's anarchist *Klassenkampen* and France's communist/leftist *L'Humanité*, have been major recipients of state aid. Overall, subsidies have proved to be important but relatively weak forms of intervention in capitalist markets which, in the absence of stronger measures to prevent media concentration, have delayed but not countered the erosion of press diversity.

The decline of a party press that was strong in Northern and Southern Europe has meant that commercial papers dominate. In Austria the party press declined from 50 per cent in 1953 to 20 per cent in 1971 and 2.5 per cent by 2001 (Trappel 2004: 5). In Finland half the newspapers in 1966 were officially linked to political groups, falling to 18 of the 199 papers in 2001 (Österlunnd-Karinkanta 2004: 60). But while this indicates some convergence between the newspaper sectors of North America and Europe, significant differences in journalistic styles and cultures and orientation remain (Chapter 5).

The death of the newspaper has been predicted since 1945, although the perceived threat has changed over the period. There has been steady decline over the period, and most commentators would agree that the challenges for the press are mounting in the digital age, yet there have also been some countervailing signs of vigour. Newspapers have adapted to new technology and new opportunities, and there is also growing convergence between newspapers and broadcasting through the internet.

Conclusion

Between the 1950s and 1970s the institutional structures of major mass media remained relatively stable, while taking very different forms in WMS. Since the 1980s, media structures have changed markedly. How far and in what ways the old coexists with the new is examined in different ways in the chapters that follow.

The technological availability of new media changed the activities of media firms and policy makers. Where technological diffusion occurred, consumers could access what was, by the 2000s, an enormous range of new media services. With DTH satellite, cable and then ADSL broadband the barriers to accessing non-domestic media also fell dramatically for the majority of the population. However, to assess the impact we need to consider actual changes in the market and take-up of services. These are examined in Chapters 7 and 8. Here we have focused on the transformation of broadcasting in Europe, the shift to marketisation and the displacement of once-dominant PSB systems. Yet, while deregulation occurred across all WMS, significant differences remained, especially between the US and the broadcasting systems of Canada and Western Europe. As Blumler (1992a: 22) remarked, Europe was being 'partially transformed' by the forces of market capitalism, but these coexisted with 'many other forces and logics'. We shall defer an overall assessment of media system convergence until these forces and counterforces have been examined further.

4 Media theory

Paradigms and power

Introduction

This chapter outlines key traditions and paradigms in the analysis of the organisation of media and media systems. First, it examines normative–critical approaches towards the organisation of media which inform not only policy and regulation but also wider debates about the values that media systems should uphold. Second, it discusses analytical approaches to explaining and evaluating power in media systems. Among the huge range of theories of the media, this chapter is concerned primarily with issues relating to media structures and institutions, arising in consideration of media policy and the political economy of the mass media, and in consideration of media performance, both political and cultural.

PART 1: PARADIGMS OF MEDIA, DEMOCRACY AND POLICY

The paradigms I shall examine in this chapter are liberal democratic theory, neoliberalism, libertarianism, and critical political economy (CPE). Mapping these paradigms provides an analytical construct that can be used to assess historical changes in the governing values that inform communications policy, for wider evaluation. There are numerous possible divisions and demarcations of media policy positions (Siebert *et al.* 1963; Picard 1985; Collins and Murroni 1996; Curran and Seaton 1997; McQuail 1992, 1994). The paradigms selected here represent the principal political–philosophical divisions concerning communications policy and encompass the main framework of political, economic, cultural, ethical and legal values that shape evaluation of media systems.

Liberal democratic theory

Liberal theory of the press holds that the primary democratic role of the media is to oversee the state. This task requires that the media are 'free' from state interference. The theory supports a free-market economic model, particularly powerful in the United States and encapsulated in the 'marketplace of ideas' formulation of the US Supreme Court (Baker 1989).[1] But it can also give rise to justifications for state action to protect pluralism and diversity of opinion.

Freedom of expression is a foundational value of democratic political systems, and constitutionally enshrined in most, while some jurisdictions, notably the US and Germany, provide specific constitutional protection to media freedom. Article 10 of the European Convention on Human Rights (ECHR) guarantees 'freedom of expression and information, without interference by public authorities and regardless of frontiers', subject to certain restrictions, and this in turn provides the basis for media and information law within the Council of Europe (Lange and Van Loon 1991; Voorhoof 1995). Different justifications for a free-speech principle carry divergent implications for the scope of legal protection (Barendt 1987: 7). The argument from truth, espoused by Mill (1998 [1859]), is that truth arises from free circulation of ideas and opinions. In turn, this has been used to underpin 'marketplace of ideas' approaches that have seen free competition as the prerequisite for the circulation of truth. In absolutist and libertarian versions, this argues for the media to be free from all restraint by the state.[2] However, as Feldman (1993: 585) states, 'political liberalism requires a degree of control over the operation of markets in order to protect liberal values against market-expressed preferences'. Justifications *for* state intervention and regulation derive mainly from arguments for democracy. In order to secure a consensus of policy, free speech is required so that there may be the greatest opportunity for differing points of view to be aired and for sufficient information to be available as a basis for making decisions (Gibbons 1998: 24). It is a test of democracy that the public has ongoing access to information on the basis of decisions and the circumstances of decisions taken by those elected to govern. By contrast, an absolutist position on freedom of expression denies the state any legitimate powers to control or regulate speech.

The debate on the true character of freedom of expression is also an aspect of long-running controversy as to whether political freedom is only a 'negative' freedom from state control or comprises positive freedoms and rights (Barendt 1987: 78). Contained in Article 10 ECHR, for instance, is the implied duty of public authorities to take measures that ensure conditions for exercising the right of freedom of expression, including sustaining facilities and resources for freedom of expression and information (Foley *et al.* 1994; Voorhoof 1995).[3] The claim to positive action has arisen in particular in the European policy context and is related to the 'general evolution and "socialising" of the European Convention's rights and freedoms' (Voorhoof 1995: 54), for instance the emphasis on states' positive duties in respect of privacy or of protection of the right to life. It arises out of the strengthening and elaboration of the democratic basis for freedom of speech, namely the rights of recipients to receive a necessary range of ideas and opinions. Politically, it is also based on the social market, public welfare principles which also shaped European broadcasting regulation. The European Convention on Human Rights, drawn up in 1950 and ratified by Council of Europe (CoE) member states at various times, specifically acknowledges in Article 10 states' rights to license and regulate broadcasting.[4]

In the twentieth century, liberalism faced imperatives to resolve for each medium the inherent tensions and contradictions between economic and political freedom, between market freedom and ensuring that media support democratic processes (see Murdock 1992b). Different political systems favoured different solutions, depending on the leading values requiring protection, market conditions, and power interests shaping policy at any one time. *As the Four Theories of the Press* tradition outlined, two main responses came to be recognised as 'social responsibility' and 'social market'. The 'social responsibility' model was best articulated by the Hutchins Commission on Freedom of the Press in 1947 in the United States (Peterson 1963). This in turn influenced the 1947–49 Royal Commission on the Press in Britain (O'Malley 1997, Curran 2000). Both combined a critique of market failure in the press with promotion of media professionalism. For Curran (1996: 99):

> The cult of professionalism became a way of reconciling market flaws with the traditional conception of the democratic role of the media. It asserted journalists' commitment to higher goals – neutrality, detachment, and a commitment to truth. It involved the adoption of certain procedures for verifying facts, drawing on different sources, presenting rival interpretations. In this way, the pluralism of opinion and information, once secured through the clash of adversaries in the free market, could be recreated through the 'internal pluralism' of monopolistic media.

This 'Anglo-American' concept rejected a purely libertarian view of the press as unrestricted freedom for publishers. In part a response to mounting criticisms of concentrated ownership and the narrow business control of editorial agendas in the US press, the Hutchins Commission also drew upon the model of broadcasting regulation. It proposed that the press should become more like 'common carriers' for diverse opinions, should be subject to a stronger code of practice than the industry had created of its own accord, and should be monitored by a new independent agency. The Committee thus accepted a role for government in supplementing a privately owned media, but its defining boundary was that no economic restrictions should be placed on private enterprise.

The alternative 'social market' model, developed in several European countries, justified state intervention in markets on behalf of democratic objectives, in particular, pluralism of voice and, later, cultural diversity. In addition to public service broadcasting, the main forms of social market intervention have been press subsidies, and grants and subsidies for other media and cultural industries. According to social market perspectives, market competition cannot guarantee the conditions for a democratic media culture. This view was trenchantly argued by the UK Conservative government when it justified maintaining 'special media ownership rules' to prevent media concentration against a strengthening lobby calling for these to be liberalised. In *Media Ownership: The Government's Proposals* (Department for National Heritage 1995: 3, 16), it justified rules 'to provide safeguards necessary to maintain diversity and plurality' arguing: 'Television, radio and the press have a unique role in the free expression of ideas and opinion, and thus in the democratic process. The main objective must therefore be to secure a plurality of sources of information and opinion, and a plurality of editorial control over them.'

Neoliberalism

Neoliberalism defines the view that social development should proceed according to the dictates of the market, with the minimum of government involvement. Modern 'free market' media theory combines libertarianism with neoclassical economic theory of markets. The free market view (or 'market model', Croteau and Hoynes 2006) has been ascendant. A neoliberal paradigm of free market competition, dominant structurally and ideologically in the US from the 1980s, has increasingly taken the form of an international standard, influencing European, and in particular UK, communications policy (Chapter 6).

The core feature of neoliberal economic theory is a belief in the efficacy of markets and of market competition to provide the best and most desirable mechanisms for satisfying consumer wants. For Adam Smith (1776), market competition ensures that the best-quality goods are produced at the lowest prices. The search for market share ensures that producers adopt the most economically efficient means of production and deployment of labour. The marketplace is conceived of as a space in which individuals enter into voluntary transactions, and where the inherently conflicting interests of producers and consumers are resolved to the benefit of both parties. In neoclassical theory '[u]nder perfect competition economic resources are allocated between different goods and services in precisely the quantities which consumers wish (their desires expressed by the price they are prepared to pay on the market)' (Whish 1989: 4). Under perfect competition four conditions pertain: together with allocative efficiency, described above, there is productive efficiency: goods will be produced at the lowest possible cost. Third, price will not rise above marginal cost (in contrast to monopolists' ability to retain high prices) and fourth, competitive markets will encourage innovation and product development, thus maximising consumer benefits.

For Adam Smith, the state should provide those services which individuals or companies found it unprofitable to provide, such as external defence, internal security, national education, and roads. Smith also recommended public intervention in the sphere of culture to increase public knowledge and generate quality entertainment (Golding and Murdock 1996: 18). With the exception of such public, non-market goods, Adam Smith famously argued against state involvement in market competition, but did so on the grounds that the state can only bring about an outcome less desirable than that resulting from unregulated self-seeking (Caporaso and Levine 1992: 201). Libertarians go further in arguing that the state has no purpose interfering in any way in the integrity and freedom of economic transactions carried out between individuals.

Libertarianism

Libertarianism combines the political concept of natural, inviolable rights and individual self-determination with an assertion of property rights. For libertarian economists such as Nozick (1974), property rights are accorded the same status as rights to personal integrity and any attempt by the state to regulate these according to principles of social justice is condemned (see also Feldman 1993: 13). In the political sphere libertarianism conceives of rights as claims to liberty and autonomy, and the state as an inherently repressive force. As Curran and Seaton (1997) show, libertarianism's antipathy to state media involvement has influenced positions on the Right and Left and so problematises any neat political schema.[5] Libertarian arguments, often instrumentally advanced by corporations (Keane 1991: 89), have laid siege to state-supported media structures such as public service broadcasting, and, far more selectively, state involvement in media and communications. More widely, certain forms of 'left' libertarianism have also challenged the basis for state regulation and intervention, in particular supporting media cultures around the internet and new communications media. Here, strains of 'radical' capitalist entrepreneurialism merge with both anti-statist and participatory democracy arguments. Finally, postmodernism and libertarianism have been mutually influencing, not least in challenging the normative basis for media policy shared by both liberal-democratic and critical political economy approaches.

Critical political economy

Critical political economy mounts a critique of liberal-democratic media theory and of the capitalist market relations on which liberalism is contingent. Shaped by Marx's critique of capitalism, the Western Marxist critique of commodification, reification and the 'culture industry' (Adorno and Horkheimer 1979 [1944]), and by theories of 'strong', participatory democracy, political economy criticises the capitalist market system for its failure to deliver economic fairness, social justice or the basis for a democratic polity (Mosco 1996; McChesney 1998; Golding and Murdock 2005).[6] In place of the sovereign individual exercising free choice in the market, critical political economists follow Marx in shifting attention from the realm of exchange to the organisation of property and production (Golding and Murdock 1996: 14). Political economy begins with an analysis of how capitalism structures and circumscribes the exercise of social and economic power. It therefore addresses how market power operates against principles of free and freely informed exchange. A core feature of political economy approaches has been the analysis and critique of the increasing concentration of corporate media ownership, a process seen as integral to the logic of capitalism and so requiring not simply anti-monopoly measures by the state but transformation of the economic system (McChesney 1998, 1999).

For Golding and Murdock (2005: 61), critical political economy approaches are *holistic*, seeing the economy as interrelated with political, social and cultural life, rather than as a separate domain. They are *historical*, paying close attention to long-term changes in the role of state, corporations and media in culture. They are 'centrally concerned with the balance between private enterprise and public intervention'. Finally, 'and perhaps most importantly', they go beyond 'technical issues of efficiency to engage with basic moral questions of justice, equity and the public good'.

Assessment: market failure

Here I will draw together some common strands among the different paradigms considered so far. For liberal democracy, individuals must have access to a wide range of ideas and opinions in order to exercise their will and judgement as citizens, albeit to different degrees according to the democratic theory espoused (Baker 2002). In the liberal legal tradition freedoms collide, notably speech rights, and carefully circumscribed constraints upon speech may be tolerated. In spite of significant contradictions and inconsistencies in media regulation, the liberal democratic paradigm is based on cherished principles of non-interference by the state in the exercise of free speech. In response to monopolisation and abuse of property rights, liberal democracy favours the media professionalism/social responsibility model and industry self-regulation. Market failures, notably concentration of ownership, which endanger the democratic process, may be further tackled through special rules (sectoral regulation) or general competition law.

State intervention, which is anathema to the libertarian wing of economic liberalism, finds justification in 'social market' approaches developed in the twentieth century. For Keynes and later advocates of social market policies, market failure necessitates state intervention. From this tradition of economic thinking, which influenced social democratic policy, especially in Western Europe, the state may intervene in the exercise of property rights in the economy in order to support public policy objectives. There are three main types of market failure recognised by modern economists: externalities, public goods and monopolies. For neo-Keynesians and social market economists, the state may use a variety of measures, including those affecting the price and availability of goods, such as subsidies and fines. The other main mechanisms are forms of regulation, including the control of licensing and the application of rule-based standards, notably competition regulation, that can be legally enforced (Chapter 6).

Social market intervention has been strongest in the 'democratic corporatist' systems of Northern and Central Europe. But it was reasserted in the 1990s in what for Hallin and Mancini is a 'liberal' tending system, the UK. The Labour government in the late 1990s was influenced by a series of arguments made by neo-Keynesian economists. In a BBC-commissioned book, co-written with Gavyn Davies (later BBC Chairman), economist Andrew Graham (1997) challenged claims that the broadcasting market alone could either adequately satisfy consumer wants or serve citizens. He advanced four main reasons why broadcasting run on purely commercial terms would be undesirable, identifying these as: market failure, citizenship and community, democracy, and industrial policy. Each critique of market provision also supported the case for public service broadcasting as a 'highly effective form of intervention'.

A market system would tend towards concentration of ownership, owing to the economies of scale and scope in broadcasting (Chapter 7). Commercial broadcasting would produce 'market failure' in consumption as well as production. In a purely market system, consumers would fragment more than they really wished, buy less good programmes than was collectively desirable and underinvest in their own long-term development. Broadcasting could give rise to negative externalities (adverse effects arising from such things as the promotion of violence) as well as positive externalities, such as cultivating education (a 'merit good'). Media concentration, for instance, might be economically desirable, but democratically undesirable by allowing dangerous accumulations of media power. What could offset the various market failures, Graham argued, was public service broadcasting. Such arguments influenced the Davies Committee report on BBC funding and are evident in a speech by British Culture Secretary Chris Smith in 2000 in which he outlined five key characteristics of PSB concerning: democracy, education, the human spirit (culture), the economy and the nation. Smith emphasised entertainment: fun and enjoyment were legitimate and essential components of PSB, so that 'mixed channels ... providing a mix of information, education and entertainment exemplify what public service broadcasting is, or should be, about'. This vision of mixed programming, while reaffirmed by his successor, Tessa Jowell, became the principal target of commercial opposition, with growing pressure to restrict PSBs to content that the market did not provide (Chapter 6). Already by the time of the Davies Committee report (1999), Graham's expansive arguments concerning 'market failure' had been narrowed and reformulated. The report identified as 'foul' trading 'the BBC's use of licence fee money to make programmes of a type which could perfectly well be left to the private sector, so there is no "market failure" case for public funding'.

The social market approach gained salience partly because it adopted the dominant language of market economics to present a social and cultural case (Hardy 2004b). Critical political economy goes further in offering a more systemic critique of market provision. Curran (1996: 92–5) set out six reasons to challenge the belief that 'the free market produces a media system which responds to and expresses the views of the people'. First, 'market dominance by oligopolies has reduced media diversity, audience choice and public control' (92). Second, rising capitalisation restricts entry to the market, creating a zone of influence where 'dominant economic forces have a privileged position' (94). Third, the 'consumer representation thesis' ignores the decoupling of the link between the media and political representation since the original formulation of such accounts in the nineteenth century, influenced by a more politically diverse press. Fourth, the claim by liberal pluralists, that 'media controllers subordinate their ideological commitments to the imperatives of the market is only partly true' (95). Fifth, the concept of consumer sovereignty ignores the variety and complexity of influences which shape media content, notably in large, bureaucratised media organisations. Sixth, the idealised notion of market democracy ignores the structuring influence of advertising in commercial broadcasting and press, which Curran describes elsewhere as a 'licensing' power (Curran 1978, 1996).

PART 2: APPROACHES TO MEDIA

Thompson (1988, 1995) argues that there are three principal 'object domains' in the analysis of mass communications:

1   the process of production and diffusion of symbolic forms (situated in specific social-historical circumstances)
2   the construction of the media message
3   the reception and appropriation of media messages (symbolic meanings).

This approximates to three interconnected foci of production, content and audience (see also Meehan 1999: 149). This section follows the selective focus of most 'media systems' analysis on 'production', by considering approaches to the organisation of media systems, the sociology of media institutions and media power. However, any such selective focus needs to be conceived within, and connected to, the larger totality of media processes including 'content' and 'audience'. This is especially the case in considering questions of media power.

Liberal pluralism vs critical political economy

Over thirty years ago, in a provocative mapping, the division between 'liberal pluralist' and radical Marxist approaches to the media was used to structure the nascent field of media studies in Britain (Curran and Gurevitch 1977: 4–5):

> The pluralists see society as a complex of competing groups and interests, none of them predominant all of the time. Media organizations are seen as bounded organizational systems, enjoying an important degree of autonomy from the state, political parties and institutionalized pressure groups. Control of the media is said to be in the hands of an autonomous managerial elite who allow a considerable degree of flexibility to media professionals ...

> Marxists view capitalist society as being one of class domination; the media are seen as part of an ideological arena in which various class views are fought out, although within the context of the dominance of certain classes; ultimate control is increasingly concentrated in monopoly capital; media professionals, while enjoying the illusion of autonomy, are socialized into and internalize the norms of the dominant culture; the media taken as a whole, relay interpretative frameworks consonant with the interests of the dominant classes, ...

In the liberal pluralist paradigm power, including media power, is dispersed; the relationship of power to media content and media discourse is contingent. In the Marxist account, media play a key role in the management of society, the relationship between concentrated power and media discourse is one of determination. In the 1970s distinctive liberal and neo-Marxist approaches dominated and structured debates in Western media theory. Through the 1980s and 1990s such a division of the field became less tenable and less acceptable to all protagonists. Radical, neo-Marxist perspectives lost ground in the midst of a broader retreat from socialist influence and ideas, towards more pluralistic accounts of media power and influence. Liberal perspectives were also strengthened by a variety of different, even incompatible, intellectual currents that shared opposition to the perceived rigidities, reductionism and determinism of neo-Marxist approaches. These included postmodernism, cultural studies approaches, liberal sociology, what Fiske (1990) calls the 'process school' of semiotics, and emerging globalisation theories.

A major criticism is that, however modified and attenuated, critical political economy sustains a reductionist account of the relationship between culture and the economy in which the former is over-determined by the latter. In its most functionalist, 'vulgar Marxist' form, this posits that the 'superstructure', including media and culture, reflects the economic base, leading to a functionalist account of the mass media as a transmitter of ruling class ideology and a usually impoverished account of determination of media performance by state power or by the economic and political interests of media owners and advertisers. Political economy approaches, critics charge, offer an incomplete and partial account of media power, mediation and of the influences on media performance, in particular by neglecting media consumption and hence audience power, by failing to account for the complex range of influences on media performance, and by downplaying the relative autonomy and creativity of media workers (see Goldsmiths Media Group 2000 for a useful survey of debates).

Determination

Three related problems in particular must be acknowledged and addressed, then: reductionism, instrumentalism and the problem of determination. By instrumentalism, Golding and Murdock (2005: 73–4) refer to accounts that conceive of capitalist media corporations as instruments of class domination, acting to ensure 'the flow of information is consonant with their interests' according to an overriding instrumental logic. Herman and Chomsky's 'propaganda model' (1994) has been the target of such criticism. Their model was derived from analysis of American news media reporting in which they seek to explain 'mechanisms by which the powerful are able to dominate the flow of messages and limit the space of contesting parties' (Herman 1999). Theirs is a radical functionalist account that describes system-supporting mechanisms for elite domination. A chief criticism of their model is that it assumes that the most important influences on media all flow in one direction, towards supporting the status quo (Eldridge 1993; Schudson 2000; Curran 2002b), a deficiency acknowledged by Herman in a later essay (1999).

Such accounts of the strategic use of power by political or corporate elites tend to underestimate contradictions in the system, and the way in which actors, including owners, advertisers and key political personnel 'operate within structures that constrain as well as facilitate, imposing limits as well as offering opportunities' (Golding and Murdock 2005: 74; see also Garnham 2000; Curran 2002b; Hesmondhalgh 2007). They also tend to neglect other forces which influence and help to explain the diversity or 'contradictions' of content and output. Herman and Chomsky argued that beyond the main 'filters' were 'secondary effects', some of which support propagandist purposes while others, such as the professional integrity of journalists, could be countervailing influences. The revising tradition of critical scholarship goes further in identifying the range of contradictory forces that the media in liberal democracies are subject to (see below).

However, critical political economists have also striven to develop a non-reductive analysis of the way in which the capitalist mode of production may be understood as determining the structure and practices of social communication. For Garnham (2000: 41) the economic system is determining in two main ways. First, because it produces results which influence and shape behaviour but which are 'systemic' in that they are beyond the action or control of individual economic actors. Second, because it is a necessary condition for the level of production and reproduction required to sustain advanced societies. Garnham, while not engaging with an ecological critique of such productivism, is nevertheless at pains to reject a crude structure–agency binarism, arguing that the system only works so long as human agents continue to act according to the 'bounded rationality' of the occupational situation in which they find themselves, itself structured according to the capitalist division of labour (Garnham 2000: 42–3).

Media sociology, influenced by occupational sociological studies and the 'ethnographic turn' (Boyd-Barrett 1995: 273), has provided a necessary addition, as well as corrective, to political economy accounts (see Boyd-Barrett 1995; Goldsmiths Media Group 2000), as well as offering a complex account of the differentiated roles of media workers and of power relations among agents.[7] Commercial media institutions are driven by core economic interests to secure future profitability and expand market share. But in addition to market forces, organisations are subject to other forces, including countervailing ones. Studies of journalistic media (Gans 1980; McQuail 1992; Baker 1994; McNair 1998; Bennett 2004) identify key influences as:

- Economic influences (including economic structure, levels of competition and ownership concentration, influence of advertising)
- Political influences (governments, politicians, pressure groups and powerful interests as well as political–legal framework and wider political culture)
- 'Sources' and interaction with extramedia social actors
- Technology
- Management control, corporate policies and organisational dynamics
- Professional culture and norms
- Gender, ethnicity, and social, cultural backgrounds of professionals and actors
- Reader or viewer preferences and influences.[8]

No media system, including that of the United States, was ever simply the product of corporate and commercial pressures. Media systems are shaped by the complex interaction of political, economic, technological, social and cultural influence, as well as by each media component's historically determined rules (McQuail 1992: 82–98).

Media ownership and influence

With the rise of conglomerate ownership, political economists have acknowledged the increasingly varied and complex forms of ownership and wider networks of corporate power (Mosco 1996: 173–99), but can be distinguished by efforts to sustain a critique of the structural implications of capitalist ownership of the media. There have been numerous challenges to the links made between media ownership and influence, ownership and pluralism, competition and content diversity (Chapter 7). Assessing the influence of ownership and proprietorial or corporate interests on media practices and content thus raises a host of critical issues and debates.

One focus has been on the nature of the controls exercised. Murdock (1982) drew on the distinction between allocative and operational control of firms, to argue that managerial elites exercised operational rather than allocative control; the latter, including control over policy, resources and dictating of editorial lines, being retained by owners. McQuail (1992) highlights the difficulties of separating allocative from operational control among the problems for analysis, which also include isolating ownership from other variables influencing content. Another focus has been upon structure–agency relationships, assessing the changes and variables affecting how far autonomy may be exercised by media workers (Golding and Murdock 2005; Beck, A. 2003; Hesmondhalgh 2007). Goldsmiths Media Group (2000) reviews the challenges made to traditional political economic accounts in pluralist, post-Fordist and other studies that indicate devolved patterns of managerial control. Such accounts have suggested that media workers in conglomerate firms may enjoy protection from owner influence, through the intermediate layers of management, and may operate with a sufficient degree of autonomy to mitigate or even cancel altogether the threat to pluralism posed by media concentration and consolidation. Such studies certainly highlight the need for micro-empirical investigations of labour. The authors, however, discern a shift from positive accounts of independence in the 1980s to more 'sober' assessments of the effects of 'insecure employment' on autonomy in the 1990s, and they conclude that '[f]or many, operations may have been dispersed, but power and profits have not' (Goldsmiths Media Group 2000: 32). Summing up the broad findings of this merged tradition, Cottle (2000b: 17) writes: '[c]hanging media structures and processes therefore shape the production contexts and frame the operations, budgets and strategic goals of media institutions, and these are condensed within senior decision making and must be professionally (pragmatically) negotiated by media professionals and producers in their daily practices'.

Media and power

There are many ways of conceiving of media power, but one of the most influential is that of 'symbolic power'. For Thompson (1995: 16), symbolic power 'stems from the activity of producing, transmitting and receiving meaningful symbolic forms'. Media power is defined by Couldry (2000a: 4) as 'the concentration in media institutions of the symbolic power of "constructing reality" (both factual representations and credible fictions)'. If symbolic power is the power of media to construct reality, then a full account of power must include content and reception – what people think and do in relation to the media meanings constructed. We can justify focus on various aspects of media power – for instance, how the resources for symbolic meaning are organised and concentrated in media organisations. These are what Herbert Schiller (1989: 156) calls the 'locus of representational and definitional power'. But meaning is the complex outcome of social interaction, and so symbolic power must be recognised in relation to the full process of meaning making (Couldry 2000a: 4).

Symbolic power, according to Thompson (1995: 17), refers to the 'capacity to intervene in the course of events, to influence the actions of others and indeed to create events, by means of the production and transmission of symbolic forms'. This is one of four main types of power (Table 4.1). Economic power stems from the organisation of human productive activity. Political power stems from the activity of coordinating individuals and from regulating the patterns of their interaction. For Weber, the capacity of states to command authority (political power) is generally dependent on their capacity to exercise two related but distinct forms of power: coercive and symbolic. States seek to retain sole legitimacy for use or threat of physical force (coercive power). State authority can be supported by the diffusion of symbolic forms which seek to cultivate and sustain belief in the legitimacy of political power, especially in democratic systems. In modern democratic societies the task of social coordination is increasingly borne by the mode of persuasion over coercion, with the crucial exception of policing minorities of various kinds. These four forms of power, then, are analytically distinct, but overlap in complex ways. This is particularly important in considering the media (symbolic power), which involves conjunctions with each other kind of power.

The concept of symbolic power is valuable in focusing attention on the range of power sources that might influence media content and on the dynamic nature of contests for access to media resources or opportunities to affect the definitional power of media. This definitional or 'discursive' power of the media is identified

Table 4.1 Forms and resources of power

Forms of power	Resources	Key institutions
Economic power	Material and financial	Economic institutions (e.g. resources, commercial enterprises)
Political power	Authority	Political institutions (e.g. states)
Coercive power	Physical and armed forces	Coercive institutions (especially the military, but also the police, carceral institutions, etc.)
Symbolic power	Means of information and communication	Cultural institutions (e.g. the church, schools and universities, the media industries, etc.)

Source: Thompson (1995: 17)

by Street (2001) as one of three main forms of media power. *Discursive power* operates through the way the media privileges particular discourses and constructs particular forms of reality. This has been explored in research on agenda setting (McCombs 2004) and framing (Entman 1993), particularly by North American scholars. In a wider use of the concept Couldry (2000a: 14) refers to the framing function of the institutional sphere of the media as a whole: '[a]ny theorisation of the media's social impacts must start from their privileged role in framing our experiences of the social, and thereby defining what the "reality" of our society is'. The second type of power is *access power*, whose voices, identities and interests populate our electronic screens and newspapers. Attention to access power includes addressing how particular interests or identities are articulated or excluded in the media (a focus of critical cultural studies) and how media institutions and systems are structured in relation to access to communication resources (a focus of critical political economy).

The third type of power is *resource power*, which refers to the ways in which media conglomerates can affect the actions of governments and states. This focuses on how media forms can use their 'symbolic power', their media resources, to secure favourable conditions from politicians, a topic discussed more fully in Chapters 5 and 6.

Revising critical political economy: synthesis, holism and humility

Synthesis

The interweaving of critical political economy, sociology and critical cultural theory has produced synthesising accounts that are more open and less deterministic, while sharing a focus on the nature and effects of power imbalances in communication resources. These approaches may be called 'radical pluralist'. They acknowledge the potentiality for creativity, agency and uncertainty within the production process, as well as its structuring limitations. In turn, structures are conceived as 'dynamic formations that are constantly reproduced and altered through practical action', so that 'analyzing the way that meaning is made and remade through the concrete activities of producers and consumers is equally essential' (Murdock and Golding 2005: 63).

Curran (2002b) reviews the various liberal and radical traditions in media sociology and puts forward a revising map identifying key forces that serve to sustain relations of power and countervailing forces. There is space only to list these here, but they are examined in more detail at various points in later chapters. Eleven main factors are identified that encourage media to support dominant power interests:

- State censorship
- High entry costs (economic barriers to mass media production)
- Media concentration
- Corporate ownership

- Mass market pressures (i.e. commercial incentive to maximise audiences)
- Consumer inequalities (i.e. provision 'skewed' towards serving affluent consumers)
- Advertising influence
- Rise of public relations
- News routines and values
- Unequal resources (unequal access to economic, social and 'cultural' capital)
- Dominant discourses.

Countervailing influences include:

- Cultural power (intra- and inter-group influences of alternative understandings/values)
- State empowerment (for instance, press subsidy systems and forms of public broadcasting)
- Media regulation
- Source power (capabilities of groups, including 'resource poor' groups, to secure media exposure or access)
- Consumer power
- Producer power
- Staff power.

Holism

A full account of media power must be inclusive and holistic. Media power is

> constituted both through institutional structures, and the unequal distribution of access to the means of media production which they entail, and the broadly cultural processes which help reproduce the media's legitimacy. There is no contradiction, therefore, between 'political economy' approaches which concentrate on the first and 'cultural' approaches which concentrate on the second. On the contrary, they require each other.
>
> (Couldry 2000a: 194)

In a related plea for better-integrated research on media production and consumption Deacon (2003: 209) argues

> [t]here is no reason why different elements of the 'the totality formed by the social relations of the communication process as a whole' (Hall 1993: 3) cannot be separated empirically – whether for positive reasons (for example, the accruing of expertise in particular areas) or out of practical necessity ... However, empirical divisibility should not become a pretext for theoretical isolationalism, in which attendance to the complexities of one phase is used to justify disregard for the other. Holism is essentially a mind-set, in which specialization should be seen as the basis for greater theoretical integration rather than a barrier to it.

Humility

While the importance of the economic and political forces shaping media production and organisation are widely acknowledged, the conclusions of critical political economic analyses are condemned as 'often predictable, portraying corporate ownership leading to rigid forms of social control' (Negus 1999: 15). The synthesising of radical media sociology and cultural theory with CPE has sought to address these criticisms (Golding and Murdock 2005; Hesmondhalgh 2007). A key response has also been to acknowledge the limitations of political economic analyses and the implications these have for studying the 'circuit of culture' (du Gay *et al.* 1997), a model designed to address the interconnectedness of aspects of culture identified as production, consumption, regulation, texts and identity. The third important component of revision, then, is 'humility', incorporation into analysis of the recognised limitations, as well as value and importance, of a political-economic consideration of media processes. US political economist McChesney (1999: 31) argues that the core 'structural factors' influencing the nature of media content in the US media system (including the overall pursuit of profit, size of firm, levels of media concentration and competition, advertiser influence, 'the specific interests of owners, managers and, to a lesser extent, employees') provide a 'context (and a trajectory)' for understanding media content, but 'can only rarely provide a detailed understanding of specific media content' (see also Mosco 1996; Hesmondhalgh 2007).

Challenges

This section has identified some key revisions to critical political economy but has not sought to situate them within the full range of alternative approaches to media. Marxian influence has declined, while much postmodernist cultural theory rejects shared assumptions of liberal and radical approaches, both of which, critics charge, share assumptions rooted in the mass media/mass society era. McNair (2006), for example, argues that CPE retains a control paradigm, while the current era is best understood in terms of a chaos paradigm. Davis (2003) challenges the presumptions of 'mass communication', and failure to revise these to address shifts to more targeted communication among elites and with publics. However, in the analysis of media institutions and public communication, the earlier mapping of liberal and radical approaches retains value and salience. Traceable to their liberal roots, theories of power as dispersed across society have come to dominate, but neither these nor accounts of assured media control by political and economic elites are satisfactory. More positively, there has been a shift from doctrinaire pronouncements to a more empirically driven investigation of how and under what conditions different kinds of power are exerted, work that has contributed to greater fusion of positions that were starkly separated in the early 1980s.

Public sphere: critical tools for analysis and evaluation

Habermas's *Structural Transformation of the Public Sphere*, first published in 1962, has had an enormous impact on Western media scholarship, especially following its translation from German into English in 1989. Habermas argued that the eighteenth-century bourgeoisie in Britain, France and Germany engaged in critical discussion through face-to-face communication in coffee houses and other shared spaces and mediated communication, especially through newspapers and periodicals. For Habermas, this early bourgeois public sphere provided a space for collective will-formation in which an autonomous public opinion was created that influenced government policy. For Habermas (1989: 36):

> *Les hommes*, private gentlemen, or *die Privatleute* made up the public not just in the sense that power and prestige of public office were held in suspense; economic dependencies also in principal had no influence. Laws of the market were suspended as were laws of the state. Not that this idea of the public was actually realised in earnest in the coffee houses, the *salons*, and the societies; but as an idea it had become institutionalised and thereby stated as an objective claim. If not realised, it was at least consequential.

Habermas's own account has been described as a 'melancholic historical narrative in two acts' (Dahlgren 1995: 7). The public sphere was destroyed by the very forces that brought it into existence, undermined by corporate and state power, as commercially driven media came to dominate and the state, political parties and other large organisations 'used their control of social resources and political power, as well as the techniques of public relations, to dominate the process of public communication' (H&M 2004a: 81). The concept of the public sphere has gained considerable currency, especially in Anglo-American scholarship. However, the term has been incorporated into a variety of different, sometimes incompatible, accounts of the media. In more liberal-tending versions, the public sphere equates to the existing public media, serving a largely descriptive purpose that draws attention to the space and processes of mediated interaction and political opinion formation. For critical political economists, by contrast, the public sphere serves as a problematic. As Golding and Murdock (2005: 77) write '[t]his general ideal of a communications system as a public cultural space that is open, diverse and accessible, provides the basic yardstick against which critical political economy measures the performance of existing systems and formulates alternatives'. Garnham (1990, 1992) provided a highly influential 'reinterpretation' of Habermas (Curran 2004: 18), extracting from the public sphere ideal and the emphasis on the material conditions for mediated democratic communication, a principled defence of public service broadcasting.

An influential model of media citizenship was thus derived from Habermas's original account of the public sphere and adopted in arguments to oppose market dominance and justify expansion of non-commodified public media (see also Croteau and Hoynes 2006). The 'public sphere' model, however, primarily addresses the informational role of the media serving the needs of rational deliberation. Criticism has been made of both the privileging of rational discourse in Habermas's model and the positing of a centred, rational subject as the agent of communicative exchange. Of the numerous criticisms (see Calhoun 1992a; Keane 1998: 157–89; Goldsmiths Media Group 2000), the treatment of non-political communication and entertainment media is particularly salient in considering media systems. The Habermassian public sphere privileges the exchange of information and opinion in line with liberal media theory. The latter, Curran argues (2002d: 237–9), neglects the entertainment activities of media on the untenable grounds that these are not part of rational exchange and not concerned with public issues. This critique is amplified by numerous media scholars (Dahlgren 1995; McGuigan 1996, 1998; Garnham 1992; Hesmondhalgh 2007). McGuigan (1998: 98) notes the 'tantalizing brevity' of Garnham's remark in 'The Media and the Public Sphere' (1992) that entertainment is 'a crucial and neglected area of media and cultural studies research', and goes on to highlight the fact that most of the actual research about the entertainment content of the media 'usually operates in a very different space from research that is grounded in a problematic of the public sphere'. Political theorists, communications and feminist scholars have challenged and deconstructed information/entertainment divisions, addressing, for instance, how politics is constituted through entertainment (Street 2001: 60–79; see Calhoun 1992a) and assessing the limitations of what McGuigan (1996) calls the 'politics of information'.

Yet, while CPE has adopted these deficiencies it also provides resources to address them. Central here is the development of a radical democratic perspective, offering what Curran (1991, 2002d) described as a third way between liberalism and Marxism. This approach is characterised by synthesising and combining market and statist strategies (Curran 1991: 46; 2004), derived from a complex, multidimensional analysis of the state[9] and addressing problems arising from both state and market provision. It rejects the radical functionalism of the 'propaganda model' in favour of a more complex account of media power. It promotes strong democratic values while critically addressing limitations of the original Habermassian public sphere, such as the failure to take adequate account of organised groupings and their relationship to media in modern societies. There are three principal features.

1 An expanded concept of citizenship

Murdock (1992b) argues that, in addition to access to the full range of information, citizens must have scope to engage with the greatest range of contemporary experience, both personal and collective; to excavate the historical roots of present conditions; to have access to the broadest range of viewpoints, expressed in the widest range of possible voices and forms. Here, the informational, political speech role of media is privileged, but this argument connects a much broader range of media provision and mediated communication to underlying values of citizenship.

2   *Critique of market liberalism*

Against market liberalism, critical political economists argue that unregulated markets cannot satisfactorily either serve the needs of citizens or satisfy the wishes of audiences (Baker 2002). The market system is inherently exclusive and inegalitarian, in tension with principles of democracy and justice. A market-orientated media system does not provide adequate means to distinguish between people's private and individual role as consumers and their public and collective role as citizens (Hoynes 2002: 3) or reflect non-market preferences. The special nature of communication goods renders the media particularly susceptible to market failures (Congdon *et al.* 1995; Graham and Davies 1997; Baker 2002). Consumer demand is only partially effective in oligopolistic, commercially driven systems, financed by advertising. Media conglomeration diminishes competition (McChesney 1999). The increasing power of private economic interests over the political process undermines democracy and further removes the market and economic agents from democratic control. However, the radical democratic approach also challenges the limitations of statist alternatives to market provision and acknowledges the value of markets in meeting market-expressed preferences and benefits arising from market competition and innovation.

3   *Complex model of how the media should be organised*

This multidimensional assessment of state and market informs radical democratic models of how the media *should* be organised that draw on another key argument, namely that there are different tasks required of media in a democratic system that can best be served by having a combination of media sectors differentially organised, controlled and financed, generating different media spaces and styles. Curran (1991, 2002d) provides the best exposition of such a normative model, proposing a core public service sector encircled by private, social market, professional and civil media sectors. For Baker (2002), this compound model is best able to serve a 'complex democratic perspective', one that combines and goes beyond elite, republican (participatory) and liberal-pluralist democratic theories. It seeks to ensure that the media system is not controlled by either the state or market, while incorporating both state regulation and private media. There are dynamic disequilibria in the system: the various sectors not only provide different purposes but also ways of influencing the performance of other sectors to strengthen media independence, enhance diversity and generate quality. Such normative models were constructed to address problems in Anglo-American media systems, and their authors would reject universalising them as a blueprint against the grain of diverse existing media systems. They provide, rather, a way of evaluating performance according to a more complex set of criteria than those shaping the *FTP* tradition.

This selective and partial survey has considered the critical–normative tradition of political economy and its interrelationship with other approaches to the analysis of media institutions and systems. The following chapters build on this analysis by examining in greater detail relationships between the media and politics (Chapter 5), policy (Chapter 6) media ownership and transnationalisation (Chapters 7 and 8).

5 Media and politics

Introduction

The relationship between the media and political power structures in society, and the changing nature of political communication are immense and rapidly changing objects of enquiry that have benefited from increasing scrutiny and comparative analysis by political science and media scholars alike. Drawing on these resources, this chapter describes key features of the dynamic and reciprocal relationship between media and politics. The first part examines the relationship between political systems and media systems, drawing upon and assessing Hallin and Mancini's (2004a) comparative analysis. Part two examines key trends and variations in political communication and the mediated communication of politics.

PART 1: POLITICS AND MEDIA SYSTEMS

Political system differences

Hallin and Mancini (2004a) ask: can stable connections be identified between media systems and political systems? Their answer is 'yes', but it is qualified by their effort to avoid positing narrowly causal explanations because of the 'preliminary' status of research and the complexity of systems. There are connections between patterns of development of media systems and key characteristics of political systems, they argue, but these are better understood in terms of co-evolution and the traceable influences of common historical roots. How political systems developed has shaped the conditions and influenced the characteristics of media systems. Their relationship is reciprocal and interlinked, especially as we consider the influence of media on politics. All Western states have formally democratic systems. However, they differ in the manner in which democratic politics is organised today and are marked by very different political histories. Several states developed democratic institutions 'early' in the eighteenth and nineteenth centuries. In the twentieth century most Western states experienced periods of authoritarian rule either by occupying powers or domestic regimes, the exceptions including the US, the UK, Canada and Switzerland. The transition to modern democracy occurred latest in parts of Southern Europe. In Greece, Spain and Portugal, authoritarianism only gave way to democratic systems in 1974–75. Another division is between 'liberal' and welfare state democracies. The post-war authoritarianism in Spain, Portugal and Greece delayed the creation of welfare systems. The ideology of social democracy on which welfarism is based was much weaker in the 'new' democracies and, when established in the 1970s, was already being challenged by rising neoliberalism. By contrast, most of Western Europe, including France and Italy, established strong welfare states after the Second World War. To varying degrees the US, Canada, Ireland and the UK adopted 'liberal' characteristics, espousing private enterprise over state intervention. There are five 'principal dimensions' through which Western political systems can be categorised.

The role of the state

How states intervene in the media (a media system variable) is clearly connected to the wider role of the state in society and to what kinds of action and intervention have political sanction and legitimacy. Particularly salient for WMS are differences between the restricted role of the state promoted in liberal-tending systems against more active state intervention in welfare state democracies. However, even in systems espousing a 'limited' role, the state has been an active agent in the development of capitalist society, including the media. The US has given vital economic and political support to communications industries, from state investment in research by media and technology firms, to political support for US interests in international policy forums. More broadly, the international competitive strategy of the US from the 1960s until the more recent embrace of greater liberalisation has been described as 'neoprotectionism', involving intensive state intervention on trade issues (Sánchez-Ruiz 2001; Chapter 6).

The majoritarian or consensus character of political systems

Lijphart (1999) distinguishes between majoritarian systems, usually dominated by two main parties competing for power to govern and represent the nation, and consensus systems, typically multiparty democracies characterised by power sharing between ruling parties and requiring mechanisms for compromise and cooperation between opposing factions. Majoritarian systems are characterised by parties seeking to represent the nation as a whole, rather than competing to increase power for particular interest groups. Such systems tend towards 'catch-all' parties seeking to appeal broadly across social divisions, although this is more characteristic of the US presidential system than the 'Westminster system' in Britain (H&M 2004a: 51).

Patterns of interest group organisation and influence (individualised vs organised pluralism; liberalism vs corporatism)

Individualised pluralism describes 'systems in which political representation is conceived and organized in terms of the relation between governing institutions and individual citizens' (H&M 2004a: 53). This can be distinguished from 'organised pluralism', where groups represent different segments of the population and are formally integrated into the policy process to varying degrees. Corporatism, a process of continuous political bargaining between state bureaucracies, political parties and interest groups, in particular representatives of labour and capital, is a defining feature of North and Central European states. It developed in the early twentieth century and comprises three main traits: 'an ideology of social partnership expressed at national level; a relatively centralised and concentrated system of interest groups'; and continuous political bargaining between political parties, interest groups and state bureaucracies (Katzenstein 1985: 32, cited in H&M 2004a).

Distinction between moderate and polarised pluralism

Polarised pluralism arises where there are significantly deep ideological divisions and a highly conflictual political life, usually with the presence of significant 'antisystem' parties challenging the legitimacy of the underlying political order, such as communist or fascist parties. Where there is greater acceptance or less challenge to the underlying order and ideological differences between significant parties are less great, political scientists speak of 'moderate' pluralism. Britain may be characterised as a moderate pluralist system. Antisystem parties include, on the far right, the anti-immigration British National Party, the anti-EC UK Independence Party, and on the left, Respect and several small socialist parties. These antisystem parties are electorally marginal and the 'Westminster' political system remains dominated by two main parties, with a smaller Liberal Democrat party, all of which support underlying principles of parliamentary democracy, a market economy, welfare state provision and judicial independence. In addition, there is a powerful Scottish Nationalist Party, an electorally weaker Welsh nationalist party (Plaid Cymru) and a legacy of extreme polarisation in the disputed province of Northern Ireland.

Clientalism vs rational–legal authority

The fifth key variable H&M describe is between the entrenchment of rational–legal authority and clientalist forms of social organisation. Rational–legal authority refers to a rule-governed system in which formal, universalistic rules of procedure are applied. The two key forms of such authority are bureaucracy, which for Weber characterised an administrative apparatus acting according to established procedures, autonomous of particular parties, social groups or individuals and instead oriented to serve society as a whole; and an independent judiciary. Clientalism is defined as a 'pattern of social organization in which access to social resources is controlled by patrons and delivered to clients in exchange for deference and various forms of support' (H&M 2004a: 58). Here, personal connections, or connections mediated through political parties, are more important than formal rules and procedures, and adherence to the latter may be weak.

Media system variables

As we have seen (Chapter 1), Hallin and Mancini identify four main clusters of media system variables. All are integral to explaining media–political relationships, but three have a direct connection to political system attributes.

State intervention in the media system

Media systems can be distinguished by the nature and extent of state involvement in the media. Intervention takes many forms, from regulation, ownership, finance, subsidies and other 'formal' controls, to informal influence (see Chapter 6).

Political parallelism

Political parallelism refers to 'the degree and nature of links between media and political parties or, more broadly, the extent to which the media system reflects major political divisions in society' (H&M 2004a: 21). It extends the notion of party–press parallellism (Seymour-Ure 1974) not only to encompass wider media but also to reflect a wider conception of the 'political', to include non-party groups and issues beyond 'established' parliamentary politics. Indicators of political parallelism include the extent to which media content reflects distinct political orientations or allegiances, and the orientation and professional practice of journalists, whether towards providing more neutral reporting, or serving a 'publicist' role in political communication. Another indicator is organisational connections between media and political parties or organisations such as churches, trade unions and civil society associations. A fourth component is the involvement of media personnel as formal political actors. A fifth feature is for the career advancement of media personnel to be conditional on political affiliations, and finally, partisanship of media audiences is another.

Professionalism

The concept of journalistic professionalism is among the more controversial and contested in *Comparing Media Systems*. As the authors are acutely aware, the legacy of Anglo-American studies has been to associate professionalism with political neutrality and 'objectivity' and, with varying caveats, to privilege US journalism as a model. Accordingly, the delinking of media from organised party or political interests is perceived to mark a higher stage of development. H&M explicitly reject and strive to avoid reproducing this triumphant evolutionist account, but only partially succeed. Some problems derive from the fact that the term 'professionalism' is used to describe many different characteristics. At a more basic level it is unavoidably pejorative to speak of more/less, weak/strong professionalism in the contemporary context of formally 'professional', salaried and trained journalism. Professionalism refers to the degree to which journalists can 'enjoy autonomy in exercising their functions' (H&M 2005: 219). Another criterion is evidence of shared norms and standards of practice (reflexivity and agreement among professionals) and the degree to which journalism has developed both as a profession and as a differentiated social 'field', in Bourdieu's terms (Bourdieu 1998). Thirdly, 'the degree to which journalists see themselves and are seen by society as serving the public as a whole rather than particular sectors or actors' (H&M 2005: 219). Political parallelism and professionalism are pivotal structuring terms for Hallin and Mancini, since their comparative account focuses in particular on the relationship of political systems with news media and political journalism. We will return to consider different notions of media autonomy and their consequences for comparative analysis below.

Hallin and Mancini: three models of media and politics

In distilling a considerable amount of accumulated scholarship, Hallin and Mancini offer a detailed analysis of the historical evolution of Western systems. Their three models focus especially on media and political relationships and provides the principal basis for the following short summary below before I critically review aspects of their analysis. It is worth repeating their emphatic caveat that countries grouped under each model all have important differences as well as similarities, that 'media systems' are internally complex, dynamic and changing, and that many can be considered as mixed cases combining elements from more than one model.

The Mediterranean or 'Polarized Pluralist' model

The 'Polarized Pluralist' model is characteristic of Southern Europe, Greece, Italy, Portugal, Spain and France, with the latter in particular representing a mixed case. These media systems shared a low-circulation, elite-centred and politicised press and high levels of state involvement in the media sector. A key characteristic for Hallin and Mancini is that journalistic professionalism developed later and more weakly in Southern than in Northern Europe and North America. Factors here included the lower status afforded to the profession of journalism and the lack of agreed and codified standards of professional practice. Professionalism is deemed 'low' principally because of the influence of politics on journalism (the relative lack of 'differentiation' between the spheres of journalism and politics) and limits on journalistic autonomy, although this has been increasingly contested by journalists. Above all, the media are subject to a high degree of instrumentalism. This refers to the use of media as an instrument to serve economic, cultural or political objectives. For Hallin and Mancini (2004a: 114, 37) the most significant form of instrumentalism has been by commercial owners, sometimes private and sometimes formally linked to the state, using media to exert influence in the political world.

In Italy, large-scale but unprofitable newspapers were established in the early twentieth century, with the backing of industrial and financial enterprises that sought to use them to enhance political influence. In Greece too, industrialists from sectors such as shipping and construction have used media acquisitions for political bargaining purposes. This long tradition is evident in contemporary owner-ship patterns and manoeuvring (Papathanassopoulos 2001). Media–political elite integration has also been strong in southern states. Political parties in Italy 'have always been involved in editorial choices and the structure of the mass media, thereby assuring their loyalty' (Mancini 1991: 139). Such political instrumentalism is connected to the interventionist role of the state in the Mediterranean model. Even where states have been weak in their capacity to govern, they have tended to be highly interventionist in regard to media, through direct ownership and control of media as well as through regulation. Partly, this has arisen because the media have been weak economically; with the exception of France, the press was economically weak and thus more dependent on state support or on the involve-ment of private interests seeking political voice and influence. Governing parties have also been interventionist and instrumental in regard to media.

All countries in this model exercised 'politics over broadcasting' systems in formative periods. In periods of dictatorship in Spain, Portugal and Greece, state instrumentalism was particularly high, as media operated under requirements to serve the ruling authority. In Portugal, under the Salazar and Caetano regimes, journalism was reduced to the level of a 'clerical sub profession' that transcribed government statements (Seaton and Pimlott 1980: 179, cited in Williams 2005). In Greece and Portugal, the connection between military dictatorship and the media persisted in the post-dictatorship period, with excessive 'intimacy' between the political elite and the media (Papatheodorou and Machin 2003). However, there were also countervailing pressures, as journalists, who played an important role in Portugal's 1974 revolution, moved to establish greater professionalism and autonomy, following a short period in which efforts were made to establish more radical workers' control in media outlets (Downing 2001). Explaining the connec-tions between the state and political instrumentalism by private media owners, Hallin and Mancini (2004a: 134–5) contend:

> The centrality of the state in southern Europe means not only that the state intervenes relatively strongly in the media institutions, but also to some extent the reverse. Because the state is so important, other social actors have a strong stake in influencing state policy, and one of the principal ways they do this is through the media. Business, in particular, often has a powerful stake in access to state contracts, subsidies, waivers of regulations, and so on. This is one of the reasons business owners have traditionally been willing to subsidize economically marginal media enterprises.

There are important variations here. France fits the pattern less well and is, at the least, a very mixed case in the schema. Although public broadcasting was highly instrumentalised under de Gaulle, it achieved greater independence from the 1980s. Polarised pluralism is reflected more strongly in the press, which 'has reflected and perhaps even exacerbated the fissures of this divided society, with newspapers taking up cudgels on behalf of one tendency or another' (Kuhn 1995: 9).

Political history and culture: transitions to modernity

The different patterns of development of media systems are traceable to broader differences in the political, economic and ideological forces shaping society, in particular between those countries where liberal, bourgeois institutions triumphed relatively early over feudalism and patrimonialism, and those where the conflict between forces of liberalism and traditional conservatism remained unsettled until well into the twentieth century. This historical difference, Hallin and Mancini argue, 'accounts to a large extent for the quite distinct patterns of media system development that prevail in Northern and Southern Europe' (H&M 2004a: 62); WMS differ fundamentally in terms of paths and processes of 'modernisation'.

In Southern Europe, dominated by powerful landed aristocracies and monarchies, the forces of the *ancien régime* were stronger than in the North. The church was a powerful political force and social influence, whether Roman Catholic (Italy, France, Portugal) or Orthodox (Greece). In mostly agricultural-based societies, the capitalist bourgeoisie and urban proletariat were small, restricting the power and influence of capitalist liberalism. The forces of liberalism thus developed relatively late and were weaker, except in France. There were other important variations, with greater industrialisation in parts, for instance northern and central Italy, and important regional variations such as the Basque country, Madrid and Catalonia as compared to the rest of Spain. When democracy was established it tended towards 'polarized pluralism', with a large number of parties, including antisystem parties, reflecting the strong authoritarian right wing, the communist left wing, as well as parties representing regions challenging central authorities. Political polarisation, as we shall examine, is closely connected with high political parallelism.

Democratic Corporatist model

The Democratic Corporatist model is characteristic of Northern and Central Europe and comprises three main groups of countries: Austria, Germany and Switzerland; Belgium and the Netherlands; and the Nordic countries of Norway, Sweden, Finland and Denmark (as well as Iceland and the Faroe Islands). The key political system characteristic is the development of democratic corporatism in the early twentieth century in all countries, with the exception of Austria and Germany, where it occurred after the defeat of fascism, through post-war reconstruction and new democratic structures. Systems of democratic corporatism developed as other countries struggled to confront the economic crises of the 1930s and avoid the conditions that led to the collapse of democracy in Germany and Austria. In Northern Europe the forces of conservatism were generally weaker, relative to the forces of liberalism; liberal institutions became established earlier and more firmly by the end of the nineteenth century (H&M 2004a: 183–186).

Democratic Corporatist systems have combined a diversity of parties and organised social interests with broad consensual agreement about the underlying political system, including processes and institutions for power sharing and decision making. As such, systems tend to have moderate pluralism, highly defined political differences combined with shared societal interests, and consensual support for 'the rules of the political game' (H&M 2005: 227). Another key feature of consensus was welfarism, as there was broad support, at least until the 1970s, for the expansion of the welfare state and state intervention on behalf of social objectives, including the media and media pluralism.

Democratic Corporatist systems are characterised by a strong commitment to media freedom and autonomy. As we have seen, these countries established a large and vibrant press sector which placed high value on the rapid flow of public information, and on political and religious liberties. Journalistic professionalism is also strongly developed according to various indices. Strong journalists' unions and professional associations developed early. Laws protecting the autonomy of journalists against 'external' interference from political or commercial interests, or 'internal' interference with editorial autonomy from owners or managers, feature in several states. However, systems are also characterised by strong state involvement in the media and high political parallelism. These systems, argue Hallin and Mancini, are thus characterised by three 'coexistences' of features which are deemed to be incompatible, according to the idealised 'liberal model' that has dominated North American media studies.

1   The simultaneous development of an economically strong, mass-circulation commercial press alongside high political parallelism, with newspapers and later broadcasting tied to political and civil groups.

2   The coexistence of high political parallelism and journalistic professionalism. Strong political affiliations in the press developed alongside a journalistic culture protecting journalistic independence and based on professional codes that transcended political affiliation.

3   The coexistence of liberal traditions of press freedom with traditions of strong state intervention in the media (the latter seen as social institutions responsible to society not as purely private enterprises). State intervention is deemed inimical to press freedom in the strong libertarian tradition that takes its inspiration from an anti-statist interpretation of the First Amendment. By contrast, democratic corporatist states are characterised by strong state regulation for social purposes, such as Sweden's ban on broadcast advertising to the under-12s, and measures such as the press subsidies introduced in the 1970s in Norway and Sweden. Such a 'positive', interventionist role for the state has been combined with a defence of 'negative' freedom – freedom from undue interference by the state and protection of access to public information.

The party press was beginning to weaken by the mid twentieth century and there has been a marked decline of party-affiliated papers. Germany's national press has distinctive political orientations (Kleinsteuber 2004: 79), but there is no longer a party-political aligned press (Schulz *et al.* 2005). In Belgium most newspapers 'lean towards one of the large political groups', but ongoing concentration has 'acted as an impetus to the removal of all affiliations between the newspapers and more or less circumscribed religious, social or political groups [the "pillars"]' (De Bens 2004: 17). Broadcasting has tended to reflect corporatist politics, with regulatory councils formally including representatives of political parties and social groups. But these are characterised as politics-in-broadcasting structures, rather than politics-over-broadcasting, due mainly to the relative absence of political instrumentalism. Political involvement has coexisted with greater formal and cultural adherence to independence and rational–legal authority.

Liberal model

The 'North Atlantic' or liberal model encompasses the US, Canada, Ireland and the UK. The contemporary political systems in all these countries may be described as moderate pluralism. All the 'liberal' countries have predominantly majoritarian systems, except for proportional representation systems in Ireland, Scotland and Wales, while in the US and Canada majoritarianism is modified by federalism.

In the UK the 'Westminster system' describes a two-party dominated system whose 'first-past-the-post' electoral arrangements have favoured single-party government over coalitions and power sharing, although the system has been modified in devolution, with the creation of a Scottish Parliament and Welsh Assembly. The US is in many respects a very different, presidential, political system, but is also dominated by two main parties. In Britain and America liberal institutions emerged early, following bourgeois revolutions. Liberal countries also saw the strong development of rational–legal authority, pursued by business and middle-class reform movements in the nineteenth century. With formal rule-making processes, the value and opportunities for businesses to use political influence to achieve favourable outcomes were diminished, although far from extirpated.

Across liberal systems the commercial press has largely displaced mass media directly affiliated to political parties or trade unions, which remain important, if residual features of some 'Polarized Pluralist' and Democratic Corporatist systems. There are important exceptions, however, for instance in the contested region of Northern Ireland, where papers were affiliated with highly polarised Unionist and Republican communities, divisions that also influenced all major media outlets. In the US, party-political parallelism in the press declined markedly in the late nineteenth century. However, the rise of polemical, mostly right-wing 'shock jocks' in radio in the 1980s and the explicitly partisan Fox News channel indicate an important counter-trend. In Britain a high degree of political parallelism characterises the tabloid newspapers, and the quality broadsheets all have clear (if changeable) political affiliations, with the exception of *The Independent*.

The liberal model of government espouses a limited role for the state. In Britain, liberalism was modified by more statist, conservative traditions and by a strong Labour movement which shifted Britain towards an active welfare state and liberal corporatism (Curran and Leys 2000). In media this is reflected in a strong public broadcasting system, relatively strong broadcasting regulation, as well as in 'illiberal' laws restricting media freedom and public access to information, now somewhat mitigated by the impact of the Human Rights Act (1998) and Freedom of Information Act (2000) (Robertson and Nicol 2002). In both Canada and Ireland, different processes of nation-state formation and efforts to support national identity through media policy modified liberalism. In Ireland, a protracted struggle for national independence, and a murderous civil war, influenced a period of post-colonial social conservatism which lasted from the 1930s until the 1970s. The independent Republic of Ireland established public broadcasting as a monopoly, although UK terrestrial television reached parts of the south-east and UK commercial television became a dominant influence from the 1990s.

Assessment: journalistic professionalism and media independence

The *FTP* tradition of comparative media analysis, especially in the United States, was tied to modernisation theory (Edelstein 1982), setting world press systems against a liberal ideal of a 'watchdog' press free from state interference or partisan affiliation. Hallin and Mancini seek to evade the *FTP* tradition in two main ways. First, they explicitly refuse to privilege one model of journalism over another, resisting traditional hierarchisations. Second, they seek to provide empirically grounded models in place of normative models. Normative questions matter, they argue, but cannot be answered in an abstract and universal manner; media models that 'work' in one context cannot be assumed to 'work' under different ones, for instance where the nature of divisions in society, political beliefs and processes are markedly different (H&M 2004a: 15).

The 'Anglo-American' model defines professionalism principally as autonomy to produce factually oriented 'objective' news without political interference or allegiance. Hallin and Mancini are careful to examine conditions giving rise to different kinds of journalism and to explain and value alternatives. In particular, they acknowledge the historical influence and normative value of politically aligned media. US 'neutral' journalism occurred under particular commercial and political conditions. In a majoritarian system where major parties share underlying values it is possible for journalists to cultivate 'neutral' journalism that aspires to provide balanced coverage of political differences between the main contending parties. Within polarised pluralism, where there are greater social cleavages expressed by parties ranged across a wider political spectrum and where 'antisystem' parties challenge the basis for 'consensus', such a neutral position is less tenable, any 'neutrality' being more readily exposed as being just another political position.

However, in majoritarian systems publicly owned media (especially monopolies) have proved 'vulnerable to capture by the dominant political tendency' (Humphreys 1996: 11), as occurred in post-war France (before 1980) and in Spain, Portugal and Greece. Humphreys notes, however, that in the majoritarian UK, broadcasting was insulated against capture by the governing party, partly as a result of strong liberal traditions favouring limited government.[1]

Hallin and Mancini make admirable advances. Yet the conceptual frame the authors adopt retains strong traces of modernisation theory. Their account of the progressive differentiation of media from politics does not avoid reproducing a stagist, evolutionist model that privileges the liberal conception of media independence as a higher stage of development, even though this model is heavily qualified rather than merely endorsed. Clientalism receded where reform movements succeeded in entrenching rational–legal authority in those systems reaching a higher stage of modernisation.

The ability of news journalists to report and comment on matters of public importance free from interference or control may justifiably be considered a foundational principle of democratic media systems. Many transnational bodies, including IFEX, Freedom House and Index on Censorship monitor the level of media freedom from constraints according to various measures. The first complication concerns which kinds of 'interference' shaping the media are considered detrimental. Here Hallin and Mancini are careful to avoid privileging the US model, decentring the Olympian, universalist perspective in favour of a more complex, historically grounded evaluation. However, tensions and problems remain; various normative values concerning media independence and autonomy are asserted or otherwise smuggled in to their analysis, which does not escape privileging features associated with the US model. Two kinds of discourse of modernisation are brought into their analysis, both of which were developed in the 1950s and 1960s: theories of the modernisation of capitalist societies and the 'development' paradigm for media. According to Durkheim's theory of modernisation, the increased complexity of society required increasing functional differentiation of activities and institutions. This was further developed by Talcott Parsons' influential structural-functionalist theory of society. For Parsons, social progress may be measured by the degree to which social systems underwent differentiation, such as the separation of the institutions of politics and religion. Parsonian theory extrapolated from and privileged the United States as an advanced and stable system, and, proposing the superiority of Western capitalist 'modernity', offered a highly conservative and ethnocentric account. Hallin and Mancini adopt, at some critical distance, the concept of differentiation. But for all the vitality of politically aligned media, they equate journalistic autonomy and 'professionalism' with dealignment from politics: 'Where political parallelism is very high, with media organizations strongly tied to political organizations, and journalists deeply involved in party politics, professionalism is indeed likely to be low' (H&M 2004a: 38).

For critical scholars, central questions are how far media serve existing dominant power relations in society; how far the media carry and create openings for the full range of information, ideas, imagery and opinion in society; and how far there is commensurate communicative space for opposition to dominant interest to be expressed. From this perspective, the cluster of associations that have dominated US liberal assumptions of journalism are deeply flawed.

1   Identification of the media's formal autonomy from the political sphere downplays the actual extent and processes of affiliation and support for powerholders and the 'status quo'. The ideology of journalistic professionalism occludes the conditions giving rise to subservience to powerful interests

in society from a nominally 'independent' media. As Downey notes, 'A good deal of commercial media across North America are clear in their support of policies to create a less state-regulated, lower taxation, free-trade, pro-business economy' (Downey 2006: 22).

2   Formal independence does not mean that political dependencies are necessarily diminished. While Schudson (2000) defends reliance on official sources as consonant with serving the democratic needs of society, critics such as McChesney characterise US news journalists as 'stenographers' for power interests. For Entman (2005), US 'objectivity' practices are dependent upon the competitive balance between the two major parties, an analysis that finely assesses media autonomy and dependencies in contrast to simple accounts of state–media relations.

3   Focus on political interference ignores wider forms of economic and cultural intrumentalisation – giving rise to a compartmentalisation that understates and undervalues the close articulation of dominant political and economic interests (Sparks 2000c).

Hallin and Mancini do also acknowledge processes of de-differentiation, namely increasing economic influence over the media whereby corporate ownership and 'bottom line' pressures have eroded journalistic autonomy (2004a: 227; Hallin 2000). They consider media commercialisation to be a central dimension of media system convergence (Chapter 9). Yet, the cluster of concepts of journalistic professionalism they adopt privileges markers of differentiation from formal politics. By contrast, CPE scholars challenge journalistic professionalism as an ideology and examine the nature of constraints on autonomy arising from corporate media ownership and commercial imperatives. Empirical studies can contribute here in testing which explanation best fits the evidence (see Benson and Hallin 2004).

Media moguls, ownership and political influence

What are the various different ways in which media owners can use media to influence politics? A distinction is usually made between efforts to intervene in order to advance the business interests of firms, and efforts to influence political opinion through content. We have already encountered what Street (2001: 236) calls 'resource power', which refers to the 'bargaining power' that media organisations can bring to bear in their dealings with governments, regulators and other agencies. All kinds of public policy, from tax to employment law, affect the business interests of large media firms, all of whom are necessarily concerned about the political and legal environment in which they operate and use resources to intervene directly in the policy process. Media firms may bargain with their economic resources, threatening to relocate their activities if unfavourable regulation is implemented, for instance.

Media can also intervene by using their content (symbolic resources) to seek to influence the opinion of key publics, electorates and policy makers, matters at the heart of concern about media power and influence. We have already encountered the conceptual distinction between instrumental and structural influences of media ownership, which is also pertinent here (Williams 1998: 229–31). Political instrumentalism may involve the personal political interests and ambitions of owners (as well as editors, journalists and other media personnel). Structural forms include the way in which market forces shape what media are viable and so influence what kind and range of political orientations are made available though public media. Political and business interests are often closely entwined and reciprocal. One simple test of political instrumentalism is whether media enterprises are run at a profit or sustained at a loss, although, as Street (2001: 134) notes, the latter does not provide incontrovertible evidence of political motives. Canadian press baron Conrad Black operated the *National Post* at considerable loss for many years before selling it to the liberal Asper family, who likewise continued to run the paper at a loss, but 'as a mouthpiece for their pointed editorial views' (Steven 2003: 57).

Berlusconi and Italian politics

The Italian media magnate and current Prime Minister Silvio Berlusconi offers an 'extreme' case (Downey 2006: 20) of a media mogul turned politician, who used accumulated media power to pursue political power. Berlusconi built up near total dominance of commercial television following Italy's 'savage deregulation', and by the end of the 1980s owned the three largest private networks, Canale 5, Retequattro and Italia 1, as well as AC Milan football club, publishing, satellite TV and other media and non-media interests. The patronage of Bettino Craxi's Socialist Party was crucial in protecting his expanding business empire in the 1980s (H&M 2004a: 137). Craxi, Prime Minister from 1983 to 1987, overturned a court order banning Berlusconi from broadcasting national network television, the so-called 'Berlusconi Decree' of 1984. His network, Canale 5, established in 1980, relied heavily in its early years on imported US programming such as *Dallas*, as well as local game shows.

By the 1990s, Berlusconi's Fininvest, through its subsidiary holding company, Mediaset, controlled Italy's private channels and had a majority share of the television advertising market. In 2006, Fininvest, which is 96 per cent-owned by Berlusconi's family, owned nearly 49 per cent of Mediaset. Berlusconi has a controlling stake (48 per cent in 2001) in Mondadore, Italy's largest publishing group, whose print interests include the influential weekly *Panorama* and *Il Giornale*, a daily newspaper which competes with L'Espresso's *La Repubblica*, and with *La Stampa* and *Corriere della Sera*, owned by the RCS group. Berlusconi's other holdings include property, financial services, multimedia, printing and telephone directories. Berlusconi deployed his considerable media assets in launching a new political party, Forza Italia, which was promoted heavily across his television, publishing and sports interests. The new party, rapidly formed in 1993, became the largest bloc in the national parliament at the March 1994 elections, and Berlusconi became prime minister (until 1995) of a right-wing coalition government. Berlusconi was re-elected in 2001, despite facing corruption charges against himself and his government, remaining prime minister until 2006.[2]

Berlusconi's use of his media empire to seek to influence voters' behaviour raised profound questions about the state of Italian democracy. In the 1994 election, Berlusconi's television channels allocated 65 per cent of the time devoted to electoral coverage in newscasts to Forza Italia (FI) and its coalition allies in the Polo della Libertà (freedom pole). This compared with 16 per cent for parties of the Left and 10 per cent for the Christian Democrats (DC). By contrast, RAI gave 38 per cent to Berlusconi's coalition, 24 per cent to parties of the Left and 29 per cent to the centre (Marletti and Roncarolo 2000). Fininvest channels were also filled with advertisements for FI (Stratham 1996). While some ascribed the 1994 election to Berlusconi's public relations initiatives or as Italy's transition to 'teledemocracy', however, the rise of FI reflected longer-term changes in Italian politics and society, Italy's gradual transition to a more majoritarian political system, as well as the crisis provoked by a wave of scandals resulting in criminal accusations against over 1,500 politicians, including two former prime ministers, in the early 1990s.

In the late 1940s and the 1950s Italy's political system had been highly polarised between the Christian Democratic party, a socially conservative party with strong Catholic roots, the Socialist party (PSI) and a mass 'antisystem' Marxist Communist Party (PCI). Post-war Italy has been described as 'a stable democracy founded on an unstable political equilibrium' (Marletti and Roncarolo 2000: 198), with short-lived governments and fragmented and polarised multipartyism (Sartori 1966). During the 1950s and early 1960s governments of the centre, centre-right and later centre-left were formed through various short-lived coalitions, with no single party gaining a sufficient majority to govern alone (Mancini 1991: 140–1). The Christian Democrats were the largest party, participating in every governing coalition, but by the 1960s their Catholic subcultural base began to erode, partly due to long-term secularisation of Italian society and politics, as well as in reaction to the church's political interventions (Marletti and Roncarolo 2000: 208–9).

Between 1946 and the mid 1970s political parties used specific media outlets as allied or dependent channels for partisan political communication. The Socialist party (PSI) had a party paper, *Avanti*, while the Communist PCI's party newspaper, *L'Unità*, achieved a circulation up to 1 million (usually around 100,000) and was one of the few papers to reach beyond a limited, elite readership (Marletti and Roncarolo 2000: 210). Party–press parallelism was high; however, up to the 1970s over 75 per cent of national newspapers were under the control of powerful economic groups, with a predominance of papers having a centre or right-wing orientation. Polemical writing was a central feature of Italian newspapers, with leading journalists writing *pastone romano*, daily commentaries on the main political developments, that were given front page prominence.

In the first two decades of Italian democracy, the DC effectively controlled the single publicly owned television channel. Although not highly partisan, this was used by governing parties to promote their perspectives and gain electoral advantage. The formation of a centre-left coalition including the PSI in 1962 led towards greater accommodation between parties and a depolarisation of the deep cleavages between the radical Left and moderate, religious Right in Italian society (between 'red' and 'white'). A second channel (RAI-2) in 1961 would, over time, come to publicise the views of the PSI and other parties in the governing coalition, while the DC controlled RAI-1, and from 1979 the creation of RAI-3 provided a platform for the PCI when it entered the governing coalition. Fully established by the 1980s, under a practice known as *lottizzazione*, sectors or 'lots' of the public broadcasting system RAI were divided up for control by the various main parties. RAI was thus integrated into the *lottizzazione* system through which the parties divided power and resources across society. The DC's direct control was narrowed to RAI-1, although the party continued to exercise broader influence through appointing RAI's director general. In contrast to the press, however, partisan bias was more heavily restrained, as television was held to strict impartiality standards by oversight boards which included representatives of all the major parties.

Changes in political party–media relations in the 1980s and early 1990s helped to undermine mass support for the old political order. By the early 1990s, parties that had previously enjoyed broad support and allegiance from certain media outlets found instead growing media scrutiny and criticism from influential and more 'autonomous' news outlets. The move from deferential styles of political reporting toward more critical, independent and increasingly cynical journalism has been a general feature of change across WMS, but its precise forms have been shaped by factors in each country. In Italy, extensive unearthing of corruption though judicial activism in the 1970s contributed to the collapse of all the major post-war parties and brought down the once-mighty Christian Democrats, opening up space for the 'new' political parties.

In power, Berlusconi broke with the *lottizzazione* practices of the 1980s and undertook a strategy to control RAI and thus acquire power over public as well as private broadcasting (television). After the election there was a purge of RAI management, whereby general managers, news directors and other top-ranking personnel were replaced by individuals allied to Berlusconi (Marletti and Roncarolo 2000: 229). Berlusconi and his coalition allies adopted a new, majoritarian approach, appointing directors and senior staff of RAI, enabling them to control public broadcasting alongside Berlusconi's grip on private broadcasting. In 1995 Berlusconi used his networks to campaign successfully against referendum proposals that would have forced him to divest part of his television empire and won a referendum to privatise RAI, which would have granted him near-monopoly control over all broadcasting. However, these efforts were halted when his coalition government collapsed later that year, and were reversed under the subsequent Prodi and D'Alema governments. On his re-election in 2001, Berlusconi moved to take control of RAI-1, controlled by the centre-left (1996–2001), which became the province of Forza Italia, RAI-2 of the Lega del Nord, while the Left's control of RAI-3 was weakened (Downey 2006). During his premierships, journalists at RAI were vulnerable to attacks from the ruling coalition. Two notorious cases involved the firing of the well-known journalists Enzo Biagi and Michele Santoro after Berlusconi publicly attacked them (OSI 2005: 64–5). From 2003 to its 2005 edition, Freedom House (2006) ranked Italy, along with Turkey, as the only country in the region to be rated 'partly free' according to its criteria of media freedom, due mainly to the constraining influence of Berlusconi's media dominance.[3]

Murdoch

By many of his critics Rupert Murdoch is widely perceived as a figure of immense power which he deploys ruthlessly to pursue his own interests, willing to sacrifice ethical, political and journalistic standards for profit, as a long list of former executives, editors, competitors and biographers attest. There are many, largely anecdotal, but well-documented accounts of Murdoch's direct proprietorial interference, by journalists (Giles 1986; Evans 1994; Neil 1997) and academics (Curran 1990; Belfield *et al.*. 1991; Williams 1996; Curran and Seaton 1997; Street 2001: 133–7). The 'demonisation' of Murdoch has undoubtedly had real effects, for instance strengthening (and personalising) resistance from some regulators to the corporate ambitions of companies in which News Corporation has a stake. However, such personalisation risks obscuring the systemic characteristics of corporate media activity (Herman and McChesney 1997).

According to Tunstall's definition (1996: 85), Murdoch is an archetypal media mogul. He owns and operates media properties, is a risk-taking entrepreneur and has an 'idiosyncratic or eccentric management style, that may involve political motives'. Murdoch is also a transitional figure, straddling what Tunstall describes as a gradual shift from the era of interventionist 'press lords' to 'entrepreneurial editors' in Britain. This is characterised by a shift from owners who privileged the political influence of newspaper ownership above business expansion to an entrepreneurial model in which profit maximisation, corporate survival and appeasing shareholders are governing priorities. One of the atypically loss-making acquisitions Murdoch retains is the *New York Post*, which, as Alterman remarks (2003: 241) 'buys him a political voice in New York and with the media elite, which is extremely valuable when he needs a favour from one of the city or state's elected politicians'.

Murdoch imposed an editorial shift in the political orientation of *The Times*, *Sunday Times*, *News of the World* and *Sun* towards Thatcher support for the New Right government. He has interfered directly politically, written or rewritten leaders and other articles (Neil 1997; Manning 2001: 88–9, Curran and Seaton 2003: 69–71). As Murdoch famously declared: 'I did not come all this way not to interfere' (cited in Curran and Seaton 2003: 70). Such interference declined somewhat in the later 1980s as Murdoch moved to Los Angeles and took much more direct control of US television and film interests and global media expansion (Snoddy 1998). Murdoch led a management-imposed shift to the right at *The Times* and *Sunday Times* in the 1980s, while in the 1990s he shifted the *Sun* (and *News of the World*) from Conservative to Labour party support, much to the anger of some staff journalists (Neil 1997: xxiv).[4] Through a mixture of threats and cajoling, employing senior managers and editors sharing his outlook and rewarded for loyalty, Murdoch has deployed various means to exert operational as well as allocative control over media interests.[5] For instance, a survey of editorial coverage in 2003 found that the most influential of the 175 newspapers owned by News Corporation worldwide unanimously supported the invasion of Iraq by a 'coalition' of the US, the UK and a few allies (Greenslade 2003). However, overt intervention is less common than more subtle alignments between the outlook of editors and their internalised awareness of Murdoch's political and other interests (Neil 1997).

Simple notions of instrumentalism cannot do justice to the relative autonomy of editors and journalists across such a diverse conglomerate as News Corporation, although this is better understood in Curran's phrase as 'licensed autonomy', journalistic independence bounded by the requirements of employing organisations (Curran 1990: 120). Proprietorial intervention also needs to be distinguished as only one factor that may explain the political outlook or 'bias' of particular media. As Street (2001: 144) puts it, 'Both the internal structure of the media outlet and the wider political structure within which those outlets are situated act to channel the flow of political influence.' The strongest case today can probably be made for Fox News, which has stridently supported US president George W. Bush and the 'war on terror' (Alterman 2003: 234–42). But this powerful corporate orientation cannot be ascribed to Murdoch's individual political preferences alone, but rather to a more complex fusion of political–ideological and business motivations to build share among the demographic groups targeted by the Fox network.

Manning (2001: 91–2) identifies three main ways in which power is exercised intentionally or instrumentally by proprietors and senior executives:

> they may exercise power internally to ensure that their news organisations produce news formats or editorial regimes of which they approve; they may exercise and accumulate power externally through their exchanges with political elites; and they may consciously exploit the advantages which accrue with the structural positions of their organisations to further consolidate resources, and undermine rivals.

He gives a valuable account of how Murdoch has exercised each type of opportunity (2001: 87–97), although he neglects cross-promotion, such as the promotion of Sky and later SkyDigital television in Murdoch-owned newspapers (examined in Hardy 2004a).

It is widely observed that corporate rather than political interests dominate corporations such as News Corporation. They intervene politically, through the formal policy process, to seek to create optimal conditions for their unhindered operations, but can use their resources, including editorial content, to support such ends. In many instances, commercial interests have predominated over political ideology. When he acquired the left-leaning *Village Voice* newspaper in New York, Murdoch refused to renew the contract of the then editor, but permitted a non-conservative replacement editor to retain the paper's editorial stance relatively unchanged. Corporate and political interests may also be closely intertwined; for instance, Murdoch's support for Reagan and Thatcher also advanced favourable regulatory structures and decisions required for the expansion of his media businesses. Other key characteristics, also informing corporate culture, have been Murdoch's opposition to public service media, the BBC in particular (Barnett 1989; O'Malley 1994: 36–46), and to traditional rationales for media regulation, as well as wider, selective opposition to 'the establishment', especially in the UK (see Shawcross 1997; Horsman 1998). Once again, this is a complex mix of business interests and political conviction, as the company has waged battles with regulators worldwide since it expanded from its Australian newspaper base in the 1960s. Claims that *The Times* carried articles criticising the BBC and advocating its dismemberment, as part of a campaign to further Murdoch's commercial interests, were rejected by the paper's independent directors (*The Times* 1985), but later research found that the 'editorial and reporting approach to broadcasting matters being pursued by News International is having a material effect on the opinions of readers' (Barnett 1989: 19) and concluded:

> Whatever the editorial intentions, concentration of newspaper ownership is clearly capable of being exploited to promote the owners' interests elsewhere. Largely, it seems as a result of reading its newspapers, significant numbers of people hold views which are patently to News International's financial advantage.

Murdoch and his many advocates and lobbyists have courted, cajoled and threatened politicians across the continents of his media empire. It took a freedom of information action in the UK to reveal the meetings between Murdoch's advocates and the Blair government in the period leading up to the Communications Act 2003, which resulted in favourable outcomes for Murdoch's cross-media interests. The relationship between Murdoch and Labour illustrates complex dependencies on each side. Securing the support of the Murdoch papers, in particular the three million readers of the daily *Sun*, was an important goal for Labour, especially following the party's third consecutive electoral defeat in 1992. Labour courted Murdoch, as symbolised in leader Tony Blair's address to News Corp executives in Cancun in 1994, after which the party abandoned policies on tackling media concentration which directly threatened Murdoch's UK businesses. Blair retained the support of the *Sun* (although not the elite *Times* and *Sunday Times* newspapers), especially as a war leader, but this was qualified by these papers' sustained opposition to EU governance, rooted in Murdoch's opposition to EU measures such as the 'social chapter' provisions for workers and trade unions, which he considered threatening to corporate business interests.

Reviewing instrumentalism across Western media systems

What are the conditions in which political instrumentalism flourishes or diminishes? Is instrumentalism more prevalent in some media systems, and if so why?

Key factors are the strength of formal rules and regulation, the wider environment and culture in which all participants interact, the values and strength of journalistic autonomy and professionalism. For Hallin and Mancini, journalistic professionalism is more likely to develop in societies with strong traditions of rational–legal authority, where 'the idea of professional communities with special qualifications, rules of practice, social functions, systems of ethics, and claims of autonomy flowing from these is widely diffused' (H&M 2004a: 194). The development of rational–legal authority reduces the tendency for media owners to form partisan alliances in order to secure business interests, and thus reduces the importance of the kind of 'instrumentalisation' that prevails in Southern European systems.

This analysis is most helpful in describing the dynamics of clientalism and instrumentalisation in media systems. However, it offers a misleading account of conditions where 'rational–legal authority' pertains. Hallin and Mancini do acknowledge the influence of political instrumentalism by figures such as Murdoch in liberal and Democratic Corporatist systems. They are also right to argue that transparent, rule-based processes of decision making reduce the risks and incentives that drive media into clientalist relations. But there is plenty of evidence that the two may coexist, and Murdoch provides a good illustration of these.

Other key factors regarding instrumentalism are the nature of the media outlet and the principal purposes of firms. An older distinction between media conglomerates and 'general conglomerates' (Murdock 1982: 199) has become less sustainable as conglomerates diversify their holdings and interests. But the configuration of media firms' main activities and interests clearly reflects on the nature and incentives for instrumentalism. One powerful mode of political instrumentalism has been the use of media as an instrument to influence political opinion (mass or elite) through content, exercised usually by or on behalf of individual owners. Its characteristic form has been a privately owned press, and later radio, with only rare instances of instrumental control of mass television channels by private individuals such as Berlusconi. Such forms of instrumentalism have become more marginal in liberal-capitalist systems, where commercial pressures and capitalisation shifted ownership from individual to corporate, and privileged corporate over narrowly political interests. However, media owners able to exercise control have included those such as Murdoch, Canadian Conrad Black, Robert Hersant in France and Axel Springer and Leo Kirch in Germany (Tunstall and Palmer 1991), driven by strong right-wing political interests and interventionist motivations.

The *need* to use editorial resources in efforts to secure firms' interests is diminished where firms can intervene in a formal policy process governed by transparent rules and procedures. However, it does not follow that editorial intervention is necessarily diminished. Murdoch's News Corporation illustrates the use of editorial content directly to support corporate interests as well as the use of media power arising from the more diffuse interdependencies with politicians. The power of such media companies to shape government policy, and politicians' fear of attack, both personally and collectively, underlies critics' fears about the creation of politically insulated and sustained, if never entirely self-perpetuating, media empires.

PART 2: POLITICAL COMMUNICATION

Are media and political systems converging in the way politics is conducted and mediated? This has been a central question within political communication research and wider debates on convergence in media systems. Through the 1980s and 1990s much debate centred on the 'Americanisation' of political communication in other systems, especially in Europe. Rapid changes affecting both political systems and media have also led to a constant need to revisit and refresh accounts within a highly volatile field of enquiry. All the main elements that make up political communication – political actors, media and the social constituencies addressed are not only internally complex and differentiated, but are constantly adapting and changing in their relationships, shaped by both internal, intranational (endogenous) and external (exogenous) forces of change. Nevertheless, there is broad agreement that some important common trends can be identified across Western systems, including a destabilisation of older patterns of political communication. The next section identifies trends and then considers evidence of the nature and limits of convergence and homogenisation in political communication. Changes in political communication involve the interaction of three broad processes:

1 societal changes
2 changes in politics and political parties
3 changes in media systems and cultures.

We will address features of each in turn and then deal in a more integrated way with questions of the nature and dynamics of change in political communication.

Societal changes and secularisation

The relationship between voters and political parties, it is argued, has shifted since 1945 from one characterised by identity, affiliation and long-term commitment to one based on party efforts to persuade voters who lack enduring political convictions. This has been described as a shift from sacred to secular politics (Swanson 2004). 'Sacred' is used in a metaphorical rather than religious sense to describe politics as an expression of community affiliation to political leaders and parties that seek to represent the collective aspirations and identity of a group of followers. Traditionally, party divisions, it is argued, were based upon socially recognised political cleavages based on a combination of class affiliation, religion, community or regional identities. Parties differed in core values such as social justice and individual freedom, but were mainly divided on economic and social welfare issues, in post-1945 Europe, between the communist and socialist left, social democratic centre and right-wing parties. Citizens recognised themselves in collective groups and identities and regarded political parties as representing and advancing the collective's interests and shared values. Parties mobilised masses of voters.

The post-industrial era, it is argued, has involved the dissolution of masses and mass societies, the weakening of bonds based on class, the creation of more segmented and fragmented collectivities and, above all, increasing individualism. The traditional base of support for political parties has been eroded. Another key term here is dealignment, which refers to voters' increasing detachment from more stable, longer-term attachments to parties and political movements. A marked transnational trend has been the decline in party membership and affiliation, and associated evidence of disengagement from electoral politics, especially among the young. Electorates are more mobile, the issues that divide voters are more personal, less fixed, and people are less likely to see their identity as contained in and expressed through membership of a collectivity. For Dahlgren and Gurevitch (2005: 378), common trends across Western systems include greater fragmentation of shared common culture as societies become more pluralistic and differentiated; a strengthening influence of consumerism, favouring individualism; growing disparities between rich and poor, undermining 'universalistic ideals of democratic citizenship'; and an erosion of support for traditional institutions.

Various factors have been identified as possible causes of growing secularisation, including rising affluence, the decline of manufacturing industries which were central to working-class organisation, and the relative stabilisation of parliamentary systems. Another factor is education. For Mazzoleni and Schultz (1999), higher levels of education have contributed to the rise of a sophisticated 'self-mobilized' citizenry, with more people formulating their own stance on current issues independently of the position of political parties. But, they argue, this social segment exists alongside a much larger group of people who are poorly informed and express a lack of interest in formal politics. Whereas, in previous times, the majority of this group relied on political parties to relieve them of the need for individually deliberated choices, political parties have now lost this orientation function, particularly for apolitical citizens, they argue. Both groups, sophisticates and apoliticals, have in common a high dependency on media, turning to mass media for political orientation and guidance.

As the foundations of social solidarity and support on which they relied erodes, political parties have had to seek support from 'a more consumerist, individualistic, volatile and sceptical electorate on the basis of issues and appeals of the moment' (Blumler and Gurevitch 2005: 105). Ideologically rooted mass parties have declined and been replaced by 'electoral-professional' parties more oriented to achieving a commanding share of the electoral market. For Hallin and Mancini (2004b: 32; 29–32), these processes of change 'probably account to a large extent for the Americanisation of European political communication', as this increasingly resembles the market-oriented and individualistic US political and media system. The 'depillarisation' of Dutch society (Brants 2004) and the weakening in the 1960s and 1970s of the highly polarised subcultures in post-war Italy are oft-cited examples of these changes. However, these are broad trends only, with considerable variation according to specific circumstances and a dynamic coexistence of shifting and countervailing trends. The US presidential election of 2004, for instance involved heightened political polarisation, increased involvement of young people, as well as increasing use of online communication for electoral and political mobilisation.

Affiliational as distinct from 'issue' voting remains stronger outside the liberal countries (H&M 2004a:133, Mancini 1991), but there are important exceptions in regions (Northern Ireland) and amongst subcultures. How far 'dealignment' has occurred is also a matter of dispute among political scientists (Street 2001: 195, Swanson 2004). Nevertheless, with the decline in mass party membership and affiliation, traditional party networks for organisation and communication, such as public and party meetings, became less influential and effective, increasing the importance of mediation through the mass media.

Parties, party organisation and political communication

In some political systems there has been a tendency for parties to become more 'catch all', seeking broader appeal and votes across a more differentiated electorate through more centrist, electorally aggrandising policies. In this model, political leaders have become more prominent, tending towards a presidential style of leadership. However, the precise organisation and communication of political parties still depends on the political conditions and culture within states. In Italy, as we have seen, a particular form of majoritarianism occurred after near-total collapse of the previous political system triggered by corruption scandals. In other systems, such as in the UK, traditional parties have remained dominant while managing their long-term decline in party membership and affiliational support. In several European countries there has been a growth of support for small, sectional and antisystem parties, including parties mobilised around anti-immigration platforms. Among the key underlying trends has been the decline of party influence relative to the growing influence of new power centres outside the formal sphere of national (or regional) party politics, including transnational corporations, transnational and national NGOs and the network of 'single-issue' campaign groups and voluntary associations (Swanson 2004: 47–8). While political responses to these challenges have varied considerably, parties have shown more commonality regarding communications. To adapt to altered circumstances, all modern parties have sought to professionalise their communications. Traditionally, parties tended to rely on paid political staff or party members but have increasingly turned to political communication specialists, notably experts in marketing, public relations, media relations and opinion polling to find out how they can appeal to voters.

Mediatised politics

Politics has become mediatised. The media have become an indispensable conduit for political information and ideas to reach citizens. The earliest studies of mediated politics began in the print era, when radio was in its infancy, their findings revised especially as post-war scholars examined the growing importance and influence of television. Today, television remains the main source of political information, but the internet, new modes of online and citizen journalism, changing patterns of media consumption and use require further revision of findings and theoretical review. The growing importance of television in politics was recognised from the 1950s, when the networks commanded mass audiences in the United States and most of Europe had monopoly providers. Political campaigning became more media driven. Party electioneering added telephone canvassing, e-mail and mobile communications to more traditional activities such as public meetings and direct mail. But television has become the principal means of reaching citizens, increasing in importance as traditional forms of party communication declined, such as meetings and events, pamphlets and party newspapers.

The majority of Europeans rely on TV for daily information, but dependence varies in accordance with patterns of media development already outlined. In 1999 the EU average percentage was 71 TV, 41 press, 41 radio. In the UK the press was cited as a source of daily information by 50 per cent, with 72 per cent for television, close to the European, and 46 per cent for radio. By contrast, in Greece the percentages were 82 TV, 16 press and 17 radio (Eurobarometer 1999 cited in Papathanassopoulos 2002: 126).

To varying degrees, parties have 'professionalised' by adapting their communications to the news values and formats of the TV environment. The reconfiguration of politics around television is described by Mazzoleni as 'videocracy', while for Castells (1996) all politics now subsists within the frame of electronic media. According to the 'media logic' thesis (Mazzoleni 1987), the technical requirements of media, journalistic professionalism, as well as commercial imperatives lead to a style of reporting that prefers personalities to ideas, simplicity to complexity, confrontation to compromise and heavy emphasis on the 'horse race' over substantive policy issues in electoral campaigns (see also Mancini and Swanson 1996). Researchers in Sweden, for instance, found that while the media attention on political leaders had remained consistently high between the 1970s and 1990s there was a qualitative shift towards 'focus on party leaders as private persons' (Asp and Esaiasson 1996: 84, cited in Street 2001). Using the medium of television, politicians must adapt to its conventions, becoming, as well as courting, celebrities so as to enhance media exposure and voter appeal (Hart 1999; Street 2001).

Comparative analysis

A major theme of media systems research has been to assess how far there are general tendencies shaping political communication, and the extent to which structural or cultural differences serve to modify or block these (Gurevitch and Blumler 2004: 334). Comparative research on political communication developed from the late 1950s in the US under the influence of Daniel Lerner's modernisation research (Edelstein 1982: 29), but Blumler and Gurevitch (1975) found an underdeveloped field with few studies when they proposed a comparative framework for political communication research. Subsequent reviews have shown considerable development in comparative studies since, mostly from the early 1990s (Pfetsch and Esser 2004).

Americanisation?

The concept of Americanisation has been used, especially by European scholars, to describe the adoption of practices in political communication seen as emanating from the United States, where the 'modernisation' of political communication appeared most advanced. The explanation of media system change as 'Americanisation' has its origins in critical discourses of cultural imperialism from the 1960s and 1970s (see Chapter 8), although 'Americanisation' was first used as a term of abuse in the 1830s (Rose 1974 cited in Negrine 1996). The focus here has been the growth of political marketing and party publicity professionalism along lines first developed and applied in the US (Newman 1999; Plasser and Plasser 2001). Sound bite, photo opportunity, news management – all have American origins (Negrine 1996). Modern Western electoral campaigns revolve around TV. One simple explanation for this is that parties and politicians copy successful techniques. The UK Labour Party, for instance, collaborated directly with Bill Clinton's Democratic Party, adopting similar campaign strategies and even slogans (Butler and Kavanagh 1997: 56–7), in turn influencing the German Social Democrats (SPD) (Esser *et al.*. 2001). However, the notion of a one-way flow of influence is problematic and limited, and since the 1990s analysts have increasingly challenged the adequacy and applicability of the term (see Negrine and Papathanassopoulos 1991; Blumler and Gurevitch 2001; Schulz *et al.*. 2005). In particular, focusing on transference *from* America, Americanisation cannot adequately address significant changes within US campaign communications themselves. Nor does it explain why such techniques evolved in the US in the first place (Street 2001: 193; Pfetsch and Esser 2004).

For Mancini and Swanson (1996), the process is better understood as modernisation, the development of professionalised campaigning techniques for managing the social complexity caused by the breakdown across Western states of old identities, hierarchies and social structures. Modernisation thus incorporates endogenous as well as exogenous forces of change, not merely the exporting of an American way of doing politics. Similar forces have led political communication to become more professionalised, and they find growing similarities in election practices, despite great differences in political cultures, histories and institutions of the countries in which they have occurred; yet the precise forms and influences of professionalism remain distinctive in each country (Mancini and Swanson 1996). Yet, if Americanisation is problematic, so too is 'modernisation', which carries an implicit evolutionist and positivist assumption of progress and collapses together dimensions of social, political and media change that need to be distinguished analytically (see H&M 2004b: 28).

Beyond important debates on the sources of change, are issues concerning the extent of 'Americanisation' in different political and media systems. On the whole, analysts agree on the diffusion of what Plasser and Plasser (2002: 343) describe as 'macro trends' including the increasing mediatisation, professionalisation, personalisation and 'negativity' of political campaigning. Analysts have shown increasingly worldwide adoption and adaption of some American styles and practices (Blumler and Gurevitch 2001). However, the degree of Americanisation differs, with most Western countries showing a 'hybrid' mixing of American-sourced and country-specific styles and practices. Thus, even where 'American' practices are present, there can be significant differences that belie convergence. One study found that sound bite length remained very different between Germany and the US. It did, though, find increasing convergence in reporting politics between

German public service and commercial channels (Schulz *et al.* 2005: 75). This finding corresponds to Pfetsch's (2001) account of macro differences between the media-driven political communication culture in the US and Germany. In the US presidential system, Pfetsch argues, the communication efforts of government have to concentrate strongly on media-oriented news media strategies. Political parties, reduced to electoral machines, cannot mobilise opinion or support in order to put issues before Congress, so media are among the few levers through which political support can be won and maintained. In Germany, party and coalition motives are prime factors in policy formation, and so governments seek support from party and party coalitions first, before attempting to mobilise public support through mass media.[6]

Comparative research has highlighted trends common, to varying degrees, in all WMS (as outlined above) including reduced ideological polarisation between established parties (Blumler and Gurevitch 2005). The broad findings of comparative research indicate growing similarities in party election practices, but significant differences remain, for instance between the party-based systems in most European countries and the electoral processes more focused on candidates, for president or other positions, in the US (Papathanassopoulos 2002: 143). Another key trend is the increasing power of market forces. All Western systems have trends towards media commercialism, but the forms such commercialism takes has crucial bearing on the mediatisation of politics. Features associated with commercialism and commercial media coverage of politics in the US have indeed become more significant in European political communication. However, commercialisation has deepened and changed within the US itself (Blumler and Gurevitch 2001: 390). 'Americanisation' is inadequate to capture the diversity and complexity of differences in political communication, including the changing dynamics and influence of media commercialism. In addition, new kinds of cross-national divergence may arise alongside ongoing processes of convergence (Blumler and Gurevitch 2001: 385).

Esser *et al.* (2001) identify six main factors shaping political communication in a given country, drawing on the work of Pfetsch (1998), Plasser *et al.* (1999) and Scammell (1998):

1 the electoral system
2 the system of party competition
3 the legal regulations of election campaigns
4 the media system (public *vs* dual *vs* private television systems, differentiation of the media system, professional roles of journalists, autonomy of mass media)
5 the national political culture
6 the degree of modernisation in society.

Blumler and Gurevitch (2001) outline a similar model which gives added emphasis to the degree of professionalisation of election campaigning, and media system variables such as market competition. The legal and regulatory environment is another important variable; US journalists benefit from First Amendment protection in attacking politicians in ways actionable in European countries (although protection has tended to be strengthened by ECHR rulings). The extent to which media systems permit paid political advertising has historically been an important difference (Negrine 1996: 156–7). The United States is exceptional, argue Gunther and Mughan (2000: 442, 12), in its 'wholesale commercialisation of the electoral process', allowing unlimited and unregulated paid political advertising. Ever since Eisenhower's successful presidential campaign in 1952 used advertising executive Rosser Reeves to devise a series of short spot adverts ('Ike for President') that ran in commercial breaks, US political campaigns have relied heavily on TV ads. The internet has increasingly been used for all kinds of fundraising and political advertising, but US television remains the main vehicle, and cost, for reaching general audiences. Despite political efforts, US broadcasting still provides no free time for election addresses, in contrast to European broadcasting systems (Negrine 1996; Blumler and Gurevitch 2001). The costs of running campaigns on paid TV advertising have grown and had a huge impact on the configuration of formal politics in the US. Paid political advertising on television is banned in the UK, France, Spain, Belgium, Denmark, Sweden, Switzerland, Norway and Portugal.

Western European systems are characterised by regulation of political advertising, electoral campaign expenditure, the allocation of broadcasting time given to political candidates, and rules on television reporting during election campaigns designed to ensure fairness to candidates. In France, under rules dating from 1969, the time allocated to political representatives is divided into thirds for government, parliamentary majority and main opposition respectively, with some allocation extended to small parties since 2000 (H&M 2004a: 109). France also has strict restrictions concerning the images of candidates that can be shown (Negrine 1996). However, such rules from the era of regulated broadcasting have an uncertain future. Both general impartiality rules and rules on election coverage are challenged by the distribution of 'unlicensed' audiovisual content via the internet. How far either media or electoral regulation will be used to address these challenges remains unclear.

Public relations and information management

The professionalisation of politics has involved increasing use of public relations strategies and personnel by political parties and governments (Davis 2002; McNair 2003). Critics have identified this as part of an increasing 'packaging' of politics (Franklin 1994), whereby public representation of politics is increasingly being managed by parties and politicians, through such figures as spin doctors (Street 2001: 185). Such critiques have a public sphere focus, often drawing on aspects of Habermas's refeudalisation thesis. Critics argue that political information is being presented, managed and manipulated in ways which undermine the capacity of citizens to reach well-informed judgements about the actions and performance of politicians and other powerholders.

Evidence of the rise in political public relations (PR) across WMS is plentiful. Parties have spent increasing sums on PR strategies and on spin doctors who operate on the porous borders between the increasingly enmeshed 'institutions' of politics and media (Esser *et al.* 2001). However, variations in the use of PR and the size of the sector connect to wider differences. The PR industry overall grew more rapidly in the US and the UK than in Europe. Miller and Dinan (2000) attribute the dramatic expansion of the sector in Britain in the 1980s to government and corporate efforts to promote free-market 'reforms', privatisation and deregulation, which in turn prompted adoption of professional PR by trade unions and other groups seeking to influence British politics and policy making (Davis 2002). A factor in the smaller growth of the PR sector in other parts of Europe was greater resistance to privatisation and deregulation, for instance in Germany and France. In general, PR and information specialists have grown in numbers more quickly than journalists, but the rate varies. In the Netherlands it is estimated that PR specialists outnumber journalists by a ratio of 2 to 1 (Bardoel 1996: 285, cited in Williams 2005: 75). In Greece and Portugal the PR sector is smaller. In Europe, the rise of governmental PR has been associated with the decline of affiliated political papers in Europe and the rise of a more independent critical professional journalism (H&M 2004b: 36–8; Williams 2005: 75).

Government media management developed earliest and is most extensive in North America and the UK (Miller and Dinan 2000). In a comparative analysis Esser *et al.* (2001) find political parties' use of PR 'spin doctors' more marginal and less developed in Germany as compared to the US and the UK. The same study found evidence in Germany of greater dependence by journalists on spin doctors, especially during election campaigns. There is a broad shift towards greater dependence on PR sources, whose 'information subsidy' is increasingly important as production pressures mount with online and 24-hour news demands and as resources are constrained for a variety of reasons. Whether this results in greater dependence of journalists on official political sources depends on how established patterns change in each country. Increasing media commercialisation can lead to greater independence and autonomy for political journalists, especially where political parallelism has traditionally been strong. On the other hand, marketisation can diminish the space for independent, investigative journalism.

Media commercialism and political communication

The expansion of privately owned commercial media has increased competitive pressures, as all media compete for audiences in increasingly challenging environments. This competitive pressure has been identified as one of the main causes of changes in the quality and range of public affairs news (McManus 1994). As well as analysis of what has changed, there is considerable debate about how such changes should be evaluated, not least as the quantity and channels of communication have increased so considerably in the last decade alone.

One core 'transformative trend' occurring across the globe arises from 'increased exposure of media organisations to unfettered market competition' (Entman 2005: 251). Closely linked is decreasing investment in serious, public affairs news by mainstream media and audiences alike (Gans 2003; Bennett 2004). There are

increasingly comparative studies of media commercialism, although much literature remains anchored in distinct North American or European foci. For comparative analysis of the transformation of media systems, these differences are of central
importance. US studies have examined the intensification of commercialism in a
predominantly commercial system, while in Europe a more protracted process of
transformation has occurred as commercialisation has eclipsed and infused major
public service institutions and cultures.

The influence of commercialism on political reporting in the US is discussed
extensively (Hallin 2000; Bennett 2004; Entman 2005; and highly critically by
McChesney 2004). For Bennett (2003: 17), 'the quest to deliver consumers to
advertisers with low-costs content has dramatically shrunk the space for even mainstream news about politics, government and policy'. The main trends identified
are increasing dominance of commercialised news and information systems and
a shift in corporate norms and values towards profits over 'social responsibility'
norms that provided insulation and support for the production of loss-making or
less profitable news journalism. Over the past 30 years, with US newspaper circulation generally flat or declining, the pressure to become more market driven has
intensified (Squires 1994). The processes of commodification and their resulting
forms in newspapers are certainly not new, as Baldasty (1992) shows in his account
of nineteenth-century US newspapers; ethics codes were established in the 1920s,
partly in reaction to the excesses of sensationalist 'yellow journalism' (McManus
1994: 201). But it was from the 1960s that one of the most successful newspaper
chains, Gannett, became a market leader after adopting new technologies,
reducing staff costs and introducing 'market-driven journalism' (McManus 1994).
Under Al Neuharth, Gannett secured stockholder investment to fund aggressive
expansion, generating profits considerably higher than most traditional newspaper owners were achieving, through a strategy of acquiring monopoly papers
and increasing advertising rates (Squires 1994; McManus 1994: 202). Since the
1970s, stockholders have come to expect high profits from newspapers held by
publicly listed companies. According to critics, many corporate investors do not
share the principles of journalistic service and professionalism which shaped the
uneasy balance between business and journalistic imperatives and which created
the historically brief 'provisional resolution' between owner intervention and
journalistic autonomy (Hallin 2000: 220; see also Bagdikian 1997; Sparks 2000b).
Journalistic professionalism, it is argued, survived largely in an economic context
where profit margins of 5–7 per cent were acceptable before returns of 15–20 per
cent were required (Squires 1994: 72–102; Hallin 2000: 222–3).

For the US television networks, news divisions were loss making, but protected
and supported for a mixture of reasons, including maintaining good relations
with the FCC and strong post-war news cultures. However, commercial pressures
increased from the 1980s as network news costs grew and audiences declined and
fragmented. CBS at the end of the 1990s was losing some $70 million per year
on its news division. This has influenced, critics argue, a shift to news as infotain-
ment, reduced coverage and quality (McChesney 2004). The long-term audience
trend has been one of declining interest in both national and international news.

Bennett (2004) cites research that only one-third of the younger demographic age bracket enjoys keeping up with the news 'a lot' as compared to two-thirds of those 65 or older. There are counter-trends, in particular a surge in demand for international news after the 9/11 terrorist atrocity, although by then news businesses had already undergone restructuring and cuts in staffing which exposed shrinking resources for expensive international investigative journalism (see McChesney 2003).

In competitive commercial systems the costs of acquiring information must be justifiable on commercial grounds. Where resources are needed to compete for market share there is a strong incentive, if not imperative, to cut down on the often considerable costs of investigative reporting and instead accept pre-packaged material. This increases media receptivity towards political public relations messages tailored for news usage and deadlines, material that provides 'information subsidies' (Gandy 1982). Media commercialisation has led to 'greater infusion of entertainment values into editorial decisions and political reporting' (Swanson 2004: 50). Competition for audiences fuels demand for 'human interest' and celebrity-based stories. The distinctions between news and entertainment have become blurred in the manner in which politicians, policies, events and issues are covered by media and promoted by parties (Delli Carpini and Williams 2001; Street 2001). These are all tendencies within commercial systems. Where such systems predominate we may predict an undersupply of the information and communication resources that citizens need (Baker 2002). According to Gitlin (1991: 129, 133, cited in Street 2001), American politics, 'raucous, deceptive, giddy, shallow, sloganeering and demagogic for most of its history', is now covered by a media that is intolerant 'of the rigors of serious arguments and the tedium of organised political life'. However, we cannot read off such 'negative' outcomes simply by identifying media as 'commercial'. The useful but vague concept of 'hypercommercialism' (McChesney 1999) is one attempt to differentiate between the commercial ownership of a media organisation per se and the effects of a predominantly commercial logic on media production, such as news, formerly governed by other values. Yet, these economic forces are only one of the many kinds of influence on the production of specific media content (Chapter 4).

There are important counterforces which can influence the content and performance of commercial firms. In general, the various forms of insulation of news journalism from commercial pressures have thinned, but commercial pressures do not necessarily mean an erosion of news and can lead to the production of higher quality news. The need to retain a valuable consumer or advertising market share by providing 'quality' is one reason. A commercial logic does not automatically operate against the coverage of politics. If audiences of high value, to advertisers or as purchasers, can be attracted by detailed coverage of politics, then it makes good business sense to provide such coverage (Sparks 2000b). But this logic tends to skew media provision towards elite audiences (Schudson 2000). Incentives to occupy a valuable market niche may also encourage high investment. An argument used to defend media concentration is that larger firms can support (often) loss-making activities such as news and cross-subsidise, as well as cross-promote, these services from their allied media. Finally, commercial media may be a powerful force for autonomy and political dealignment. 'Free' commercial media may be less prone to succumb to politicians' demands, in contrast to state-regulated systems (Semetko 1996). A guiding hypothesis for Semetko *et al.*'s research (1991: 7–8) was that competitive market pressures would render the media more audience oriented and less aligned with politicians' needs and sensitivities (see also Blumler and Gurevitch 2001: 382). Papathanassopoulos (2001: 512) links the rise in market-led journalism in Greece with higher salaries and greater resources for journalism contributing to journalists becoming more detached and 'professional', and more critical and interrogative of those in positions of power. Commercialisation has thus been identified as a force for convergence, but also for enhancing the professional status and authority of journalists. Here, as discussed in Chapter 1, analysts have sought to move beyond normative debates on the general merits of state versus market provision to examine empirically how state or market pressures influence and interact in shaping specific media performance within media systems.

In Europe, the growing commercialisation of media formed a key aspect of the 'crisis' of public communication discussed in the 1980s and 1990s (Blumler and Gurevitch 1995). Commercialisation has transformed both print and electronic media, most dramatically in undercutting public service systems since the 1980s. Similar trends to those found in the US are evident in newspaper journalism, for instance in Denmark (Mortensen 2004: 44). The decline of the party press and of papers rooted in the world of politics, and shifts towards 'catch-all' commercial papers with more politically neutral reporting, are the most obvious markers. Another is a general reduction in space devoted to parliamentary and public affairs coverage. Yet, patterns are complex even within a single national media sector. Studies of British newspapers, for example, show that such a decline has occurred over a long period (Curran and Seaton 2003), with predicted variations across elite and popular papers. Politicians' concern about shrinking parliamentary coverage is equally long-standing when, by the 1980s, news content became more varied to attract larger groups of potential readers, less space was devoted to coverage of debates and speeches by politicians, and the short summaries of parliamentary speeches transmitted by news agencies became acceptable for the majority of newspapers (Ward 1989: 25).

In British broadcasting, growing commercialisation was illustrated by ITV's decision in 1998 to move its main evening news from 10pm to a later slot, in order to free the schedule for more lucrative prime-time entertainment (a move subsequently reversed in 2007). The channel lost two million news viewers through the change but earned a reported £70m more per year in advertising revenue through screening films and entertainment programmes more attractive to advertisers. Studies have shown the decline of UK public affairs television and documentaries (Barnet and Seymour 1999; Curran and Seaton 2003). However, trends are certainly not unidirectional, especially with media proliferation and diversification. For instance, television and radio broadcasts of the UK Parliament did not begin until the 1980s. In 1992 a dedicated Parliamentary Channel was established by UK and US cable operators, and was acquired and relaunched by the BBC in 1998 as BBC Parliament. Both the quantity and diversification of such political information refutes early Habermas's refeudalisation thesis (see Webster 2002), but evidence of the negative impact of commercialisation on 'traditional' mass media institutions is nevertheless compelling. The deregulation of European broadcasting led to an expansion in the number of commercial channels, with an increasing share of viewing (Chapter 7). As programme supply has become much more entertainment oriented, 'viewers have allotted an increasingly larger share of their daily television consumption to entertainment at the expense of infor- mation programmes' (Schulz *et al.* 2005: 65). As we have seen, competitive and market pressures have also led PSBs to adopt more commercial, tabloid strategies, although the extent of all these trends varies and important differences between PSB and commercial stations remain (Chapter 9). Neveu (1999) highlights increasing trivialisation and personalisation in political reporting on French televi- sion, criticisms developed in Bourdieu's (1998) trenchant if generalised critique of French television. Trends toward tabloidisation are found across WMS, for instance in Belgium (De Bens 2004). However, lack of systematic cross-cultural content analysis of news media in Europe makes it difficult to reach definitive conclusions about the precise nature and extent of tabloidisation and 'dumbing down' (Sparks and Tulloch 2000). The research available 'does not show clearly a continuous decline of serious news and programming and the rise of tabloid news and entertainment', but does show that the 'balance between the serious and the sensational is changing' (Williams 2005: 78, 79).

Political communication, culture and journalism

How have cultures of journalism changed? How has the content, tone and mix of journalism altered? Is there convergence towards an 'Anglo-American' form of journalism? If there is any such convergence, what are its characteristics in regard to the communication of politics? As we have seen, different forms and tradi- tions of journalism developed across WMS. Historical and comparative analysis in recent years has helped to show the conditions giving rise to different kinds of journalism and aided the decentring of the so-called 'Anglo-American' model from its universalising pretensions.

By 'Anglo-American', what is generally meant is news-driven journalism in which factual reporting and information is privileged, and reporting and comment are kept recognisably separate. From its nineteenth-century origins the Anglo- American press emphasises speed and accuracy in the delivery of news (Smith 1979; Chalaby 1996) and 'objectivity', detachment and neutrality in recording news (Schudson 1978). While this helps to identify a cluster of characteristics, the term is problematic. It is misleading because there are important differences between US and UK journalism, and it lacks precision regarding characteristics. The political partisanship and agitational style found in British newspapers, partic- ularly in political and public affairs coverage in the tabloids, is quite at odds with the political 'neutrality' in most US newspapers. Across Europe, other models of journalism developed, placing greater emphasis on interpretation, analysis and opinionated commentary (Chapter 2). There are also very important differences between different kinds of journalism within each media system, differences across sectors but also within different sections of a newspaper or news programmes, for instance, which are not adequately captured.

Adversarialism

Across both the US and Western Europe there has been a recognised shift since the 1960s away from a deferential style of journalism to one more sceptical and critical of established institutions and elites. Padioleau (1985), in a comparative study of *Le Monde* and *The Washington Post*, termed this more independent style of journalism 'critical expertise'. Ornebring (2003; cited in Williams 2005) identifies a shift in current affairs debate programmes in Sweden from 1956 to 1996 from a journalism marked by courtesy and deference to authority, towards a 'popular' form emphasising conflict and criticism, with journalists as self-appointed champions of ordinary people. However, levels of journalistic adversarialism are related to the influence of media management strategies by politicians and their interaction with journalists. PSB systems (especially monopoly ones) used to guarantee access for politicians, controlled on their own terms to varying degrees. The multichannel world guarantees much less privileged access.

The interaction between politicians and journalists has led to what Moog and Sluyter-Beltrao (2000: 51) describe as 'negative dialectics'. As the airtime dedicated to policy and political statements shrinks, politicians respond with efforts to manage the news and catch attention: '[b]ut such manoeuvring, especially when aided by the professional tactics of pollsters and marketing experts, becomes news itself, as journalists' attempts to deconstruct the public relations strategies of politicians become a central staple of news coverage'. Journalists, seeking to resist manipulation and assert independence, adopt an increasingly adversarial relationship, described as the journalistic 'fight back' (Blumler and Gurevitch 1995). Research on news frames in the US has emphasised journalists' focus on the 'horse race' and public relations wars, on popularity and ratings of politicians. Studies show such meta-discursive coverage has increased in other countries, such as Germany, but Esser *et al.* (2001) explain that it exists there among a mix of diverse styles of reporting. By contrast, Benson and Hallin (2004: 18) found the French press more focused than the US press on what they call the 'political game'.

Semetko (2004: 364) highlights the importance of assessing how and why common elements in media content may nevertheless be refracted through different political and media cultures:

> Television news in Europe, as in the United States, is also predominantly 'episodic,' but the content analysis of European political news revealed that at the same time, responsibility was often attributed to the government and not the individual ... the way in which responsibility is framed ... is influenced by the political cultures and social contexts in which the news is produced. In

Western European democracies, unlike the United States, where the welfare state is comparatively strong, the government is expected to provide answers to social problems.

Murdock's (2000) analysis of differences between US and European PSB talk shows draws a similar conclusion about the framing of social problems, while illustrating the importance of extending analysis of political communication to entertainment formats and cultures.

The features of Anglo-Saxon public spheres involving particular relations of journalism to majoritarian political systems have been universalised (Mancini 1991). European countries show alternative models of advocacy journalism as the 'voices of organised groups' (Mancini 2000: 271). Williams (2005: 65) concurs in describing a 'European' model of journalism that remains more ideological and politically committed than its Anglo-American counterpart. Hallin and Mancini (2004a) identify several factors that have helped to weaken the connections between journalism and politics in European journalism, bringing it closer to the more 'information-oriented' journalism of the Anglo-American model. Williams (2005: 68–73) identifies the impact of technology, commercialisation and the rise of public relations in making professional journalistic practice more similar across Europe. Commercialisation has contributed to weakening 'European' models of journalism and to greater convergence, but journalistic practices in WMS still fall considerably short of homogenisation. Mancini (2000) finds that journalists are still heavily influenced by traditions in their countries which in most European countries continue to emphasise political engagement and commitment in journalism. Continuing differences in political, social and cultural contexts in different countries act as barriers to the influence and adoption of the Anglo-American model.

Donsbach's (1995) research in the 1990s confirmed key differences in journalists' attitudes. US journalists were least likely to believe it is important for them to 'champion particular ideas and values', aspiring instead to influence politics and the public through information and not advocacy (of their ideas, values and beliefs). By contrast, most respondents among Italian and German journalists favoured advocacy 'where each news organization tries to promote its own particular point of view': Germany (71 per cent), Italy (74), Britain (45), Sweden (36), US (21) (Donsbach 1995: 29–30). Further, Mancini (2000: 266) finds that Italian journalists misrecognise their own levels of attachment with Anglo-American norms being espoused while in real practice 'journalists are advocators and close to different social powers'.

There are also important counter-trends. Within US journalism trends towards a more European model of reporting have been identified in which the press is more politically active and aggressive (Donsbach 1995; Bagdikian 2004: 15). As Hallin and Mancini (2005) note, political parallelism is starting to re-emerge in the US, particularly in radio, cable TV, the internet and in the explicitly partisan, right-wing agenda of Fox News.[7] So while there are forces of convergence in political communication and media reporting, there remain significant differences in journalistic styles and cultures, which are linked both to established traditions of reporting and to changing influences from political systems and cultures. Benson and Hallin (2004: 20) conclude: 'journalistic professional practices are bound to be strictly limited by the political culture and system in which they operate'.

There is, however, another common trend across WMS: declining trust in journalism. Journalists' relations with the public have changed considerably over recent decades. EU surveys have revealed public trust of journalism across Europe is falling; in 2001 62 per cent of respondents said they tended to trust radio and TV, compared to only 46 per cent for the press, with TV news presenters trusted more than print journalists (Eurobarometer 2002, cited in Williams 2005). News journalism is losing its privileged status as an institution (Allan 2004). Commercialisation is an important factor here, but perhaps even greater is the impact of new digital media.

Political communication and new media

The internet has not only become a major new source for political information and opinion but also serves as an additional distribution channel for print, radio and television. This 'amplifies the mediatization of election campaigns through a multiplication of messages while simultaneously blurring the borders between the channels of voter accessibility' (Schulz *et al.* 2005: 80). The internet has provided unrivalled opportunities for the expansion and deepening of political communication. This promise, particularly in contrast to the perceived failures of off-line media, has provided inspiration since the early 1990s (Rheingold 1993), now tinged with more sober reflections of how the net has actually developed (Schiller 2000, Mosco 2004).

The internet is a heterogeneous space with multiple tendencies, possibilities and constraints (see Bennett 2003), both integrated into established systems of political communication and being used to challenge established structures of power, including media power and the role of gatekeepers and editors (Couldry and Curran 2003). The speed and extent of developments is perhaps sufficient justification to assert the net's transformative potential. However, claims arising from the potential of the internet need to be matched to the actual development and impact of new media.

The internet and new digital media are contributing to the transformation of modern politics, with characteristics of interactivity, immediacy, resistance to hierarchical mediation and the fact that the mediatisation of political discourse is itself a part of the cultural shift in politics. The boundaries between 'professional' and other journalism, and established media–source relationships, are changing with online journalism, citizens' media and weblogs. This is affecting the production of journalism and the privileged institutional space journalism has occupied between the political sphere and citizens, with some forecasting an 'end' of journalism (see Williams 2005: 73–5). However, compared to other aspects of new media, the impact on most citizens of changes to modes of political communication has so far been modest, beyond a minority segment of networked political 'sophisticates'. A much stronger case can be made for the internet's influence over 'new politics', both issue-based and organised around new social movements, operating in attenuated interaction with 'formal' politics (Dahlgren and Gurevitch 2005: 383–6). Here the extension of 'horizontal communication' and forms of civic interaction and participation point towards realisation of 'digital democracy', but considerable deficiencies regarding access and other exclusions must be set alongside the wider distribution of communicative power.

The internet generates countervailing forces to those of dominant commercial media and enables the creation of new and alternative public spaces for some 'alternative public spheres' (Dahlgren 2001b; for a critique see Sparks 2001). On the positive side has been an enormous increase in the range and diversity of political voices circulating, once various barriers to access are overcome. The internet has aided in the creation of new modes of political engagement and definitions of what constitutes politics. Against this optimistic assessment must be placed those analyses of the fragmentation and erosion of shared public space, with political communication geared to smaller and smaller target groups (Blumler and Gurevitch 2005). This trend dovetails with more general patterns in commercial media whereby media audiences are increasingly characterised by fragmentation (horizontal differentiation) and stratification (vertical differentiation) (Dahlgren and Gurevitch 2005: 382; see also Turow 1997). However, these trends are blocked, in Blumler's phrase, in other systems. Schulz *et al.* (2005: 68) argue that although German audiences have fragmented with increased media diversification, the large audiences for televised debates in the 2002 federal election campaign 'proves that fragmented audiences do not necessarily lead to a fragmentation of the public sphere'. Increasing media commercialisation is undermining media systems where public service and other non-market values formerly prevailed, but in various ways and to varying degrees. In particular, important differences remain evident in the reporting and discussion of public affairs between public service and commercial media (Chapter 8).

Assessments

If there is reasonably broad agreement about underlying macro trends in media coverage of politics, there is much less agreement about how these should be assessed (Street 2001: 186–7). Positions may be divided between pessimists, optimists and sceptics, the latter questioning the extent to which trends do in fact dominate in particular media systems (see Axford 2000). Some see news management and professionalisation of communication as necessary in complex modern environments and as containing beneficial features, including the capacity to 'reconnect' politics with people in ways that traditional media forms either did not achieve or can no longer achieve (Negrine 1996). Within media studies, culturalists generally tend towards 'cultural populism' valuing the shift from elite discourses (for instance Hartley 1999), while critical political economists, as well as conservative critics from quite different perspectives (Postman 1987), both tend to be more critical of the 'dumbing down' of politics. Across studies of North American and

European media the principal 'negative' trend found is an erosion of the quality of political coverage where commercial logic prevails. Features include a decline in truthfulness and the explanatory mission of political communication. Commercialisation strengthens the forces of private capital coalescing under a prevailing neoliberal order, drawing power away from the formal democratic political arena. The dominance of market forces in shaping media content in the US, Entman argues (2005: 251), has a specifically partisan effect: augmenting the ability of political parties that most thoroughly embody the interests of large corporations to dominate news agendas and government policy decisions. Elsewhere, however, such forces meet countervailing ones within media and political cultures.

Assessing the quality of political communication in any system requires not only examination of media output and diversity but also assessment of 'audiences' and the contribution of media towards political understanding and engagement. We have focused largely on 'macro' structural issues, but these matter, ultimately, because they shape media messages and their circulation, the political effects of which arise from their interaction with 'micro' level characteristics of recipients.[8] The latter requires much more detailed consideration than can be afforded here, but some findings of comparative research can serve to illustrate connections between structure, cultures, content and audience in particular temporal–spatial instances. In a comparative analysis of awareness of international political events, Dimock and Popkin (1997: 218) conclude that US citizens are in general less knowledgeable than citizens in other advanced industrial democracies 'in part because American television is less informative than television in other countries' regarding such international news. Americans had the highest media consumption overall and the highest dependence on television as a source of news among seven WMS studied; by contrast, Germans spent less time on TV news and more time reading newspapers (221). The study found that people who reported that they got most of their news from newspapers were significantly more knowledgeable than people who got their news from TV in every country save Canada.

Other research comparing the effects of public service and commercial media in the Netherlands on public opinion and political action found that watching television news regularly on the public service channels had positive effects on political learning, feelings of political efficacy and tendency to vote, whereas regularly opting for commercial television news had consistent and significant negative effects on these variables. All such research has considerable difficultly in isolating causation, however. More reliable is comparative analysis of commercial and PSB channels in regard to the amount of policy-relevant information conveyed to viewers and listeners (Semetko 2004: 439), although complex judgments of 'quality' remain.

Conclusion

There is some convergence within political communication towards characteristics found in the US market-dominated system. However, political communication is shaped by cultures and structures that differ markedly across WMS and which influence some of the ways in which politicians and media actors and citizens interact. The field of interactions is thus highly diverse, and is transversed by international media and communications to an extent that challenges traditional systems perspectives (Dahlgren and Gurevitch 2005). If there is convergence towards any one 'system' it is that of the United States. But there remain significant differences in the way politics and political communication are organised and conducted across Western systems, and between the US and Europe. Common elements reflect shared processes of 'modernisation' in political communication and media commercialisation, but these interact with the institutionalised cultures of politics and media across each system. The main media system variables include the historical traditions of media and governing professional norms of journalists and editors. Other key variables are the manner and extent to which 'market' regulation and formal law and regulation shape media performance. The latter are the focus of the next two chapters.

6   Media policy and regulation

Introduction

Media policy and regulation has adapted with increasing rapidity to changes in the organisation, delivery and consumption of media. But policy has also been a key force driving change, and regulation always influences the circumstances in which media services are provided. We have examined different perspectives on the values that should guide media policies and traced how some of the more settled arrangements for organising and regulating mass media have been challenged and transformed, especially since the 1980s. This chapter maps key changes in communications regulation and then examines national variations and transnational influences in selected policy areas of media ownership, broadcasting, and trade in audiovisual services to ask: how has national policy and policy making changed, especially since the 1980s and in the context of digitalisation and convergence from the 1990s? How is media policy being reshaped in the context of globalisation and internationalisation? Has the national level of media regulation diminished in scope, relevance and influence? Is there growing homogenisation in Western media policy?

PART 1: MAPPING CHANGES IN POLICY

Over the last quarter-century three main aspects of changes in communications regulation can be identified.

Shifts from the separate regulation of discrete media ('sectoral' regulation) towards convergence

Media systems are moving from an 'analogue' era in which different media have been subject to divergent forms of regulation to one in which the convergence and integration of media challenge the viability and suitability of such approaches. New methods of delivery of content via satellite, cable, internet, PDAs and other devices, and the expansion and interconnection of media, arising from privatisation of broadcasting and telecommunications, have led to boundaries between industries increasingly dissolving.

Shifts in governing values and purposes

Technological convergence may have necessitated regulatory reform, but how policy has changed cannot be explained, much less justified, by appealing to technological capabilities alone. Rather, there has been a 'paradigm shift' in governing values, but one accompanied by contestation over regulatory changes, resulting in varying degrees of 'openness', volatility and unpredictability in these decisions.

Geopolitical changes – changes in regulatory powers and effectiveness between national and transnational regulation

Through most of the twentieth century mass media regulation of newspapers, radio and television was mainly organised and authorised at the level of nation-states. Accompanying the transnationalisation of media has been a shift in authority from nation-states to supranational bodies. This shift is unmistakable, yet the contemporary scene is still better understood in terms of interplay between different levels of national, supranational and subnational regulation rather than as a unidirectional transference from national 'level' to supranational.

From sectoral regulation to convergence

The 'old' analogue world comprised different, largely incompatible communication technologies. Media were subject to different types of 'sectoral' regulation, based on different industries that were usually distinguished on the basis of their technologies of distribution: radio and television broadcasting, print publication, phonography, film and telecommunications. The main characteristics of 'old' analogue regulation included:

- regulation structured along vertical lines (production to distribution to consumption/use) or industry lines
- regulatory frameworks based around delivery platforms
- different regulatory bodies responsible for different media
- divergence – regulation directed towards achieving different objectives for different media.

Sectoral models of media regulation

The press

The liberal 'free press' model is one of legal libertarianism and non-interference with property rights of media owners. This ranges from the 'absolutist' constitutional protection of the First Amendment in the US, to the more qualified protection of the European Convention on Human Rights, where freedom of expression is subject to limitations (known as 'derogations') which are themselves strictly limited. These must be

> prescribed by law and ... necessary in a democratic society in the interests of national security, territorial integrity or public safety, for the prevention of disorder or crime, for the protection of health or morals, for the protection of the reputation or rights of others, for preventing the disclosure of information received in confidence, or for maintaining the authority and impartiality of the judiciary.
>
> (Article 10 (2) ECHR)

As we have seen, the democratic importance of the press has given rise to justifications for public policy interventions affecting property rights, notably in measures to tackle concentration of ownership; anti-monopoly measures; and 'positive' state interventions through systems of subsidy. The press is nowhere free from state intervention, since the latter takes a variety of forms, from economic benefits (tax laws and postal concessions) present in liberal systems, to specific (sectoral) measures. In addition, the press is subject to general laws and media laws affecting the collection, reporting and dissemination of information and images. However, regulation of editorial content is characterised by voluntarism. In most Western states the editorial conduct of the press is governed by self-regulation, through press councils usually comprising a mixture of industry and lay representatives. In Britain successive governments have upheld press self-regulation, but governments have periodically intervened to direct changes, such as replacement of the Press Council with a Press Complaints Council in 1991, and to apply the threat of statutory intervention to bring about changes by industry 'self-regulation'.

Broadcasting

Historically, broadcasting has been subject to controls by each of the three main types of regulation: structural, content and behaviour (Feintuck and Varney 2006: 68). Structural regulation refers to measures affecting the ownership and provision of services by firms. In broadcasting, the main kinds of structual regulation have been licensing and rules on ownership and control. Content regulation can be divided between 'negative' rules restricting content, for instance to protect against 'harm and offence', as the UK regulator Ofcom (2005) puts it, and 'positive' content regulation. The latter has been a core feature of PSB regulation and may involve requirements that general standards of programming are maintained or that specific programme types are broadcast, notably news, current affairs, children's programmes and programmes for religious, linguistic, ethnic or cultural sections of society. The US networks do not have any comparable PSB obligations; provision of news, education and cultural programmes is dependent on what is in these channels' commercial interests. The third type of regulation, behavioural, refers to measures governing the competitive behaviour and interaction of firms in markets. Its most characteristic form, competition regulation, has become increasingly important within liberalised media markets. During the high point of influence between 1945 and 1980, the 'broadcasting model' was characterised by regulation for access, universal service requirements and public service, although with considerable variation between the US and PSB systems.

Telecommunications

We can identify a 'common carrier' model (McQuail 2005a: 238), which relates to communication services such as postal, telegraph and, later, telephone services. In Europe, common carrier services were mainly provided by state-run enterprises, the PTTs or others. In the US widespread opposition to government-run enterprises led to the innovatory model of a private monopoly (AT&T) subject to close regulatory supervision (FCC). The basic telecoms model has been regulation of carriage, that is, distribution and networking standards, and very minimal content regulation. The main rationale for regulation has been to ensure efficient management of resources. Conceived as 'natural monopolies', telecommunications have historically been subject to public interest regulation concerning access to services, cost and quality and 'universal service provision'. However, as value-added services were developed for business users or affluent domestic market segments, widening gaps have opened up between these services and provision of basic telephony. In the traditional 'telecoms model' there has been strong regulation of ownership and infrastructure, but not of content.

Convergence, digitalisation and media policy

The analogue telecommunication systems in place as the post-war era began have been gradually replaced by digital systems that allow the intermeshing of telecoms systems, computing, broadcasting and all forms of digitalised media. Unlike analogue, digital information is independent from any specific transportation medium and can be conveyed over all available networks, including satellite, cable, high frequency wireless, DTT and digital subscriber lines (DSL). From the 1980s fibre optic cable and advances in computer technology (including processing, storage, compression and packaging of data) greatly increased carriage capacity. The ability to carry rich audiovisual content via telecommunications networks lies at the heart of mass media convergence. With technological convergence, the same digital media can be carried via different platforms and each platform can carry a range of different media forms. The distinctions that have shaped regulation and the rationales for divergent treatment have consequently been profoundly challenged, although some may also be defended.

Convergence, the coming together of different technologies and industries to create new ways of producing, distributing and using cultural goods and services, entered policy debate in the 1980s, although the term was used in its modern sense from the 1950s. Technological convergence remains the most manifest dimension, but to understand the policy debates the term needs unpacking. Murdock (2000) usefully delineates three convergence processes: the convergence of cultural forms, as formerly distinct forms of expression can be combined and recomposed; the convergence of communication systems as different network platforms can start to carry the same kind of services; and the convergence of corporate owner-ship. Garnham (1996) provides a longer list, encompassing convergence across production, circulation and consumption, while the UK regulator, Ofcom (2006a), identifies device convergence (accessing different services from the same device), billing convergence and platform convergence. Comparing Western and other high-tech economies, it finds that platform convergence is the most advanced and fastest growing, enabling consumers 'to access multiple products and services over a single platform and often over one device with a single operator relationship' (Ofcom 2006a:14) such as VoIP telephone and TV via mobile devices.

From the early 1980s policy makers and analysts began to anticipate the future convergence of communications industries and consider which models of regula-tion were most appropriate – debates which intensified in the 1990s as govern-ments began to radically reshape communications regulation. The Bangemann report (1994) argued that Europe should develop a strong commercial communi-cations market capable of competing worldwide. To achieve this, national rules on media concentration and cross-ownership should be swept away and broad-casting should be liberalised to facilitate the creation of large companies capable of financing and building the information infrastructure required for Europe's economic growth. Opponents argued that it did not follow from technological convergence that the social and cultural purposes justifying communications regu-lation should be abandoned. In Europe debate focused on the appropriate appli-cation of broadcasting (content and carriage) or telecommunications (carriage) regulation for converged communications (Tongue 1999; Marsden and Verhulst 1999). These ongoing convergence debates are best understood in broader histor-ical context. The next section offers a summary of changes that draws especially on accounts of media policy paradigm shifts (Hoffman-Riem 1996a; Van Cuilen-burg and McQuail 2000) and the internationalisation of media policy (Ó Siocrú *et al.* 2002).

Phases of communications regulation

Phase 1: Mid nineteenth century to Second World War (1939–1945)

Press, periodicals, book publishing, theatre and the arts have been subject to varying forms of political and legal control since their inception. States have also intervened in the running and regulation of communication services, from the movement of people, animals and goods, to postal services, for several centuries. We can begin to identify as communications policies in the modern, specialised sense the efforts of states to manage the operations of commercial/industrial enterprises in respect of the emerging electronic technologies, beginning with the electric telegraph (Van Cuilenberg and McQuail (2000: 111). Phase 1 covers a period from 'no policy' to the adoption of measures to regulate and influence the development of communication systems. The main policy goals were to promote industrial and economic develop-ment, whether by the state or private capital, in ways that served the interests of government and nation. During this phase there was institutional development of law and regulation for telegraphy, radio and television, film, cable transmission, phonography and associated media. In this 'analogue' phase, separate regimes were established for different technologies. These features were common to both North American and European approaches, which otherwise diverged significantly in terms of ownership and control. In the United States the model of government-regulated private monopoly was established. When the main telegraphy company, Western Union, was permitted to merge with AT&T in 1913 the federal government granted the new company an effective monopoly on long-distance telephony and telegraphy, subject to anti-monopoly (anti-trust) measures to ensure competition at local levels. In exchange for its state-secured monopoly, AT&T accepted government regulation of prices (tariffs) and 'legislated divergence' (Winseck 1998), whereby it was not permitted to compete with broadcasting services in content creation and distribution. In Europe, telegraphy and telephony were developed in the mould of postal services, provided as monopoly services by states directly or through authorised institutions.

This was also a phase in which international cooperation was formalised for emergent communication services. Addressing the need for multinational cooperation in the telecommunications sector, the International Telegraph Union was founded in 1865 to coordinate interconnection and technically effective communication across national boundaries. Later, governments agreed arrangements for allocating radio frequencies, in Berlin in 1906, aiming to support technical standards for interconnection. In July 1926 a Geneva Plan for European spectrum was adopted, and by 1929 agreement was reached whereby national administrations (including the Soviet Union) would make detailed allocations from the total wavelengths allotted to them (Briggs and Burke 2002: 163). In 1932 the international bodies governing radio and telegraphy were merged to form the International Telecommunication Union (ITU). The ITU later became a United Nations body, making it a condition of membership that governments license the use of spectrum for broadcast and satellite systems. Another key concern for international cooperation was intellectual property rights to address unauthorised copying of works or use of patents and trademarks. The Paris Convention for the Protection of Industry Property (1883) and the Berne Convention on literary and artistic works (1886) formed the basis for the subsequent creation of World Intellectual Property Organization (WIPO) in 1967.

In phase 1 communications were generally treated as branches of industry, subject to medium-specific regulation focused on technical concerns and with the main policy goal, such as it existed, being the perceived 'national interest' of states. This is a transitional phase, however, and regulation to serve socio-cultural purposes began to emerge with the regulation of cinema and radio broadcasting. In particular, as we have seen, the concept and institutionalisation of public service broadcasting began in this period, forming the characteristics of the next phase of policy. Internationally, the main driver of cooperation was the facilitation of economic benefits from international media trade and operations. Societal and cultural concerns did inform some international measures, but were considered to be matters of national sovereignty.

Phase 2: Public service media policy (1945–1980/1990)

Phase 2 marks the period of dominance of public service broadcasting in most of Western Europe and Canada and the privileging as 'public interest' of social, cultural and democratic values in media policy and regulation. This phase has been described as 'characterised more by normative and political than technological considerations and by the search for national coherence and stability' (Van Cuilenberg and McQuail 2000: 112). Key values shaping policy were national integration, the promotion and extension of liberal democracy and, in the period of Cold War divisions and decolonisation, drives to foster greater international solidarity, structured under Western dominance. Broadcasting was harnessed to processes of political and social integration and democratic nation (re)building involving both emancipatory and social control/management features. More broadly, regulation shifted from technical and industrial concerns to address notions of communication welfare and the promotion of social and cultural goals.

There are notable variants in press policy in this period. Criticism of the press had grown from the early decades of the twentieth century, notably in the US (see McChesney and Scott 2004) and the UK. The capitalist press was criticised by socialists and within liberal opinion as disproportionately representing right-wing opinion, dominated by irresponsible 'press barons', and biased against progressive social reform. Arguments for press reform had limited influence in phase 1, but in the reconstruction period after the Second World War press policy was influenced by criticisms of a monopolistic and 'irresponsible' capitalist press than had grown from the early decades of the century. Some social democratic administrations were emboldened to introduce measures designed to tackle concentrated corporate ownership. Such criticism also strengthened support for public broadcasting as a counterweight to private media failures.

Media policy, while often arbitrary and inconsistent became more institutionalised. Legal–rational authority was entrenched, especially in democratic corporatist systems (H&M 2004a). Government intervention on behalf of social purposes was legitimised (Van Cuilenberg and McQuail 2000: 121). Most media regulation remained resolutely national in scope, focusing on broadcasting structures and content. Likewise, public policy debate was largely nationally (or subnationally) orientated. However, states and firms engaged in a growing internationalisation of some policy areas and by the late 1960s and 1970s international and intercultural issues were being mobilised in dramatic new ways. At the international level the key development in phase 2 was the creation of the United Nations system. The failure of the League of Nations and the destruction and trauma of the Second World War underpinned the urgent case for new institutions of global governance and international economic and social cooperation. Societal and human rights came to prominence at an international level, although these soon reflected divisions and Cold War bifurcation over the relative claims of civil and political rights championed in the West and social and economic rights claimed in the East. A new body, the United Nations Educational, Scientific and Cultural Organization (UNESCO), founded in 1945, began to promote the international circulation of media, protection of journalists, and promotion of Article 19 of the UN Declaration of Human Rights (1948). UNESCO's subsequent development was shaped by two major geopolitical processes – the emerging Cold War between the US-led West and the Soviet Union, and struggles for independence and decolonisation by southern states from centuries of domination by European powers. During the 1970s UNESCO became the forum for opposition to 'cultural imperialism' and calls for a new world information and communication order (NWICO), led by 'non-aligned' states over whom the two superpowers fought for influence (Chapter 8).

During this period there was some international cooperation and regulation of communications technologies, notably telecoms satellites. Intelsat, the International Telecommunications Satellite Organisation, was created in 1964 and established formal intergovernmental agreements. The Soviet Union, excluded, created Intersputnik with seven members, while Intelsat had 89 by 1975 (Briggs and Burke 2002: 292). The use of satellites with transmission footprints that covered large sections of the globe challenged international regimes for radio spectrum allocation and required agreements concerning scarce geostationary orbital slots. The newly independent countries and less-developed nations that made up a majority on the ITU voted in 1971, against Western opposition, in favour of equal rights for orbital access for all countries. Even today, many less-industrialized countries have not been able to occupy their allocated slots, lacking both technical and financial resources.

Phase 3: Communications policy

While some institutional arrangements have certainly persisted, the characteristics of a new phase, marked by a paradigm shift in governing values, became discernible in many systems from the early 1980s. Internationally, the NWICO movement, which had called for action to redress inequalities in the flow of information and culture, was defeated. The US-sponsored doctrine of 'free flow' of information and communication, which fused 'media freedom' with 'free trade', was re-established within UNESCO (Ó Siocrú *et al.* 2002: 123–4). Phase 3 is marked by processes of internationalisation, digitalisation and growing convergence of communications and of regulatory regimes. In this phase, economic goals tend to displace social, political and cultural values (McQuail 2005a: 240). The chief new governing values are:

- market competition (transparency of ownership and control; industry self-regulation; accountability to 'markets' for public intervention);
- commercial competition (driving technological and service innovation);
- consumer welfare – defined as 'consumer choice' (access to goods and services; prices).

The paradigm shift in communications regulation may be summarised as one from societal regulation to industrial regulation, from sectoral towards general competition regulation, and from broader public policy considerations towards limited regulatory intervention on economic and consumer welfare grounds.

Market mechanisms, industry self-regulation and general competition regulation are favoured, with content regulation limited mainly to broadcast media. General tendencies have been the promotion by national governments and supranational agencies of market developments favouring economic objectives. Policy action on behalf of socio-cultural goals and citizenship has been disfavoured, with a growing presumption against 'intervention' or 'interference' with market mechanisms.

International trade agreements are 'moving the locus of media governance from national, discretionary and industry-specific forms of regulation, towards internationalized, legally binding and generic forms of media governance' (Flew 2002: 119). International and supranational regulation has become more powerful and influential relative to the former dominance of nation-states in phase 2. The major international institutions have been mainly concerned with trade in goods and services to facilitate 'free trade' and to strengthen international adherence to rules protecting property rights and trade, notably intellectual property rights. Another key feature has been international governance of communications for technical standards, interoperability and competition. Leading international institutions in this phase have been the World Trade Organisation (WTO), focused exclusively on international trade issues, and successive trade processes, notably GATT and GATS (see below). The new phase is characterised also by efforts, led by large corporations, to establish more effective regulation and enforcement of copyright and other intellectual property rights through WIPO. Societal regulation at international level has been limited (Ó Siocrú *et al.* 2002).

Summary

The internationalisation of communications policy did not begin in the 1970s but in the mid nineteenth century. Yet from the early years of radio, policy actors and debate focused on mass communications, organised mainly within national boundaries. Regulatory power was distributed among governments and parliaments, regulatory agencies and the judiciary, with varying levels of influence and accommodation for organised social groups. Cultural regulation of broadcasting was a matter of national sovereignty, even though the allocation of radio spectrum was and remains a matter requiring international cooperation to minimise interference and 'spillover' effects. From the 1970s, however, internationalisation of telephony (beyond international connectivity of mainly monopoly national services) and broadcasting was accompanied by a shift towards transnational policy regimes. Key trends in phase 3 include:

- a shift from national to transnational regulatory authority
- erosion of distinctions between different media through convergence, conglomeration and new media developments
- strengthening of private media industry rights, especially in intellectual property rights (IPRs), with global rules imposed on national-level regimes
- media ownership increasingly private, multimedia and transnational, with firms market-orientated and subject to 'light touch' regulation and oversight

- shifts from 'command and control' regulation towards industry self-regulation and co-regulation.

However, such an aerial reconnaissance cannot show the rough terrain underneath. Actual policy change is invariably more complex, uneven and contested, as the next section illustrates and examines.

PART 2: COMPARING POLICY AND REGULATION: NATIONAL AND TRANSNATIONAL VARIATIONS

Political, economic and technological changes are transforming how states intervene in policy making. Regulatory powers are pluralising, especially at supranational levels but also, in some cases, through devolution from national to subnational arenas. Whether the power of nation-states to regulate their territorial space is being eroded is a highly contested issue within globalisation debates. We examine such theories more fully in Chapter 8, but concentrate here on specific issues of media policy.

One of the principal factors in regulatory convergence is the shift in some areas of authority from nation-states to supranational bodies such as the World Trade Organisation and the European Commission. All WMS are now members of various international membership bodies and increasingly adopt common rules and policies. Yet, even where subject to the same rules, how these are implemented, the performance of regulatory authorities and the interaction of policy actors all reflect national specificities. While some differences are eroding, important differences remain among WMS which continue to influence how regulation develops at both national and supranational levels. Different market conditions and institutional arrangements have influenced the variations in regulatory regimes. Differences in states' regulation and organisation of media markets are clearly connected to more general differences in the role of the state in society (H&M 2004a: 49). Here, an underlying difference is between more liberal-tending states, and the welfare state democracies in Europe, between neoliberal and regulated economic systems (Curran and Park 2000b). As Hallin and Mancini (2004a: 283) note, differences between the US and more interventionist states may be sharper in media policy than in other areas, given the primacy awarded to private actors in the US First Amendment legal tradition.

Variations in rational–legal authority (Chapter 5) affect the implementation and enforcement of regulation. France and the UK remain highly centralised, with central government retaining most powers over media policy. In Germany, Belgium and Switzerland regional authorities are more important, while the US has a mixed system for broadcasting regulation involving both federal and state governments. All WMS today have regulatory agencies with formally independent status. While legislation remains the preserve of parliamentary institutions, independent regulatory bodies are entrusted with increasing responsibility for rule-making decisions as well as implementation. Powers and functions vary, but can include licensing, monitoring and enforcing rules, exercising judicial powers, advising government and, more rarely, appointing top media personnel (d'Haenens and Saeys 2001: 28–9). EU member states are now bound by Directives which require that National Regulatory Authorities (NRAs) be independent of industry, audiovisual media service providers and national governments. However, institutional arrangements and cultures vary considerably from country to country. Most regulatory institutions responsible for broadcasting across Western Europe are required to report to the relevant ministry, and some government ministers retain powers to control independent regulators (Iosifides *et al.* 2005: 68–9). According to one study (OECD 2000), the degree of independence is influenced by factors including the personality of the head of the regulatory body, but mostly by political traditions.

In France, with traditions of strong state authority, an independent regulator for broadcasting was only created in 1982, many decades after the US, the UK and Germany. The Conseil Supérieur de l'Audiovisuel (CSA) has been criticised for the political dependence and suspected bias of its commissioners, all of whom are appointed by political authorities (OSI 2005: 49). In Italy, legal provisions bar members of the regulator, AGCOM, from conflicts of interest, yet the voting structure gives greatest power to the president of AGCOM, a government appointee, leading to doubts about 'whether these provisions guarantee the independence of the regulator' (OSI 2005: 49). In Greece, efforts to provide the regulator with some autonomy from the Ministry of Press and Mass Media were only introduced in 2000 (Iosifides *et al.* 2005: 69).

The establishment of the UK regulator, Ofcom, been described as 'ensuring a proper cooperative relationship between Government, industry and regulators, a situation not found anywhere else in Europe' (OSI 2005: 49). Ofcom's procedures undoubtedly demonstrate a high level of rational–legal authority, and it meets its obligations to undertake public consultations in an exemplary fashion. Technically, the appointment system leaves room for state interference, but Ofcom operates in a political culture that upholds broadcasters' independence from political interference as a fundamental value. Nevertheless, Ofcom's chief executive Ed Richards was a former government adviser (1999–2003) and key architect of the Communications Act 2003, which established Ofcom's powers. For many critics, the problem is less proceduralism or crude forms of regulatory 'capture' by political or corporate interests, than the body's engineered pursuit of its pro-competition legislative mandate in ways that serve the powerful interests of commercial media over its (weaker) requirements to serve citizens.

The Canadian Radio-television and Telecommunications Commission (CRTC) is another regulator at 'arm's length' from government, although the 1991 Broadcasting Act extended government control. The CRTC also established a high level of democratic participation in regulation, for instance with public hearings and consultations on broadcast licence renewals, although this has been weakening (Lorimer and Gasher 2004: 148–57).

Concentration and convergence: national policies

Nation-states continue to reveal important differences in their approaches to media ownership and concentration. This area of regulation also reveals some of the shifts in regulatory values and in state–supranational relations in finer detail. Diverse ownership rules were created in different systems, but common elements have been:

- anti-monopoly controls to prevent undue concentration in media markets
- rules on cross-media ownership
- rules governing what persons or bodies may own media (notably, rules on foreign ownership).

From the 1980s national media ownership rules have been relaxed in all Western states. Over the past 30 years certain arguments on all sides have lost relevance or persuasive power as market conditions changed, but liberalisation has been fiercely contested. This may be illustrated by considering two starkly opposing accounts of US deregulation since the 1980s. The first argues that technological change is transforming existing media and communications systems and industrial structures, and making traditional ways of regulating those industries increasingly redundant. Technological developments in communications have undermined the rationale and the capabilities of (state) regulation to prevent media concentration (Price and Weinberg 1996). US communications policy, especially from the 1980s, has been reshaped according to this view, influencing European communication policy and emerging as an international standard. The contrary view, expressed by a long-standing critic of US neoliberalism, Herbert Schiller, is that it is not technology so much as the willingness of governments to allow industries and firms to combine and merge which has changed, as governments reverse laws and policies designed to safeguard the public interest. Concentration of capital has had a deepening impact in shaping government economic and social policy, reversing or overturning laws and regulations that originated from pressure for anti-monopoly measures in the pre-Second World War depression years. In advancing this proposition, Schiller (1996: 249) states:

> The merger and concentration movements in the United States over the last 25 years have derived mainly from successful corporate efforts to achieve deregulation of their activities. New technologies have played, at best, a supplementary role in accounting for the powerful combinations that have emerged.

The first, technological determinist account, then, emphasises the need to respond to essentially technological changes and adjust regulation accordingly. The other sees 'convergence' policies as one phase in a longer process of liberalising re-regulation in which governments have adjusted policy to the interests of powerful corporate players. Schiller may be rightly criticised for imputing a coherence of purpose to capital, offering an inverted account of corporate triumph that fails to fully acknowledge complex and contradictory market dynamics (Thompson 1995; Tomlinson 1999; Hesmondhalgh 2007). Nevertheless, Schiller's critique should alert us to question the technological deterministic thinking which has dominated much policy debate. He emphasises that the process of 'convergence' has been neither seamless nor predetermined, but rather actively shaped by regulatory intervention serving organised interests. Instead of conceiving of convergence as a single imperative process, it is important to identify the interaction of specific forces and actors shaping different kinds of convergence, and the unevenness of change. It is because outcomes cannot be read off deterministically but are, nevertheless, constrained and shaped by powerful forces (industrial, economic, institutional, political and technological) that policy and regulation are so important.

By the 1990s it was clear that 'convergence' challenged existing regulatory arrangements and divisions, which would have to be renegotiated. At the same time convergence became the major policy issue around which new entrants competed to establish a stake in media markets while established players sought to preserve their position or extend their influence. Defining the terms of debate and the new rules of the game is central to this contest for power (Murdock and Golding 1999). The now dominant view, held by all 'liberal model' governments (the US, Canada, the UK, Republic of Ireland), the most powerful sections of the European Commission and other European states, and asserted across all branches of the communications industries, is that specific measures to prevent convergence and concentration of firms should be phased out. We can identify five key arguments which make this case.

1   *Pluralism.* There is an explosion of choice and diversity in the media – pluralism is secured. The need to retain regulations designed to bring about pluralism either externally (through ownership regulation) or internally (public service broadcasting, effective codes for journalistic integrity, etc.) is diminished. New technologies enabling an expansion of media and interactivity also overcome the problem of power of voice inherent in a limited range of one-to-many mass channels of public communication.

2   *Competition and consumer welfare.* According to neoliberals, competitiveness and 'consumer welfare' are best secured by an unfettered market system. Further, the alternatives represent unacceptable (or inappropriate) interference in the market and unjustified restraints on the property rights and speech rights of media owners.

3   *Economic viability.* The expansion of media has increased competition for advertising or consumer revenue. In order to preserve the economic viability of national media firms and maintain threatened media outlets, concentration and cross-ownership may be necessary, and may be beneficial, in sustaining media diversity.

4   *Global competitiveness.* Firms need to be larger to compete globally. Hampering their growth will have an adverse impact on the economy and jobs. One variant emphasises the need to retain cultural influence in globalising markets

by encouraging the growth of national firms and reducing the risks of foreign acquisition. Another variant links the relaxation of rules on growth to enabling private firms to generate the resources required to deliver the 'global information infrastructure' required for the information society. This has shaped EC policy following Bangemann (1994), together with the argument that regulatory restrictions should be relaxed to stimulate the creation of large firms capable of competing with foreign (principally US) cultural producers.

5   *Convergence.* The media are converging – and increasingly globalised – so for a variety of reasons (technical, legal and political) governments and regulators cannot (even if desirable) tackle media concentration and corporate media power. Regulation of media ownership is hopelessly obsolescent before it is even implemented. Alternatively, nation-states and even supranational bodies such as the EC must accept globalisation as an imperative. Any regionally imposed regulation is likely to be ineffective in preventing abuse and, worse, is likely to hamper firms' competitiveness in the global economic system.

Balanced against the risk to cultural diversity and the public sphere from media concentration are the perceived benefits of economically strong companies that can 'withstand external pressures ... act as public watchdog on the European scene, promote European standards, content and diversity and create a European alternative to cultural imports' (CoE 2004; see also DTI/DCMS 1998). The leading argument today is that digital abundance is overcoming scarcity, so that market mechanisms will ensure diversity of supply without the need for structural intervention. According to UNESCO (1997: 11, cited in Thussu 2006),

> The world of communications is gradually changing from an economy of scarcity and government-structured controls to a free economy oriented towards abundant supply and diversity. This change quickens the pace of the elimination of monopolies in the delivery and distribution of information, in both telecommunications and the audiovisual field.

From a contemporary vantage point the argument that ownership regulation would become increasingly untenable may appear amply justified, and there is certainly no return path to many of the rules designed for an earlier era. There are also challenging judgements and trade-offs to be made concerning concentration, as indicated above. However, ownership continues to be one of the most sensitive issues in media regulation and a principal means to influence the operations of private media firms in markets, and so rules remain in place across most states.

The United States

Until the Reagan presidency (1981–89), the Federal Communication Commission (FCC) adopted a presumption in favour of diversity of ownership and against media concentration. The FCC was expected to protect against abuses by semi-monopolists and to confine licensees, in particular the TV networks and AT&T, to their licensed area (Winseck 1998; Tunstall and Machin 1999: 41). Diversification of ownership was an acceptable policy goal into the early 1980s, as Schiller (1996: 261) describes. Acquisitions and mergers in network TV were forbidden by the FCC until 1985 (Tunstall and Machin 1999). Once they were permitted, however, all three networks changed ownership in 1986. Congress passed little significant communications regulation between the break-up of AT&T in 1984 and the 1996 Telecommunications Act (Tunstall and Machin 1999: 40–1); deregulation arose, rather, from inaction or non-enforcement by the FCC and declining use of anti-trust powers.[1]

Telecommunications Act 1996

The 1996 Telecommunications Act endorsed the principle that telecoms and other companies should be allowed to advance into neighbouring businesses (McChesney 1999; Tunstall and Machin 1999; Aufderheide 1999). Before the Act, a single entity was limited to national ownership of 12 TV stations and 30 AM and 30 FM radio stations. The Act set a new maximum of between two and eight stations in each local market and eliminated the national cap on radio ownership, a move followed by a wave of consolidation in the industry. Removing market entry barriers, the Act permitted local telephone companies, the so-called Baby Bells, to enter long-distance markets while opening up competition in their own markets, resulting in a shakeout of firms and growing concentration (Tunstall and Machin 1999: 56). It relaxed charges on cable TV companies. Broadcasters were allocated free spectrum, subject to minimal restrictions, and new rules gave them greater security of licence tenure.

The Act retained ownership rules (including limiting cross-ownership of cable systems and broadcast outlets, newspapers and broadcasting, and restricting TV station ownership to one station in all but the largest markets), preventing the economic logic of consolidation from completely determining market structures. It provided that a single entity could not own TV stations reaching more than 35 per cent of national households,[2] although subsequently both Time Warner and Viacom were granted waivers by the FCC when their share exceeded 35 per cent. Calls by major media owners for complete elimination of the rules had met strong opposition from politically influential smaller media whose survival was threatened if ownership limits were abandoned, as well as opposition in Congress (McChesney 2004: 53–4). Yet the Act established a mechanism, and pressure, for the FCC to periodically review and liberalise rules as market conditions changed. In 1998 the FCC had reviewed, but retained, newspaper–broadcaster cross-ownership restrictions. For the 2002 review, under new Chairman Michael Powell, the FCC announced a review of all media ownership rules with the presumption they be replaced by reliance on general anti-trust enforcement. However, the FCC action was met by a campaign that mobilised public and political support which, aided by court rulings, succeeded in halting moves to deregulate (see McChesney 2004: 252–97).

Canada

The last vestiges of 'legislated media divergence' in Canada were swept aside in 1996, and all residual restrictions on telecommunications operators' authority to deliver broadcasting and cable services were removed. The Canadian broadcasting industry lobbied successfully for rules limiting ownership to one AM and FM station to be replaced by a multiple licence model from 1998 (Parnis 2000: 237). However, bordering the culturally dominant United States, with its long history of involvement in Canadian media markets, has given rise to cultural protection measures designed to restrict foreign (US) ownership and dominance over Canadian cultural industries (see below). Newspaper ownership regulations, for instance, prevented foreign companies from owning more than 25 per cent of a Canadian newspaper.

Western Europe

Ownership regimes vary considerably across Europe. Countries with specific rules on newspaper ownership and cross-ownership include the UK, Netherlands and Italy, while Ireland restricts newspaper ownership/concentration only. Belgium, Spain and Germany have no specific regulation governing newspaper concentration. Finland has no special media ownership rules (Österlunnd-Karinkanta 2004: 59). Direct aid systems for newspapers remain in force across Scandinavia, although on much reduced scales than in the 1970s and 1980s, in Finland, Norway and Sweden but not Denmark; and, to a lesser extent in Austria, France, the Netherlands, Portugal and Italy also. In the UK a formally strong interventionist system of anti-monopoly controls has, in practice, proved woefully inadequate in preventing newspaper concentrations, and ownership rules have been relaxed through successive Acts of Parliament (1990, 1996, 2003). In Sweden efforts to establish a law against concentration failed and there are no regulations governing cross-ownership: the large Bonnier group owns three of the six daily papers in the capital, Stockholm, as well as radio stations and a national TV network (TV-4) (Hultén 2004). Summing up newspaper ownership regimes across Europe, Sánchez-Tabernero and Carvajal (2002: 130) write: 'In practice, the ownership of the daily press in Europe is almost completely subject to general legislation and … market laws.'

Multisectoral ownership

With the expansion of private broadcasting in Europe, legislators established limits on ownership of radio stations and television channels. Many countries began with a limit of 'one owner, one outlet', but have since developed different and more complex rules, as the following selection illustrates. In 2001 limits on television ownership and cross-ownership remained in place in most of the 15 EU member states, with the exception of Finland, Luxembourg, Portugal and Sweden (see Iosifides *et al.* 2005: 60). There are several detailed studies available of media ownership rules, although the pace of change requires continual, detailed mapping (see Ward *et al.* 2004). The following illustrates the variety of national rules and approaches.

France

No legal person can hold more than a 49 per cent share (of capital or voting rights) in a nationwide terrestrial television service. Newspaper owners may not exceed a 30 per cent circulation share of the same type of dailies. Audience share thresholds are used to control concentration, and apply to radio, local/regional television and cable TV. In addition to audience and capital share limits, there are also numerical limits on the number of broadcasting licences that can be held by the same person. In 2003 operators could hold one licence at the national level and two for satellite television services, while the maximum holding for Digital Terrestrial Television was five licences, and the 49 per cent capital share limit does not apply. France has cross-ownership restrictions based on a 'two out of four' rule: operators may not hold interests in more than two of the following sectors: terrestrial TV, cable TV, radio or press. Turnover is not used as a criterion to control media concentrations in France.

Germany

Concentration in the press, radio and television sectors falls under the scope of general competition law. There is additional sector-specific legislation to safeguard plurality in television. There are no numerical limits on channel ownership, but operators are prohibited from reaching a dominant opinion-forming position with their programmes. A dominant opinion position is assumed to exist when an operator has an audience share of more than 30 per cent, although this may be disproved in specific cases, and even where found, a dominant position can be granted approval. The Broadcasting State Treaty of the Länder, in its July 2002 version, allows various factors to be taken into consideration when examining whether a dominant opinion-forming position exists, such as the position of the operator in related markets that are relevant for the media. Germany also has rules requiring broadcasting of programmes made by independent producers, so-called 'window programmes', where broadcasters have more than 20 per cent of total viewer share. Germany does not have specific national cross-ownership regulations, although there are some restrictions at the Länder level on newspaper–broadcasting cross-ownership.

Italy

As we have seen, legal confusion and political interference in the 1980s enabled Berlusconi to own the three main private television networks. Up to 2003 owners were not permitted to exceed a 20 per cent share of the overall daily newspaper circulation or more than 50 per cent of the total number of regional dailies. Italy limits the number of terrestrial television licences that can be held by one person, currently two licences and only one nationwide terrestrial pay-TV. Limits on turnover also apply, and terrestrial, cable and satellite may not accumulate more than 30 per cent of the resources in their respective markets, as defined by delivery technology. The cross-ownership regime is based on limiting the financial resources which an operator can accumulate: owners in the radio or broadcasting and newspaper or magazine sectors cannot hold more than 20 per cent of the total resources obtained from commercial communications, subscription and sales revenue across these markets.

Norway

The Media Ownership Act of 1997 aimed to promote media pluralism and diversity. A Media Ownership Authority has powers to prevent acquisitions in newspapers or broadcasting enterprises if the acquirer would gain a significant ownership position in the national, regional or local media market, usually one-third, that was deemed contrary to the purpose of the Act. Norway has no specific rules on cross-ownership.

United Kingdom

There were no cross-ownership provisions from when commercial television was introduced in 1954, until 1963, but cross-ownership became a more significant and controversial issue after the 1990 Broadcasting Act set rules that failed to restrict Murdoch's joint ownership of Sky and News International newspapers. The 2003 Communications Act relaxed ownership rules, allowing the creation of a single ITV and adopted one of the most liberalising approaches to foreign ownership of broadcasting. Against stiff parliamentary opposition, the government removed restrictions on foreign ownership of broadcasting assets and embraced a shift away from the protection of national champions towards market liberalisation. However, pro-market deregulation was balanced by a social-market defence of public service broadcasting, provisions to reject newspaper concentrations, and rules on television ownership (Curran 2003b).

Summary

There remains considerable variation in media ownership regulations enforced at national level. The composition of governments and assemblies influences legislation (and to varying degrees the decisions of regulatory agencies), and this is particularly evident in the politically sensitive areas of national concentration, multisectoral integration and foreign ownership. In Mediterranean systems, changes in government have sometimes resulted in significant structural changes in media ownership, a pattern less evident where there is greater rational–legal authority and autonomy for regulators. There are important differences both in the formal scope for political intervention by ministers and in the actual degree to which rules and processes are adhered to.

For commercial players, obtaining favourable ownership rules for business interests and against competitors necessitates close involvement in the policy process. In all systems powerful commercial firms or industry groupings seek favourable regulation, liberalisation to facilitate business expansion, or regulatory 'protection' to restrict competition. No political administration is free from commercial influence, but patterns arc certainly affected by the extent to which clientalist or rational–legal authority prevails. In Spain the PSOE in government had ignored media ownership laws to allow the media empires of PRISA (owned by Jesús de Polanco) and Antonio Asensio (owner of Antena 3) to expand. After the Conservatives won power, charges were brought against de Polanco, while Asensio sold Antena 3 to Telefónica de España, maintaining he was threatened with prison if he did not do so. For Hallin and Mancini (2004a: 137) this illustrates the legacy of clientalism where 'a relatively party-politicized judicial system makes it easier for governments to use the legal system to selectively enforce regulations'.

Across the EU, criteria to determine ownership levels vary from limits on the number of licences, to turnover, audience share or equity. Efforts to set legal limits have often been confusing, ineffective or inadequate in tackling concentration (Sánchez-Tabernero and Carvajal 2002: 131; Iosifides *et al.* 2005: 61–3). The means of applying and enforcing sector-specific ownership rules has also varied considerably. These may be enforced by government departments under ministerial control, by the courts, by media regulatory bodies, by 'general' competition tribunals or, usually, by a combination of these powers. The main shift has been from sectoral rules towards the application of general competition regulation (although some competition regulators, like the UK's, also apply 'media specific' rules). All WMS have tribunals authorised to rule on competition matters within their jurisdiction. In the UK and many Northern European states there has been a strong tendency towards technical decisions based on economic analysis and away from more loosely defined 'public interest' considerations. In Southern Europe, as Sánchez-Tabernero and Carvajal (2002: 129) point out, decisions may be more influenced by political considerations where control of competition is more discretionary. However, across the EU national competition regulation must be compatible with the higher authority of EU law, which has been an increasingly active force in media regulation. The general trends are clearest if we first examine supranational regulation in greater detail.

European Union policies

European Union (EU) media policy has arisen through a complex interplay of political interests, diverse and often contradictory objectives, jurisdictional constraints and legal and regulatory competencies.[3] Policy has been shaped by conflicts and compromises between member states, rival power centres within the various institutions and within the Commission itself, where at least 6 of the 24 Directorates General initiated policies concerning communications in the 1990s (Goldberg *et al.* 1998: 147; Collins 1994).

There is an extensive literature charting the limited emergence of European policy on media concentration and ownership (Collins 1994; Humphreys 1996; Doyle

2002a; Sarikakis 2004; Harcourt 2005). During the 1980s members of the European Parliament called for the adoption of measures to tackle concentration. There was considerable debate about what mechanisms should be used to determine concentration and what, if any, action should be taken at EU level. The Council of Ministers approved in principle a regulation on control of concentrations in December 1989 (Council Regulation No. 4064/89). In the early 1990s the European Commission put forward two initiatives, a Green Paper on pluralism and media concentration in the internal market (European Commission 1992), followed by further proposals for action (European Commission 1994). Both were rejected by the European Council (a ministerial-level body comprising all EU member states). The Commission's proposals were opposed by member states who claimed to have full competence in this area and also failed because of lack of harmonisation of the criteria used in the different countries to 'measure' concentration (CoE 2003). In particular, the different countries did not accept that the Commission's proposed criterion for measuring audience share could be adjusted to the requirements of each country. The result was a lack of agreement on structural regulation of media ownership (Harcourt 1996; Doyle 2002a). No firm policy was agreed and the subsequent policy agenda was increasingly shaped by liberalisers. The Bangemann Report (1994) presented to the Council of Ministers in June 1994 contained an uncompromising message that deregulation should be pursued in order to establish a Europeanised version of the Gore/Clinton US 'Information Superhighway', an 'Information Society'. The report described a 'market-led passage to the new age' but warned of urgency:

> competitive suppliers from outside Europe are increasingly active in our markets … if Europe arrives late our suppliers of technologies and services will lack the commercial muscle to win a share of the enormous global opportunities which lie ahead. Our companies will migrate to more attractive locations to do business …
>
> (Bangemann 1994: 8)

The report argued for a sharp break with the past. An inconsistent patchwork of national ownership rules had tended to 'distort and fragment the market', impeding companies from taking advantage of opportunities offered by Europe's expanding market, especially in multimedia. The role for the EC should be to prevent 'divergent national legislation on media ownership [from] undermining the internal market' and establish instead competition policy that would safeguard pluralism but was also 'especially important for consolidating the single market and for attracting the private capital necessary for the growth of the trans-European information infrastructure' (Bangemann 1994: 20). In place of fear, and opposition to Americanisation evident elsewhere in European cultural policy, Bangemann embraced America as a model to emulate: its expansion of commercial entertainment media was seen as the driver of demand and revenue for infrastructure investment. In the landscape the report mapped out there was no sign of public service media.

European policy has followed this pro-market, deregulatory path. But it has been modified quite significantly by the continuing strength of support for public service media, action on media concentration, and defence of social and cultural regulation. A report by consultants KPMG, commissioned by DG XIII, argued that in place of the presumption for regulation the guiding principle should be that of no restrictions on businesses. However, there was significant resistance to what were perceived to be 'Anglo-Saxon' solutions at odds with Europe's traditions of cultural welfare. Opposition to deregulation was expressed in such reports as *The Protection of Minors and Human Dignity* (Whitehead 1997). The European Parliament also supported by a large majority the Tongue Report on Public Service Broadcasting (European Parliament 1996), which argued for PSB to be sustained and strengthened in the digital age. The accession of Sweden, Finland and Austria to the EU in 1995 added to the number of member states that viewed broadcasting as a national and culturally specific activity.

The European Parliament has maintained public debate on the need for EU-level regulation on ownership. It initiated the first directive on pluralism, drawn up by the European Commission in 1996, which was heavily defeated and hastily withdrawn (Chakravartty and Sarikakis 2006: 102). The Commission subsequently stated that it found no legal basis for legislation at EU level against concentration on grounds of media pluralism. However, there have been several initiatives since, including in 2003–4 when the Commission invited comments on proposals for European media ownership control to be made as part of the Green Paper on Services of General Interest COM (2003) 270 final (see CoE 2003). Media pluralism also formed part of the Commission's consultations on the new 'Television Directive' in 2006 and the EU established a Task Force for Co-ordination of Media Affairs, required to reconcile promoting economic growth and jobs in the media industry with promoting media diversity and pluralism. However, there are no measures to limit media concentration in the amended Television Directive.

In contrast to the European Union, the Council of Europe has been much more pro-active, producing a series of binding Declarations, together with weaker Recommendations and Resolutions for its members, but it has much more limited powers of enforcement here than the EU. The Advisory Panel on Media Diversity (AP-MD), a working group established after the 6th European Ministerial Conference on Mass Media Policy (Cracow, June 2000), monitors developments and produces reports, including *Media Diversity in Europe* (CoE 2003) and *Transnational Media Concentrations* (CoE 2004). These proposed measures including ongoing monitoring of ownership; and action at member-states level, including support for PSB, community media, a clear separation between political authorities and media, and measures to safeguard editorial independence. The reports also urged action at international level, including a new Convention. Specific media ownership regulation remains predominantly national, however. National governments on the whole want to retain control and competence, and industry generally prefers ownership matters to be dealt with at national level (OSI 2005: 122). Large commercial groups have been mostly successful in persuading politicians in Europe to allow them to expand across sectors and develop new media technologies (Humphreys 1996: 171; Hoffman-Riem 1992: 152; Iosifides *et al.* 2005: 65–6). In Greece, for instance, cross-media concentration increased considerably after press barons lobbied successfully for the relaxation in 1990 of rules preventing them from expanding into broadcasting. Hickethier (1996) argues that there has been lack of political will to tackle concentration in Germany, with Bertelsmann closely allied to the SPD and German commercial TV dominated (until 2002) by Leo Kirch, a strong supporter of the political right.

There has been no harmonisation of media ownership rules at EU or CoE level. Instead, the regulatory vacuum has been partly filled by competition regulation. It is this development which justifies the claim that the 'weight of regulation referring to concentration and pluralism … [has] passed, in part, to the EC from national governments' (Sánchez-Tabernero and Carvajal 2002: 114).

EU competition law and policy

In the absence of specific legislation for the regulation of media concentration (Harcourt 1996; Trappel and Meier 1998; Doyle 2002a), the Commission has relied increasingly on the competition provisions of the Treaty of Rome. Community law takes precedence over national law and applies where there is a community dimension. Member states retain their powers to protect legitimate interests, including media pluralism, provided the measures taken are compatible with European competition and other regulation governing the internal market. Merger Control Regulation (MCR), which came into force in 1989 'has probably become the most significant weapon for Community regulation of media concentration' (Barendt and Hitchens 2000: 259). The Competition Directorate (DG IV) has acted against mergers and concentrations deemed to be anti-competitive, in the face of generally considerable corporate, national, intra- and inter-institutional pressures (Levy 1999: 97–9). Of the 18 concentration operations prohibited by the Commission between 1989 and 2002, five involved the communications sector (Levy 1999; Sánchez-Tabernero and Carvajal 2002: 121). The assertion of competition powers, compared to the deregulatory pro-market stance of DG XIII, surprised many firms operating in telecommunications and media sectors. DG IV has navigated a delicate path between efforts to stimulate competitive markets and to act against anti-competitive practices.

The Commission prevented the creation of MSG Media Services, a joint venture between Bertelsmann, Taurus (owned by Leo Kirch) and Deutsche Telecom to provide technical services for pay-TV in 1994. The following year it rejected two other mergers, Nordic Satellite Distribution and an alliance between Holland Media Group/RTL/Veronica and Endemol. Competition Commissioner Karel van Miert identified as a common theme in the rejected mergers that each involved 'network operators, enjoying essentially gatekeeper functions extending dominance into related broadcasting and content markets' (Van Miert 1997, cited in Levy 1999: 88). However, the Competition Directorate has tended to look favourably on cross-border alliances that involve companies whose main geographic markets lie elsewhere, leading to approval of several transnational mergers. For instance in 1995 the directorate approved a 50:50 joint venture between Compagnie Luxembourgeoise de Télédiffusion (CLT) and Disney to set up a new Disney channel in Germany, clearing the deal on the basis that although CLT was a powerful broadcaster in Europe, Disney was not. In 1996, the Commission approved all nine mergers in the media sector that it considered, including that of Audiofina and its subsidiary CLT with the television and radio interests of the Bertelsmann Group (through UFA), creating what was then Europe's largest broadcasting organisation.

There continues to be critical debate about the adequacy of competition regulation as a substitute for media ownership regulation (Doyle 2002a). Competition Commissioner Van Miert stated in 1997: 'My personal opinion is that I am convinced of a need for European legislation on media concentration ... We cannot use competition rules to govern democratic issues' (cited in Barendt and Hitchens 2000: 264). In assessing market power through economic considerations, competition law is unable to grasp more complex operations of cultural or symbolic power which regulation of media pluralism has traditionally sought to address. Competition policy 'may tolerate monopoly or oligopoly so long as markets are (economically speaking) "contestable" ... [and so] allow for conditions that still endanger pluralism' (Humphreys 2000: 90). In contrast, the public policy concept underpinning anti-monopoly measures concerns the effects of concentration on the public interest rather than on competition. By the 1990s, however, the deficiencies of existing sectoral rules and enforcement were also increasingly evident and today many, including supporters, see no realistic prospect of ownership regulations being re-established. Deregulatory policies and weak restrictions on concentration have enabled media conglomerates to consolidate their position and expand into new markets (Chapter 7). As a recent study of European television puts it: 'Even where anti-monopoly legislation is in place and ceilings on ownership are enforced, television corporations have taken advantage of permissive laws, legislative loopholes or weak regulatory mechanisms to maintain and even increase their ownership share' (OSI 2005: 67–8). Entrenched market positions, lobbying power and the (varying) ability of large media companies to use media to influence the political process makes it 'rather hard to imagine how any policy can be pursued that can break away from the now well-secured status quo of ownership' (Chakravartty and Sarikakis 2006: 102). That view is certainly open to challenge, but accurately reflects majority opinion among policy makers and scholars.

For some analysts the formidable challenges are predominantly technological and market oriented, rather than political, and arise from the difficulties of maintaining or justifying rules which are easily bypassed or rendered obsolescent by the pace of developments. Digitalisation renders the practice of licensing a restricted number of suppliers increasingly untenable. However, while increasingly difficult to tackle except through transnational coordination, these are ultimately political, not technical, questions. As a Council of Europe report (CoE 2004: 14) concludes:

> The liberalisation and globalisation of markets, the rules governing digital technology and the licensing system in telecommunications seem to make legislators inclined to consider that, given the expected unlimited access to the market of many operators, there will be no further need to establish rules for

safeguarding pluralism, and to underestimate the importance of the criteria of evaluation (resources, networks, audiences) used until now in legislation. This happens despite the fact that, on the one hand, operators are more and more frequently private companies and the media tend to concentrate, and that, on the other hand, the shortage of content suggests that the same sources, instead of a diverse range of them, will be used.

Broadcasting and digital media

If the organisation and regulation of broadcasting is our focus for comparing Western media systems, there is an overwhelming case for American exceptionalism. By contrast, if we took a global perspective, the public service systems of Canada and EU states are the exceptional arrangements, with broadcasting dominated elsewhere by a variety of state, commercial or combined controls. The US system has no regulation based on genre or quality of programmes broadcast by commercial channels. Some European systems similarly have negligible regulation for commercial broadcasters (Italy, Spain, Portugal), but all EU states are bound by a Directive that sets minimum standards for commercial broadcasters and most have heavily regulated PSBs whose audience share is considerably greater than the US public broadcasting service's 1–2 per cent. Some systems are characterised by broad PSB intervention combining public funding for PSB channels with positive programme obligations on licensed commercial channels. These include Germany, the Netherlands, Sweden and the UK.

Television content regulation, justified because of the pervasiveness, invasiveness and influence of the medium, ranges from general standards of protection for quality and from harmful material to detailed requirements for programme output by genre. One important addition since the 1970s has been in policies for cultural diversity. These include measures for inclusion in employment practices (such as in the Canadian Broadcasting Act 1991) and programme requirements (promoted in European policy and required in national legislation in many states). Several systems also include 'cultural exception' measures such as quotas for domestically produced programmes. In Sweden 70 per cent of channel output must be for domestic programmes on national channels, in France 60 per cent must be of European origin and at least 40 per cent original French-language programmes.

European audiovisual policy

There have been five main areas of EC intervention in the audiovisual industry (see Levy 1999; OSI 2005: 90). First, the 'Television without Frontiers' Directive (1989, 1997) has been designed to ensure the free flow of programmes within the EU; second, financial and other support has been given to the European AV production industry; third has been industrial policy, such as the effort to create a High Definition Television Standard in the 1980s (although the EU has since become less directive, adopting principles of 'technological neutrality' in its convergence policy); and fourth, the operation of competition law. A fifth area, of increasing importance, is action on behalf of European interests in international policy forums such as the WTO. EU media policy has developed in accordance with the broader objective of establishing a regulatory framework for realisation of the single market (OSI 2005: 90). Policies have also been influenced by changing and contradictory cultural objectives, in particular tension between fostering 'European' identities and support for cultural difference and diversity. Schlesinger (2001: 102–4) examines how national levels of production and distribution were seen by EU policy makers as an obstacle to be transcended in the interests of forging 'Europeanness', although since the late 1980s this 'public culturalist model' has been supplanted by an industrial logic to strengthen European AV services in global markets.

The 'Television without Frontiers' Directive

Between 1982 and 1996 the number of commercial channels in Western Europe increased from 4 to 217. During the 1980s there was growing recognition of the need for Europe-wide arrangements for satellite TV. The origins of the Television Directive lie in the work of DG IV, the powerful Directorate responsible for the internal market, which in 1984 produced a Green Paper supplanting DG X, the Directorate responsible for audiovisual policy (Collins 1994; Harcourt 1996). The Television Directive took nine years to evolve from the initial proposals put forward by the Hahn Report for the European Parliament in 1982 (which declared that national media controls were a barrier to European integration) to the coming into force of the Directive in 1991 (Tunstall and Machin 1999: 204). It was adopted on 3 October 1989 (89/552/EEC), amended in 1997 (97/36/EC) and then substantially revised to create the Audiovisual Media Services Directive (EC 2007a).

The Directive, incorporated into each member state's national legislation, is the main instrument in the EC regulatory framework for AV services. It applied to television broadcasting the broader goal of ensuring equal access to markets, establishing a legal framework governing the free movement of broadcast services. Member states could continue to impose regulations on domestically licensed services but could not impede the 'retransmission' or reception of broadcasting from other EU countries, all of which were subject to minimum harmonised rules. States retained exceptional powers to prohibit programmes which 'seriously impair the development of minors' and so infringe Article 22 of the Directive. However, under the 'country of origin' principle, broadcasters need only comply with national law of the member state in which they are located, without being subjected to secondary control by the receiving state. The Directive lays down minimum content standards, rules on advertising and sponsorship (and from 1997, teleshopping and self-promotion). Following various political interventions from MEPs and supporting NGOs, it also included measures to protect consumers and minors.

The Directive's objectives included the promotion of the European audiovisual industries, with the goal of increasing their share of global markets. It established cultural protection measures, in particular the requirement that 51 per cent of television transmission time should be for 'European works'. Under lobbying pressure, not least from the powerful US Motion Picture Association steered by Jack Valenti, who regarded the measure as a protectionist barrier against US films and television programmes, the phrase 'where practicable and by appropriate means' was incorporated into Article 4, weakening the quota rule. The Directive thus restricted national protectionism while upholding European protectionism (Näränen 2005), although its effect was to support the expansion of pan-European satellite TV, whose heavy reliance on US programming led to a growing cultural trade deficit (Levy 1999, Tongue 1999; Chapter 8). In his detailed study of EC audiovisual policy, Collins (1994: 23) writes:

> Two themes therefore distinguish the development of European Community broadcasting and audio-visual policy: creation of a well functioning, integrated, competitive European *market* for broadcasting and the audio-visual and *intervention* in the Community's audio-visual and broadcasting market(s) to redress what have been perceived as undesirable outcomes of the single market. Broadcasting and the audio-visual has therefore been a notable site where one of the 'grand narratives' of the Community has been played out, the battle between interventionists and free marketers, between '*dirigistes*' and 'ultra liberals'.

The Television Directive was an achievement of liberalising re-regulation (McQuail and Siune 1992; Humphreys 1996) which nevertheless contains *dirigiste* elements, arising from the political conflicts and compromises of its making. There were tensions between advocates of liberalisation (the UK, Germany, Luxembourg and Denmark) and opposition led by France with support from Italy, Belgium and Spain (Levy 1999: 40–2). The UK, in particular, along with the US government, has continued to lead calls for liberalisation since the late 1980s. The Directive was predominantly a victory for commercial forces, it 'conceived of broadcasting as a private service to be determined by consumer demand, ignoring the wider political issues of pluralism and cultural diversity' (Radaelli 1999: 125). There were no specific measures on PSB or media ownership and content rules were minimal and limited.

The Audiovisual Media Services Directive

The revision of the Television Directive was a lengthy, two-year process initiated by the Commission in 2005. On 24 May 2007 the European Parliament and Council reached agreement on the Directive, which entered into force later that year, giving member states 24 months to transpose the new provisions into their national law. At the heart of debate has been the issue of extending rules for television beyond 'linear services' such as conventional broadcasting, live streaming and near-video-on-demand (NVOD) to 'non linear' audiovisual services such as video-on-demand (VOD) and interactive AV content accessed via a range of devices. The Commission's stated aim has been to establish a modern, pro-competitive framework for TV and TV-like services to take account of rapid changes and convergence in technologies and services, with the addition of internet TV, TV on mobile phone devices, the expansion of pay-TV, on-demand services and new advertising methods. Different rules are established for linear broadcasting as opposed to on-demand content, but the latter include measures to protect minors, encourage cultural diversity, prevent incitement to hatred and offer basic consumer protection. These measures, while covering public media only, are anathema from a US libertarian perspective and mark a sharp and continuing divide between US and EC policy.

Recognising that non-linear services may replace linear services in future, the Directive argues that the former should also promote the production and distribution of European works 'where practicable', by such means as financial contributions to the production and rights acquisition of European works, a minimum share of European works in VOD catalogues, or 'the attractive presentation of European works in electronic programme guides' (EC 2007b: 18). While extended to new media, these provisions are accompanied by a shift from 'command and control' regulation to encouragement. Indicating the limits of 'convergence' policies, the new Directive also excludes from its provisions electronic versions of newspapers and magazines (as well as audio-only transmissions).

One of the principles of European regulation has been the separation of advertising and content. The Television Directive (1989/1997) upheld the 'separation principle' and prohibited surreptitious advertising. Although 'product placement', the paid placement of branded goods or services in programmes, was not specifically named, many member states have national rules that prohibit it. The new Directive accedes, albeit partially, to the wishes of a powerful coalition of media and advertising interests and permits member states to allow product placement except in news, current affairs and children programmes, subject to rules requiring that such programmes are identified to viewers (for instance by on-screen identification) and that editorial independence is not thereby undermined. Commercial lobbies argued that maintaining the rules threatened competitiveness against countries that permit product placement, notably the US and Japan. Justifying the change, the Commission (EC 2007b) states that

> providing a clear legal framework for product placement will secure new revenue for Europe's audiovisual industry, help to boost Europe's creative economy and reinforce cultural diversity. Product placement is a reality on European TV screens today, but operates essentially to the benefit of non-European content producers and without viewers being informed.

The privileging of economic interests over viewers is clear in the Directive specifically excluding identification requirements on any non-EU content containing product placement (EC 2007b). This important issue highlights greater convergence between Europe and America, marking a shift from strong principles of separation and enforcement found in most EU states towards permitting commercial integration in a manner normalised, among influential professionals at least, in the United States (Hardy 2004a). At the same time, the extension of advertising rules to internet and on-demand AV content pulls Europe in the opposite direction from the US. Permitting greater integration of 'commercial communications' in editorial content also highlights some underlying contradictions in neoliberal media policy, whereby consumer protection measures are removed in accordance with a rationale justified by 'consumer welfare'. EU states retain powers to continue to prohibit product placement in programmes produced under their jurisdiction, but not retransmission from any other EU states. Entry to any one European market thus allows US suppliers access to the total EU market without encountering any remaining barriers of national regulation.

Regulating digital television

Digital Television (DTV) has been one of the main drivers of regulatory convergence, combining as it does the technical and content regulation of traditional broadcasting with telecoms and ICT regulation. The main framework for many regulatory issues has been competition regulation in regard to licensing, provision and control of key services (digital equipment, conditional access systems and the use of proprietary or open software). The EU has also established Framework Directives for Electronic Communication Networks and Services that have been incorporated into member states' national laws. One, the Access Directive, requires national authorities to impose obligations on operators to provide access to application programming interfaces (APIs) and electronic programme guides (EPGs) on fair, reasonable and non-discriminatory terms. The Competition Directorate has also intervened to reverse the actions of national governments. It took action against the Italian government's subsidising of digital set-top boxes, which was deemed likely to consolidate the dominance of the two main licence holders RAI and Mediaset. The EC has also established a framework for digital switch-over, publishing proposals in 2005 to accelerate the transition to digital (COM2005, 204 final), proposing a deadline of 2012 for switch-off in all EU states and imposing constraints on the reuse of spectrum.

Global media governance

The latest phase of communications policy has involved an enhanced role for international institutions in media governance, creating a 'complex ecology of interdependent structures' (Raboy 2002: 6). Global institutions include various United Nations bodies (UNESCO, ITU) and newer, commercially focused bodies such as the WTO and WIPO. There are multilateral exclusive 'clubs' such as the Organisation for Economic Cooperation and Development (OECD) and the Group of Eight (G8) grouping of powerful nation states. The European Union and Council of Europe form 'regional multistage groupings', as does the North American Free Trade Agreement (NAFTA) between the US, Canada and Mexico. An important difference, however, is that the European Union is a politically integrated institution of global governance, with the European Parliament providing a level of democratic deliberation absent in the WTO and weaker in NAFTA (Chakravartty and Sarikakis 2006: 87). Among the diverse regulatory issues addressed, an underlying theme and tension has been between values of 'trade' and 'culture' (Harvey 2002). This is reflected in struggles over nation-state authority and supranational regulation or cooperation. The national–international dynamic is traversed by another dimension concerning the democratic capabilities of policy forums and processes of cultural and social inclusion in policy making. Chief concerns here have been the powerful influence of transnational private sector organisations and the extent to which deliberations have been open to democratically elected political actors and to civil society organisations.

The World Trade Organisation

The WTO, along with the World Bank and International Monetary Fund, has been one of the principal instruments of neoliberal policy. The WTO is charged with administering a multilateral trading system that involves 151 countries (July 2007). It was established in 1995 as the successor to the General Agreement on Tariffs and Trade (GATT), which had been established in 1947 to deal with commercial policy and to seek to reduce tariffs, trade barriers and preferences between a small number of powerful countries (initially, 23 representing around 80 per cent of world trade). The WTO is very different from its predecessor: it is a permanent institution; it has much greater powers to ensure compliance with WTO agreements, which are binding on all members, and in handling trade disputes. The place of media within the WTO regime is a matter of some complexity and ongoing dispute. WTO trade issues now include trade in services, trade in ideas (intellectual property rights) and liberalisation of telecommunications. Among the WTO-administered agreements, the TRIPS Agreement (Trade-Related Intellectual Property Rights) and, to a lesser extent, the ITA (Information Technology Agreement) have implications for the audiovisual sector. However, there have been strenuous efforts by some member countries, and the EU trade delegation, to keep their audiovisual trading out of the WTO rules. By contrast, WTO agreements covering books and magazines already prevent member governments from introducing measures that would tend to favour national products over imports, on the grounds that such measures distort competition.

When it was first established, the GATT acknowledged the role of AV products in reflecting national cultural values, permitting governments to apply production and screen-time quotas. In the Uruguay Round of GATT negotiations (1986–94), the US argued for the inclusion of AV products into the newly established framework for trade in services (GATS), and for the import quotas and state subsidies common in Europe to cease. It had already challenged the quota provisions of the European Television Directive of 1989, just as it had previously challenged film import quotas established in the 1947 GATT negotiations, and European restrictions on US television imports in the 1960s (Pauwels and Loisen 2003:

293). The French government, strongly supported by its film and TV industry, was a leading force of opposition. Its national screen quotas were considered by elites to be vital in protecting against US-style commercialism, although there was evidence of softening of this position in the 1990s (Pauwels and Loisen 2003: 308). Fiercely fought exemptions have been maintained but are under continual pressure from powerful advocates of liberalisation, and have also been undermined by the growth of transnational corporations whereby US subsidiaries can claim the subsidies and quota status of European-originated production (Thussu 2006: 161–2). As one Council of Europe report puts it (CoE 2003: 9–10):

> Within the framework of the World Trade Organisation, there is an attempt to treat culture as an ordinary commercial good or service … Should such efforts succeed, there is a danger of narrowing cultural diversity down to one or a few dominant cultures which will serve global audiences through the global dominant media … The European tradition, which has been strengthened over the last decade, is to acknowledge the value of European cultural diversity … to protect and promote minority cultures … based on a belief that culture and cultural expressions transcend the notion of being a merchandise, and that cultural diversity contributes profoundly to European identity and democracy.

How far any 'cultural exception' for audiovisual services can be meaningfully sustained remains unclear. Lobbyists for companies seeking access to lucrative semi-protected markets in Europe and Canada continue to press the US government to create the conditions for further liberalisation. The European Union and its member states have preserved some room for manoeuvre within the GATS agreement by making no commitments concerning National Treatment and Market Access for the audiovisual sector. In addition, by June 2005 only 26 WTO members had made commitments or offers in audiovisual services, while 122 WTO members had made none, illustrating efforts to maintain national authority over cultural policy. However, with growing media convergence, audiovisual sector policy is coming increasingly into contact with other services covered by the WTO, notably e-commerce, providing routes to dismantle the protective measures for audiovisual (Pauwels and Loisen 2003). The US, critics maintain, only insisted on trade liberalisation once its dominance of world markets was firmly established. It also retains barriers to international trade in AV services, including limiting foreign ownership of broadcasting (Sánchez-Ruiz 2001: 107). Section 310 of the US Communications Act, amended by the Telecommunications Act 1996, sets limits on foreign ownership of television or radio licences to 20 per cent and indirect investment to 25 per cent (although the FCC has discretion over these limits).

Canada and cultural exception

The US position on international trade remains challenged by two of its major trading partners, the EU and Canada, as well as the vast majority of WTO members. Among the bodies calling for audiovisual services to be exempted from total liberalisation have been the Council of Europe and the European Broadcasting Union (EBU). In the European Parliament support for *dirigiste* intervention has weakened somewhat, following elections in 2004 that saw the political composition of the parliament move to the right. The accession of states from Central and Eastern Europe may accelerate greater accommodation with the US.

The Canadian government has used a range of measures including 'financial incentives, Canadian content requirements, tax measures rules on foreign investment and intellectual property tools to promote Canadian culture' (SAGIT 1999: 1). Canadian policy has been shaped by an acute sense of the risks of losing cultural identity to the much more dominant US media along its long border (Chapter 7). Cultural industries were formally exempted from the Canada–US Free Trade Agreement (CUSFTA). Yet, the agreement did impact on cultural issues in several areas all of which favoured the US and established the principle of commercial retaliation if one party's cultural policy harmed the other country's industry (McKercher 2001: 195; Pauwels and Loisen 2003). Canada's 'cultural exception' was nevertheless retained in the NAFTA agreement. Canada has operated a grant system for domestic television production, together with tough quotas requiring broadcast of Canadian 'priority programmes'. This system has proved successful in raising domestic production output, although it has also sent some television viewing underground: 'an estimated 20% of Canadian multi-channel viewers illegally watch U.S. satellite TV, rather than Canadian-licensed platforms' (McKinsey and Co. 2004: 3).

For Magder (1998: 15) the 'high water mark for Canadian cultural nationalism' was Bill C-58, passed in 1976, which banned foreign (i.e. US) split runs for magazines and made advertising in foreign magazines non-tax deductible for Canadian businesses. Canadian magazines' share increased by 10 per cent to 40 per cent between 1975 and 1985, although US magazines continued to dominate sales. Laws preventing foreign ownership also contributed to increasing concentration across print media. By the late 1990s Conrad Black's Hollinger International owned 60 per cent of daily newspapers and, through its subsidiary Southam, published over one hundred Canadian magazines and speciality publications.[4] When Canada extended its magazine provisions in 1996 the US took the issue to the WTO; Canada was heavily defeated and subsequently created a direct subsidy system for the magazine industry as its main tool to assist with the anticipated loss of $98 million per year in advertising revenue (see McKercher 2001: 197–9; Lorimer and Gasher 2004: 184–5). Canada has had a long history of measures to protect domestic cultural industries and promote Canadian culture. However, while leading calls for cultural exception at international levels, critics argue that successive Conservative and Liberal governments since the 1980s have pursued deregulation across federal government activities, including media.

European cultural protection and state aid

After 'trade in services' became part of the WTO mandate, the WTO launched attacks on state aid for national industries including public service broadcasting, and has called for complete liberalisation of the audiovisual market. According to WTO rules there should be no national subsidies for the production of goods and services that would distort competition. From a US policy perspective, European licence fees are 'subsidies' that create unacceptable trade barriers for US companies operating in the European broadcasting market. The US–EU conflict over the issue has continued without clear resolution through the Doha Round of trade negotiations and the agenda of the World Summit on the Information Society (WSIS) in 2003. The European Commission's position on state aid has been complex and changeable in emphasis ever since commercial broadcasters, from the early 1990s, mounted arguments that financing public service broadcasting violated European competition law and that licence fee 'subsidies' gave PSBs unfair privileges. The European Council, urged by PSBs and supportive MEPs, agreed the insertion of a short Protocol in the Treaty of Amsterdam (EC 1997), designed to protect PSB funding from the general prohibitions on state aid. The Protocol states that PSB is 'directly related to the democratic, social and cultural needs of each society and the need to preserve media pluralism'. Reflecting European governments' efforts to retain PSB services while also acknowledging private broadcasters' interests, it reaffirms member states' competence to provide funding insofar as this is granted 'for the fulfilment of the public service remit as conferred' and does not affect trading conditions and competition in ways 'contrary to the common interest'.

Member states thus retain the right to determine the mission and system of remuneration for their PSBs, but this operates in increasingly uneasy tension with the competition and market policies of the EC. In 1998 the Competition Directorate (DG IV) issued proposals for discussion that would have prevented PSBs from providing state-aided programmes if such programmes were already being provided by the market. A rearguard action prevented the entrenching of an overly narrow 'market failure' definition restricting PSBs to that which the market would not itself provide. In terms of the contradictory pressures on PSB outlined earlier (Chapter 3), such approaches risk consigning PSB to a marginal role in a predominantly commercial system with a thin programme diet whose restricted appeal would threaten the continuing legitimacy of state support. On the other hand, a popular programming strategy also risks erasing the distinctiveness on which PSB is justified under the growing threat of regulatory intervention, driven largely by commercial opposition. Drawing back somewhat from intervening over the definition of national PSB remits, the Commission has focused on combating any perceived over-compensation by states that might lead to 'market distortion' (Hujanen 2005: 61; European Audiovisual Observatory 2006b: 57). Several states have been required to take action, from reviewing rules to stopping payments, and in some cases PSBs have been required to pay back public aid deemed illegal. Jakubowicz (2003) describes the emergence of a two-tier system of accountability in which PSBs are accountable to national public authorities while member states are accountable to the European Commission for the way in which they confer and finance the public service remit.

Surpanational EC regulation has thus intervened in states' organisation of PSB and represents one facet of a broader shift in regulatory power from national to supranational. The PSB Protocol at once grants nation-state competence while setting market and competition criteria that are determined at European level (see also Chakravartty and Sarikakis 2006: 90–9). However, the shift towards EC regulation has not opened up significant policy divisions with member states. As we have seen, states differ considerably in their support arrangements for PSB but all have introduced pro-market liberalisation and required internal reform of PSBs.

Lobbying

The significant political role played by actors with key economic interests in 'deregulation' policies during the 1980s and 1990s has been examined in accounts of UK and European policy (Dyson and Humphreys 1990; Tunstall and Palmer 1991; O'Malley 1994). This process is usually complex, since corporate actors in different media sectors seek outcomes favourable to their predicted economic interests and *against* those of competitors, while even apparently homogeneous interests may have complex, conflicting subdivisions. For instance, commercial broadcasters failed to develop a common position regarding the first EU Television Directive (Tunstall and Palmer 1991). In Europe, powerful groupings of commercial media organisations include the European Publishers Council, the Association of Commercial Television in Europe and the Association Européenne des Radios. Their membership is overwhelmingly West European, with the exception of the Polish publishing group, Agora, and ARCA, the Romanian commercial radio association.

Another coalition, the International Communications Round Table (ICRT), represents 25 leading media, computer and communications companies, including Time Warner, Walt Disney, News Corporation, Reed Elsevier, Sony Entertainment, Bertelsmann, Philips, Siemens and Microsoft. This grouping urged revision of the 1997 Television Directive, opposing EU quotas as no longer viable or justifiable in a global, technologically converging environment. There has continued to be extensive lobbying of Brussels by national and transnational industry interests (Sarikakis 2004; Harcourt 2005; Williams 2007). For instance, in the ongoing challenge to state aid for PSBs one report, *Safeguarding the Future of the European Audiovisual Market* (2004), argued that publicly funded broadcasters received state aid of more than €82.2 billion between 1996 and 2001, making it the 'third most subsidised "industry" in Europe'.

Evaluation: convergence trends and counter-trends

Is there growing convergence in media policies and regulation? Is this convergence towards a 'liberal model'? Is there an erosion of nation-state powers?

Nation-states remain lead players in the design and implementation of media policy. As Straubhaar (2002: 187) writes: 'Nation-states still structure most ground rules of media, such as national market structures, ownership rules, production incentives and subsidies, financial rules, frequency assignments, technical standards and content rules.' For example, the new AV Directive extends content regulation at EU level but TV content regulation remains a national prerogative (Marsden and Ariño 2005: 6–27). However, institutions of supranational governance have increased their influence. States are differentially involved in and affected by supranational bodies from issue to issue, but they are increasingly constrained by supranational agreements on market openness, competition and trade. Yet states may be key agents here, depending on the flows of influence, not merely acted upon 'from above'. Individual states may succeed in influencing 'supranational' regulation. States may also manage domestic opposition by presenting supranational decisions that they have actively pursued as being imposed. What is clear, though, is that the capacity to implement national rules in certain areas is becoming more limited.

Policy convergence is a predicted consequence of convergence in media systems as the forces of the global market 'tend to displace the national political forces that once shaped the media' (H&M 2004a: 276). Shared processes of internationalisation, digitalisation, convergence and market expansion influence the adoption of similar, if not always common, policy solutions. Supranational agreements impose uniformity, as does the creation and diffusion of global governance norms. The influence of powerful market actors is also increasingly transnational and borderless. Powerful lobbying by transnational corporations and industry bodies shapes policy convergence, as do, to a much lesser extent, civil society coalitions and networks. There are common trends and features, as we have seen, in the latest phase of communications policy. Policy makers have favoured the convergence, consolidation and integration of communication companies. Cross-ownership and integration have become an increasingly accepted norm despite opposition from civil society groups, some political actors and bodies such as the Council of Europe. Processes of digitalisation and technological convergence, while complex and uneven, have undoubtedly influenced the weakening of sectoral regulation and of command and control measures (such as entry control) which have underpinned broadcasting regulation. Technological change, it is argued, has undermined the rationale (scarcity, market failure), desirability and capacity of sectoral regulation, in particular content regulation. International trade agreements are 'moving the locus of media governance from national, discretionary and industry-specific forms of regulation, towards internationalized, legally binding and generic forms of media governance' (Flew 2002: 119).

Yet the value of identifying common macro trends must be set against the ever-present risks of reproducing seamless accounts of regulatory change. The shift in policy towards neoliberalism has been powerful and pronounced. Large transnational media corporations have been the clear beneficiaries, enabled to expand across national borders and create powerful multisectoral operations. National capital has also benefited from deregulation, but calls for liberalisation here have been accompanied by calls for policies that provide protection. The protectionist efforts of France can be interpreted in this way, although they are defended as benefiting cultural values, not merely the economic interests of firms. One of the most significant challenges to the powerful, trade-based approach of the WTO has been the effort to support cultural diversity through UNESCO, a strategy pursued by countries such as Canada (SAGIT 1999) and France, recognising that this offered potentially more durable protection than that provided by defence of 'cultural exception' exemptions within the WTO. The UNESCO Convention on the Protection and Promotion of the Diversity of Cultural Expressions (UNESCO 2005b) states that 'cultural activities, goods and services have both an economic and a cultural nature, because they convey identities, values and meanings, and must therefore not be treated as solely having commercial value'. The European Council established a Convention based on the UNESCO provisions, which entered into force on 18 March 2007. Another important counter-trend has been efforts to democratise media governance at various levels. The most notable at supranational level has been the efforts of NGOs, scholars and activists at the World Summit on the Information Society (Chakravartty and Sarikakis 2006).

Within mass media policy, approaches to broadcasting continue to mark the most decisive differences in regulatory approaches. US policy seeks further deregulation of digital services within the broader liberalisation of e-commerce (United States 2000). By contrast, the EU Audiovisual Services Directive extends AV regulation to digital and online services. There is speculation that the EU's proactive stance has been taken against further anticipated deregulation. Nevertheless, it is significant that on-demand services are included in regulations despite very considerable opposition from internet and AV businesses. The EU also opposed, unsuccessfully, the continued US-based administration of the internet through the private entity ICANN.

This chapter has examined three main areas of media policy: media ownership, broadcasting regulation and the redefinition of cultural content in terms of multinational trade regulation. In the case of the first two there is ample evidence of continuing differences in regulation within nations but also increasing supranational control and trends towards regulatory convergence. Trade has become the most powerful framework for media policy at international level, but this also highlights significant divergence between the US, Canada and the EU. The counter-trend, reasserting national cultural policy on behalf of cultural diversity, may falter, but it highlights that future paths remain, to a significant degree at least, open, unpredictable and changeable.

7 Media markets

Introduction

Communications markets have undergone fundamental structural changes since the early 1990s. This chapter focuses on the organisation, provision and consumption of various cultural resources in media markets, including patterns of expansion and interaction of firms. It assesses variations in media markets across WMS and does so with particular focus on patterns of media ownership and concentration, mass media and digitalisation, and digital television.

Characteristics of media markets

Market has three main meanings: (1) It describes the place where buyers and sellers meet to exchange goods and services; (2) it describes the demand, actual or potential, for a product or service; (3) it describes the aggregate forces that shape trade and commerce in a specific service or commodity. 'Place' is a key characteristic and variable regarding media markets. Until electronic media developed, starting with telegraphy, all media forms required physical transportation. The shoft from atoms to binary digits has enabled some place-based limitations of distribution to be overcome (Negroponte 1995): digital editions of newspapers, radio and television programmes can be accessed by consumers instantly, anywhere. But market 'place' remains important in considering the resources, content, audience and distribution patterns of media. A market consists of both buyers and sellers. Flew (2007) identifies three main markets for media:

1 the market for creative content
2 the market for financial resources
3 the market for audiences/readers/users.

This may be simplified further into two main sets of markets: product markets (selling products to consumers) and resource markets (i.e. the markets for labour, finance and other resources to enable firms to supply products).

Variables and differences in Western media markets

All markets are bounded. One of the most important kinds of boundary is geographic (local, regional, national or transnational markets). What marks the boundary needs to be carefully distinguished, however, since the 'hold' of different markers of boundary is precisely at issue in contemporary cultural debates. First, there is physical geography, the physical markers which have contributed to the human processes of marking out territories and the physical and geological features that have influenced the creation, transportation and electronic transmission of media. The physical size of a territory, its properties and natural resources, the routes of access both to neighbouring territories and within, can all influence the production, carriage and circulation of media. A second kind of boundary is that of legal–jurisdictional or other forms of political authority. The third kind of boundary is, broadly speaking, cultural, comprising language and also cultural affinities and commonalities. All these market characteristics are vital in understanding not only domestic cultural production but also the nature and influence of transnational media and cultural flows. For Albarran and Chan-Olmsted (1998:15) the unique economic, political, geographic and cultural characteristics as well as 'historic events' of a country or region may be presented as the context in which media markets are analysed. Yet it must also be emphasised that culture is shaped by mythic as well as 'real' histories, by conflict and contestation, by reconstructed legacies from below as well as nationalist, 'invented traditions' from above (Hobsbawm and Ranger 1983).

Country size, properties and 'pecking orders'

The size of a country's media markets clearly depends on economic resources and cultural factors within market segments, not merely on the total population size of a territory. But there is an evident correlation between total population or total 'market' size and the scale and range of domestic media production that can be sustained economically. Country size is also, crucially, relational. The relationship between small and large countries is the central feature, argues Tunstall (2008), of the 'world pecking order'. This is especially the case where there is physical, linguistic and/or cultural proximity between small and large countries.

The United States has by far the largest population of all Western states. It achieved this pre-eminence early in the twentieth century, before the expansion of mass media. By 1913 the US had a larger population than any Western European country (97.6 million), enabling media industries to benefit from the profitability of large-scale mass production. Domestic market conditions were the springboard for US pre-eminence as a cultural exporter worldwide.

The total estimated population of 18 Western states is set out in Appendix 1. After the United States (305,826,000), there are five large European states: Germany, France, the United Kingdom, Italy and Spain. All are larger than Canada (32,876,000), which is twice as large as the next largest Western state, the Netherlands (16,418,000). The 'big five' European states make up some 66 per cent of the EU's 457 million population. Tunstall (2008: 247) argues that all five 'want to promote and export their national culture and media' and share a marked reluctance to import media and culture from each other, although all import from the United States. The 'media trade pecking order', he argues, 'involves cultural nationalism; in most countries, most politicians and most people want to export their national media. In particular most nations do not want to import much media from their major regional rivals, and they especially do not want to import from smaller neighbors' (235).

Four of the five, France, Germany, Italy and the UK remain the most important countries in the television industry at the pan-European level. The top ten broadcasting companies in 2003 originated from these countries and commanded combined revenues of €22.7 billion. (OSI 2005: 41). The media pecking order reflects hierarchies, recognised by all countries, that are relatively stable and based on 'established facts of population, language, and cultural tradition' as well as 'political and cultural alliances and antagonisms' (Tunstall 2008: 235). However, Tunstall does not systematically address the precise correspondence between these different dimensions of geopolitical and cultural status. Country size and geopolitical or cultural status are not synonymous, and so rigorous analysis would need to isolate each independent and dependent variable here. In particular, the causes of cultural dominance, and any other form of dominance, cannot be reduced entirely to economic relationships, much less to population size. Nevertheless, Tunstall offers a shortened but incisive mapping of cultural power relations. Larger countries have significant economic advantages where market size sustains media industries that can export and expand overseas.

The cultural pecking order can be further illustrated by considering proportions of national and non-national fiction broadcast. Overall, by 2005 the hourly volume of non-national European fiction in thirteen older EU member states was similar to the volume of national fiction broadcast. Non-national European programming accounted for 13.4 per cent of total hours broadcast. Among the big five there was a higher proportion of national fiction, ranging from 17 per cent in Italy to 27 per cent in France.[1] The percentage of national fiction was less for medium-sized countries such as the Netherlands, Norway and Finland (between 9 and 11 per cent) (European Audiovisual Observatory 2006b: 151). In Austria, Belgium, Ireland, Denmark, Sweden and Ireland the proportion of national fiction was less than 5 per cent.

Geocultural markets

Language has an important bearing on the boundaries of media markets. Newspapers have overwhelmingly provided a mono-linguistic product that corresponds to the readers' first language. The extent to which newspapers have served minority language groups has depended largely on their market size and their concentration for the purposes of production and distribution. Producing and distributing services for different language groups have been technically easy in the case of free-to-air broadcasting, so provision has been shaped by commercial or political decisions.

The concept of 'geolinguistic' markets is particularly associated with discussions of transnational communications and the accelerated movement of peoples worldwide. There are an estimated 110 separate linguistic 'peoples' in Europe (Tunstall 2008: 247). All modern Western states comprise a diversity of linguistic communities, but there are important differences. Some states have more than one major linguistic community. Canada has two main language groups (English, French). Belgium has three officially recognised languages – Dutch, French and German, all of which cross state boundaries. Some states share the same language as larger and more dominant neighbours, as Finland, where the Swedish language is spoken.[2] Geocultural has been preferred over geolinguistic to describe media markets on the grounds that language is only one of the potential cultural connections between places and people (Hesmondhalgh 2007: 220–1). Certainly, culture is broader and can also replace the problematic notion of a homogeneous linguistic 'community' with an appreciation of both deep-rooted connections and also the diversity and complexity that characterise contemporary cultural formations.

For Straubhaar (1997; 2002), television is undergoing 'regionalization', rather than globalisation, into multicountry markets linked by geography, language and culture. Germany, for instance, has over 82 million inhabitants living with high population density in a territory of 349,520 sq km. With German spoken in Austria and parts of Switzerland, the common language and media market is some 100 million (Kleinsteuber 2004:78). Geocultural (rather than regional) captures this best, since 'not all these linked populations, markets and cultures are geographically contiguous' (Straubhaar 1997: 285). Yet language is especially important in considering media flows.

Newspapers are sold in mono-linguistic markets and while they may incorporate translations of foreign-language texts (as many of the earliest European papers did), printing fully translated newspapers is exceptionally rare. The magazine sector is marked by greater internationalisation of brands and formats and the production of editions aimed at different geocultural and advertising markets (Usherwood 1997). In broadcasting, there has been a range of ways of localising material for different language markets, including subtitling, dubbing and reshooting formats.

In predominantly mono-language states, national media cultures have generally provided only limited resources and access for minority language groups, state recognition and regulatory policies being key factors in the level of support. Where minority languages are those of larger geocultural groups served by media, then there are incentives for providers and minority groups to import foreign media to the extent they are able to do so. Linguistic groups' demand for culturally relevant programming or content in their own language may be met by market provision where it is economically viable, by public investment arising from policy, or by a combination of both.

Patterns of linguistic dominance

Several European languages have geocultural influences across the world, marked by the tracks of imperial expansion, conflicts, trade and migration (French, Portuguese, Spanish, Dutch). Anglophone dominance remains pre-eminent, powerfully combining the historical legacy of the British empire with the twentieth-century hegemony of the US, whose film and cultural exports capitalised on the global penetration of English. English is the second language of most of the world's populations. The mainly anglophone countries of the US, Canada, UK, Australia and New Zealand constitute the richest and most influential geocultural market in 'Western' media (Sinclair *et al.* 1996; Tunstall 2008).

Cultural affinities

Media use and consumption reflects different patterns of life in different regions and cultures (Williams 2005: 12–13). Such patterns include the division of labour in the workplace and also in domestic environments, the organisation and space of leisure, the patterns of the work-day and working life. Key influences on media consumption patterns include environmental factors (climate, terrain), sociocultural resources and competencies (the nature of the education system, traditions of politics, the distribution of capabilities to access media), class, lifestyle and the distribution of economic resources, power and privileges across society.

Media market characteristics and national markets

The following briefly illustrates how features and variables identified above shape different media systems.

The United States

The United States has been the largest national media market among WMS since 1918. It remains the largest market for total consumer spending and advertising revenue. Overall, market size has enabled the US to sustain considerably greater levels of media production than any other Western country. According to Bagdikian (2004:16), 'The 280 million Americans are served, along with assorted other small local and national media, by 1468 daily newspapers, 6,000 different magazines, 10,000 radio stations, 2,700 television and cable stations, and 2,600 book publishers' (based on 2001 figures).

Communications spending is expected to be the fourth fastest-growing sector of the US economy in the 2004–2009 period, at an annual rate of 6.7 per cent, reaching $1.109 trillion in 2009 (Veronis Suhler Stevenson 2005). Strong domestic growth has enabled US-based companies to treat overseas markets as a source for further profits. Film and television industries could invest heavily in production and then sell abroad, at differential prices for each market, programmes whose budgets and production values exceeded most countries' domestic production capabilities (Chapter 8). Globally, television is the fastest-growing sector within the US communications industry, with a growth rate of 7.2 per cent per annum since 2001, above telecoms (5.7 per cent) and radio (3.9 per cent). Revenues reached £164 billion in 2005 (Ofcom 2006a: 4, 33). Overwhelmingly, the largest communications industry (by revenue) is the US (£75 billion in 2005), followed by Japan (£19.5 billion) and the UK (£10 billion) (Ofcom 2006a: 4).

Canada

Canada has the 'fortune, good or bad' to border the United States (Herman and McChesney 1997: 156). Most of its cities lie within 50 miles of the US border and so within easy reach of US broadcasts, a major influence on the development of anglophone broadcasting in Canada (Browne 1999: 8). By contrast, broadcasting for Canada's second major language group, French speakers, is much less influenced by the US, which produces and broadcasts negligible amounts in French. Canada's population is divided into two main language groups: approximately 7 million French speakers, mostly concentrated in the province of Quebec, and 22 million English speakers (Attallah 1996). American television, widely available and popular, sets the production standards, but the Canadian market is too small to sustain equivalent programme costs (Attallah 1996: 165).

Europe

Europe, including Western, Central and Eastern Europe, is the largest single consumer market (Williams 2005:15). The 27 member states of the enlarged EU, together with Russia and the remaining ex-Communist countries of Eastern Europe, plus Norway and Switzerland (outside the EC) make up a potential market of nearly 700 million people, almost three times the size of the US domestic market.[3] Europe has also been the largest market, in economic terms, for audiovisual goods.

Broadcasting

Of the 50 leading European television companies (by operating revenues in 2005), the 'big five' dominate, with Germany (13), Britain (11), France (8), Spain (5) and Italy (3); all the others have one or fewer. The largest company based outside the big five is SRG-SSR in Switzerland (ranked eighteenth). The big five, except Spain, also have the largest public broadcasting companies. The BBC domestic service (UK) is the largest (€44,827 million in 2005), followed by RAI (Italy), ZDF (Germany), France 2 and France 3, the German channels WDR, SWR and NDR, Channel 4 (UK) and SRG-SSR (European Audiovisual Observatory 2006b: 29). With the advent of DTV several countries now offer upwards of 250 channels. France went from 6 analogue terrestrial channels to 18 digital channels, the UK from 5 to more than 30.

Radio

The US is the largest radio market (annual revenues of £11 billion in 2005), followed by Germany (due largely to considerable investment made by public broadcaster ARD). The UK is the fourth largest market, after Japan, but radio remains more popular in the UK than in the US or 'big five'. Digital radio is increasingly popular and DAB roll-out is also most advanced in the UK, with 85 per cent coverage and 200 stations in 2005. The highest share of PSB listening is also in the UK (55 per cent in 2005). The internet is having a positive effect on radio listening. Around one-third of adults with broadband connections listened online every week, while fewer than one-fifth claimed to have reduced offline radio listening as a consequence (Ofcom 2006a: 5). Digitalisation has increased the number of radio stations offered in most Western countries, with 300 to 500 being the norm, except in the US.

The press

The daily paid newspaper has continued to decline. Within Western Europe, only Ireland saw substantial growth (29 per cent) in daily newspaper sales between 2000 and 2005. Elsewhere circulations have declined, by as much as 10 per cent in Germany and the UK over the same period (World Press Trends 2005). In Denmark, adult newspaper readership fell 90 per cent in the 1970s, among the sharpest declines in the world, to an average of 75 per cent in 2001, dropping to 65 per cent for those under 30 (Mortensen 2004: 44). Newspaper revenues have been under pressure from advertising competition and falling readerships. This has mostly led to a reduction in titles, although some countries (Greece) have seen an increase in titles despite continuing falls in circulation.

With data accurate up to 2002, Kelly *et al.* (2004) provide useful reports on media markets across Europe (for Europe the European Journalism Centre provides updated profiles). There is space here for only bare thumbnail sketches of selected countries. While it perpetuates unjustified patterns of neglect, for reasons of space the section below concentrates on television and newspapers, mostly ignoring radio, periodicals and other media.

Germany

Germany has over 82 million inhabitants living with high population density in a territory of 356,954 sq. km. Germany is a diverse, multicultural society with around 10 per cent non-German immigrants. The newspaper market is characterised by a predominance of local papers (often monopolies) and four major national papers. The highest-circulation paper, *Bild-Zeitung*, is a politically right-wing tabloid or 'boulevard' paper with national coverage through regionalised editions and a total circulation of 4.4 million (2001 figures). The Axel Springer company, the largest publishing house in Europe, has an almost 24 per cent share of the newspaper market. Migrant communities are served by foreign papers printed in Germany, especially Turkish.

Over 90 per cent of households receive TV programmes via satellite or cable, with most receiving over 30 German-language programmes 'free', a factor making the market especially difficult for pay-TV. The public channels (ARD-1, ARD-3 and ZDF) have been supplemented by specialised channels such as ARTE and children's channel Kika. The main commercial channels are Bertelsmann's RTL, RTL-2, Vox and Sat-1, Pro-7. Global media corporations have become active in the large German market, notably in television services (Kleinsteuber 2004: 87).

France

France has over 60 million inhabitants. Newspaper readership is at the relatively low rate of 150 per 1,000. The press comprises 10 national dailies, 10 specialist dailies (business, sports, etc) and 61 local and regional titles (Charon 2004: 66). Public television comprises three PSB networks held by France Télévision (France 2, France 3 and France 5) and joint French–German channel ARTE. Private channels include TF-1, LCI (24-hour news), M6 and Canal+, the internationally successful pay-TV service which also provides Canal Satellite.

Italy

Italy has over 58 million inhabitants. Some 90 per cent of the 138 newspapers are regional or local and there is significant diversity of ownership (110 press enterprises in 2002), although the most important dailies are owned by major groups. Italy has a well-developed popular magazine market but no tabloid newspaper segment.

In television RAI controls three terrestrial channels (46 per cent share of viewing in 2002), five free satellite and seven pay-TV channels. Berlusconi's Mediaset dominates commercial television, while a new channel, La7 (owned by Pirelli), began broadcasting in 2001. Similarly in radio, RAI controls three national channels and has around 50 per cent of the market, with 14 major commercial networks (Mazzoleni 2004: 132). News Corporation's Sky Italia remains the sole provider of digital satellite, but Italy has rapidly established digital television services (see below).

Spain

Spain has a population of 40.4 million. There are eight national dailies, three general newspapers (*El Pais*, the highest-circulation, with 485,000 in 2005, *ABC* and *El Mundo*) the others being sports or business papers. There are some 140 newspapers published, including six Catalan and one Basque paper (De Mateo 2004). Circulation has gradually fallen to around 4.2 million and is among the lowest in Europe, although a higher percentage read newspapers (36.3 per cent in 2000, according to De Mateo 2004: 227), available in restaurants and other public places, than the 10 per cent who buy them. The daily press is concentrated into twelve main groups and 20 papers have about a 70 per cent share of total circulation.

Radiotelevisión Española (RTVE), established by statute in 1980, operates the two public national television channels (TVE-1 and La 2) as well as TVE Internacional (broadcasting by satellite to Europe and Latin America) and digital

television channels available via by satellite. There are ten regional PSB channels. Spain has no licence fee and all channels depend primarily on advertising
revenue, but the public broadcasters can receive aid from the central state or
regional governments in the seventeen autonomous regions. As such, Spanish TV
is heavily entertainment oriented, although more serious cultural progammes are
shown in the minority audience channels La 2 and regional Canal 33. Telecino and
Antena 3 dominate private television. DTT, discussed further below, is accessed
by nearly one in five TV households in Spain (19.4 per cent) (Ferreras 2007).

Key trends and processes

It has been argued that trends in Western media 'illustrate more commonalities
than differences with regard to business practices among the nations' (Albarran
and Chan-Olmsted 1998: 331). Central to these trends have been the growth
of large media corporations that have exploited new opportunities to establish
multiple media ownership nationally and to transcend national boundaries in
ownership and operations. A central claim by critical political economists is that
large media corporations can exercise an unhealthy degree of market control in
a manner detrimental to societies and cultural exchange. Little in the contentious debates concerning media concentration is agreed, about either the facts
of concentration and market dominance or how their effects on content diversity, quality or media 'independence' should be evaluated (Chapter 4). We shall
examine different aspects further, but first it is useful to identify some terms and
processes of media concentration and consolidation. In their analysis of structural
trends in the US media industry, Croteau and Hoynes (2006: 77–115) identify
four broad developments: growth of corporations; integration; globalisation; and
concentration of ownership.

Corporate growth and integration

The underlying economic dynamics of growth are inherent in capitalist market
economics. What is particular to media markets is the wider cultural and social
significance that arises from the market dynamics of growth: commercialisation,
concentration, internationalisation and expansion into foreign media markets.

Horizontal integration refers to the process of acquiring competitors in the same
industry or sector. Horizontal growth occurs where two firms engaged in the same
activity combine forces, usually through acquisition, takeover or merger. This
process is evident in the 'chain' ownership of US newspapers in the late nineteenth
century. There is no necessary connection between horizontal expansion and market
concentration. However, when a firm attempts to secure as large a market share as
possible, the usual 'successful' outcome is greater concentration. The UK national
press, for instance, remains dominated by a handful of firms; the ten titles are owned
by seven large media companies all with substantial other media interests. The top
four companies control nearly 90 per cent of the total market.

Vertical integration refers to the acquisition or control of companies in different stages of the 'value chain' leading from production to circulation and consumption. Again, the process is not new. The Hollywood studio system in the 1920s is the classic example, notable also as a system dismantled in part through regulatory pressure when the US Supreme Court ruled in 1948 that the studios must give up their exhibition operations, and then subsequently reconstructed from the 1970s (Miller *et al.* 2005; Schatz 1997). However, vertical integration was a leading feature of changes in corporate organisation and business strategy from the 1980s.

Other forms of integration include multisectoral, cross-media and multimedia integration. An older term, 'diagonal', indicates patterns of integration across product sectors as firms diversify into new businesses, but industry-based distinctions are becoming less tenable with accelerating convergence. Since the mid 1980s there has been a relentless phase of concentration in multimedia companies and merger mania. In 1999, for instance, 72 per cent of media companies operating in Europe were involved in some form of merger or acquisition activity. The growth of media companies has very often involved acquiring other media firms, to form ever larger conglomerates (Sánchez-Tabernero *et al.* 1993: 94).[4]

Following a sustained phase of merger activity since 1986, nine major global multimedia companies now dominate US media according to McChesney (2002; Herman and McChesney 1997). These firms have responded to the dynamics and imperatives of capitalist accumulation and economic, institutional and market conditions, forcing them to become larger, integrated and increasingly global. Bagdikian, in his preface to the 1997 edition of *The Media Monopoly*, noted: 'Only fifteen years ago, it was possible to cite specific corporations dominant in one communications medium, with only a minority of those corporations similarly dominant in a second medium' (xxv).

Growth and consolidation patterns may be illustrated by a selective record of merger activity:

- 1985 Murdoch's News Corporation buys Twentieth Century Fox
- 1986 Matsushita acquires RCA for $6.4 billion (then the largest non-oil acquisition in history)
- 1989 Sony acquires Columbia Pictures (and Tristar) (Japanese electronic hardware company buying entertainment software)
- 1990 Time and Warner merge
- 1991 Matsushita acquires MCA
- 1994 Viacom acquires Paramount ($8 billion) and Blockbuster ($8.5 billion)
- 1995 Westinghouse acquires CBS ($5.4 billion)
- 1995 Disney acquires ABC/Capital Cities ($19 billion) (vertical integration)
- 1995 Seagram acquires Universal Studios
- 1996 Time Warner acquires Turner Broadcasting ($7.4 billion)
- 1998 AT&T acquires TCI (including Liberty) (telecoms–media convergence)
- 1999 Viacom and Columbia Broadcasting System (CBS) merge ($80 billion)
- 2000 Vivendi acquires Seagram/Universal ($35 billion)
- 2000 AOL acquires Time Warner ($166 billion) (ISP–media conglomerate)

- 2003 News Corporation buys a controlling interest in Hughes Electronics (DirectTV) ($6.6 billion) (US satellite/global satellite TV)
- Sony and Bertelsmann merge music units into Sony BMG ($5 billion)
- 2003 General Electric (NBC) buys Vivendi Universal Entertainment ($5.2 billion)
- 2006 Disney acquires Pixar.

Media merger and acquisition activity has been part of a wider trend across industries. For instance, 1986, the 'year of the deal' saw 3,300 corporate acquisitions in the US. A sustained period of growth and consolidation in US media culminated in the AOL–Time Warner merger. Valued at around $160 billion, this was nearly 500 times larger than any previous media deal and, at the time, the largest in business history. In the period 2000–2002 a series of shocks affected media corporate growth, notably the collapse in internet stock value, a short worldwide advertising recession and the impact of the 9/11 terrorist attacks. The dot.com stock collapses of 2001 revealed AOL–Time Warner's over-inflated value, the company reported heavy losses for AOL in 2002 and reverted to 'Time Warner' the following year. The year 2001 marked a general slowing in corporate growth and some spectacular failures (including several of the early developers of digital television services in Europe), although this shakeout itself gave rise to further consolidation and acquisitions. Growth picked up with the expanding market for digital devices and the corporate rush to occupy new spaces of communication and congregation, such as social networking sites MySpace.com, purchased by News Corporation in 2005 for $580 million, and YouTube, acquired by Google in 2006 for $1.65 billion.

Dynamics of corporate integration

Several economic characteristics of media markets encourage concentration and consolidation and it is the intensification of this market 'logic' that prevails in commercial media systems today. In particular, the benefits of economies of scale and scope are often considerable. Economies of scale occur when the cost of providing an extra unit (of a good or service) falls as the scale of output expands. Economists refer to average cost (AC) as the total costs involved in providing a particular product or service divided by the total number of consumers. Marginal costs (MC) refer to the cost of supplying a product or service to one extra consumer. Economies of scale exist where the marginal costs are lower than the average costs. Such economies are prevalent because many media industries have high initial costs of production combined with low marginal reproduction and distribution costs (Picard 1989: 62–72; Doyle 2002b: 13–14). Film, broadcasting and print media are all characterised by high 'first copy costs', while the cost of bringing additional copies to market is low, in some cases zero. When the gap between first copy and second copy costs is large there tend to be economies of scale. Beyond break-even point, the volume of sales at which total revenues equal total costs, the profits made from selling additional units can be considerable. Where fixed costs of production are high, firms need to achieve significant sales to spread the costs across a large number of consumers. This means there is a strong orientation towards 'audience maximisation'.

As in other industries, large media companies enjoy scale benefits when long-run average costs (LRAC) decline as output and plant size increase (Picard 1989:122). Such benefits include larger production runs, cost savings on bulk purchases, automated assembly and a specialised division of labour. Achieving economies of scale means that existing firms with high volume will usually operate at lower cost per unit than a new firm entering the market, creating a 'barrier' to market entry. Of course, competitors may have other advantages, but where entry to market is difficult there tends to be concentration. Historically, this has fuelled concerns that the major means of communication would tend to be owned by the powerful and wealthy – because the strategies for profitability required huge resources. High barriers preventing market entry has certainly been an important factor in newspaper concentration. After the closure of *Le Matin*, Wallonia no longer has a progressive, left-oriented newspaper, despite strong socialist traditions in this region of Belgium. In Belgium 27 papers disappeared between 1950 and 2002 and all new ventures failed (De Bens 2004: 18).

The situation of free-to-air broadcasting is somewhat different, since this industry creates what economists term 'public goods'. Whereas private goods, such as a sandwich, are exhausted in the act of consumption, public goods such as free-to-air broadcasting are not. As Chan-Olmsted and Chang (2003: 217) put it 'most media content products are nonexcludable and nondepletable public goods whose consumption by one individual does not interfere with its availability to another but adds to the scale economies in production'. This has underpinned the rationale for a shared tax on users (licence fee) (Graham and Davies 1997) in public service systems. It also underpins efforts in commercial systems to create scarcity in order to realise value (pay-TV) or, for network television, achieving profits through 'syndication, networking and general distribution' (Picard 1989: 66).

Achieving economies of scope has been another important driver of corporate merger activity. Economies of scope arise when activities in one area either decrease costs or increase revenues in a second area. Such economies usually arise 'when there are some shared overheads or other efficiency gains available that make it more cost effective for two or more related products to be produced and sold jointly, rather than separately' (Doyle 2002b: 14). Savings can be made if the creative and other inputs gathered to make one product can be reused in another (repurposing). In addition, product and brand extensions can increase the scope for profits. The Scandinavian Broadcasting System (SBS), for instance, cut production costs through the simultaneous production of a variety of programming formats targeted at different national markets (Iosifides *et al.* 2005: 84). The SBS broadcasting group, based in Luxembourg, has expanded from its Nordic market base and now controls channels in Northern and South-Eastern Europe. Firms use other means to achieve scope benefits, including licences, alliances and joint agreements. Where first copy costs are high, there are incentives to sell the product or associated products in as many formats or 'windows' of opportunity as possible. This underlies the dynamics of branding and merchandising and the more recent developments of content repurposing that the internet and digitalisation have greatly facilitated.

Herman and McChesney (1997: 54) identify two main kinds of 'profit potential' driving merger activity. The first is cost savings arising from 'fuller utilization of existing personnel, facilities and "content" resources'. The second is the combined benefits of synergy, 'the exploitation of new opportunities for cross-selling, cross-promotion, and privileged access'. Synergy, like convergence, was presented (especially during the 1980s and 1990s) as an imperative to justify liberalisation of communications policy and, like 'convergence', it provided a more palatable description for monopolisation and concentration. The lustre and hype surrounding synergy has since diminished somewhat, as claimed benefits failed to materialise or 'megabrands' flopped (see Negus 1997; McChesney 1999: 25; Doyle 1999). Some firms that merged during the 1990s found it difficult to achieve profitable synergies (Baker 2007), leading to demergers and sell-offs. Spectacular corporate failures, such as Vivendi in 2002, prompted something of a reversal of synergy hype, although corporate integration has, if anything, increased since.

Globalisation and growth

A common factor reshaping media systems has been the growth and influence of transnational media corporations in national markets. The search for growing amounts of capital to invest in media technologies and services, and the imperatives on firms to compete in increasingly liberalised international markets have encouraged the expansion of multinational media corporations. A transnational corporation (TNC) 'is one that maintains facilities in more than one country and plans its operations and investments in a multi-country perspective' (Herman and McChesney 1997: 13). Such firms tend to internationalise both products and production processes, which in turn contributes to dissemination and adoption of professional practices (H&M 2004b).

Multinational expansion may be constrained by national rules on foreign media ownership and investment. This is one reason why firms may seek strategic alliances with local firms to 'integrate operational functions, share risks, and align corporate cultures to achieve a collective market advantage' (Albarran and Chan-Olmsted 1998: 334). Alliances can offer the best opportunity to capture an already developed customer base, or overcome barriers to market entry. Alliances are also driven by the need of TNCs to localise media content and services (Chapter 8). Overseas expansion is also connected to domestic market and regulatory conditions. As one report puts it (CoE 2004: 10):

> Media firms move into other countries when their home market is saturated, to attain critical mass, to pool resources and to share risks. In several cases firms have turned to other countries because the competition authorities refused to let them go ahead with a national merger for fear that it would create a dominant position or a monopoly.

The US is a well-developed market and its largest firms expanded operations significantly from the 1980s. In Europe, regional and international expansion had taken place as firms rebuilt after 1945, but the main phase of internationalisation began later, in the 1990s.

Patterns and profiles of conglomeration

News Corporation

While News Corporation is not the largest, it can claim to be the most integrated global media corporation, owning a wide range of media interests that straddle five continents. Rupert Murdoch remains the single most prominent international 'media mogul' today, in Ben Bagdikian's (1989) phrase, 'the lord of the global village'. For Herman and McChesney (1997: 70), News Corporation provides 'the archetype for the twenty-first century global media firm in many respects and ... the best case study for understanding global media firms' behaviour'. From his origins running inherited newspapers in Adelaide, Australia, Murdoch established News Corporation as a global conglomerate with interests across satellite and cable television, film, newspapers, magazines and book publishing. News Corporation owns the largest number of English-language daily newspapers around the world. Ownership includes the Fox Broadcast network (35 stations across the US in 2005), Fox News Channel, Twentieth Century Fox, film studios, TV channel FOXTEL in Australia, together with newspapers; the National Geographic channel; HarperCollins and numerous other book publishers. Murdoch owns Star TV, which reaches more than 300 million people across Asia, the Middle East and in India, where it is the most popular channel. News Corporation has a minority stake in Phoenix Satellite TV, based in Hong Kong and targeted at mainland China, as well as stakes in other Chinese media, including newspapers (People's Daily Newspaper) and the internet.

Murdoch owns Direct TV, the largest pay satellite DTH service in America, with over 13 million subscribers. This long-cherished ambition led to the creation of Sky Global Networks, with satellite TV services now available worldwide, and efforts to integrate Star and BSkyB with Fox's programme and on-demand content to create a global media infrastructure. News Corporation's expansion has occurred in various phases (see Flew 2007: 88–90) and has involved cross-media integration that has variously circumvented national anti-monopoly and ownership rules. In 1985 Murdoch became an American citizen so that he could overcome laws prohibiting foreign ownership of television assets, launching Fox as a fourth TV network. The FCC waived the cross-ownership rule to allow Murdoch to acquire a TV station in New York, where he also owned the *New York Post* daily newspaper. In 1985 Murdoch's move into satellite television was financed from his newspaper operations, including ownership of four UK national newspapers (and briefly a fifth, *Today*), while Sky's takeover of the ailing BSB to form the hugely successful British Sky Broadcasting occurred in a legislative hiatus tolerated by the outgoing Prime Minister Margaret Thatcher (Goodwin 1998). Initially Sky was a highly risky and hugely costly venture which nearly led to corporate collapse (Horsman

1998). However, Murdoch bought up premium content, in particular live sports rights and US films, pioneering 'pay-per-view' sports television in Europe. BSkyB became Europe's most profitable private broadcaster (with operating revenue of €53,840 million in 2005) and continues to be a leading innovator in digital media services, with Sky Digital (1998) and Sky+, the leading UK provider of personal video recorder (PVR) and interactive services. In 2006, Sky Broadband and Sky by mobile were introduced, confirming the company's position as a leading innovator in developing and exploiting the convergence of digital and interactive TV, wireless and internet communications. Through subsidiaries, News Corporation expanded into continental Europe. Europe's second-largest digital TV packager, Sky Italia, was created from News Corporation's and Telecom Italia's acquisition of Telepui in 2003. Using mostly Direct Broadcast Satellite (DBS), a 'logical cross-border communication technology' (Albarran and Chan-Olmsted 1998: 332), and strategic alliances, News Corporation has become a major competitor in many regional and national markets. The US remains News Corporation's primary market, accounting for 74 per cent of revenues in 2005, and since 2004 became the headquarters of News Corporation, which moved from its carefully protected Australian base to be registered on the US Stock Exchange.[5]

Time Warner

The New York-based conglomerate Time Warner is the world's largest media entertainment and information company, with major businesses in movies (Warner Bros. Entertainment Inc, New Line Cinema), cable TV, publishing (Time Inc) music and the internet, merchandising, retail and product licensing.[6] Properties include Cable News Network (CNN) and Turner Broadcasting, including Cartoon Network. Time Warner owns HBO (Home Box Office), the largest pay cable channel in the world, which produces high-quality shows for its premium subscription channels that have been acquired internationally, eagerly consumed and critically acclaimed, including *Sex and The City*, *The Sopranos*, *The West Wing* and *ER*. Time Warner was formed in 1989 when the film and television group Warner Communications Inc. merged with Time Incorporated, and became the largest media firm in 1996 when it acquired Turner Broadcasting. The merger of America Online (AOL) and Time Warner in 2000 created a multimedia corporation worth an estimated $350 billion, then ranked fourth-largest corporation. Huge losses followed, but Time Warner re-established its pre-eminence although with less spectacular annual growth, dropping to 48 from 40 in the Fortune 500 US companies in 2007.

Viacom

Viacom is a first-tier media conglomerate with interests in film production, music, theme parks, video/DVD rentals, broadcasting and publishing. Brands include MTV Networks, VH1, Nickelodeon, Nick at Nite, Comedy Central, CMT: Country Music Television, Spike TV, TV Land, Logo and more than 130 networks around the world, BET Networks, Paramount Pictures, Paramount Home Entertainment, DreamWorks and Famous Music. CEO Sumner Redstone engineered a hostile takeover of Viacom in 1987 for $3.4 billion. Redstone outbid Barry Diller for Paramount (1994), swallowed Blockbuster Entertainment the same year, and merged with CBS in 1998, his largest deal, at $34 billion. On 31 December 2005 CBS was spun off as a separate publicly traded company. CBS Corporation took with it the UPN broadcast networks, Showtime cable, TV stations, radio, billboards and publishing. However, Redstone controls both CBS Corporation and Viacom, as chairman and as majority owner of both companies' voting shares.

Consolidating corporate power? Contradictions, counter-trends and risk

Corporate strategies include efforts to create scarcity in order to realise value, to minimise risk and maximise returns, and to derive advantages from being large, dominant across multinational markets and vertically integrated across the supply chain. Thus economies of scale and scope both create market advantage and barriers to market entry. In open and competitive markets, new firms will enter the market and compete. According to the theory of imperfect competition, however, cost advantages associated with size will dictate that an industry should be an oligopoly unless either some form of market intervention or government regulation prevents firms from growing to their most efficient size. The trends outlined above help to explain tendencies towards growth and consolidation of corporate power. On their own, the tendencies indicate the steady accumulation of market power that underlies critical arguments about media power. However, much is disputed in the latter account and we need to pursue various contested issues further. First, it is argued that 'market intervention' is precisely what is occurring as new media open up opportunities to challenge or bypass incumbents. There are disputes concerning the empirical evidence, analysis of trends, evaluation of consequences and the wider value framework in which these matters should be assessed. At issue is the extent of changes in the ownership, structure and size of media industries, including the basis of evidence and measurability, and differences in how to evaluate developments. Are media markets (becoming more) concentrated? Does it matter? Is there greater corporate media ownership? Does it matter who owns the media? Does media concentration and integration restrict or enhance media content diversity? Do the activities of transnational corporations enhance or threaten cultural diversity and creative autonomy?

If tendencies towards integration are clear, corporate strategies and market processes have also involved disintegration, demergers, fragmentation and the creation of new kinds of networks and interdependencies between firms. All these processes must also be understood in the context of uncertainties and risks, the unpredictability and high levels of failure of ideas, products, firms and operations. This is essential in order to understand market dynamics and corporate strategies as well as to account for their highly varied performance and outcomes in the face of competition for audiences and resources (Croteau and Hoynes 2006; Hesmondhalgh 2007).

The media mergers of the 1980s and 1990s have been described as largely defensive moves (Curran 2002e), and as 'bulking up for digital' (Tunstall and Machin 1999: 53), attempts to manage the costs and risks associated with establishing and maintaining strong market positions. Financing is another source of risk. Financing growth through 'retained earnings', revenue derived from sales, generally enables control over media organisations to remain with those who currently have it. However, increased need for investment has necessitated greater use of debt and equity. With debt financing, firms risk control passing to banks or financial institutions if they are unable to service (manage repayment of) their borrowing. With equity investment (selling tradeable shares in the company) there are risks of shareholders launching a takeover bid (see Flew 2007: 10). More generally, firms need to manage the demands of investors, those institutions and individuals who hold shares in the company.

Assessing trends in ownership and media concentration

United States

According to Bagdikian (2004: 3), five 'global-dimension' conglomerates own most of the newspapers, magazines, book publishers, film studios and radio and television stations in the United States. They are Time Warner, Disney, News Corporation, Viacom and Bertelsmann. In the first edition of his book *The Media Monopoly*, Bagdikian identified which companies held the largest shares, up to 50 per cent of total, in each market and calculated that 50 firms dominated across the media as a whole. The total dropped in each subsequent edition of the book. According to McChesney (2004: 178), the major media markets of television networks, cable TV, music, film, newspapers, magazines and book publishing are 'almost all classic oligopolies with only a handful of significant players in each market'. The two largest firms in radio broadcasting, Infinity (owned by Viacom) and Clear Channel have a greater market share than the firms ranked 3–25 combined. Clear Channel Communications, run by Randy Michaels, a former ultra-right-wing 'shock-jock' DJ, embarked on an acquisitions spree after radio ownership restrictions were lifted by the Telecommunications Act 1996. By 2002, Clear owned 1,225 stations. In a formerly diverse cable TV industry six companies now control over 80 per cent of the market. Four firms sell almost 90 per cent of US recorded music, while six companies account for the same share of industry revenues (McChesney 2004).

Transnationalisation of ownership and operations

By the end of 2006, eight major companies dominated US media, including three newer players (Microsoft, Yahoo and Google). Conglomerates with US headquarters also dominate the 'global oligopoly'. Herman and McChesney (1997) describe a global media market dominated by 'ten or so vertically integrated media conglomerates'. By 2002 the top tier comprised nine companies: General

Electric (owner of NBC), AT&T/Liberty Media, Disney, Time Warner (then 'AOL–Time Warner'), Sony, News Corporation, Viacom, Vivendi and Bertelsmann. Between them, these firms owned '[m]ajor US film studios; US television networks; 80–85 per cent of the global music market; the majority of satellite broadcasting world-wide; all or part of a majority of cable broadcasting systems; a significant percentage of book publishing and commercial magazine publishing; commercial cable TV; European terrestrial television' (McChesney 2002: 151).

The breakdown by nationality of the top 50 audiovisual companies worldwide (ranked by turnover in 2005) is as follows: United States (18), Japan (7), UK (5), Germany (5), France (4), Spain (3), Italy (2), Canada (2), Austria (1). Apart from Japan (with 4 of the 20 largest companies), only Brazil, Mexico and Australia reached the list with one each (European Audiovisual Observatory 2006b: 8).[7] McChesney (2002: 154) argues that many media systems are dominated by a combination of first-tier firms and a handful of 60–80 large regional operators who make up a second tier

Arguments about the market and cultural dominance of TNCs are considered further in Chapter 8, but the core political economic critique of media concentration has been challenged on numerous matters of fact and value, evidence and evaluation (Compaine and Gomery 2000). Is there (growing) concentration in media markets? Regarding the United States, Compaine (2000) acknowledges growing concentration in some sectors (newspapers) but argues that, taking media as a whole, there has been an expansion of outlets. However, scholars disagree over the appropriate measures to identify concentration (Iosifides 1997). Baker (2007) challenges the manner by which concentration in markets is calculated by Compaine and others, while Kunz (2007) provides a detailed account of growing concentration in the US film and television industries. Additionally, proving the effects of concentration on content diversity and quality has been inconclusive to say the least. Picard (1989), reviewing empirical studies of the US newspaper industry, concludes that they provide little direct evidence that market structure in itself has any significant effect on news and editorial content (see also Entman 1985; McQuail 1992: 116). The political economic critique, however, is principally that certain kinds of market concentration threaten media and cultural diversity – where supply is dominated by firms sharing a market-driven logic.

European media markets and concentration

Meier and Trappel (1998) reported very high levels of concentration in newspapers, television and book publishing in EU countries. Overall, the newspaper market has continued to become more concentrated as it has continued to contract. In Austria, 53 papers closed of the 66 existing since 1945; the top-selling *Neue Kronen-Zeitung*, with 43 per cent of the market in 2001, dominates the popular 'boulevard' sector, although there is some competition among quality and regional segments (Trappel 2004: 5). In Denmark the number of papers fell from 123 in 1945 to 29 in 2002 (Mortensen 2004: 43). However, newspaper concentration patterns vary and studies have shown mixed trends (Sánchez-Tabernero *et al.* 1993). There has been growth in some sectors, such as free newspapers. Parts of the magazine sector have also shown growth, benefiting from technology, market segmentation and internationalisation.

By 2004 there were more than 3,000 television channels available in the 15 EU member states, as well as around 1,900 regional and local channels (European Audio-visual Observatory 2004: 6). National and transnational channel numbers rose from 103 in 1990 to nearly 1,100 by 2003, and 1,678 by 2005 (European Audiovisual Observatory 2005: 12–13). For market advocates this is powerful evidence of success. European TV industries are far more competitive today than ever, argue Compaine and Gomery (2000). Across Europe, channel choice has increased from a handful of public and private stations to 400 or so over the last two decades. There has been a growth of national and local radio in most national markets. Access to radio and, more recently, television services via the internet provides an enormous expansion of consumer choice and, say advocates, illustrates the benefits of competition. Despite the proliferation of channels, however, market concentration remains significant. TV markets across Europe remain highly concentrated in terms of ownership and view-ership (OSI 2005: 22). In most countries the three largest channels grab the bulk of the audience. Ownership of private broadcasting tends to be highly concentrated. According to one EC study of media pluralism (EC 2007c:15):

> The increased number of channels does not necessarily mean increased media pluralism. Many are either the result of thematic diversification of bigger channels or of large media companies. Many are held by incumbent broadcasters and a very large majority (around 80%) have a micro audience and therefore small means. The number of news channels remains also quite limited (less than 10% of the total).

Despite lower barriers to entry, the European DTV landscape is characterised by the formation of large companies and concentrated power (Iosifides *et al.* 2005: 107). Digital satellite, the largest platform for digital TV in Europe by consumer market share, has significant concentration. There is only one operational plat-form in all 'big five' countries. In Spain, Canal Satellite and Via Digital merged in 2002 to form Digital Plus. In France, the government authorised the absorption of TPS by Canal Satellite (30 August 2006), subject to 59 commitments aimed espe-cially at maintaining market access for service providers. Across Western Europe, competition is only found in Nordic countries (European Audiovisual Observa-tory 2006b: 90), although proposals by satellite operators to become distribution platforms may increase competition in future.

Europe's cable industry, longer established than satellite, has undergone consolida-tion over many years, intensifying in 2005–2006. As a result, a single dominant operator is now the norm in each national market. In Ireland, for example, the American group Liberty Global, which owned the country's second network Chorus, was permitted to take over the principal operator NTL. In France, Cinven (which with Warburg Pincus owns a significant share of cable subscribers in the Netherlands) acquired three of the largest operators (France Telecom Cable, Numericable and UPC Noos). In the UK the two main companies, NLT and Telewest, completed a merger in March

2006 (NTL Incorporated), becoming the UK's largest provider of residential broadband. On 4 July 2006, NTL completed its acquisition of Virgin Mobile, operating under the brand Virgin Media, creating the first opportunity for UK customers to buy a so-called 'quadruple-play' service comprising TV, internet and fixed and mobile telephony services from a single operator (Ofcom 2006b: 114–15)

There is also considerable cross-ownership between broadcasting and publishing among major companies in Europe, notably Mediaset, News Corp, Swedish company Bonnier, Bertelsmann/RTL and Axel Springer. Between 1985 and 1995 leading national print groups expanded into national television and several of these press–TV groups then acquired media properties in neighbouring markets. Egmont (Denmark), Bonnier (Sweden), Schibsted (Norway) and Kinnevik-MTG (Sweden) all expanded into other Scandinavian countries (Tunstall 2008: 264).

The presence of small firms

Among the counter-tendencies to concentration, it has been argued, is a flourishing of small firms (Hesmondhalgh 2007). The creative conception stage of the production of cultural products in some industries (music) remains small-scale, with low barriers to entry. The internet has dramatically lowered some market barriers, enabling a massive growth of commercial and non-commercial content providers (see below). At issue, however, is the extent to which large firms can exercise an unhealthy influence over the system as a whole. Concentration is one indicator of the ability of firms to exercise market power. However, it is the relationship between firms that matters, not merely the number operating in and across media markets. A commonly found pattern, consistent with the capitalist development of cultural industries, is for the 'profit seeking sector' to be dominated by large conglomerates, alongside which are clustered small and medium enterprise (SME) creative industries, a two-tiered market structure in which there is a limited oligopoly of firms controlling between 75 and 90 per cent of revenue/ market share, together with a number of smaller firms on the other tier fighting for a small percentage of the remaining market share (Albarran 2004). Such market analysis cannot account for the cultural vitality and diversity within these markets, nor indeed offer any detailed account of content. Hesmondhalgh (2007: 175) is surely right to highlight that small companies with limited market share may be important sources of creativity, innovation and diversity as well as employment.

Critical arguments

Markets and competition

Whether markets are competitive or not is a concern shared across neoliberal, liberal and critical perspectives. What marks the differences between them is how the problem is formulated and what remedies are promoted or tolerated (Chapter 4). One line of argument within critical political economy, as we have seen, is to challenge free-market nostrums by highlighting how 'market regulation' can lead to oligopoly, barriers to competition and anti-competitive behaviour of firms. This justifies the case for democratically sanctioned regulation to prevent concentration and to address the problems that arise where concentrated markets are unavoidable (McChesney 2004: 208–9).

A different set of critical arguments concerns market-dominated production of symbolic content. Here again there are concerns about content diversity arising from corporate structures. The issue of consumer power focuses on the core tendency of commercial market systems to favour profitable consumer markets and under-serve less profitable consumer markets. Advertising finance tends to favour commercially friendly media content, large aggregate audiences or affluent niche audiences, and disfavour less popular content and the preferences of those constituting poorer groups, or interests, in society (see Baker 2002; Gandy 2004). Commercial markets fail to register the full range of people's preferences, which include non-market values and preferences (Baker 2002). More fundamentally, commercial markets are considered an insufficient basis for all media provision because the principles of market provision are inherently in tension with principles of democratic participation, equality and universality (Murdock 1992b). Here, critical concerns move beyond competition or concentration per se to address problems of commercialism. A further set of critical arguments (Chapter 8) concerns the adverse effects of transnational corporatisation on the plurality and diversity of global media cultures, 'by undermining cultural sovereignty and accentuating the already deep divisions in terms of information resources between and among nations' (Thussu 2006: xviii).

Traditionally, the critique of media concentration made by both liberals and radicals focused on the consequences for democracy. The private concentration of symbolic power potentially distorts the democratic process (Curran 2002e). Other concerns focus on cultural pluralism, while the importance of diversity in entertainment, in ideas and imagery has been a growing focus (Murdock 1992b; Andersen 2000). Reviewing the US media, Bagdikian (2004: 6) argues: '[o]ne result of this constricted competition is that the thousands of media outlets carry highly duplicative content'.

Defending concentration

Oligopolistic media markets may be defended by mainstream media economists as tolerable, particularly in the context of opposing interventions other than those of competition regulation (Compaine 2000; Albarran 2004). Concentration and conglomeration may be justified on grounds of consumer welfare if they result in greater economic efficiency that benefits consumers (see Doyle 2002a: 37–41). Baker (2007: 50) makes the criticism that social benefit cannot be based on such narrow measures but must take account of 'externalities' to assess social benefit – here 'cost saving and profitability can systematically diverge from efficiency and social welfare'. Concentration may safeguard diversity. Stronger and more efficient firms may ensure the viability, and vitality, of media that would otherwise fail. The EC report cited earlier, for instance, noted the 'paradox ... that high market share – concentration – may be helpful for funding certain types of programming considered important for pluralism, notably expensive drama series or investigative journalism' (EC 2007c: 15). However, the report's call for 'new business models to secure a continuing supply of the high-quality programming that European audiences seek' (15) is made without reference to PSB, the model originally devised to answer this 'paradox'.

As we have seen (Chapter 6), a variety of arguments for concentration have been advanced by policy makers. These arguments return us again to underlying differences on the goals to be served and whether neoliberalism or public policy intervention best achieves them. But these debates also point again to efforts to avoid a reductive binarism of state versus market and instead seek to include the strengths of different ways of organising media within a mixed system (Curran 2002d).

European corporate players: selected profiles

Meier and Trappel (1998) identify the growth of new European media empires whose characteristics are that they are transnational in scale and have a strong presence in several European markets, mostly operating among the top firms in each sector. Some date from the early nineteenth century, such as Havas and Hachette in France and Bertelsmann in Germany, others are more recent, such as Murdoch's News International from the 1960s and Berlusconi's Mediaset from the late 1970s. Some examples follow. Formerly monomedia companies such as Bertelsmann, Bonnier (Sweden) and Egmont (Netherlands) have become large multimedia conglomerates. Most major broadcasters and newspapers have internet editions, publishing houses have bought broadcasting enterprises and broadcasters production companies. One reason for such developments is the need to secure a broad industrial base in view of the uncertainty linked to developments in the media sector (CoE 2003).

Bertelsmann AG

Bertelsmann is one of the largest media enterprises in Europe and the only one in the top tier of global media groups. It has operations in 63 countries covering television and radio; book publishers; magazines and newspapers; music labels and publishers; print and media services; book and music clubs. Bertelsmann owns the RTL Group, the leading European broadcaster. After acquiring US publisher Random House in 1999, it is now the world's largest book-publishing group. It owns Gruner + Jahr, Europe's biggest magazine publisher; Arvato, which provides media and communication services, including mobile entertainment, through 250 subsidiaries; and Direct Group, which bundles Bertelsmann's worldwide direct-to-customer businesses. It owns 50 per cent of Sony BMG Music Entertainment with Sony, the second -largest recorded music company worldwide, having sold off BMG Music Publishing to Vivendi in 2006. Bertelsmann's 2006 revenue was €19.3 billion, of which US: 19.7 per cent; Germany: 30.6 per cent; Europe (excluding Germany): 44.1 per cent; other countries: 5.6 per cent.

The origins of the company established by Carl Bertelsmann in 1835, lie in religious (Protestant) publishing. It expanded into fiction between the two world wars and in the 1930s developed through close ideological and economic ties with the Nazis (National Socialists). After the Second World War the company printed schoolbooks for the Allied military government, diversified into selling recorded music, and then expanded in the 1960s and 1970s through product diversification and acquisitions beyond Germany into book clubs, magazines, film and television. In the 1980s Bertelsmann broke into the US market, buying publishers Bantam Books and Doubleday and RCA Records, and held a stake in the first commercial TV station in Germany, RTL plus. It moved into online media in the 1990s, setting up AOL Europe with America Online. In 2000 Bertelsmann sold its internet access businesses to concentrate on media content, direct-to-customer businesses and media services. It invested in over 100 internet activities, mostly joint ventures with worldwide partners, but these included notable failures, including its online books and music seller Bertelsmann Online (BOL), sold in 2002. In January 1997, Bertelsmann merged the Ufa Film- und Fernseh-GmbH with CLT, creating Europe's largest television company, with CLT–Ufa doing business in radio and television in Germany, France, the Benelux countries, the UK, Sweden and the Czech Republic. The RTL Group resulted from the merger in 2000 of CLT–Ufa with the British company Pearson TV. By 2006 RTL Group operated 38 TV channels and 29 radio stations in ten countries and was European market leader in ad-financed (free) television and TV production. Its production subsidiary Fremantle Media made *Baywatch*, *Good Times*, *Bad Times* and the successful 'Idols' format. Channels include RTL Television, Super RTL, Vox or N-TV in Germany; M6, France's most profitable advertising-financed private channel; Five in Great Britain; Antena 3 in Spain; RTL 4 in the Netherlands; RTL TVI in Belgium; and RTL channels in Hungary and Poland. Bertelsmann has benefited significantly from the privatisation of media in Central and Eastern Europe following the reunification of Germany. Buying back the remaining shares of RTL in 2006, financed partly through the sale of BMG's music-publishing division to Vivendi, enabled Bertelsmann AG to operate as a privately held company with no external shareholders for the first time since 1973.[8]

Lagardère

Hachette Filipacchi Presse is part of French industrial conglomerate Lagardère (cars, munitions, telecommunications, aerospace), whose founder, Jean-Luc Lagardère, died in 2003. It has interests in the book, magazine and multimedia publishing industries, and it has a European presence through licensing its titles for local editions. Hachette Filipacchi Médias (HFM), the news and magazine division, is the world's largest magazine publisher, with 238 titles in 36 countries, including *Elle*. More than half its sales are outside France in the US, Asia and across Europe. Lagardère Active includes film and television production and radio broadcasting and the group also owns Interdeco, the leading media buyer in France, and Hachette Filipacchi Global Advertising.

Scandinavian Broadcasting System (SBS)

SBS Broadcasting S.A. was established in 1989 as a US-owned company. With cross-media interests in print and broadcasting, by 2006 the company owned 19 commercial TV stations, 20 premium pay-TV channels, 15 radio networks and 8 stand-alone radio stations across western, central and eastern Europe. In its original geographical business area it operates TVNorge (Norway), TV Danmark and Kanal 5 (Denmark) and Kanal 5 (Sweden) as well as the leading Nordic pay-TV service C More, which owns rights to live sports and premium US films and programmes. The company's strategy has been to target the most attractive demographic segments by mixing popular local and international content, news and sports. Already large some years ago, the company expanded further by acquiring radio and television businesses throughout Europe. SBS also invested heavily in multimedia, from online download functions to mobile services and live streaming of AV and IPTV. For instance, SBS launched a music service, The Voice, targeting 12–24 year olds on TV, radio and with interactive programs, SMS/MMS and multi-media applications. SBS was controlled by two major private equity firms, Permira and KKR, until it was acquired by the German AV group ProSiebenSat.1 Group in June 2007 in an operation valued at €3.3 million.

Media and finance

The main sources of earned income for media companies are consumers and advertisers, variously secured by:

- direct payment by customers (subscription, retail, e-commerce)
- advertising revenue (from paid communications controlled by advertisers)
- direct advertiser finance (e.g. advertiser-financed media production)
- sponsorship or joint agreements (with advertisers, third parties or 'intra-firm').

Most commercial media have a dual revenue source and are said to operate in a 'dual product market' (Picard 1989:17). They sell media products to consumers who expend time (always) and money (sometimes). The second market is the advertising market, selling audiences (access to audiences, as measured by ratings, circulation and marketing research) to advertisers. In such markets, producers respond to market signals from at least two different sources. This undermines any simple equation between product supply and consumer demand, or the belief that commercial media systems are straightforward expressions of popular (much less 'democratic') will. Media that sell to advertisers do so in a huge variety of ways and with varying levels of dependence on advertising finance. Some forms of advertising have been separated from content, by regulation or custom, such as classified and display advertising in print media. However, the integration of advertising into media content is increasing under a combination of competitive pressures and dependencies, technological opportunity and regulatory changes.

Market size

The size of the advertising market varies considerably across WMS. The size of the TV advertising market in 2004, for example, was €230 million in Finland compared to €4,235 million in Germany, €4,124 million in Italy and €5,537 million in the largest market, the United Kingdom (EC 2007c: 32). The 'big five' sustain large commercial media sectors, whereas the viability of external pluralism, for instance in television broadcasting, diminishes as the advertising market shrinks. In Italy TV's share of total media advertising is highest at 54 per cent, compared to Germany where print has greater dominance and TV's share is 29 per cent. Globally, advertising expenditure reached £251 billion in 2005, of which television advertising accounted for 45 per cent (£112 billion) and radio 8 per cent (£19 billion).

Worldwide, television still takes the largest share of advertising revenue (37.8 per cent in 2005, followed by newspapers with 29.8 per cent, according to Zenith Optimedia). Television has shown market growth overall with proliferation of commercial TV channels, but this fragmentation has eroded the advertising share of individual channels. In Britain, ITV and Channel 4 have both lost share, leading to cuts in programme services and threatening their future viability as commercial public service providers. TV's share of total advertising was predicted to fall from some 20–22 per cent in 1996 to 17–19 per cent in 2016. The UK has seen slow growth in TV advertising revenues, but significant growth in other revenue. In 2006 subscriptions exceeded advertising revenue by a margin of 10 per cent. EU broadcasting revenues declined in 2002 (generating €65.4 billion, a drop of 1.3 per cent on 2001) after a period of steep economic growth. By 2005, television advertising saw growth in several countries: Ireland (21.4 per cent), Norway (10.6 per cent), Sweden (10.3 per cent), Spain (9.9 per cent) (European Audiovisual Observatory 2006b: 65). For television revenue, the largest growth sectors have been home shopping (€2,261 million in 2004, up nearly 18 per cent on the previous year), TV packagers (increased 21.3 per cent to €1,1405 million in 2004) and Thematic channels (up 14.4 per cent to €4,214 million) (European Audiovisual Observatory 2006b: 56; OSI 2005: 40, 135).

Public broadcasting still commands the largest share of the total EU market (€28,299 million in 2004, 38 per cent of broadcasters' net revenue). Total revenues for European PSBs rose from €27.5 billion in 2000 to nearly €30 billion in 2004. Public revenues increased by an average 3.6 per cent (from €17.6 billion to €20.2 billion), while commercial revenues declined by 0.6 per cent on average (European Audiovisual Observatory 2006b: 56).

Total industry revenues for television from advertising and subscription correlate to the size of the consumer market in each country, although public funding is less dependent. Ofcom (2006a: 109) calculates that the US market is best funded at £253 per head, the UK is second (£188) followed by Japan, Sweden, France and the Republic of Ireland. In 2005 public funding of television was highest per capita in the UK (£40), followed by Germany (£37). In Germany, PSBs are dependent on public revenues (85.7 per cent) compared to Spain where commercial revenue is the largest share (77 per cent). The UK was the second-best funded PSB (£2.9 billion in 2005) after Germany (£4.9 billion), with France (£1.8 billion) and Italy (£1.6 billion) third and fourth, while US public funding for TV was some £220 million (Ofcom 2006a: 124–5). In global terms, public funding is a small and diminishing proportion of TV revenues, but it remains an important source of finance in most European countries (except Spain). There has been a shift from licence fee to subsidies in several countries, including the Netherlands and Belgium (except Wallonia), while in Portugal a tax on electricity usage was introduced in 2003 to fund AV services.

Private broadcasters in Europe have invested significant effort in diversifying revenue and limiting dependence on their primary revenue stream, whether advertising or subscription. Traditional 'linear' broadcasters have diversified by developing new modes of media consumption, including VOD, and acquisition or partnerships with social network/videosharing services. Another source of income, and controversy, has been so-called 'participation TV', such as ITV Play, where income is derived from call fees and quiz entry. Other broadcasters have diversified into networks, telecoms and internet markets either by becoming broadband (BSkyB) or mobile operators (M6), aiming to exploit their brand power and advantages of cross-promotion. Commercial broadcasters such as M6 have also moved into electronic commerce, taking over one of France's leading discount traders Mistergooddeal. It has become easier for operators to have an internet presence, act as ISPs or offer mobile services (Ofcom 2006a: 16). However, advertising and sponsorship still accounted for 91 per cent of global TV revenues in 2005.

Newspapers and advertising

Newspapers remain the second-largest medium by ad-spend. Newspapers' share of total advertising has tended to decline, but share of some ad sectors, such as classified advertising, job recruitment, information-rich and display advertising remained high until the challenge of the internet in the 1990s. The biggest shift over the last 15 years has been online advertising, which has grown at an average rate of over 60 per cent per annum between 1995 and 2005, reaching £12 billion. Global internet ad spending was predicted to grow by 28.2 per cent in 2007, with the medium's share of total spend overtaking radio by 2009 (Zenith Optimedia 2007).[9]

In the UK, online advertising revenues increased almost eightfold, from £170 million in 2001 to £1.3 billion in 2005. By then online advertising was already three times greater than radio and over one-third that of television, which was £3.8 billion in 2005. Advertisers are increasingly tapping into the web and diverting revenues from other media. By 2006 in the UK nearly 10 per cent of all advertising spending was on the internet, the highest share among WMS including the US. Increasingly, newspaper publishers are turning to the internet as an additional route for delivering both editorial and advertising content to their readers. The number of newspaper websites grew by 20 per cent in 2005, while online newspaper ad revenue was up by 24 per cent – the highest growth rate for five years (WARC 2006).

Even with declining audiences, mass media and new specialist niche media can command high advertising premiums and assert control. Where there is greater competition among an expanding range of outlets for the same advertising finance there has tended to be a shift in decision-making power to advertisers. Put another way, in such conditions there tends to be greater media dependence on advertisers. The result has been greater efforts to accommodate advertising and offer promotional packages and inducements. On the changing relationships of power and dependency between advertising and media see McAllister (1996, 2000) and Hardy (2004a). Changes in the advertising industry are also important aspects of media systems impacting on industries, markets and policy. Features include corporate consolidation and continuing domination of the ad industry by US-headquartered corporations, including Omnicom Group, WPP Group, Interpublic Group and Publicis (Mattelart 1991; Thussu 2006: 127–9) as well as integration of advertising and PR groups with media production businesses.

Internet and digital media

The patterns of diffusion of the internet across WMS replicate those of mass media in significant respects. First, the US has been the leading technological and market innovator. US predominance has gradually declined as more have gone online internationally, although in 2000 one-third (154 million) of the 406 million users were American (Norris 2001: 47). Second, the patterns of diffusion conform to other key patterns of development. In her analysis of internet diffusion across Western Europe, Norris (1999: 6) concludes that '[f]ar from equalizing the playing field between European societies, the adoption of new technology has so far exacerbated a north–south divide that already existed in traditional patterns of mass media use'. European nations that have adopted the internet most extensively tend to be those that are already heavy consumers of the printed press.

In spring 1999, 39 per cent of the population were internet users in Northern Europe as compared to only 8 per cent in Southern Europe. Overall, Europe lagged behind the US, which had 49 per cent online, although Sweden had the highest percentage of internet users (61 per cent). Between individual countries the 'digital divide' was even starker, 44 per cent of Danes compared to only 5 per cent of Portuguese and 7 per cent of Greeks (Norris 1999: 4–5). Movement towards an 'information society' encompassing access to a wide range of mediated and interpersonal communication technologies has been very uneven across and within countries (Van Dijk 2005; Thussu 2006), with huge socio-economic inequalities in access (Murdock and Golding 2005). Internet connection levels in 1999–2000 were 18 per cent lower averaged across black and Hispanic households than for all homes in the US (Raphael 2001: 203). The young have also been among the early adopters and most active users. In the UK, the strongest factors influencing online entry have been found to be age and class, with usage highest among 16- to 24-year-olds (Curran and Seaton 2003: 280). Language and culture, as well as economic disparities and gender, have been important factors shaping access and adoption. In 1999 more than three-quarters of internet pages (78.3 per cent) were presented in English, while the combined share for three other major European languages (French, German and Spanish) was 5.9 per cent (Murdock 2000: 54).

Initially the roll-out of broadband was very slow in Europe, except in Denmark, but take-up increased rapidly. The number of broadband connections in the EU-25 + 2 (Norway and Iceland) reached 60.5 million at the end of 2005, 50.6 million of which were in the EU-15 (EC 2006). Broadband access was an estimated 29 per cent across the 25 EU countries by winter 2006, up from 23 per cent the previous year. But access remains highly uneven. Internet access was highest in the Netherlands, Denmark and Sweden but less than 20 per cent in Greece. Slightly over half of Europeans (54 per cent) have a computer in their household. The average percentage is significantly higher in the EU-15 member states (58) compared to the twelve accession countries (39), but below average in Portugal (40) and Greece (36) (Eurobarometer 2007). Revenue from online content is predicted to reach €8.3 billion by 2010 in Europe, a growth of over 400 per cent in five years, with online and mobile games expected to generate particularly high revenues (€2.3 billion). As for newspapers and magazines online, revenues are expected to amount to €2 billion in 2010, almost exclusively from online and mobile advertising. The fastest-growing market is online video and movies, with an expected growth of revenues from €30 million in 2005 to €1.2 billion in 2010, slightly above the prediction for digitally distributed music (€1.1 billion) (Nordicom 2007).

The internet and 'old' media

The growth of the internet and broadband have been unprecedented and their long-heralded impact on the production and consumption of media will undoubtedly be profound. We are now some way past the mix of techno-utopianism, technological determinism and the confluence of entrepreneurial capitalism, anti-statist libertarian anarchism and postmodernist theory that offered influential visions in the early 1990s (for a critical analysis see Mosco 2004; Streeter 2004). From issues of politics and democracy to culture, communities and identities the rise of the internet poses insistent challenges requiring new thinking. The internet is the gateway to a vast storehouse of information and entertainment and a platform and resource for social interaction and connectivity. It has provided a means of self-expression and collective exchange in ways which far exceed the capabilities of one-to-many systems, such as conventional, linear television. Our focus here is limited to considering briefly the implications of new media for mass media systems. Here, there are strong grounds to reject 'year zero' thinking about digital media in favour of a longer-range analysis of change.

Sparks (2004; 2000) offers a very useful analysis of the ways in which the internet challenges core aspects of mass media production and consumption (see also Freedman 2003; Hesmondhalgh 2007: 248). The internet entails a common technology and converged content: digitalised information. According to Sparks, internet delivery erodes established patterns of media consumption. The advantages of physical space, for instance those which enable a newspaper or broadcast station to dominate consumer and advertising markets in a particular geographical area, are eroded. The internet also erodes advantages of production and distribution based on time. The advantage of market dominance in production of a morning newspaper or prime-time news are eroded, as internet content is available any time. Journalistic media based on professional routines and deadlines have been particularly affected, with many firms seeking 'productivity' gains to feed and compete with 24-hour news that critics say leave journalists more desk-bound and dependent on sources.

The internet is a competitor for consumers' time and money and for advertising revenue. A study of online behaviour in 2002 found that a quarter of US internet users were watching less television, with 14 per cent reporting a decline in newspaper reading (Pew Internet Project 2002: 4, cited in Freedman 2003). Sparks (2004) highlights how the internet provides many ways to disaggregate content, for example reading only part of a 'newspaper', and to disaggregate content from advertising. At the same time, the internet has significantly advanced the erosion of boundaries between editorial and advertising, between telling and selling, speech and commerce. Conventions and regulations that apply in the offline world to distinguish editorial and advertising are established only to a limited extent online.

Production and distribution on the internet lowers entry barriers for some media. The costs of production of symbolic content remain, but distribution costs are much smaller, with no licensing or transmission charges. Lowering entry barriers can allow new players to challenge entrenched interests. For Negroponte (1995: 57), 'Guaranteed plurality might require less legislation than one would expect because the monolithic empires of mass media are dissolving into an array of cottage industries'. This heavily espoused notion of digital plenitude has been used to justify liberalising media ownership rules (Chapter 6). By contrast, McChesney (2000) sets out several reasons why the internet 'won't sink the media giants', including:

1   Media companies' willingness to take heavy short-term losses in order to protect long-term interest and to test markets by investing in internet start-up companies.
2   Media companies' ability to exploit their brands and plug content into the web at little extra cost. Such content includes what Anderson (2007) calls the 'long tail' of material that can be profitably sold to micro, niche markets.
3   Cross-promotion, including the ability and advantages of 'leveraging' audiences from established media to the internet and to current markets to ease the transition into new ones. Mergers have been driven, or at least justified, by executives in terms of synergies arising from repurposing content, building brand awareness and cross-promoting and cross-selling.
4   Advertising – large media companies can exploit their relationships with advertisers, for instance offering (or requiring) advertising packages that combine old and new media platforms.

By 1998, more than 2,700 newspapers internationally had online businesses, of which 60 per cent were US-based, up from only 496 worldwide in 1995, but the failure rate was also significant, with high creation/production costs and low advertising revenues cited as key reasons for failure. Online expansion has involved an ever-changing mixture of opportunity and threats. The prospect of fewer users accessing traditional media content was a key driver for firms to create content sites and portals.

Newspapers have been challenged by alternative content and competition for their vital advertising markets, but many have been able to create sizeable, if rarely profitable, online operations. Some of the settled business models that evolved for each medium will not be reproduced in the online environment. The online world alters the ways in which all the media are produced and distributed, the ways in which they can be consumed by their audiences, and the technical, temporal and geographic boundaries that have until now helped to structure analogue industries. The mass media industries initially most affected by the internet have been those with low-bandwidth music and sound, text and low-resolution image (newspapers, magazines and 'print' media, music and radio broadcasting) (Sparks 2004). The impact on high-bandwidth media (high-resolution audiovisual content such as films and television) has only begun to be felt from the early 2000s with technological developments and the growth of broadband consumer markets, but is expected to lead to far-reaching changes in business and consumer models. Yet media industries bring their strong competitive advantages online: economies of scale and scope, including those aided by digitalisation, available content and ease of 'repurposing' and marketing advantages. There will be increasing scope for newcomers, for 'first mover' advantage and new sites of 'competition', but it is naïve to presume that the major established companies lack the accumulated resources to continue to command media markets.

The expansion of production and consumption of alternative sources such as weblogs, alternative news organisations and 'radical' online media are important developments. Nevertheless, news consumption online is still heavily dominated by traditional news suppliers. FCC research (2002: 20) found the share in the US to be MSNBC (22.4 per cent), CNN (19.1), Yahoo! (17.9) and AOL (13.3). A global listing of the ten most-visited news websites included four search engines (Yahoo! and Google sites), the BBC, CNN, MSNBC and the New York Times (Alexa 2007). The situation is fast changing, predictions become rapidly obsolete and none can be guaranteed. Political-economic analyses of the internet must be alert to contradictions (Raphael 2001) and 'paradoxes' (Rice 1999), and be concerned about opportunities and potentialities (especially for the expansion of voices, pluralisation and democratisation of media); changing social usage; and sites of resistance to established media power (Bennett 2003; Couldry 2003).

The internet is dialogic and interactive in its technical structure, allowing, in principle, greater user participation and co-creation than any other media form alone permits. It enables 'disintermediation', bypassing of established gatekeepers (such as editors) (Poster 1997) and can enable resource-poor organisations to overcome many of their disadvantages to communicate and network with millions. More broadly, as Jenkins (2001: 93) puts it: 'Media convergence fosters a new participatory folk culture by giving average people the tools to archive, annotate, appropriate and recirculate content.' Contradictory forces thus push towards a greater diffusion and concentration of symbolic power. New opportunities, however, also remain largely structured by resources, capabilities and 'visibility' in the offline world, and only idealist thinking brackets out, resolves or ignores these deepening inequalities.

'The creation of the internet', argues Curran (2003a: 287), 'has injected new pluralism into the media system because it is still not fully commercialised, and entry costs are lower than in most other media sectors.' However, the view that the rise of new media has greatly enhanced pluralism must still be 'heavily qualified' (Curran 2003a: 288).

As Canadian scholar Dwayne Winseck (1998: 325) wrote: 'The struggle to find a workable business model that will permit profitable online operation is likely to result in the continued, or even increased, domination of the supply of media artefacts by the same large corporations that dominate offline media'. A decade on, there is arguably greater market volatility and undoubted expansion in the diversity of content providers, but the large corporations, for now at least, remain dominant forces.

Changing patterns of media consumption and use

The internet has grown more rapidly than any previous medium. From a mere 500 computers connected in 1983, by 1998 there were more than 16 million registered host computers. According to Nua, a leading internet trends and statistics research group, the worldwide online population grew from 119 million in mid 1998 to 580 million by early 2003. This represents an astounding increase of 461 million internet users in just five years. Yet, overall, the internet is supplementing, even aiding, rather than replacing consumption of other media, with internet users combining their consumption of radio, television and other online activities, with increasing use or adoption of converged technologies (desktop and personal computer devices, integrated digital televisions and games consoles, and mobile phones). This also applies to user-generated content (UGC). In the US, user-generated material accounted for 47 per cent of the online video market in 2006. Screen Digest predicted it could rise to 55 per cent by 2010, but even then would account for no more than 15 per cent of total online video revenue, most of it coming from advertising (Snoddy 2007). In the US the largest media sectors by revenue in 2005 were entertainment (films, video games, DVDs, etc.) and pay-TV, followed by newspapers and broadcast television. The consumer internet sector is fifth largest but, as Freedman (2003: 283) points out, some two-thirds of this spending is on access fees (to ISPs, telecoms companies) rather than on content or advertising. The most common uses of the internet remain for information and interpersonal communication.

Of course, attention to revenue changes may serve to mask more profound shifts in share of time, with long-term consequences for traditional media. Yet, in terms of media consumption by time spent, television has so far maintained its appeal as the leading medium overall. Incorporating new media has increased total media use/consumption, but more time is still devoted to watching television across the population as a whole in all WMS than to any other medium. Consumer survey research on media usage tends to have a relatively high error rate, since much relies on self-assessment, often over an extended period (Hesmondhalgh 2007). According to research for Ofcom (2006a), only a minority of those with broadband at home said they watched less TV, ranging from 21 per cent in the US to 41 per cent in Italy. A minority also reported watching TV more, the highest being in Italy (11 per cent). The proportion who reported reading a national newspaper less (again, a very imprecise categorisation) was between 23 per cent in Italy and 30 per cent in Germany.

Among the 15 EU states (prior to enlargement), 97 per cent of citizens watched television, 60 per cent listened to the radio and 46 per cent read a newspaper, all on a daily basis (CoE 2004: 9). Overall, television viewing actually increased in the early 2000s. In Western Europe, the average viewing time for adults increased from 195 minutes in 1995 to 217 in 2003 (and in Central and Eastern Europe from 208 minutes in 2000 to 228 minutes in 2003). Southern Europeans still watch most television, while the Nordic countries (Denmark, Sweden and Finland) continue to have the lowest viewing rates, averaging only 162 minutes in 2003 (OSI 2005: 39). In Southern European countries, including Greece, Portugal, Cyprus and Malta, virtually all households have television (100 per cent) while Germany records the lowest rate (93 per cent) (Eurobarometer 2007: 99). Italy had reached 100 per cent during the 1960s despite the relatively late introduction of television in 1954 (Marletti and Roncarolo 2000: 202).

After years of growth, television viewing plateaued in 2005, falling in Denmark (–8 minutes per day) and in Eastern Europe, but remaining high elsewhere. Comparative figures for 2005 were US 271 minutes, Italy 237 minutes, the UK 219 minutes, France 206 minutes (Ofcom 2006b: 30). There are thus important variations between countries. depending on factors such as programme offer, the provision and influence of other media, and political, social and cultural factors in the country. Viewing time in Germany increased dramatically following deregulation and the increase in commercial channels, rising from a daily average of less than 120 minutes in the early 1980s to 210 minutes in 2002 (Schultz *et al.* 2005: 65). In Germany, over a decade after unification, East Germans, who were more affected by unemployment, tend to watch more television than the former West Germans, 249 minutes as compared to 217 in 2004. Among the 15 largest West European countries, average daily TV viewing increased between 1995 and 2005 except in Denmark and Ireland, where it fell slightly (European Audiovisual Observatory 2006b: 142).[10]

Figures from the UK show that in 2005, 16- to 24-year-olds spent on average 21 minutes more time online per week, sent 42 more SMS text messages, but spent over seven hours less time watching television than the general population (Ofcom 2006b). However, while important, these trends can be easily exaggerated: viewing among young adults has always been lower than the average (Hesmondhalgh 2007: 249). In the UK, average hours of viewing of television have remained fairly constant, despite the introduction of DVDs, broadband-enabled services, video games and other competing interests on leisure time. Young people watch less than older people (an hour less than average viewers per day), watch more digital channels and now watch significantly less public service broadcasting output than ever before. The share of viewing for all terrestrial channels among 16- to 24-year-olds fell from 74.3 per cent in 2001 to 58 per cent in 2005.

Declining TV viewing among the young is evident across all WMS, yet this is far short of a predicted collapse of television viewing. Instead, what has occurred is an increasing audience shift to new digital channels. The impact this has had on public broadcasters' share has depended on their appeal, the nature of competition and the strategies they have adopted. In increasingly competitive environments older public and private channels are losing share to new entrants, especially foreign channels in some countries. However, some European PSBs are managing to maintain a significant, even majority, share, due to the success of their thematic digital channels. In Britain in the first half of 2006 households receiving the digital terrestrial platform Freeview spent more time watching the new digital channels than the five established channels. However, lower audiences for BBC1 and BBC2 were offset by the growing success of digital-only channels BBC3, BBC4 and the children's channels CBeebies and CBBC. BBC3, a youth-oriented channel established in 2003, invested in new fiction and, having tested shows in its 'narrow-casting' environment, successfully migrated some to its main broadcast channels. Such digital channels can rely on established brands and programme archives as well as cross-promotion and marketing to support niche programming. Their success is also due to high-quality original production and absence of advertising. In the Netherlands, where PSB share was declining, NOS has launched five thematic channels (focused on news, history, documentaries, youth and parliamentary affairs) (Ofcom 2006a: 113). By contrast, in countries where PSBs have not developed thematic channels, audiences are generally declining in favour of new private offerings.

Digital television: comparing patterns of development

The transition to digital television (Chapter 3) continues to follow different routes across WMS depending on conditions in each national market that include different patterns of roll-out, regulation, supply and take-up of the various technologies: DTT, DTH digital satellite, Digital cable, and the digitalisation of networks and broadcasting over broadband networks in ADSL (IPTV). TV reception via terrestrial aerial, satellite, cable, digital terrestrial television (DTT), or via telephone network differs considerably across Europe (see Eurobarometer 2007). In the UK a majority of homes access digital TV via digital terrestrial, following the success of Freeview (launched 2002). Elsewhere, Germany, the US and Sweden among others rely mainly on cable distribution (both digital and analogue). In the Mediterranean countries a majority still rely on analogue terrestrial television (ATT): Italy 66 per cent, Spain 60 per cent and France 58 per cent in 2005, although all are committed to switching off analogue signals by 2012. All WMS have targets for the digital switch-over, when analogue broadcasting systems will be switched off. Sweden and Germany have started a phased process in different regions, to be completed in 2007 (now due 2008 and 2009 respectively). All WMS have set completion dates between 2009 (United States) and 2012 (United Kingdom and EU completion date).

There are also significant differences in modes of consumption and payment. Majorities in the UK, France and Italy rely more on free-to-view services. In countries where TV is received mainly through cable a higher percentage of people pay for channels, as in the US. A high percentage pay in Netherlands (91 per cent cable; 1 per cent aerial) and Belgium (92 per cent cable; 2 per cent aerial). The correlation between satellite TV and payment is relatively weak (the UK's monopoly pay service BSkyB is an exception, although BSkyB and the BBC both launched free satellite services in 2007). An estimated 24.4 per cent of EU households were equipped to receive digital television by the end of 2005, but persistent north–south differences remain. In Northern Europe (Sweden, Finland, Denmark) DTV penetration has been high, while in Mediterranean and in many smaller countries DTV has not secured a significant share of the market. The striking exception is Italy. News Corporation's Sky Italia remains the sole provider of digital satellite but has been banned from broadcasting digital terrestrial channels (Gardini and Galperin 2005: 327). By July 2007 DTT was received by 19.5 per cent of TV households (Pekic 2007). DTV take-up has been most successful in countries where a majority previously only accessed analogue free-to-air (France, the UK, Italy, Spain) compared to countries with a majority of multi-channel households accessing satellite or cable (Germany, Austria and the Benelux countries) (Marsden and Ariño 2005: 7–8). By 2005 the UK was a European and world leader in DTV, with over 60 per cent of households reached.

Internet (and) television

The integration of the internet and television through IPTV and broadband now allows the merging in significant consumer markets of the two main media of the late twentieth century. The television signal is delivered over broadband data networks via a dedicated set-top box or an ADSL modem using the internet protocol that supports the internet (hence IPTV). This has profound technological implications for the entire model of linear, scheduled broadcasting, although it does not follow that consumer demand for the latter will necessarily collapse. IPTV is distinct from placing TV content online as some broadcasters do – for instance, Channel 4 (UK) simulcasts all its proprietary content online while ABC (US) offers online versions of its most popular shows. IPTV is typically supplied using a closed network infrastructure (providing encoded television over the Digital Subscriber Line – DSL) and is distinct from and competes with the delivery of television content over the public internet. IPTV services challenge satellite and cable operators especially, but initially at least, providers have granted very limited access to channels other than those offered on the other platforms (European Audio-visual Observatory 2006b: 91). IPTV has so far mostly been received via television sets rather than the computer, although multi-platform set-top boxes (STBs) feed the signal to either, facilitating greater convergence. The commercial bundling of IPTV, internet access and fixed-line telephony is known as 'triple play', with mobile telephony added for 'quadruple play'. There were more than 60 IPTV services operating in Europe by the end of 2006, with most offering VOD as well as distributed television services.

In the UK, BBC, BSkyB, Channel 4, MTV and AOL had all launched IPTV services or pilots in 2005–2006. Whether consumers will pay for on-demand, broadband delivery of television has been less heavily tested, as much IPTV content is currently free. Nevertheless, TV over broadband will alter the business and regulatory models that have governed television. Across the European 'big five', subscriptions to IPTV services were expected to jump from 3 million to 5.7 million between 2006 and 2007. According to Screen Digest, the number of IPTV subscribers in Europe is expected to reach 8.7 million in 2009, up from 658,000 in mid 2005 (European Audiovisual Observatory 2005b: 77). The market, however, is dominated by an oligopoly of six brands: Orange, BT, Telefonica, Free Telecom, Neuf Telecom and Fastweb (Italy), which accounted for 60 per cent of Europe's total IPTV market at the end of 2006.

Conclusion: convergence in media markets?

Is there growing convergence in media markets? That question is best answered after further consideration of transnationalisation (Chapter 8) and media system convergence (Chapter 9). To answer the question fully requires answering a number of other questions. What are we comparing? What is the basis for determining commonality or difference? World-systems theory (WST) is among several theories that argue that the nation-state as a unit of analysis and basis of comparison should be replaced by 'historical systems' as an object of study (Wallerstein 2006: 16). For Wallerstein (2006: 17), the 'modern world-system' is a capitalist world economy, one comprising a 'spatial/temporal zone which cuts across many political and cultural units, one that represents an integrated zone of activity and institutions which obey certain systemic rules'. It is a collection of many institutions 'the combination of which accounts for its processes, and all of which are intertwined … The basic institutions are the market, or rather the markets; the firms that compete in the markets; the multiple states, within an interstate system; the households; the classes; and the status groups' (Wallerstein 2006: 24). For Wallerstein, too, the world system is structured by drives towards universalism and 'anti-universalism', the latter structuring the allocation of work, power and privilege.

The general tenet that modern capitalism is global and manifests common economic drives and processes is accepted across mainstream and radical scholarship. Underlying commonality in capitalist media markets is axiomatic. What, then, is the status and significance of 'differences'? As we have examined in this and earlier chapters, common trends can be readily identified with common forces, even if the conjunction of forces in any one instance is much more challenging to analyse. The forces of media capital have become increasingly transnational. The media have, in general, become more exposed to market forces, which has tended to accelerate commonality and convergence in media markets. Put another way, the forces that have tended to insulate media from market forces and competition have generally become weaker, including national policy, but also various market barriers. Yet clearly, differences remain evident across and within national systems. As Seaton (2003: 311) argues, 'nationality still remains a very robust way of categorizing systematic differences in the use and content of the media themselves. Viewing habits, computer preferences, film tastes, where and how the media are brought into home by whom they are used and for what purposes, are all remarkably different.'

What has explanatory value here will depend on what specific research questions we ask about similarities and differences in production, circulation, consumption and 'meaning making'. To do so usually involves transcending the 'container thinking' of the nation-state to examine processes and forces whose origin and extent is by no means coterminous with nations. But that is not the same as neglecting concrete interactions between institutions and actors within nation-states that result in differences in the characteristics of media markets. At an even broader level, we can adopt, as Hallin and Mancini (2004a) do, a historical perspective to ask whether and why certain differences across markets have diminished, and whether new ones have emerged. Key differences between the three models are evident in contemporary media markets. Media consumption patterns show the highest television consumption and lowest newspaper share in Mediterranean countries. Differential patterns of development have persisted in regard to the internet and broadband. Market patterns are shaped by the distribution of economic resources. These resources are traceable to the historical development and interaction of countries and regions, including imperial expansion, war conquest, trading and cultural diffusion and interaction. But important factors such as market size (country size and wealth) cut across the three models. The size of the economy is the major differential in contemporary Western media markets, even though English linguistic imperialism still structures the overall 'pecking order' across Euro-American media.

In media production, we have examined trends towards concentration of ownership, conglomeration and integration. In consumption, this chapter has argued that the shift from old media to new media has been overstated and needs to be corrected. There is an underlying, most likely unidirectional, shift in consumer expenditure of time and money from printed newspapers and from linear television towards non-linear digital media, from 'traditional' to 'new' media. But there are no grounds yet for dismissing the continuing influence and importance of public media and the likely importance of the delivery of such packaged content for decades ahead. Television audiences have fragmented (Turow 1997), but television remains the most significant medium in terms of size of audience and the time it absorbs. Assessing the UK, Curran (2003: 24–5) finds that the 'core media system' is changing more slowly than accounts of fragmentation suggest: in 2001 four terrestrial channels were responsible for 80 per cent of prime-time consumption. Clearly, TV is declining and how long it will remain dominant is uncertain. But television's enduring appeal is a powerful rejoinder to claims of fully realised demassification or new media substitution.

If this is so, it continues to matter enormously how such media power is organised and controlled. The issue of media concentration has been a focus in this and previous chapters. A recent EC report (2007c: 16) repeats the claim that internet users are more active than traditional media consumers, and are likely to be members of several non-commercial media communities as well as several of those run by major media players. Consequently, 'even if it is still too early to draw any conclusions in relation to media concentration and media pluralism, one can already argue that, theoretically, internet media seem promising for pluralism' (EC 2007c: 16). The case appears strong. There is evidently much greater content, more easily available (once cost barriers are met) than in any previous era. But we need to take account of diversity losses as well as gains (Curran 2003: 289). Firms dominating 'old' media maintain a grip on the consumption habits and market structures of media industries in general. The creation of scarcity in premium sports and movies that drove sales of pay-TV packages also meant the loss of live coverage, once available free on PSBs. The internet allows some communication resources to be spread more deeply and widely, and control is relatively dispersed, but we must not confuse these important challenges to established patterns of media production and consumption with the predicted demise of commercial media conglomerates. The range of content and 'interactivity' available on digital television has been mostly shaped by logics of commodification, commercialisation and concentration. For this reason, among others, media ownership continues to matter. In the next chapter we shall examine these issues further in the context of transnational media and cultures.

8 Western media and globalisation

Introduction

Up to the 1990s world media markets in print and broadcasting were still dominated by national enterprises, whether public or private. A central claim of theorists we examine in this chapter is that the dominance of state-based national media has been eroded. This can be formulated as a key question: is the global and transnational eroding the national and local? It is a question of immense importance but, formulated thus, it also invites a zero-sum analysis in which the transnational is either shown to weaken and displace the 'national' or instead we 'prove' the durability of the national media. This chapter argues that we do need to rebut certain, influential globalisation claims and redress a bias in the literature, but that we also need to try to better understand how diverse processes interact in the transnationalisation and transformation of media systems.

We can distinguish analytically three main aspects of media transnationalisation:

1 the transnationalisation of businesses and operations
2 the transnationalisation of media content (flows, texts, symbolic meanings)
3 transnationalisation of cultural identities (cultural practices and meanings).

The focus of this book is on understanding the nature and implications of transnationalisation for media systems. Here we must also address what lies outside the frame of 'vertical' national media systems and consider aspects of minority, diasporic, and radical and alternative media. Exploring how the circulation of media texts is contributing to the formation and reconfiguration of cultural identities and identifications is beyond the scope of this book. However, to address even the first two aspects of transnationalisation, we must bring together both political economic and cultural traditions of analysis.

Assessing transnationalisation: frameworks

Two rival polarities have structured debate on media transnationalisation. The so-called 'cultural imperialism thesis' focused on the nature and consequences of inequality in the flows between nations of cultural products, technologies and symbolic meanings, and it connected relations of dominance and dependence in media and cultural flows with geopolitical and capitalist economic power relations. This critical approach was influential on media analysts and some governments and policy forums, reaching the height of its impact in the late 1970s; it was challenged, was weakened and lost ground in the 1980s. Various critiques coalesced with emergent theories of globalisation to shape a 'cultural globalisation' thesis that has largely dominated Western media scholarship since the 1990s. This account is sometimes framed, therefore, as one of linear transition from a crude, neo-Marxist model of cultural imposition and 'one-way' flows to a sophisticated appreciation of the complexity of multidirectional cultural flows. Some important aspects of contemporary debates are lost in such self-serving caricatures. From the late 1990s, theories of cultural domination have been revisited and 'reformulated' because of the enduring, and arguably growing, issues of inequalities in the flow of media and communications and media power which gave rise to the original thesis. There is now an immense literature on these debates (see Thussu 2006; Hesmondhalgh 2007), so what follows is a necessarily brief outline before bringing these different frames to bear on our key questions.

Cultural imperialism

The concept of cultural imperialism was produced by radical scholars in the context of the NWICO struggles of the 1960s and 1970s that arose against a background of decolonisation (Mosco 1996: 75–6; D. Schiller 1996). Its achievement was to challenge the then dominant 'modernisation' paradigm (Chapter 1; Nordenstreng 2001). In place of a benign account of Western modernisation, radical scholars argue that 'Western culture' was being imposed on newly independent states in the 'third world', eroding cultural autonomy. Their core claim was that the imperialism had not ended with the withdrawal of direct political economic domination (Said 1993). Rather, colonial powers had found other means to sustain relations of dominance, including cultural imposition and the unequal exchange of cultural products, technologies, skills and resources. Cultural domination was seen as a 'strategy to generate demand for Western goods and to compound subordination and inequality between producer and recipient cultures' (MacKay 2000: 64). Scholars drew on dependency theory, grounded in neo-Marxist political economy, which argued that core nations maintained peripheral nations in relations of economic and political dependence. Transnational corporations, mostly based in the North, exercised control over developing countries in the South through setting the terms of global trade and exchange, aided by the active support of their respective governments.

What is labelled the 'cultural imperialism thesis' was in reality a short-lived formulation which was criticised 'from within' by critical scholars such as Tunstall (1977) and Mattelart *et al.* (1984), within an ongoing, revising tradition of critical political economy. However, three kinds of criticism, in particular, informed what became the 'revisionist orthodoxy' of cultural globalisation theory in the 1990s (Curran 2002a: 171).

(1) Multiple flows

The notion of predominantly 'one-way' flows from the US, or the West to the rest, was challenged by evidence that global flows were always but increasingly 'multidirectional' and so, it was argued, not reducible to a dependency model that conceived influence emanating from 'core' nations to 'peripheral' ones (Sreberny Mohammadi 1996; Baker 1997). There were 'reverse flows', a 1980s term for phenomena such as Latin American telenovell as from companies such as TV Globo in Brazil and Televisa in Mexico, then cheaper than most US imports, being shown on commercial channels in Italy, and especially in Portugal, where they became extremely popular. In place of US domination of a single global market, Sinclair *et al.* (1996: 5) described multiple regional and geolinguistic markets justifying 'a dynamic regionalist view of the world [that] helps us to analyse in a more nuanced way the intricate and multi-directional flows of television across the globe'.

In his 'generic' concept of media imperialism Boyd-Barrett (1977: 120) identified transnational flows as taking four main forms:

1   the shape of the communication vehicle
2   a set of industrial arrangements
3   a body of values
4   specific media contents.

Dissemination ranged from hardware and content to professional values as well as domination of international news reporting by Western agencies. Later scholars extended analysis of the range of cultural flows (Sreberny Mohammadi 1996), acknowledging media as only one part of broader cultural interconnectedness (see Held *et al.* 1999). Above all, multidirectionality came to be emphasised, and by the late 1990s at least was confirmed by the growing media influence and 'software' exports of East Asia (Japan, South Korea), Latin America (especially Brazil and Mexico), Australia, India and China (Tunstall 2008).

(2) Media audiences

The second main area of critique focused on the failure to analyse and appreciate audience reception, meaning making. While much can be said about media and cultural flows, the *implications* for those who consume them remained largely obscure. In his criticism of Herbert Schiller (1992) Thompson (1995: 171) argues:

> Schiller tries to infer, from an analysis of the social organization of the media industries, what the consequences of media messages are likely to be for the individuals who receive them. But inferences of this kind must be treated with scepticism. Not only are they very speculative but, more importantly, they disregard the complex, varied and contextually specific ways in which messages are interpreted by individuals and incorporated into their day-to-day lives.

Early studies, argues Madger (1993) assumed that the transnationalisation of cultural production led to transnationalisation of reception.

(3) Cultural domination

The third main challenge concerned the notion of *imposition* of culture, usually conceived as Americanisation or Westernisation. By contrast, it was argued that cultural imports, whether products or ideas, are indigenised, hybridised, modified, in sum appropriated in various ways that transform their meaning. Where cultural imperialism had feared growing cultural homogenisation, it was argued that more complex processes of differentiation were taking place. Insofar as there *was* a predominant flow of 'cultural discourse' from the West (or North) this should not be regarded as a form of domination but as a multiply directed transition to global modernities.

Globalisation theories

Cultural globalisation must be situated in the wider context of globalisation debates. The growing interlocking of the world has been theorised in a large number of competing ways, including the capitalist world market (Marx and Engels), imperialism, world-systems theory (Wallerstein), modernity and postmodernity (Waters 1995). 'Globalisation theory' provides another explanation, one generally opposed to neo-Marxist theories of capitalism and imperialism (Tomlinson 1999; see Sparks 1998a). Almost everything about the notion of globalisation remains highly contentious, including its conceptualisation, causation, periodisation, impacts and trajectory (Held *et al.* 1999). The term refers to the intensification of relationships between social activities on 'local' and global scales and increasing consciousness that 'the constraints of geography on social and cultural arrangements' are receding (Waters 1995: 3). Central to our concerns in this chapter is the claim that 'Globalisation is all about the dissolution of the old structures and boundaries of nation states and communities' (Robins 1997: 12). Globalisation generally refers to processes leading to the erosion of the nation-state and increased economic, political and cultural interdependence. Key aspects include the expansion of international trade and of multinational corporations, international finance, international communications and the transnationalisation, for some 'homogenisation', of consumer culture.

In their useful mapping Held *et al.* 1999 (see also Held and McGrew 2000) distinguish between hyperglobalist, sceptical and transformationalist positions. Hyperglobalists, or what Flew (2007) calls 'strong globalization' advocates, argue that global forces are bringing about a denationalisation of economies. State sovereignty and autonomy are being eroded and nation-states are becoming less powerful, less relevant and, for some, increasingly untenable. Hyperglobalists include those with diametrically opposed perspectives, dividing between neoliberals, for whom globalisation marks the triumph of individual autonomy and market forces over state controls, and neo-Marxists, for whom it marks the triumph of oppressive global capitalism. What strong globalisation theorists agree upon is that changes in the economic, political and cultural dynamics of societies are profound and qualitative and that the analytical tools required to understand them are fundamentally different from those that were applicable to earlier twentieth-century societies (see Flew 2007).

Sceptics (sometimes called 'traditionalists') include CPE analysts who variously challenge claims regarding the novelty, scale, intensity and direction of 'globalisation' processes. For some, the historical evidence confirms only heightened levels of internationalisation (Hirst and Thompson 1996; Weiss 1998). For sceptical critics, globalisation serves as a myth (Ferguson 1992), a politically convenient rationale for implementing unpopular neoliberal economic strategies and disguising relations of dominance. The so-called 'transformationist' position offers a self-proclaimed sophisticated take on globalisation which it views as the driving force for a 'massive shakeout' of relations formerly governed by nation-states, but one whose trajectory remains uncertain.

Cultural globalisation

Globalisation, argues Giddens (1999), is only partly Westernisation. Globalisation is becoming increasingly decentred, not under the control of any group of nations, still less of the large corporations. Such arguments recast earlier critical discourses, such as cultural imperialism, by describing a process that is decentred, lacking a 'fixed' dominant power centre. Cultural processes are also recast. One leading critic of cultural imperialism, John Tomlinson (1991, 1999) argues that to identify the spread of Western goods with the emergence of a capitalist monoculture is to offer an impoverished view of culture, one that reduces culture to its material goods:

> Culture simply does not transfer in this unilinear way. Movement between cultural/geographical areas always involves interpretation, translation, mutation, adaption, and 'indigenisation' as the receiving culture brings its own cultural resources to bear, in dialectical fashion, on 'cultural imports'.
>
> (Tomlinson 1999: 84)

However, if the cultural imperialism thesis may rightly be accused of assuming negative cultural influence (or passivity), this account assumes too much. How is the interaction structured? Is there always 'indigenisation', and if so, where is the evidence? Cultural globalisation theory '[f]ails to capture the agency of large profit making corporations in affecting, but not completely determining the new cultural world order' (Hesmondhalgh 2007: 238). In doing so, it reflects a 'blind spot' in revisionist cultural globalisation theory, a reluctance to critically address economic power (Curran 2002a: 174).

However, cultural imperialism will not do either. One set of ultimately insurmountable problems derives from the fact that the concept of cultural (or media) imperialism is an 'evocative metaphor' rather than a 'precise construct' (Sreberny 1997: 49). Imperialism and empire are primarily of a political nature, describing rule by a central authority over physical territories. A strength of the cultural imperialism tradition has been to highlight how political authority and economic power are intertwined; nevertheless extending the concept of imperialism to transnational corporations is problematic. For Pieterse (2004: 34) the idea of 'corporate imperialism' 'is a step too far and a contradiction in terms, for it implies non-state actors undertaking principally political (not just economic) projects'. This is certainly not to argue that corporations do not support political regimes or 'projects', or that political power is not used instrumentally to further corporate interests. Rather, he argues that the combination of the language of imperialism and colonialism with culture has been vague, confusing different kinds of power and agency which, while interlocking, still need to be distinguished analytically. Most transnational corporations, Pieterse argues (2004: 34), 'can achieve their objectives without control over sovereignty; economic influence of the type provided by the IMF, World Bank, and WTO regulations suffices, along with lobbying and sponsoring political actors'.

Boyd-Barrett (1998) asserts that a key virtue of the concept of 'imperialism' is that it focused on agency, but his original formulation (Boyd-Barrett 1977) conflated structure and agency, 'imbalance of cultural resources (structural and instrumental)' with 'cultural invasion', as 'imperialism could result through either deliberate export or through unintentional influence'. This problem was not resolved in his otherwise important effort to 'reformulate' media imperialism, which sought to replace the international, territorially based concept of imperialism with one of 'colonization of communications space', the latter taking greater account of the increasing hybridity of media systems (Boyd-Barrett 1998: 167).

One way of making sense of these debates is to recognise them as located within and mobilising different sets of concerns. The tradition associated with cultural imperialism is primarily concerned with *cultural resources*: who has access to the resources to produce, circulate, consume and use cultural forms. Its principal concerns are the distribution of resources for production; access for users; media pluralism and diversity of information, ideas, imagery; the conditions for people to exercise and enjoy freedom of expression; democracy (including media democracy, the ability to participate in decisions about how media and communications are organised). The cultural globalisation tradition is primarily concerned with *cultural processes* – how culture makes us, individually and collectively, and how we make use of culture. Its principal concerns are meaning, identity, consumption, the use and appropriation of culture. The notion of cultural imperialism has been challenged for its inadequate understanding and account of cultural processes. Its continuing relevance is in foregrounding questions of inequalities in cultural resources (and so issues of power and control of media and culture) and is at its best when pursuing investigation in an open, evidence-based manner.

'Strong globalisation' theories

How do contemporary media theorists assess the relationships between transnational, national and local media? I want to frame this discussion by outlining two very different accounts which nevertheless share characteristics of 'strong globalisation' theses. Herman and McChesney (1997) describe the ascendancy of what Herbert Schiller (1996) called 'transnational corporate cultural domination' in their three-tier model of global media. Theirs is an analysis of a shift from American hegemony to what Thussu (2006: 64) describes as 'a world communication order led by transnational businesses and supported by their respective national states, increasingly linked in continental and global structures'. This is not an Americanisation thesis, McChesney (2002: 157) writes, 'the notion that media are merely purveyors of US culture is ever less plausible as the media system becomes increasingly concentrated, commercialised and globalised'. Instead, the global system is better understood as 'advancing corporate and commercial interests and values and denigrating or ignoring that which cannot be incorporated into its mission' (McChesney 2002: 157). Globalisation here is largely conceived of as a process driven 'from above', by the activities of transnational communication conglomerates supported by neoliberal states and supranational institutions such as the WTO and EC. Herman and McChesney (1997: 9):

> regard the primary effect of globalization process ... to be the implantation of the commercial model of communication, its extension to broadcasting and the 'new media,' and its gradual intensification under the force of competition and bottom-line pressures.

As these are the most powerful forces shaping media, to grasp them, analysis must no longer begin with national media systems, but with the global level, and then factor in national variations.

A central claim of cultural globalisation is deterritorialism, the 'loss of the natural relation of culture to geographical and social territories' (Tomlinson 1999: 107). The influence of place, in the sense of geographic location, as a foundation for individual and collective identity is fading, argue Lorimer and Gasher (2004: 301). This involves a broad range of processes and most analysts are careful to avoid a mediacentrism that would see these changes as emanating from media influences alone. Nevertheless, the media figure centrally. Broadcasting is seen as inherently global in reach. Once its 'containment' within national systems was challenged, television, in particular, has served to disseminate global cultural meanings which have contributed to deterritorialism. The internet has allowed even greater global distribution and aided the formation of new (non-territorial) identities. For Castells (1996) the global proliferation of new forms of information and entertainment through digitally networked ICTs means 'the end of mass media', and hence of the association of nationally based media with the development of national cultures. The global 'space of flows' erodes the significance of a variety of forms of historically based and locally grounded forms of culture. For Flew (2007: 149), the notion that media 'work towards a territorially defined cultural mandate has therefore been under challenge for some time, and the case for deterritorialization seems to strengthen with each new media form'. Like most, Flew does not see this process as simply unidirectional. Rather, globalisation involves a dialectic of disembedding and re-embedding as local identities have been reasserted. Bounded cultures and ethnic 'resilience', including nationalist sentiment, coexist with less-bounded 'trans-local' cultures (Pieterse 1995). However, 'strong' cultural globalisation theories tend to see the 'local' as residual, weaker, and reactionary, globalisation is both stronger and normatively embraced as more progressive 'cosmopolitanism'. At its best, however, this tradition rejects an opposition between cosmopolitan and local, seeing the global and local not as 'cultural polarities but as combined and mutually implicating principles. These processes involve not only interconnections across boundaries, but transform the quality of the social and the political inside nation-state societies' (Beck 2002: 18). For Beck (2002: 18; 2003), cosmopolitanism focuses on growing interdependencies (cultural, social, political) between global and local, and provides 'a methodological concept that helps to overcome methodological nationalism and to build a frame of reference to analyze the new social conflicts, dynamics and structures'.

Others highlight broader cultural flows and interaction arising from migration and mobility, including, notably, the relocation of 'Third World' cultures in the metropolitan centres of the West. For García Canclini (1995), migration and modernity have broadened cultural territory beyond the traditional nation-state. According to Thompson (1995: 175), 'As symbolic materials circulate on an ever-greater scale, locales become sites where, to an ever-increasing extent, globalized media products are received, interpreted and incorporated into the daily lives of individuals'. In addition, many texts circulate on the basis of transnational cultural affinities rather than nation-based interests or concerns (Hesmondhalgh 2007: 219). According to cultural globalisation theories, the global and transnational is eroding the national. Above all, this constitutes a shift from the dominance of national media, such as national broadcasting, to a new media order whereby '[a]udiovisual geographies are thus becoming detached from the symbolic spaces of national culture, and realigned on the basis of the more "universal" principles of international consumer culture' (Morley and Robbins 1995a: 11).

Two radically different perspectives, then, agree that transnational media are eroding national media. They differ. One focuses on production – the global flow of mass media output – while the other focuses on reception, the production of cultural identities. But both agree that national cultural space is being significantly eroded

Both tend towards, without fully endorsing, a one-way unilinear model of change. Both 'strong globalisation' arguments tend to focus on processes eroding state-based media from above. The alternative perspective we shall examine argues instead that we need to be much more careful and discriminating in assessing the nature and influence of transnational media flows. This perspective offers a critique of both, but by no means a dismissal of either. Within cultural globalisation a critical tradition has opened up the field of transcultural studies discussed below. Herman and McChesney's remains an indispensable analysis for understanding corporate media dominance and one bound to their case for democratic media reform and media activism from below. McChesney co-founded Free Press, which has pursued and popularised a radical media reform agenda in the US (McChesney 2004), and joined international initiatives such as Voices 21 (Raboy 2002). Nevertheless, there is a need for a stronger corrective to top-down accounts of global processes. Both strong globalisation theories address 'localisation'. In the neo-Marxist account localisation tends to be viewed as corporate efforts to modify content sufficiently to maximise share across different geocultural markets. For cultural globalisation, 'localisation' carries much greater weight as a rejoinder to critiques of cultural imposition, serving as the complex interface of global and local influences. Both, however, tend to bypass the 'national' in this account and the status of the 'local' is often indeterminate.

The local can mean different things. First, as Sparks (2002a: 79–80) points out 'there is social space for a number of different levels below that of the state, and it is not clear which of them is pertinent to the global/local discussion'. There are common distinctions between the regional (here meaning a subnational unit) and the local, defined geographically and sometimes also culturally. But the terms are indistinct; regional and local are used to describe a variety of very different social constructions, and important categories such as metropolitan cities are displaced. In addition, the common use of 'local' is spatial, with 'local' linked etymologically and semantically to 'locality'. This 'old' sense of locality as 'a relatively small place in which everyone can know everyone else' (Featherstone 1996: 52 cited in Sparks 2002) is associated with a place-based notion of 'common culture', and with patterns of life embodying 'structures of feeling,' some of which predate capitalism (Williams 1977; Sparks 2002: 81; see Couldry 2000b). The 'new' sense of the local is one in which similar kinds of 'structures of feeling' exist among dispersed communities, independent of their physical separation and of geographical location. This new sense of 'local' is associated with ethnic and diasporic identities and with the

> emergence of new subjects, new genders, new ethnicities, new regions, new communities, hitherto excluded from the major forms of cultural representation, unable to locate themselves except as decentred or subaltern, [who] have acquired through struggles, sometimes in very marginalized ways, the means to speak for themselves for the first time.
>
> (Hall 1991: 34)

Of course the loss of a 'natural' relation of culture to geographical and social territories occurs under highly differentiated experiences, from relatively benign processes of transculturation to forced migration.

With the expansion of modern communications, Western media systems are becoming more pluralised and hybridised. Alongside nationally organised 'vertical' media there is a greater circulation of 'horizontal' media. There can be no simple measure of the value and significance of access for different recipients. But we can use measures of market and audience share and of cultural flows to help to address how, and how rapidly, 'national' media systems are being transformed by transnationalisation.

Transnational media flows: North America and Europe

The US was a major presence in European film theatres by the 1920s. This domi-nance over the British, French and German industries, which began in the silent film era, accelerated with the devastation of the First World War, the introduc-tion of sound, and the massive advantages of the US economy after the Second World War. Advantages in production and marketing continued with television, although exports did not take off until the 1970s.

By the end of that decade the United States exported around 150,000 hours of programming a year (Held *et al.* 1999: 359). According to a study by Waterman (1988), during the 1980s, 80 per cent of US audiovisual exports products went to just seven countries: Australia, Canada, France, Germany, Italy, Japan and the UK. More recent data on audiovisual and related services shows that the US is the largest exporter of cultural services, with US$6.7 billion, far beyond the United Kingdom, which is the second-largest exporter, with US$1.5 billion (UNESCO 2005a). By the 1980s the cost of acquiring one hour of *Dallas* would pay for approximately one minute of original Danish drama (Gitlin 2002: 25). As well as the considerable economic advantages for US firms, the state played an active role by promoting its cultural industries abroad and by promoting liberalisation policies. Schiller (1998) describes how US representatives in international forums such as UNESCO pressed for implementation of the 'free flow' doctrine, which called for markets to be opened up to TNCs and limits on national government regulations of their activities, policies pursued in the post-Cold War institutions such as the WTO.

The political–economic dimensions of production help to explain the domi-nance of US cultural exports, but their appeal and success has also depended on demand-side factors (Morley and Robins 1995a; Gitlin 2002). The influence and cultural reach of its film industry has been a major contributing factor in US domi-nation of global entertainment markets (Miller *et al.* 2005; Thussu 2006: 156–8). Hollywood influence has created a globally recognised image bank. As Gitlin (2002: 22) writes, American popular culture has become the 'closest approxima-tion there is today to a global *lingua franca* drawing especially the young, urban and urbane classes of most nations into a federated cultural zone'. American popular culture has become the 'central bank of international mythologies, circulating two major dreams: the dream of freedom and the dream of wealth' (22–3). More broadly, successive US media forms established styles, formats, conventions and professional cultures that have spread and been partially transformed worldwide (Tunstall 1977).

It has been argued that US success has derived from the need of its cultural industries to serve a diverse 'melting pot' of cultures in its domestic market. For Gitlin, while the US draws on an Anglo-European cultural base,

> much of what makes its audio-visual products so successful in global markets is their hybridization of those cultural roots with other cultures represented in late-nineteenth- and twentieth-century immigration into the United States

by Eastern European Jews, Arabs, Latin Americans and Asians. Exported popular culture has been 'pre-tested' by a heterogeneous public.

(Gitlin 2002: 25)

However, this argument needs to be qualified by consideration of the variable, and often narrow, range of cultural expression in US exports, which underlies continuing concerns about Americanisation and cultural homogenisation. What is clear is that American popular culture absorbs and recombines a diverse flow of cultural influences. But the differences between US diversity and cultural homogeneity can be easily overstated and questions of cultural diversity need to be considered text by text. The US has also benefited from its large, relatively homogenised TV market while European markets are highly diversified in both language and cultural tastes (De Bens *et al.* 1992).

Concerns about cultural imperialism were given support by studies of global television markets showing that programming flows were dominated by US capital. A UNESCO report found that more than half the countries studied imported over 50 per cent of their television, most of which was entertainment, and most imported from the US (Nordenstreng and Varis 1974; Straubhaar 2002: 194). However, as we have seen, dependence has varied considerably according to underlying market features and changing market conditions (Chapter 7). Tunstall (2008: 250) identifies three phases of media trade between the US and Europe since 1980. Up to the mid 1980s European television had few channels, little advertising and 'quite modest imports of American programming'. By the mid 1990s there was a large increase in US programming hours as television expanded and new cable and satellite stations emerged. The USA accounted for 75 per cent of all TV programme exports worldwide in 1995 (Hoskins *et al.* 1997: 29). The mid 1990s were a high point, peaking around 1997 when major European channels were scheduling at least 30 per cent of time with US programming. The trade deficit between the US and EU countries was estimated by DG X to be $5,658 million in 1996 (Tongue 1999).

US influence also increased in this period through ownership of trans-European companies such as SBS. New European commercial TV channels were more dependent on imported programming, especially from the United States. Sepstrup (1989, 1990) found strong correlation between the dependence on US programmes and commercialism on European channels. The transition to multichannel television in Europe was 'heavily influenced by American companies, American policy, American programming, and American investment' (Tunstall 2008: 272). But a number of factors altered a pattern of increasing one-way US influence, as this was met with a countervailing strengthening of European defences, including regulatory efforts to protect and strengthen European production. By the early 2000s (Tunstall's third phase) European television companies were making more of their own programming and the overall US share of European audience time had declined. Some programme genres, such as daytime chat shows and soaps, were becoming cheaper to produce domestically than to import. In addition, many European commercial channels now had increased resources to produce high-quality programming for prime time, with investment on a par with premium US shows. Disparities in resources between the US networks, production companies and leading European private channels were reducing. By 2005, the three main US networks' share of the vast US market had fallen from 30 per cent to around 10 per cent of TV households. '[M]ost Hollywood TV series by 2005 no longer had much bigger production budgets than those of TV series in the larger European countries' (Tunstall 2008: 276), with the important exception of premium 'pay' channel output, notably HBO. However, as Tunstall reports, these shows were often carried by European networks that were only ranked fourth or fifth in national audience numbers (for example the UK's Channel 4). The shift also reflected strong audience demand in Europe for domestic production within certain types of programming.

The ratio of non-European to European broadcasting hours varies across genres. In 2005 the highest ratio of non-European to European broadcast hours was animation (77 per cent), followed by feature films (74 per cent) and TV films (62 per cent). The only category where the imbalance was less than 60:40 was short films (51 per cent) (European Audiovisual Observatory 2006b: 149). By genre, the heaviest dependence has been in media fiction. In a study of 36 stations across Europe De Bens and De Smaele (2001) found that nearly two-thirds of fiction broadcast was North American. Much of the heaviest European dependence has been on US movies (in all windows and formats). The proportion of US fiction broadcast on channels in selected European countries in 1997 was as shown in Table 8.1 (De Bens and De Smaele 2001: 56).

The US remains the main source of non-European feature films and fiction, although its share fell from 71.8 per cent in 1998 to 62.3 per cent of total imports in 2004. That decline, however, masks increasing US involvement in international co-productions (co-productions with non-European input or mixed co-productions), which went up from 3.1 per cent in 1998 to 13.4 per cent in 2004, most of them based on initiatives originated by North American companies (European Audiovisual Yearbook 2005b: 94). Yet the European Observatory also found that in 2002–2004, among the European 'big five', there had been a marked trend

Table 8.1   Proportion of US fiction broadcast in selected European countries (1997)

	US percentage of prime time TV fiction		*US percentage of all TV fiction*	
	Public	*Commercial*	*Public*	*Commercial*
UK	39.4	33.4	53.7	53.7
Germany	4.1	69.2	19.6	76.3
France	20.2	52.7	52.9	60.7
Belgium				
Flanders	38.2	82.3	44.4	79.5
Wallonia	14.6	63.0	34.4	75.6
Netherlands	31.6	67.6	36.1	78.8
Italy	52.2	73.0	42.3	61.9

away from intercontinental as well as inter-European co-production. It noted the 'paradox' that in an era of globalisation European fiction had become 'more domestic and local than ever' (2005b: 65).[1]

The European 'big five', France, Germany, Italy, Spain and the UK, remain the leading world market for Hollywood movies, TV, video and music output (Tunstall 2008: 257). What has changed, however, is levels of 'dependence' on imports. In 1983 France, Germany and the UK took around 12 per cent of total TV output from the US (see Varis 1985). By 1995 the US share was estimated to have doubled to 25 per cent, but it then declined to around 15–20 per cent by 2005. Southern European countries (Spain, Italy, Portugal and Greece) have been among Europe's biggest importers of American programming (Tunstall 2008: 277), as well as of Latin American. Yet, low take-up of cable and satellite services has meant comparatively fewer homes with multiple US channels than in Northern Europe.

Private channels financed by advertising broadcast the largest amount of non-European fiction (83.5 per cent), the least amount of national fiction (8.8 per cent) and the least amount of non-national European fiction (7.7 per cent) (figures for 2005, European Audiovisual Observatory 2006b: 149). In a sample of 125 channels in EUR 13 the proportion of fiction was as shown in Table 8.2.

A sample of thematic channels broadcast in Europe (most of which were children's channels) found that the proportion of non-European fiction was 70 per cent. Non-national European fiction accounted for less than 10 per cent. Such aggregation masks important variations: some PSB channels, for instance, also show a high proportion of national fiction.

European AV production

Changing patterns of European dependence on US imports reflect both supply-side and demand-side factors. During the 1990s some European commercial operators had become successful, profitable companies able to invest more heavily in European programme production. RTL devoted 30 per cent of its programming budget to original production in 1990 but had increased this to 80 per cent by 1994. But companies also met demand (both regulatory and consumer) for domestic production by developing cheaper, 'localised' formats. Most notably,

Table 8.2 Proportion of fiction broadcast on a sample of 125 European channels (2005)

	Number in sample	National (%)	Non-national European (%)	Non-European (%)
Commercial channels	40	8.8	7.7	83.5
Pay TV film channels	19	11.2	14.9	73.9
Thematic channels	19	19.5	9.8	70.8
Public service channels	47	25	24.5	51.2
Total	125	15.2	13.4	71.7

Source: European Audiovisual Observatory (2006b)

where channels had previously relied on US talk shows such as *The Oprah Winfrey Show* and *Donahue*, they developed cheaper, domestic versions filling day-time slots. There has been a significant increase of new national fiction in off-prime-time slots, 'light' and low-budget types of fiction produced for day-time audiences (European Audiovisual Observatory 2005b: 65). In addition, domestic reality programmes became prominent in European prime-time schedules in the early 2000s, with 21 reality shows across the top networks in France, Germany, UK and Italy in 2003. This also reflected a shift away from fiction to factual and reality programmes (of 8 per cent between 2003 and 2004).

A downward trend in programming of domestic fiction (2002–2003) was reversed from 2004, but a complex and varied picture has emerged in different European countries' programme types and scheduling. The strongest recovery in 2004 among the 'big five' occurred in Germany, Italy and the UK (European Audiovisual Observatory 2005b).

Assessing changing patterns of dependence on US programmes

US programmes still capture the majority of non-domestic viewing hours in most European television systems, based on total programme hours. Non-domestic European programming has a high share in countries with shared language or strong historical interconnections. But most European countries import very little from countries 'beneath' them in the 'cultural pecking order' (Tunstall 2008). The cultural pecking order can be further illustrated by considering proportions of national and non-national fiction broadcast. Overall, the balance in 13 older EU states is 53 per cent national fiction, with a higher proportion of national fiction in large states (Germany France, Britain and Italy) and less in medium-sized countries such as the Netherlands, Norway and Finland (between 9 and 11 per cent). The proportion in Austria, Belgium, Ireland, Denmark, Sweden and Ireland was less than 5 per cent (European Audiovisual Observatory 2006b: 151).

Patterns of dependence of US programming vary across WMS. To account for variations we would need to include consideration of industry development, the extent of support policies and the impact of sectoral and general legislation. Both smaller Western and ex-Communist Central European countries tend to import media from the United States and also from the 'big five' European countries. While US films and premium content continue to draw large audiences in prime time, most US imports were used to fill non-peak schedules on European TV. Here, economics is the main factor in channel dependence on US material. For peak programming, with the important exception of 'premium' US production, the domestic tends to be more appealing and hence profitable, attracting increased investment. The audience share for channels with predominantly US content is not high.

During the 1990s the main satellite and cable channels featuring the largest amounts of US material – Sky, MTV, CNN – all had low regular viewership (Browne 1999: 449). The evidence for unidirectional adoption of US programming is thus not strong. Rather, the trends confirm Tunstall's analysis of a relative decline in US influence as measured by audience share and programme flows for exported programmes. With patterns of integration, however, it is becoming harder to identify the full extent of cultural importation, due to the increasing merging of operations, personnel, cultural forms and influences.

UNESCO (2005a) data on audiovisual and related services shows that the United States remains the largest exporter of cultural services, with $6.7 billion in 2002, far beyond the United Kingdom, which is the second-largest exporter, with $1.5 billion. While the US remains the world's leading exporter of programmes, the UK has become the leading exporter of TV formats. In 2004 the UK exported 64 formats, France 56, Germany 50, the US 46 and the Netherlands 46 (Ofcom 2006a: 118). The format for *Who Wants to be a Millionaire?* has been sold to at least 106 countries, and the *Pop Idol* format has been shown in countries as diverse as Iceland, Kazakhstan, and Lebanon. France earned ECU108 million ($136 million) in 2004 with worldwide sales of its animation series *Totally Spies*, including to Time Warner's Cartoon Network, as well as documentaries and dramas.

Overall, there has been an important shift in Europe away from dependence on imported US programming, and increases in the amount of domestic content scheduled in prime time on mixed channels, especially in the 'big five'. But we cannot infer much about shifts in the cultural influence of US programming from even careful analysis of programme flows and viewing share alone. Further, the nature of cultural flows has become much more varied and complex than was the case when early analyses of television flows were produced in the 1960s and 1970s. Media imperialism analysts were certainly attuned to various kinds of flows, influence and imposition beyond acquisition of programmes. Boyd-Barrett (1977) and others examined the influence of models of journalistic professionalism and the way these were inculcated through education and other kinds of 'exchange'. Yet, the international flow of personnel, finance, cultural influences and formats has certainly become more difficult both to track and to assess. We can distinguish flows of trade in tangible products and services (software and hardware), trade in intangibles (intellectual property, including programme ideas and formats) and the flow of influences on institutional practices and cultures (such as journalistic professionalism).

One outcome of European efforts to protect AV production in order to diminish the US–EU trade imbalance was to encourage US firms to establish European operations for a mixture of incentives, including bypassing quota barriers and accessing European production subsidies. After the Television Directive (1989) and the 1992 single market process, co-productions and other joint programming ventures became a common occurrence for US programme exporters (Albarran and Chan-Olmsted 1998: 13). US firms localised for commercial as well as regulatory purposes. More broadly, as Waters (1995: 159) notes, 'Most of the large U.S.-based media firms are in the process of moving from a "U.S.-centric production and an international distribution network" model to a more transnational production and distribution model.' The increasing imperatives on media giants to 'localise' their content are encouraging them to 'establish wider international bases'. This has made it more difficult to ascribe country origination. For cultural analysts, such efforts are inherently problematic in any case. MTV is often cited as a prime example of such localisation. MTV Europe, a satellite service whose footprint stretched from Iceland to Israel, initially found it hard to localise, not least as European firms developed competitor services which began to chip away at its market share (Sturmer 1993). MTV developed regional programming, then services, and moved on to greater multimedia segmentation. Roe and De Meyer (2000) provide a valuable account of the nature and limits of localisation (of VJs and some content), while for critics, 'MTV is a well-developed commercial formula that Viacom has exported globally, by making small adjustments to account for local tastes' (Croteau and Hoynes 2006: 103).

The essentialist notion of the export of a culture has long been challenged by cultural analysts and cannot be sustained. CPE scholars have tended to replace an essentialist notion of 'Americanisation' with transnational corporate capitalism to emphasise how globalised content and production patterns from commercially driven corporations, many but not all US-based, have extended their reach and influence. However, this reformulation has been criticised in turn. For Thompson (1995: 169), Schiller's (1992) 'transnational corporate cultural domination' 'still presents too uniform a view of American media culture (albeit a culture which is no longer exclusively at the disposal of American capital) and of its global dominance'. Cultural analysts have traced more carefully the processes of cultural adaption and hybridisation shaping specific cultural production. In addition to the cultural arguments about what is 'American' about American cultural goods, transatlantic relationships in areas such as co-production, co-ownership, as well as 'transla-tion, franchising, reversioning, and piracy' (Tunstall 2008: 251) make the task of distinguishing the originating sources, much less linking these to 'national' cultural characteristics, increasingly difficult. For Tunstall, (2008: 251) 'the complexities of ownership' are evidence of the 'gradual emergence of a single Euro-American media bloc'. Both material and symbolic hybridisation underlie the need for caution in reading off cultural influence from data capturing economic flows. But, equally, we should not let growing complexity obscure consideration of the deep, underlying imbalances in cultural flows.

Reassessing transnationalisation of television

To the extent that it is occurring, what is being globalised? Globalisation of media is transforming 'media fiction and music' argues Curran (2002a: 179) 'rather than news and current affairs' (2002: 179). Across WMS, US premium fiction commands the greatest share of imports, but the maturation of commercial networks in Western Europe 'has dented the appeal of US fiction as audiences demonstrate liking for home-grown programming' (Iosifides *et al.* 2005: 6). 'Audi-ences in Europe – and around the world – prefer their own national entertainment in their own national language' (Tunstall 1995: 12). This preference for 'cultural proximity' (Straubhaar 2002) is an important corrective to strong globalisation theories, although the pattern varies, as national cultures and cultural production vary in their appeal to domestic audiences.

National broadcasting has been pivotal to debates on media globalisation, in particular the perceived weakening of the operational base and influence of national broadcasting vis-à-vis transnational. As Wang and Servaes (2000: 7) point out, however, the predicted demise of local cultures and cultural industries as a consequence of the importation of television programmes was shown to be wildly inaccurate: '[b]y the 1990s it has become evident that the theories have suffered from lack of evidence'. Transnational television has proved increasingly popular in Europe. But the hope or fear of a unidirectional transition from bounded national-based television to transnational has not transpired. Such claims, which carry considerable weight in globalisation arguments, are inaccurate and misleading.

Erosion of national broadcasting?

In 2001, BBC1 and ITV accounted for 63 per cent of prime-time television viewing and the combined prime-time share of four terrestrial channels (BBC1, BBC2, ITV1, Channel 4) was 80 per cent. By 2005 their share across all homes was 70 per cent (Ofcom 2006b: 232–3), each channel's share had fallen by between 7–9 per cent in homes with Freeview, and fell in other multi-channel homes. Nevertheless, the market share of terrestrial television in Britain remains high in spite of the enormous expansion of media. Britain, though, has a well-funded and supported public service system. In other systems, PSB's share has fallen further. From 1985 to 2005 national public broadcasting in smaller European countries declined from as high as 100 per cent to 35–40 per cent audience share (most of the fall occurring by 1995) (Tunstall 2008; see also MacKay 2000: 66–7). In smaller countries the ability to sustain economically viable domestic production has been harder, yet, where available, demand for domestic programming remains high. Despite the increasing availability of US programming, the top 10 or even 20 ratings in nearly all major industrialised nations show a clear predominance of 'homegrown' product.

There is limited transnationalisation in terms of the circulation of European television within Europe. With the exception of sports and some regional variations, the audiences for non-domestic European programming remains small. There have been cultural and linguistic barriers to PETV (pan-European TV) despite the efforts of the European Commission and the EBU's offerings, including Euronews and Eurosports. National audiences have proved unreceptive to subtitled or dubbed imports from other European states.

Finally, an important counter-trend to the predicted shift from 'national' to transnational has been the expansion of local broadcasting. In Europe local broadcasters are a relatively new development produced by political and economic action during the last two decades. Browne (1999: 452) traces this development to the growing recognition of the importance of 'microcultures' within and across nations, a recognition fuelled to some extent by EC, CoE and UN declarations and policies supporting what the EC calls 'subsidiarity'. Decentralisation has been triggered by policy deregulation and the rediscovery of autonomy by communities within a state, giving rise to 'proximity television' (de Moragas Spà and López 2000). The decentralisation of broadcasting is evidence of a challenge to existing national authority, often driven by strong cultural identifications and political claims, including nationhood. Decentralisation represents a cultural challenge to nations and efforts towards national 'inclusion', but it is also mainly accompanied by and realised through action by nation-states. From the perspective of assessing media systems, the decentralisation and localisation of broadcasting shows an important role for the state through regulation, and often subsidy, not a withering away of nation-state authority, even though among the most successful local broadcasting services have been those linked to 'nations' without states. As de Moragas Spà and López (2000) show, whether the market works for or against 'proximity television' depends on the strength of cultural and linguistic factors, with the greatest success being in 'nations without a state' (de Moragas Spà *et al.* 1999).

Such proximity TV is evidence of localisation but not of deterritorialism. Local news services and coverage of local political and cultural activities are the principal services, and of course ones in which local channels can secure market advantage (Sparks 2000a: 88). The rise of the 'local' does not necessarily contradict globalisation theories, many of which characterise global–local interactions as a dialectic process eroding the national from above and below. Nevertheless, the rise of proximity broadcasting does challenge the adoption of smooth narratives of progression to the transnational and transcultural.

News

The example of local television also serves to highlight a major bias that needs to be redressed in the media globalisation literature, the neglect of national and local news media. News outlets remain overwhelmingly national or local. The production and consumption (as opposed to gathering) of news remains largely organised around the nation-state and locality. The audience for global news channels such as CNN has been small and has remained predominantly elite. While terrestrial broadcasters' audience share has certainly eroded, this 'has not to any significant extent been caused by the rise of a global news service taking viewers for their national products as part of the growth of a global public sphere' (Sparks 2000a: 84). Cross-border press readership is mostly small and elite (Hafez 2007), with the important exception of minority ethnic and diasporic press readerships. There is increasing consumption of global news via the internet, but this is largely an additive for heavy media consumers, not a substitute for accessing news from established sources.

Local media also tend to be relatively independent of the global media operators, as described by Herman and McChesney (Sparks 2000: 86). While these authors are right to claim that national or local firms may be in relations of dependency, their tiered model is too generalised to deal adequately with different operations and business models. In particular, as Sparks argues, 'national' capital in news tends to be less connected to patterns outlined by Herman and McChesney. The press sector in Western Europe remains predominantly national (or subnational), although in Central and Eastern Europe it is increasingly dominated by foreign media owners. Newspapers do circulate beyond the borders of nation-states and, via the internet, they become place-less if only in distribution and consumption. But there are very few transnational newspapers. According to Sparks (1998b: 118) only two aim to circulate globally: the *Financial Times* (UK) and the *Wall Street Journal* (US). These, like the *International Herald Tribune*, have a mainly national market with a supplementary, mainly elite, international readership. The over-whelming majority of newspapers are aimed at national or subnational audiences in both their print and online forms.

Assessing contemporary British terrestrial television, Curran (2003a: 285) writes that it 'promotes national identification by giving prominence to symbols of the nation, providing a shared social experience for the nation, and a news service strongly shaped by national news values (even down to its definition of the "weather")'. The argument that British television is weakening national iden-tity should be 'turned on its head'. The problem, rather, is that British television journalism remains 'excessively parochial and nationalist'. Coverage of European and global politics lags behind and journalism has failed to 'respond adequately to the decline of the British state and the transfer of some of its sovereignty to global markets and agencies'. This analysis proposes a variety of corrective lenses to the vision of inexorable denationalisation of the media. Attention to news media high-lights not only the persistence of national and local news but also attendant prob-lems of their continuing dominance in the promotion of a 'nationalist and localist perspective of human affairs' (Curran 2002a: 180).

Even the most well-resourced news media appear not only to favour domestic issues, as repeated studies of news values confirm, but also to neglect the interna-tional. In Britain a study of current affairs output in 1997–98 found that only 19 per cent addressed issues outside Britain, mostly on minority channels (Barnett and Seymour 1999). Further, studies of domestic coverage of international news stories suggest that they tend to be interpreted through national frameworks that privilege news salience and strategic geopolitical interests (Lee *et al.* 2005). However, studies need to be continually revised and updated, with several of the above pre-dating the post 9/11 world.

Transnational and diasporic media

The national media systems framework describes the institutional organisation of national and subnational media. The bias within this framework has been its focus on vertical relationships between national, regional and local media. Considera-tion of horizontal relationships has been weaker or neglected altogether. This has been compounded by an already existing neglect of minority media production within nations, of issues of race, and of the complexity of cultural flows and identity formations across 'national' borders. Issues of cultural integration within national societies and the contribution of media have been properly contested issues within 'media systems' analysis, but the framework has tended towards an assumed homology between national media systems and cultural processes connected to state-based media.

As Thussu (2006: 63) points out, research emphasis is shifting from considering the contribution of media in 'the vertical integration of national societies' to studying information flows which show patterns of transnational horizontal integration of media and communication structures, processes and audiences. But media systems are changing too, with transnational media and cultural flows that challenge and traverse 'national' media systems. In understanding transnationalisation, the contribution of cultural globalisation or, more precisely, critical cultural studies, has been much more positive.

A growing literature on media and migration attests to the expansion of diasporic media and challenge to its neglect (Cottle 2000a; King and Wood 2001; Karim 2003). Historically, diasporic peoples have used various different media to communicate, from letters, books, newspapers and magazines to audiotapes and videos and DVDs. From the 1980s satellite TV opened up possibilities for transnational broadcasters to cater to specific geocultural groups, and new communications technologies have since enabled physical and economic barriers to be more easily overcome. Analysts have insisted on carefully distinguishing, for political and ethical as well as analytical reasons, differences regarding the experience of immigrants, guest-workers, ethnic and 'racial' minorities, refugees, expatriates and travellers (Cottle 2000b). These writers also emphasise the need to avoid presenting homogenised accounts of diasporic 'communities', which conflate or ignore disparities in education, wealth and class status, differences in cultural identities and power relationships. In particular, intergenerational differences in cultural tastes and affiliations are often considerable. State policies, the educational system, national media and cultural processes have tended to ensure that the second and third generations become increasingly assimilated into the receiving country's main language and culture (Tunstall 2008: 358). However, this pattern is less assured in a period of increasing cultural conflict and volatility.

Historical patterns have usually involved initial dependence on home-country media where some means of importation, legal or otherwise, exists. When communities have become larger and more established they have tended to create their own media in host countries (Tunstall 2008: 357). Small weekly papers can grow to become daily, a few hours of radio time may expand into entire radio channels. Geographic concentrations begin to provide a viable market for media products and services (video stores, screens in multiplex cinemas, satellite editions of home-country newspapers, local cable companies carrying channels, alongside 'two-way' media such as e-mail, the internet and 'cheap' phone calls). However, by no means all migrant groups are supplied with abundant media in their mother tongue.

According to UN figures for 2005, Europe (Western and Eastern) had some 56.1 million migrants, making up a 7.7 per cent share of the population. In North America the share was 12.9 per cent, with 40.8 million. Europe's large outflows of population in the nineteenth century have been replaced by a preponderant inflow. The United States is the biggest receiver of population flows, while Europe overall has the largest number of foreign-born inhabitants. However, as Tunstall (2008: 355) notes, only about 3 per cent of today's world population lives outside their country of birth or citizenship.

National deregulation of broadcasting has been a catalyst for the extension of private television networks and also made it possible for satellite broadcasters to aim beyond national borders (Thussu 2006). Apart from the major Western powers whose broadcasting had an international dimension, most state broadcasting was organised for domestic audiences and confined within state borders. Transnationalisation from the 1980s has been driven by private channels more interested in markets and advertising revenue, although some also had a more liberal political–cultural agenda. This basic difference between state-centric and market-oriented broadcasting has been a key factor in the expansion of many Southern broadcasters into lucrative Northern markets, aiming to reach diasporic communities (Thussu 2006: 186). The technical extension of satellite footprints and the growth of DTH has enabled networks such as Zee to operate in an increasingly global communication environment. Zee was 'one of the first Indian companies to recognise the potential of broadcasting overseas to geo-cultural and diasporic populations and currently claims to reach 250 million viewers in 120 countries' (Chadha and Kavoori 2005: 95). By 2001 Indians and Pakistanis resident in the UK could subscribe to some 18 South Asian satellite or cable channels (mostly from Zee, Sony and Star). Diasporic communities can also use satellite receivers to access an enormous range of transnational channels. Turkish peoples across Western Europe are served by a variety of satellite stations. Turkey's TRT launched TRT-INT in 1990 which reaches Turkish-speaking populations in Western Europe via Eutelsat. Chanel 18 (KSCI TV) broadcasts in 16 languages to minority communities in the United States.

Market regulation (supply and demand) interconnects with state-based regulation and the patterns of provision for minority cultures by mainstream media. All of these vary across WMS, although some general patterns are discernible. Demand for transnational media of all kinds reflects lack of provision for minority communities by mainstream media, argues Thussu (2006: 188). In Britain, non-domestic channels and programmes aimed at black Americans have proved very popular among black Britons. Another important issue for comparison is nation-states' responses to minority and diasporic media, which relates to broader state policies on citizenship rights and immigration status, social, political and cultural recognition, provision of services, and approaches towards social 'integration' of minority ethnic communities.

Germany, with a significant Turkish population, permits the importation of programmes from Turkish domestic radio and TV services, as does the Netherlands. By contrast, France attempted to discourage satellite distribution of TV services from Arabic-speaking nations in North Africa to North Africans living in France (Browne 1999: 11).

New technologies have facilitated an expansion and diversification of media serving minority communities in Western multicultural states. It may be assumed that the share of 'proximate' media will increase and that of national media decline. But how national media 'matter' to individuals from minority ethnic groups requires ethnographic and other research to answer. Diasporic media represent an important aspect of the pluralisation of media systems. The 'horizontal' expansion of transnational media is contributing to the emergence of 'diasporic public spheres' (Appadurai 1996). There has been a much longer history of interaction between 'horizontal' media and cultural influences, and the 'vertical' structures of national press and broadcast media. As we have seen, Western PSBs were challenged to 'open up' broadcasting and some began to provide or acquired domestically produced programming aimed at minority ethnic communities from the 1960s. How successfully, and under what conditions national broadcasting has opened up space for foreign or domestic content aimed at minority ethnic and cultural groups are important questions beyond the scope of this study. What is evident, however, is that 'diasporic' channels are not watched in any significant numbers by members of the host majority. There is little evidence of greater cultural mixing or intercultural awareness in patterns of viewing for non-domestic channels aimed at minority ethnic groups. Their output remains relatively small and their global impact is restricted to the diasporic communities, their primary target, contributing to fragmentation and 'ghettoization of minorities' (Thussu 2006: 189, 205). The media of diaspora, neglected in traditional constructions of 'national media systems', are becoming more pervasive. These are undoubtedly influencing important changes in media use and consumption. However, there is much less evidence that they are influencing consumption and use among majority groups. This is not to deny the high positive benefits that transnationalisation may bring, but to suggest that, if these values matter, then it is all the more important to be alert to problems and deficiencies in mediated communication.

Radical and alternative media

Traditional focus upon 'vertical' nationally organised media has also tended to neglect radical and alternative media (Downing 2001, Atton 2002). Some radical media is strongly national, regional or local in orientation, focused on articulating political–cultural concerns that are marginalised in mainstream media. In other cases, radical media may be transnational in focus or circulation. Comparative study of media systems has tended to eclipse the wide spectrum of small-scale, community and alternative media, through to those oppositional media forms that emerge in critique of, or critical dialogue with, mainstream media. There is no space here to offer a comparative study of these forms or do justice to their influence and importance. But this must be acknowledged as a lack that future comparative studies can remedy.

Evaluating state, nation and national media systems

Informing the clash between cultural globalisation theorists' enthusiasm for globalisation and the radical political economists' critique of globalisation as a neoliberal ascendancy are often unstated differences in conceiving of the state. Globalisation theory tends to assert that nation-states are becoming irrelevant economically, and national governments politically. For critics, this analysis 'slips with deceptive ease from a description to a proscription' (Seaton 2003: 311).

In the cultural globalisation account, globalisation is seen as a largely emancipatory force enabling new identities and solidarities to be forged that enable a new progressive politics to come into being. Global capitalism is viewed as an enabling force for cultural pluralisation and decentred, grounds to challenge the oppositionist arguments of cultural imperialism. But in this secular prolepsis hope for a more democratic distribution of cultural power is contingent on market-driven media. This is further compounded by dismissal of nationally based media and of the capacity of the state to influence communications space.

The cultural globalisation literature associates the nation with 'invented tradition, manipulative ideology, hierarchical control, intolerance, conformism and nationalism' (Curran 2002a: 178). Nationalism is pathologised (Bhabha 1994: 5) and cosmopolitanism celebrated. This literature tends to equate pluralisation of cultural offering with empowerment, and associates 'national' culture with imposition, violence and exclusion of otherness. For Bhabha (1994: 5):

> The very concepts of homogenous national cultures, the consensual or contiguous transmission of historical traditions, or 'organic' ethnic communities – *as the grounds of cultural comparativism* – are in a profound process of redefinition. The hideous extremity of Serbian nationalism proves that the very idea of a pure, 'ethnically cleansed' national identity can only be achieved through the death, literal and figurative, of the complex interweaving of history, and the culturally contingent borderlines of modern nationhood. This side of the psychosis of patriotic fervour, I like to think, there is overwhelming evidence of a more transnational and translational sense of the hybridity of imagined communities.

As progressive, anti-essentialist cultural theory and politics, there is considerable value in deconstructing myths of cultural homogeneity. In such analyses, though, transnational media serve as vehicles for cultural pluralisation and progressive identifications. While criticism of corporate media is articulated, this tradition offers a broadly 'panglossian' reading that equates capitalism with cultural democratisation. By contrast, the state is associated with the construction and maintenance of hegemonic (cultural) power. A liberal democratic tradition grapples with the balance between state supervision and market freedom but tends to support some degree of state intervention to protect democratic and cultural values. In modern form this justifies limited state action to protect domestic cultural production, especially where this serves the public sphere. Within CPE there are wider divergences between strong anti-statist and anti-nationalist strands, but most share a general conception of the democratic state as a key agency in the realisation of social and economic objectives. The nation is viewed as the place where democracy is and can be practised, a view accompanied by an interest in the capacities for supranational democratic governance but a profound scepticism about its realisation, especially at a global level (Sparks 1998; Seaton 2003). Morris and Waisbord (2001) seek to redress under-analysis of the state within writing on media globalisation. They argue that it is premature to conclude that the state is withering away and to assume a post-state world. States remain fundamental political units retaining significant law-making powers. Globalisation has challenged but not eliminated states as power centres, as sets of institutions where decisions are made regarding the structure and functioning of media systems.

Is the global and transnational eroding the national? To address the implications of globalisation we need to disaggregate issues and assumptions that are often fused together in debates: the power and influence of nation-states; nation-states' capacity to shape (communications) policy; media production and consumption patterns; cultural influence and identities; the importance and influence of national media institutions vis-à-vis transnational institutions. One set of questions concerns the powers and importance of nation-states. These must be broken down, since it does not follow that erosion of power over economic management means the same kind of erosion over communications or cultural policy. Here it is more useful to think of globalisations (Pieterse 2004) and carefully assess changes in the capacity of nation-states and in the shifts and transfers of power between institutions of governance.

Conclusion

'Strong globalisation' claims need to be modified to take much greater account of the persistence of national media, that is, media institutions and content organised at or below the national level that are subject to some degree of nation-state regulation and supervision. While this challenges some key claims, it also helps to clear the ground for a better appreciation of the merits of different perspectives and research agendas. We do not yet have a fully synthesising account. What is clear is that there are diverse, divergent and convergent trends and trajectories interacting across media systems. The notion of global–local interaction captures the richness of some of these processes but has tended to offer a poor account of national media systems (Chadha and Kavoori 2005). In a more diverse and complex media environment it is perhaps easier to move beyond earlier debates framing the interaction of global and local, particularly those cultural theories that have tended to associate deterritorialism with a progressive cosmopolitanism and the local (collapsing the national into the local) with ultimately reactionary identifications. From a critical political economic perspective, tendencies to globalisation and localisation are mutually constitutive in that the same technologies and the capitalist pursuit of profits drive both the globalisation and the localisation of public media.

There is confirmation for aspects of the 'strong globalisation' CPE analysis. In particular, there is evidence of significant and enduring imbalances in cultural flows between WMS, even before we begin to address 'Euro-American' dominance globally. There are powerful trends towards transnational corporate dominance. Yet the thesis of unidirectional, top-down change needs to be modified. National media resources (institutions, production, markets and regulation) are highly variable but often strong counter-forces. Localisation is driven by not only economic imperatives but also social, cultural and political dynamics. Older patterns of national media public spheres are being transformed under transnational, transversal, and decentralising and localising forces. These forces may certainly diminish a national public sphere over time and they certainly challenge its adequacy and universalising pretensions. But it is not clear that hybrid cultures and diasporic and transnational communities have yet made such significant inroads into mainstream national cultures and identities to suggest such dismantling is advanced. Most media, in their content, institutional organisation, distribution and reception remain, in MacKay's phrase (2000: 48), 'stubbornly local and national'.

The increasing range of transnational and transverse media choices available 'allow for the growth of other than national loyalties, affiliations and affinities – the "communities of mutual interest" that can exist on a nongeographical basis' (Browne 1999: 453). Transnational media can support and help to constitute other 'imagined communities' than those framed within nation-based configurations. Individual and social benefits (pleasure, sociality, understanding, emancipation) have been delivered in large part through market-based commercial media. But the claim that these are or will replace national-based media is overstated, too generalised and highly misleading when it suggests a consumer/citizen-driven pluralisation of media industry production.

For CPE critics, the undoubted benefits also need to be set alongside disbenefits. A commercially driven, deregulated system is more likely to create fragmentation than to aid cultural or civic interaction. The deficiencies of narrowly nationalistic media need to be met by an extension and pluralisation of public media, not their abandonment. That national public service broadcasting has been a vehicle for nationalistic and exclusionary discourses is undeniable, but it does not follow that we must accept (much less welcome) the loss of capacity for democratic control over cultural resources for intercultural communication and interaction. Nation-states remain important forces in shaping space for circulation of information and cultural interaction. There is, unfortunately, no lack of evidence that the state can be a repressive force (seeking to control flow of information, images and ideas), using media in efforts to legitimise rule or seeking to impose an exclusionary 'national' identity. But the state remains for many 'the best hope for harnessing media-driven media globalization' (Morris and Waisbord 2001: xi).

9 Assessing Western media systems

Introduction: media system convergence?

Are Western media systems converging? Hallin and Mancini (2004) conclude that the differences between their three models (and variations between nation-states) were quite dramatic up to the 1970s but have 'diminished substantially over time' (2004a: 251). At the beginning of the twenty-first century, 'the differences have eroded to the point that it is reasonable to ask whether a single, global media model is displacing the national variation of the past' (251). There is, they argue, growing convergence towards the liberal model, whose main features are a strong role for markets, weak government intervention, weak political parallelism and the privileging of a particular, Anglo-American conception of journalistic professionalism. Their focus is on media–political relationships and they find a central aspect of growing homogenization to be 'the separation of media institutions from the strong ties to the political world that distinguished both the Democratic Corporatist and Polarized Pluralist from the Liberal Model' (294). Other key features of convergence are shifts towards market regulation, with some diminution in states' role as media owners, funders or regulators (291). Above all, commercialisation is identified as the single most powerful force for homogenisation and globalisation in media systems (Hallin and Mancini 2004a: 273; 2004b: 38–9). There are, however, limits to homogenisation as well as important counter-trends. Differences between national political systems remain substantial and are likely to prevent complete homogenisation of media systems for the foreseeable future.

To answer the question of media system convergence we need to distinguish different aspects of media systems. Analytically we may distinguish:

1   media–politics relationships
2   the structure of media markets (production and consumption)
3   state policy and regulation of media markets
4   the ownership and organisation of media institutions
5   culture and cultural processes.

There is a productive tension between distinguishing and connecting these aspects in order to examine the complexity and unevenness of 'system' convergence both within and across WMS. We have examined a variety of convergence theses, which focus on some of the aspects identified above. It is a characteristic of all comparative studies that they do not examine and articulate all these relationships with anything like equal attention. There are clear dangers and a legacy of error in totalistic accounts, especially in the absence of empirical research. But consideration of holism can usefully highlight gaps that serve as productive indicators for future work. It can also highlight deficiencies in all accounts of media globalisation. It is an unwarranted leap, for instance, for Hallin and Mancini (2004a: 294) to assert that a 'global media culture is emerging' in an analysis that largely brackets out entertainment media. The point here is less to be critical of gaps, which are inevitable, than to caution against the strong tendencies to generalise about change. It is less that the micro always complicates and qualifies the macro, than that these differences matter hugely in how we identify and evaluate variations across media systems that challenge smooth narratives of globalisation, convergence and commercialisation.

Review of Hallin and Mancini's three models

Hallin and Mancini provide the most well-developed analytical framework so far for understanding the relationship between media and political systems. A major convergence trend they identify is declining political parallelism within Northern European states (democratic corporatist systems). Party-affiliated newspapers now barely exist among mass-circulation newspapers. However, political parallelism persists in Southern Europe, although journalistic styles have shifted somewhat towards 'Anglo-American' practices. There are some discernible counter-trends, such as the rise of partisan, advocacy journalism in the United States, such as politicised radio and TV talk shows (H&M 2004a: 286) representing convergence towards a more 'European' model in which 'neutral' journalism coexists with political partisanship.

Their focus is on changes in media–politics relationships and news journalism. What are the consequences if our focus shifts to include broader aspects of media markets and cultural production? Pivotal to their comparative analysis is the development and treatment of newspapers. What changes if broadcasting (audio-visual media) is made the central focus? Finally, their analysis seeks to examine the distinguishing characteristics and conditions of national media systems in historical formation. What changes if greater consideration is given to more recent developments in media systems?

If broadcasting is made the salient axis, there are good grounds to revise the three models. We would then have three models but a fourth category of American exceptionalism, or alternatively, four models. The liberal model is strongly market dominated in the case of the press, but the divisions between the commercial model of US broadcasting and the state-regulated public service systems established in Britain, Ireland and Canada are too great to be held together under one ideal-type category. PSB has been of a minimal type in the US, with no regulation by genre or quality of programmes broadcast by commercial channels and with public funding under $30 per head (McKinsey and Co. 2004). Historically, the differences in the formation of broadcasting are clear (and fully acknowledged by Hallin and Mancini). They write (2004b: 39):

> The most dramatic change, however, has clearly been the commercialization of European broadcasting. There is no doubt that starting with the end of the Second World War a process of progressive weakening of the relatively separate national cultures had already commenced, faced with the growing global flow of messages, products and institutional forms, mainly coming from the United States. An important restraint to this flow, however, and one which also had consequences for other means of communication, was the prevalence of the public service broadcasting across Europe.

The case for convergence towards a 'liberal model' has much greater weight if presented, as they do, in conjunction with the argument that PSB is a weakened and weakening force. Certainly, commercial broadcasting is increasingly dominant, commanding a majority share (in the liberal systems and all WMS except Denmark and Austria, according to their figures (H&M 2004a: 42). Market forces are forcing PSBs to 'adopt much of the logic of the commercial system'. Audiences for national public broadcasting are being eroded by competition from within (beginning with pirate radio in the 1970s) and by transborder broadcasting. Policy changes have favoured the transnationalisation of media industries, and global market forces ('economic globalisation') have tended to displace the national political forces that once shaped the media. All the forces of commercialism are correctly identified here. Their analysis is in line with critical scholarship in the 1980s, 1990s and beyond which examined the erosion of PSB and increasing marketisation. In addition, changes in technology and modes of consumption and payment for content challenge the financial arrangements and identifications on which PSB has traditionally depended. Yet the analysis needs stronger qualification than Hallin and Mancini offer. In particular, it overestimates the weakening of PSB institutions and institutional support for public media.

Reassessing public service media

Comparative analysis highlights the variation in the conditions and fortune of PSB occurring at any one point in national systems. Nevertheless, in broad outline all PSB systems have been under increasing pressures since the 1970s and how they have fared has been shaped by national and supranational governance, market conditions, popularity and legitimacy in the midst of broader social and cultural changes. It is uncertain whether PSB can survive long into the new century but the presumption that they cannot be sustained is open to challenge.

First, although systems vary considerably, PSB continues to offer a powerful countervailing force to full media commercialism. The normative case *for* PSB is powerfully argued by Graham *et al.* (1999). PSBs are necessary to counter the market failure arising from reliance on purely commercial media and commercial decision making. A commercial system cannot realise the full benefits of technology for society as a whole since it is based on calculations and exclusions driven by the search for profit, not social benefit. PSBs are a positive force and necessary counterweight to private concentration of media ownership. In continuing to deliver 'universal' national coverage they can counteract the fragmentation of audiences. They are large enough to influence the market, for instance by driving up the standards of competing services. PSBs widen choice by complementing the market through the pursuit of public service purposes (Graham *et al.* 1999).

During the twentieth century, the bi-media development of PSBs in radio and television has been an important source of their strength, identity, popularity and independence. PSBs continue to offer a variety of radio services in most EU countries, and national, regional or local radio news, in particular, competes with TV as a trusted news source. Of course, any such claims must be considered alongside actual performance and take account of consumer demand, popularity and public support, all of which vary. Yet, countering the thesis of media homogenisation, Gunther and Mughan (2000: 439) argue that free market systems still differ significantly from PSB in regard to the volume and detail of policy-relevant information conveyed to viewers and listeners. They argue that it is unlikely that political programming or citizens' viewing patterns in other democracies will go the way of the United States because of the strong commitment to PSB on the part of states. While media entertainment has become less differentiated across broadcasting, even here differences between PSB and commercial are still 'detectable' (Browne 1999: 456; see also Hesmondhalgh 2007: 274–5). News output and informational programming has fallen on some PSB channels, indicating the weakening of PSB specificity under intensifying commercial pressures (Chapter 3). However, while news output is generally falling, the pattern is mixed. In Sweden, for instance, news output fell by nearly 25 per cent between 2003 and 2004, although news and information programmes still made up 34 per cent of output on SVT1 and SVT2. In, Ireland it increased by nearly 14 per cent between 2003 and 2004, making up 31 per cent of RTE 1 and RTE 2 output, and by nearly 20 per cent across the Netherlands' PSB channels to 27 per cent of output (European Audiovisual Observatory 2005b). Overall, PSBs' supply of domestic and international news and information, while variable, remains higher than for comparable private channels and a continuing marker of difference.

The pressures on PSB systems have increased. Among the key trends in European television identified by Dahlgren (2000) are increased fragmentation and segmentation of audiences, marginalisation of less popular cultural and informational programming, reductions in public funding and government regulation alike. For Dahlgren (2000: 31), writing at the end of the1990s, the future of PSB is unclear, 'it is a vision formulated and institutionalised under different historical circumstances than exist today. It must be revitalised if it is to offer a compelling direction for television's future in the next century'. For many contemporary analysts the migration of audiences and activity, especially among the young, away from linear television viewed on TV sets to alternative activities such as social networking, and alternative modes of consumption of programmes, marks the point of irreversible decline for traditional television. But against the expected and generally accepted narrative of decline have been some counter-trends that show the continued vitality, even revitalisation of aspects of PSB. My argument is that most of the PSB systems have shown continuing popularity, resilience and expansion in the digital age.

Despite fears about the impact of multi-channel TV, publicly funded broad-casters, including France Télévision, RTVE (Spain), ZDF and ARD (Germany) and the UK's BBC have maintained their audiences. All have diversified into new digital initiatives, launching digital channels and developing online activities. In 2006 Germany's ARD and ZDF audience share was 44 per cent, Italy's RAI 43 per cent, France 2, 3 and 5's share 37.6 per cent, while Spain's TVE was 25.4 per cent (EBU 2006: 13). Overall, PSBs' audience share of domestic channel viewing between 1998 and 2005 increased in Denmark, Norway, Flanders and Greece, and fell in other West European countries. It fell slightly in the UK (from 51.1 to 50.9 per cent), France, Germany and Italy, and fell more sharply in Austria (from 62 to 49 per cent), Spain (51 to 43 per cent), Portugal (38 to 27 per cent) and Ireland (52 to 41 per cent) (European Audiovisual Observatory 2006b: 143).

As we have seen, decentralisation and localisation of broadcasting has been cited as a challenge to national PSBs 'from below'. Undoubtedly, there are consider-able challenges but these are predominantly cultural. The institutional structures of PSB have not been diminished and in many cases have been strengthened by decentralisation. Hafez (2007: 57) points to the further evolution of national and regional media now that digital media have eliminated the shortage of terrestrial frequencies.

Television remains 'inseparable from the national democratic project, but it must adapt as "the nation" historically evolves' (Dahlgren 2000: 32).

> Public broadcasting should both contribute to the dominant consensus in a society and support the process whereby alternative, minority identities and sets of values can be put forward ... In programme language this means: a combination of programmes for 'everyone', specific programmes for minorities, programmes that highlight and strengthen the national cultural heritage and programmes which recognise minority (ethnic, gender, class) cultural identities as valuable to society as a whole.
>
> (Brants and de Bens, 2000: 17)

PSBs have certainly found it difficult both to foster a 'common culture' and to address domestic audiences as they become more heterogeneous and individu-ated. But arguably, these institutions are even more burdened with the responsi-bility of doing so within increasingly fragmented and segmented media systems.

Even where strong today, PSB's relative competitive advantage may not be long lasting. The BBC, for instance, benefited from a generous licence fee settlement in 2000 during a period in which its commercial competitors battled with rising costs and often substantial reductions in advertising income. The BBC has since received a below-inflation licence fee settlement for 2007–12, as costly obligations

236 Western Media Systems

for digitalisation have been imposed, prompting a further round of cuts in jobs and services. PSB, whatever its merits, is certainly a 'parochial' and Eurocentric concern. The world's largest and single most influential system is very predominantly commercial. Nevertheless, in distinguishing among WMS it remains the most important difference and one which directly and indirectly influences broader policies and media markets.

Differences across national media systems are certainly diminishing. Media systems are converging towards some of the characteristics of 'liberal' systems. Media commercialisation is the single most powerful force for homogenisation. Commercialisation has contributed to the reshaping of media cultures, political communication and journalistic norms, leading to weakening political parallelism and the rise of 'critical professionalism' in news and political journalism. The expansion of commercialism in Western European systems has brought them nearer tendencies most evident in the US media system. The realisation of such convergence will depend, though, on the marginalisation of state-supported public media.

Western media in global context

This book has sought to provide an introduction to the development and transformation of Western media systems. It has considered transnational exchange mainly in regard to Western media markets and systems, rather than looking outwards to the influence of the West on other media systems. Efforts to overcome both the universalising pretensions of the *FTP* tradition and the parochialism of Western media theories has come at a time of increasing international and comparative research and exchange. It has also occurred as the 'American century', and US-led Western dominance in geopolitics and 'global culture' is giving way to more multi-polar configurations of power. Whether it is valuable or appropriate to sustain such a 'unit' of analysis as 'the West' depends on our purposes. For comparative analysis of historical changes in 'similar' systems which share important common historical–cultural roots and features, it is. However, the boundaries of any comparative study need to be carefully considered and justified. Increased interaction with the post-Communist states of Central and Eastern Europe is transforming 'Europe' politically and culturally. The interaction of South and North America is also gradually transforming this 'Western' zone. Yet, enduring disparities of economic, political and cultural power remain the overriding features when we bring Western (or Euro-American) systems into global comparisons. The common, if highly unevenly distributed, feature of Western states is their concentration of economic, military, political and symbolic power.

Continuing value of a national framework

Is it still relevant and useful to examine 'national' media systems? We need to distinguish national media systems from national media institutions. The latter, especially news media and broadcasting, have been subject to 'vertical' kinds of supervision or control by states. Through the period from the 1940s to the 1980s, such institutions were the main focus of analysis of countries' media systems. This equation is no longer sufficient and is becoming less 'central' according to some, if not all, measures by which this hierarchy has been justified explicitly or tacitly – total domestic audience share, market share, cultural role, media–political relations, reach and influence of symbolic communication, ritual, state involvement, and so on.

In addition, 'container' thinking, which orders phenomena and relations around the presumed centrality of the nation-state has been powerfully repudiated. The analytical challenge is combined with an ethical–political stance that rejects the exclusions of 'nationalism' in favour of cosmopolitanism. Yet, the notion that a global media system is *replacing* national media systems is seriously flawed. Instead we need to examine how the national and transnational are implicated and interact in three main areas:

1 the activity and capacity of states to affect mediated communication within their jurisdiction
2 the ownership and control of media institutions
3 media consumption and use ('transnational', national and subnational).

What is needed is less a repudiation or displacement of the national than an analysis of transformations. The national framework retains salience. Media organised at or below the national level still matter. It helps us to compare what is happening in different countries. It has always been necessary to recognise transnational and transverse forces in any adequate analysis of 'national' phenomena, even if this appears more pressing and inescapable in an era of globalisation. But questions of agency and influence 'within' nations are especially important wherever these can or do influence the nature and range of mediated communication.

Our approach has been to identify the national as a locus of analysis, to construct 'national media systems' for analytical purposes. The value of this construction is its focus on various kinds of consideration of the relationship of mass media to socially shaped environments. There are, though, both benefits and dangers in continuing to use such presumptive frames. Whereas the national frame has tended to privilege vertical media relationships, this needs to be combined with much greater attention to horizontal relationships, to transnational and transverse media and cultural relationships. The vertical frame has also reinforced tendencies to endorse a top-down account of media power and influence. Comparative analysis can, and needs to, put the national into question in order to assess patterns and processes that are misread from a narrowly national frame, but it also can redress the errors of displacing the national. It is the basis for continuing the study of the transformation of media systems. Analysis of transnational media flows or of diasporic communication must necessarily cross national boundaries. However, the nation-state remains an influential force. The political, legislative, cultural and social dimensions of the state are not simply diminished by globalisation. Rather, they are important, sometimes predominant, factors in how media transnationalisation trends are realised.

Media and democracy

In *Communications* (first published in 1962) Raymond Williams argued that the extension of communications was part of the extension of democracy. 'Yet in this century', he went on, 'while the public has extended, ownership and control of the means of communication have narrowed' (Williams 1962: 26). From the vantage point of the present, there has been an undoubted advance, leading many to propose that the problems of 'control', scarcity and media ownership are much-diminished, if not redundant, fears in the digital age. Access to communication technologies and resources has been transformed. 'Symbolic power', the power to make and distribute meanings, is now distributed more widely and with potentially greater effects than ever before. Yet power imbalances over publicly mediated communications are enduring and in many ways strengthening. To address this, we need to avoid generalisations of optimism or pessimism. The point, rather, is to continue to ask searching, critical questions about media power as part of an effort to fully understand and appreciate the constraints as well as possibilities of the 'digital age'.

As we have shown, concentration of media ownership remains a significant feature of WMS. Problems of market and media power persist alongside pluralisation. As one Council of Europe report argues (CoE 2003: 4):

> The development of digital technology poses new challenges to pluralism which results from, among others, the use of proprietary systems by operators. The trend towards media concentration is strengthened with digital convergence. Liberalisation and globalisation of markets increase the pressures for concentration on the national scale. States need to strengthen national regulators and authorities responsible for ensuring and protecting media pluralism.

It proposes a variety of measures including media ownership rules, support for PSB and efforts to ensure diversity of content sources.

We have also examined the relationship between democracy and communications in media policy. Commenting on the liberalising re-regulation of communications policy in Canada and the UK, Winseck (1998: 354) writes:

> Although these [government/private sector] initiatives may realign the ties between culture, markets and technology in ways that further the viability of information highways, the opaque and manipulative nature of these strategies is difficult to reconcile with any meaningful understanding of democracy, let alone the hyperbole of deregulation and free markets. The silence of all those who have derided the paternalism of state-centric communication policy and public broadcasting but turned a blind-eye to these more invasive and far-reaching efforts is disturbing.

For Ó Siocrú *et al.* (2002: 31):

> the extraterritorial nature of global media keeps them beyond the reach of national media governance structures and practices. There are few policy options available to a government wanting to support development of national media in this environment ... and few meaningful fora for people who question this new world order to express their views.

The trajectory of global regulation is one of strengthening neoliberalism. Yet it is mistaken to see these processes as unidirectional and merely cumulative, let alone inevitable. As Ó Siocrú *et al.* also point out (2002: 127) 'the balance of factors is relatively fluid and dynamic, and in a future phase its guiding rationale could look very different again'.

Policy and media reform

Comparative analysis can help to overcome the pitfalls of a simplistic identification and evaluation of the respective merits of 'state' versus 'market'. It can help us to understand better the specific conditions under which 'state' or 'market' may be said to have beneficial impacts (H&M 2004a: 14–15). Yet these remain irreducible matters of value. The challenge to take mass media seriously is unavoidably a challenge to connect the analytical with the normative and critical, if not at the beginning (and the normative is always at the beginning of our enquiries, assumptions and emotions) then certainly at the end.

There have been notable efforts to construct agendas for democratic media reform at national and transnational levels. What is clear to advocates is the importance of action by nation-states. State remains the most powerful of social actors and many states, including all WMS, are subject to some democratic control. Defending and extending the public sphere remains a central democratic task and the role that states can play here through regulation, subsidy and support remains integral to its realisation (see Sparks 2000a: 92–3). Some urge that the quest for emancipation through publicly regulated media must be rethought in a post-national media scene. Instead, I think that the longer view of communications requires us to consider how brief and how fragile has been the period of broadly social democratic influence over the organisation of mass media. It has always been deficient; the actual public has all too often been ignored, displaced and patronised, but it has provided an idea that was consequential, as Habermas writes of the bourgeois public sphere. The notion that public communication should be subject to democratic control and should be responsive to, accountable to and legitimated by public interest and utility was briefly dominant. In place of this notion there has been a reassertion of private interests and controls, corporate media concentration and a narrower, market-based definition of public interest providing legitimacy.

For the critical tradition, we need not and should not settle for a world shaped this way. Instead, we need to find effective ways for democracy to intersect with media.

What characterises that struggle for media democracy today is that it combines critical concern about trends towards media concentration and control with an awareness of the importance of both mass and alternative media for networks and groups in civil society, of the openings that exist and can be expanded, as well as those that must be struggled for politically.

Appendix: Comparative country data

	Land area (sq km)	Population (2005) (000s)	Population (2007 estimated) (000s)
Austria	82,444	8,185	8,361
Belgium	30,278	10,364	10.457
Canada	9,093,507	32,805	32,876
Denmark	42,395	5,432	5,442
Finland	304,473	5,223	5,277
France	545,630	60,656	61,674
Germany	349,520	82,431	82,599
Greece	130,800	10,668	11,147
Italy	301,230	58,103	58,877
Ireland, Republic of	68,890	4,016	4,301
Netherlands	33,883	16,407	16,419
Norway	307,442	4,593	4,698
Portugal	91,951	10,566	10,623
Spain	499,542	40,341	44,279
Sweden	410,934	9,002	9,119
Switzerland	39,770	7,489	7,484
United Kingdom	241,590	60,441	60,769
United States	9,161,923	295,734	305,826

Sources: Land Area: CIA World Fact Book 2007; Population at 2005: US Census Bureau, Comparative International Statistics 2007; Population estimates for 2007: UN World Population Prospects 2006, UN Department of Economic and Social Affairs.

Notes

1 Explaining Western media systems

1   Blumler and Dahlgren (2005) advocate combining a systems and a 'cultural' approach, in part to overcome the former's tendency to focus on formal actors within political communication and ignore other forms of mediated communication in which politics can be relevant and important – e.g. films, talk shows etc.

2 Media systems evolution

1   The Fairness Doctrine ran parallel to Section 315 of the Communications Act of 1937, which required stations to offer 'equal opportunity' to all legally qualified political candidates for any office if they had allowed any person running for that office to use the station. Section 315 exempted news programmes, interviews and documentaries which were covered by the Fairness Doctrine. Section 315 was federal law, whereas the Fairness Doctrine was simply FCC policy.

2   In 1960 only six countries had more than 100 TV sets per 1,000 inhabitants: the US (310), Canada (218), the UK (211), Sweden (137), Denmark (119), Australia (108). Source: UNESCO (1963: 26).

3 Transformations and continuities in media systems (late 1970s to 2000s)

1   The first evening's viewing included speeches, classical and pop music and two ITV programmes: the documentary *World in Action* and the soap, *Coronation Street* (Briggs and Burke 2002: 294).

2   A Broadcasting Act 2001 set out the regulatory framework for a commercial DTT network but no commercial operator emerged from the process. A government-initiated pilot DTT service began in August 2006 and DTT is expected to be rolled out in 2008, following new legislation.

3   Colin Leys (2001:136) provides a detailed examination of what he described as the 'reconstitution of broadcasting as a field of accumulation, rather than as a set of primarily political institutions' and identifies four prerequisites of such change: the conversion of services into commodities; the creation of demand for those commodities; the conversion of the labour force into one willing to produce profits; and the intervention of the state to lower the risks of investment.

4   See O'Malley (1994). This charge had also been made under the previous Labour administration (Donoghue 1987: 62).

4 Media system theory: paradigms and power

1 Baker (1989) provides a detailed, critical discussion of marketplace of ideas theory. This was enunciated by US Supreme Court Judge Holmes in Abrams v. U., who argued that all truths are relative and can only be judged 'in the competition of the market' [250 US 616, 630-1 (1919)].
2 Seaton (1998) argues that Mill's argument can be interpreted as supporting pro-active measures by the state to secure diversity and so ensure the conditions for freedom of expression.
3 Feldman's (1993: 606) account of US press freedom concludes 'it is still essentially a negative rather than a positive right ... it limits the range of circumstances and ways in which it is legitimate for public authorities to interfere with free expression. It usually makes no obligations on the State to make available the facilities and materials which people need in order to take advantage of the freedom'.
4 The eighteen larger Western European states ratified the European Convention in the 1950s, with the exception of France, Switzerland and Greece (1974), Portugal (1978), Spain (1979) and Finland (1990).
5 Curran and Seaton (1997: 356) distinguish four main approaches to media policy: traditional public service, free market, social market and radical public service. These approaches are defined according to a division between advocates of the free market and supporters of public service. In addition, the four approaches are traversed by another key division of opinion between paternalistic and libertarian approaches to media law. Arising from the twin axes of free market/controlled market and paternalism/libertarianism are a 'complex mosaic' of public policy positions.
6 Critical political economy (CPE) is the more accurate term to distinguish the tradition examined above, which challenges mainstream, orthodox economics, but 'political economy', or in places CPE, is used for the sake of brevity. For a detailed introduction to the tradition see Mosco (1996) and Mosco and Reddick (1997).
7 For instance, in their study of journalists accompanying the British Forces during the Falklands War, Morrison and Tumber (1988) argue that 'insufficient attention has been paid to how the journalist as an individual exercises his [*sic*] judgement in negotiating his role' arising from what they see as a research tradition shaped by defining news as the reproduction of dominant ideology.
8 Shoemaker and Reese (1996) identify the main kinds of forces influencing journalistic independence and control as being: personal attitudes and orientations of media workers; professionalism [organiSational routines]; corporate policies; corporate ownership patterns; economic environment; advertisers; ideological influences; influence of the audience.
9 For a useful summary see Held (1996: 225).

5 Media and politics

1 For Entman (2005) the insulation provided by professional journalistic norms in the US has been badly eroded, as commercial media haVE been captured by a dominant political tendency of Republican rule.
2 In April 2008 Berlusconi, one of Italy's richest men, won a third term as Prime Minister, leading a centre-right alliance, People of Liberty, following the collapse of Romano Prodi's centre-left coalition government.
3 In January 2007 the centre-left government announced plans to reform the governance and finance of RAI, involving the creation of separate licence fee- and advertising-funded public companies and with Parliamentary recommendation replacing direct government control over the appointment of board members (Screen Digest 2007).
4 For a summary account see Barnett and Gaber (2001: 27–9, 66). On Murdoch's relations with New Labour see Freedman (2003: 158–9).

5   Murdoch's pursuit of business interests in China and Asia in the 1990s led to some much-criticised instances of proprietorial influence. These included the removal of Andrew Neil as *Sunday Times* editor following that paper's investigations into the Pergau Dam affair, which threatened Murdoch's precarious business interests in Malaysia (Curran and Seaton 1997: 82). In 1994, News Corporation's Star TV dropped the BBC World News from its satellite service under pressure from various South-East Asian governments, contradicting Murdoch's assertion in his 1993 Mansion House speech that satellite television and telecommunications would threaten totalitarian regimes by allowing the 'information hungry residents of many closed societies to by-pass state-controlled television' (Hird 1994).

6   Such findings highlight the value of 'systems' approaches that examine relationships between the character of political communication and differences in political systems, although their limitations in capturing the complexity of media and political cultures are usefully reviewed by Blumler and Dahlgren (2005) and Blumler and Gurevitch (2005).

7   The commercial success of Fox News is connected to wider changes and deepening political and cultural divisions in US society. McChesney (2004: 79) acidly notes Fox's strategies to reduce costs 'by replacing expensive conventional journalists with celebrity pontificators'.

8   The patterns of interaction between macro and micro variables can vary considerably between countries, prompting Gunther and Mughan (2000: 43) to conclude that the political effects of the media are 'highly conditional on … institutional, social-structural and micro-level factors'.

6 Media policy and regulations

1   As one branch of US competition law, the FCC also contributed to a move away from vigorously pursuing anti-trust cases (Alger 1998). Anti-trust law enforcement is undertaken by the Bureau of Competition of the Federal Trade Commission (FTC) and the Antitrust Division of the Department of Justice and, indirectly, by the Federal Communications Commission exercising its powers in media matters.

2   Section 202(c)(1) of the Telecommunications Act directed the FCC to modify its rules to eliminate the numerical limit on the number of broadcast television stations a person or entity could own nationwide and to increase the audience-reach cap on such ownership from 25 per cent to 35 per cent of television households.

3   The European Economic Community, established by the Treaty of Rome (1957) became the European Community (EC) in 1993 following the Maastricht Treaty. The Treaty also brought the three Communities (Euratom, ECSC, EEC) together under the newly created European Union.

4   In 2000 Hollinger sold many of its Canadian media assets, including most of its community weekly papers and smaller dailies.

7 Media markets

1   The sample did not include Southern Europe, so there are no figures for Spain.

2   See Anderson (1991: 37–46) on the discontinuities and interconnections between 'national print-languages', national consciousness and nation-states.

3   The six members of the EEC in 1958 (Belgium, France, West Germany, Italy, Luxembourg, Netherlands) were joined by Denmark, Ireland and the UK in 1973, Greece (1981), Portugal and Spain (1986), Austria, Finland and Sweden in 1995 (EU-15). In 2004, Cyprus, the Czech Republic, Estonia, Hungary, Latvia, Lithuania, Malta, Poland, Slovakia and Slovenia joined the enlarged EU, followed in 2007 by Romania and Bulgaria.

4   A conglomerate is a collection of firms or operations dealing in different products or services that is subject to central ownership and control.

5   For further reading see Thussu (2006: 86–92), Street (2001), Chenoweth (2001) and Page (2003).

6   Ranked by audiovisual turnover only, Time Warner was the largest media group worldwide until 2003, when Walt Disney overtook it. Time Warner's turnover in 2005 was $21,535 million, just behind Disney's $22,921m. The ranking for other media groups was (3) Sony $17,910m, (4) News Corp $16,258m, (5) NBC/NBC Universal $14,689m, (6) DirectTV group $13,165m, (7) CBS Corp $11, 440m, (8) Vivendi Universal $10,600m, (9) Viacom $9 325m, (10) Bertelsmann $8,546m, (European Observatory 2006b: 6-7).

7   This identifies companies by nationality of registered headquarters. News Corporation has since registered on the New York Stock Exchange. Sony, ranked third, includes several US acquisitions such as Metro-Goldwyn-Mayer.

8   For more information see McPhail 2006; Thussu 2006: 104–5.

9   The European Advertising and Media Forecast for 2007 was between 17 and 28 per cent growth for internet advertising (European Audiovisual Observatory 2006b: 66).

10 Portugal is not included in the data.

8 Western media and globalisation

1   The decline was modest in 2004 (three titles) but marked in 2003. One factor was France's channel M6 abandoning its partnership arrangements with American producers.

Bibliography

(Some book subtitles have been omitted for reasons of space.)

Adorno, T. and Horkheimer, M. (1979) [1944] *Dialectic of Enlightenment* (trans. J. Cummings), London: Verso.

Advisory Committee report on Public Interest Obligations of Digital Television Broadcasters (1998) *Charting the Digital Broadcasting Future*. Available at www.benton.org/publibrary/piac/report.html (accessed 2 March 2007).

Albarran, A. B. (2004) 'Media Economics', in J. Downing *et al.* (eds) *The Sage Handbook of Media Studies*, London: Sage.

Albarran, A. B. and Chan-Olmsted, S. (1998) *Global Media Economics*, Ames, IA: Iowa State University Press.

Alexa (2007) 'Top sites'. Available at www.alexa.com (accessed 10 September 2007).

Alger, D. (1998) *Megamedia*, Lanham, MD: Rowman and Littlefield.

Allan, S. (2004) *News Culture*, 2nd edn, Maidenhead: Open University Press.

Alterman, E. (2003) *What Liberal Media?* New York: Basic Books.

Altschull, J. H. (1984) *Agents of Power: The Role of the News Media in Human Affairs*, New York: Longman.

—— (1995) *Agents of Power: The Media and Public Policy*, New York: Longman.

Amin, S. (1988) *Eurocentrism*, London: Zed Books.

Andersen, R. and Strate, L. (2000) *Critical Studies in Media Commercialism*, Oxford: Oxford University Press.

Anderson, B. (1991) *Imagined Communities*, London: Verso.

Anderson, C. (2007) *The Long Tail*, New York: Random House.

Appadurai, A. (1996) *Modernity at Large: Cultural Dimensions of Globalization*, Minneapolis, MN: University of Minnesota Press.

Asp, K. and Esaiasson, P. (1996) 'The Modernization of Swedish Campaigns: Individualization, Professionalization, and Medialization', in D. Swanson and P. Mancini (eds) *Politics, Media and Modern Democracy*, New York: Praeger.

Attallah, P. (1996) 'A Brief History of Canadian Television', in J. Sinclair *et al.* (eds) *New Patterns in Global Television*, Oxford: Oxford University Press.

Atton, C. (2002) *Alternative Media*, London: Sage.

Aufderheide, P. (1999) *Communications Policy and the Public Interest: The Telecommunications Act of 1996*, New York: The Guilford Press.

Axford, B. (2000) 'The Transformation of Politics or Anti-Politics', in B. Axford and R. Huggins (eds) *New Media and Politics*, London: Sage.

Bagdikian, B. (1989) 'Conquering Hearts and Minds: The Lords of the Global Village', *The Nation* (New York), 12 June.

Bagdikian, B. (2004) *The New Media Monopoly*, Boston: Beacon.

Baker, C. (1997) *Global Television*, Oxford: Blackwell.

Baker, C. E. (1989) *Human Liberty and Freedom of Speech*, London: Oxford University Press.

—— (1994) *Advertising and a Democratic Press*, Princeton, NJ: Princeton University Press.

—— (2002) *Media, Markets, and Democracy*, Cambridge: Cambridge University Press.

—— (2007) *Media Concentration and Democracy*, Cambridge: Cambridge University Press.

Baldasty, G. J. (1992) *The Commercialization of News in the Nineteenth Century*, Wisconsin: University of Wisconsin Press.

'Bangemann Report' [High-Level Group of Experts on the Information Society] (1994) *Europe and the Global Information Society: Recommendations to the European Council*, Brussels: EC.

Bardoel, J. (1996) 'Beyond Journalism: A Profession Between Information Society and Civil Society', *European Journal of Communication* 11: 283–302.

Barendt, E. M. (1987) *Freedom of Speech*, Oxford: Clarendon Press.

—— (1993) *Broadcasting Law*, Oxford: Clarendon Press.

Barendt, E. M. and Hitchens, L. (2000) *Media Law*, London: Longman.

Barker, H. and Burrows, S. (eds) (2002) *Press, Politics and the Public Sphere in Europe and North America, 1760–1820*, Cambridge: Cambridge University Press.

Barnett, S. (1989) *Cross-media Ownership and its Impact on Public Opinion: A Case Study*, London: Broadcasting Research Unit.

Barnett, S. and Gaber, I. (2001) *Westminster Tales*, London: Continuum.

Barnett, S. and Seymour, E. (1999), *A Shrinking Iceberg Travelling South ... Changing Trends in British Television*, London: Campaign for Quality Television.

Beck, A. (ed.) (2003) *Cultural Work*, London: Routledge.

Beck, U. (2002) 'The Cosmopolitan Society and its Enemies', *Theory, Culture & Society*, 19 (1–2): 17–44.

—— (2003) 'The Analysis of Global Inequality: From National to Cosmopolitan Perspective', in *Global Civil Society 2003 Yearbook*. Available at www.lse.ac.uk/Depts/global/yearbook03chapters.htm (accessed 2 February 2007).

Belfield, R., Hird, C. and Kelly, S. (1991) *Murdoch: The Decline of an Empire*, London: MacDonald.

Bennett, W. L. (2003) 'The Internet and Global Activism', in N. Couldry and J. Curran (eds) *Contesting Media Power*, Lanham: Rowman and Littlefield.

—— (2004) *News: The Politics of Illusion*, 6th edn, New York: Longman.

Benson, R. and Hallin, D. (2004) 'How States, Markets and Globalization Shape the News: The French and American National Press, 1965–1997', paper presented at ICA 2005 Conference, New York [for a revised version see *European Journal of Communication* 22 (1): 27–48].

Benton Foundation (2007) *Public Interest Obligations of Digital Television Broadcasters Timeline 1995–2007*. Available at www.benton.org/index.php?q=node/4754 (accessed 28 October 2007).

Bhabha, H. (1994) *The Location of Culture*, London: Routledge.

Blumler, J. (ed.) (1992a) *Television and the Public Interest*, London: Sage.

—— (1992b) 'Before the Commercial Deluge', in J. Blumler (ed.) *Television and the Public Interest*, London: Sage.

Blumler, J. and Dahlgren, P. (2005) 'Political Communication in a Changing World', in J. Curran and M. Gurevitch (eds) *Mass Media and Society*, London: Hodder Arnold.

Blumler, J. and Gurevitch, M. (1975) 'Towards a comparative framework for political communication research', in S. H. Chaffee (ed.) *Political Communication*, London: Sage.

Blumler, J. and Gurevitch, M. (1995) *The Crisis of Public Communication*, London: Routledge.

—— '"Americanization" Reconsidered: US–UK Campaign Communication Comparisons Across Time', in W. L. Bennett and R. Entman (eds) *Mediated Politics*, Cambridge: Cambridge University Press.

—— (2005) 'Rethinking the Study of Political Communication', in J. Curran and M. Gurevitch (eds) *Mass Media and Society*, London: Hodder Arnold.

Boddy, W. (1998) 'The Beginning of American Television', in A. Smith (ed.) *Television: An International History*, Oxford: Oxford University Press.

Born, G. (2004) *Uncertain Vision*, London: Secker & Warburg.

Bourdieu, P. (1998) *On Television and Journalism*, London: Pluto.

Boyd-Barrett, O. (1977) 'Media Imperialism', in J. Curran, M. Gurevitch and J. Woolacott (eds) *Mass Communication and Society*, London: Arnold.

—— (1995) 'Early theories in media research', in O. Boyd-Barrett and C. Newbold (eds.), *Approaches to Media*, Arnold, London.

—— (1998) 'Media Imperialism reformulated', in D. K. Thussu (ed.) *Electronic Empires: Global Media and Local Resistance*, London: Arnold.

Brants, K. (2004) 'The Netherlands', in M. Kelly *et al.* (eds) *The Media in Europe*, London: Sage.

Brants, K. and de Bens, E. (2000) 'The Status of TV Broadcasting in Europe', in J. Wieten, G. Murdock and P. Dahlgren (eds) *Television Across Europe*, London: Sage.

Brants, K. and Siune, K. (1992) 'Public Broadcasting in a State of Flux', in K. Siune and W. Truetzschler (eds) *Dynamics of Media Politics*, London: Sage.

Brenner, R. (1998) 'Uneven Development and the Long Downturn: The Advanced Capitalist Economies from Boom to Stagnation, 1950–1998', *New Left Review* 1 (229): 1–267.

Briggs, A. and Burke, P. (2002) *A Social History of the Media*, Cambridge: Polity Press.

Brown, A. and Picard, R. G. (eds) (2005) *Digital Terrestrial Television in Europe*, Mahwah, NJ: Lawrence Erlbaum.

Brown, L. (1998) 'The American Networks', in A. Smith (ed.) *Television: An International History*, Oxford: Oxford University Press.

Browne, D. R. (1999) *Electronic Media and Industrialized Nations: A Comparative Study*, Ames, IA: Iowa State University Press.

BRU (Broadcasting Research Unit) (1985) *The Public Service Idea in British Broadcasting*, London: BRU.

Butler, D. and Kavanagh, D. (1997) *The British General Election of 1997*, Basingstoke: Palgrave.

Calhoun, C. (ed.) (1992a) *Habermas and the Public Sphere*, Cambridge, MA: MIT Press.

—— (1992b) 'Introduction', in C. Calhoun (ed.) *Habermas and the Public Sphere*, Cambridge, MA: MIT Press.

Caporaso, J. and Levine D. (1992) *Theories of Political Economy*, Cambridge: Cambridge University Press.

Castells, M. (1996) *The Information Age, Vol 1: The Rise of the Network Society*, Oxford: Blackwell.

Chadha, K. and Kavoori, A. (2005) 'Globalization and National Media Systems: Mapping Interactions in Policies, Markets and Formats', in J. Curran and M. Gurevitch (eds) *Mass Media and Society*, London: Arnold.

Chakravartty, P. and Sarikakis, K. (2006) *Media Policy and Globalization*, Edinburgh: Edinburgh University Press.

Chalaby, J. (1996) 'Journalism as an Anglo-American Invention: A Comparison of the Development of French and Anglo-American Journalism, 1830s–1920s', *European Journal of Communication* 11 (3): 303–26.

—— (1998) *The Invention of Journalism*, Basingstoke: Palgrave.

—— (ed.) (2005) *Transnational Television Worldwide*, New York: I. B. Tauris.

Chan-Olmsted, S. M. and Chang, B.-H. (2003) 'Diversification Strategy of Global Media Conglomerates: Examining Its Patterns and Determinants', *Journal of Media Economics* 16 (4), 213–33.

Chapman, J. (2005) *Comparative Media History*, Cambridge: Polity Press.

Charon, J.-M. (2004) 'France', in M. Kelly *et al.* (eds) *The Media in Europe*, London: Sage.

Chenoweth, N. (2001) *Virtual Murdoch*, London: Secker and Warburg.

Clifford, J. and Marcus, G. E. (eds) (1986) *Writing Culture*, Berkeley, University of California Press.

Cockburn, C. (1991) *Brothers*, 2nd edn, London: Pluto.

CoE (Council of Europe) (1997) *Report on Media Concentrations and Pluralism in Europe*, (MM-CM) Strasbourg: Council of Europe.

—— (2000) *Case-law Concerning Article 10 of the European Convention on Human Rights*, DH-MM 6, Strasbourg: Council of Europe.

—— (2003) *Media Diversity in Europe*, Strasbourg: Council of Europe.

—— (2004) *Transnational Media Concentrations in Europe*, Strasbourg: Council of Europe.

Cole, B. and Oettinger, M. (1978) *Reluctant Regulators*, Reading, MA: Addison-Wesley.

Coleman, J. and Rollet, B. (1997) *Television in Europe*, London: Intellect.

Collins, R. (1994) *Broadcasting and Audio-Visual Policy in the European Single Market*, Luton: John Libbey.

Collins, R. and Murroni, C. (1996) *New Media, New Policies*, Cambridge: Polity Press.

Collins, R., Garnham, N. and Locksley, G. (1988) *The Economics of Television*, London: Sage.

Compaine, B. (2000) 'The Myths of Encroaching Media Ownership', OpenDemocracy, at www.opendemocracy.net/media-globalmediaownership/article_87.jsp, (accessed September 2007).

Compaine, B. and Gomery, D. (2000) *Who Owns the Media?* Mahwah, NJ: Lawrence Erlbaum.

Comstock, G. (1989) *The Evolution of American Television*, London: Sage.

Congdon, T., Graham, A., Green, D. and Robinson, B. (1995) *The Cross Media Revolution*, Luton: John Libbey.

Cottle, S. (ed.) (2000a) *Ethnic Minorities and the Media*, Maidenhead: Open University Press.

—— (2000b) 'Media Research and Ethnic Minorities: Mapping the Field', in *Ethnic Minorities and the Media*, Maidenhead: Open University Press.

Couldry, N. (2000a) *The Place of Media Power*, London: Routledge.

—— (2000b) *Inside Culture*, London: Sage.

—— (2003) 'Beyond the Hall of Mirrors? Some Theoretical Reflections on the Global Contestation of Media Power', in N. Couldry and J. Curran (eds) *Contesting Media Power*, Lanham, MD: Rowman and Littlefield.

Couldry, N. (2005) 'Comparing Media Systems: Three Models of Media and Politics', *Political Studies Review* 3 (2), 304–16.

Couldry, N. and Curran, J. (eds) (2003) *Contesting Media Power*, Lanham, MD: Rowman and Littlefield.

Croteau, D. and Hoynes, W. (2006) *The Business of Media*, 2nd edn, Thousand Oaks, CA: Pine Forge.

Cunningham, S. and Flew, T. (2000) 'De-Westernizing Australia? Media Systems and Cultural Coordinates', in J. Curran and M.-J. Park (eds) *De-Westernizing Media Studies*, London: Routledge.

Curran, J. (1978) 'Advertising and the Press', in J. Curran (ed.) *The British Press*, London: Macmillan.

Curran, J. (1986) ' The impact of advertising on the British mass media', in R. Collins, J. Curran, N. Garnham, P. Scannell and C. Sparks (eds) *Media, Culture and Society: A Critical Reader*, London: Sage.

—— (1990) 'Culturalist Perspectives of News Organizations: A Reappraisal and a Case Study', in M. Ferguson (ed.) *Public Communication*, London: Sage.

—— (1991) 'Rethinking the Media as a Public Sphere', in P. Dahlgren and C. Sparks (eds) *Communication and Citizenship*, London: Routledge.

—— (1996) 'Mass Media and Democracy Revisited', in J. Curran and M. Gurevitch (eds) *Mass Media and Society*, London: Arnold.

—— (ed.) (2000) *Media Organisations in Society*, London: Arnold.

—— (2000) 'Press Reformism 1918–98: A Study of Failure', in H. Tumber (ed.) *Media Power, Professionals and Policies*, London: Routledge.

—— (2002a) *Media and Power*, London: Routledge.

—— (2002b) 'Renewing the radical tradition', in J. Curran, *Media and Power*, London: Routledge.

—— (2002c) 'Rival Narratives of Media History', in J. Curran, *Media and Power*, London: Routledge.

—— (2002d) 'Media and Democracy: The Third Way', in J. Curran, *Media and Power*, London: Routledge.

—— (2002e) 'Global Media Concentration: Shifting the Argument', OpenDemocracy, www.opendemocracy.net/media-globalmediaownership/article_37.jsp (accessed September 2007)

—— (2003a) 'New Media in Britain', in J. Curran and J. Seaton (eds) *Power Without Responsibility*, London: Routledge.

—— (2003b) 'Central Debates in Media Politics', in J. Curran and J. Seaton, *Power Without Responsibility*, London: Routledge.

—— (2004) 'The Rise of the Westminster School', in A. Calabrese and C. Sparks (eds) *Toward a Political Economy of Culture*, Lanham, MD: Rowman and Littlefield

Curran, J. and Gurevitch, M. (1977) 'The Audience', *Mass Communication and Society Block 3*, Milton Keynes: Open University Press.

—— (2005) *Mass Media and Society*, 4th edn, London: Arnold.

Curran, J. and Leys, C. (2000) 'Media and the decline of liberal corporatism in Britain', in J. Curran and M.-J. Park (eds) *De-Westernizing Media Studies*, London: Routledge.

Curran, J. and Park, M.-J. (eds) (2000a) *De-Westernizing Media Studies*, London: Routledge.

—— (2000b) 'Beyond globalization theory', in *De-Westernizing Media Studies*, London: Routledge.

Curran, J. and Seaton, J. (1997) *Power without Responsibility: The Press and Broadcasting in Britain*, 5th edn, London: Routledge.

Curran, J. and Seaton, J. (2003) *Power without Responsibility*, 6th edn, London: Routledge.

Dahlgren, P. (1995) *Television and the Public Sphere*, London: Routledge.

—— (2000) 'Key Trends in European Television', in J. Wieten, G. Murdock and P. Dahlgren (eds) *Television Across Europe*, London: Sage.

—— (2001a) 'The transformation of democracy', in B. Axford and R. Huggins (eds) *New Media and Politics*, London: Sage.

—— (2001b) 'The Public Sphere and the Net: Structure Space and Communication', in W. L. Bennett and R. Entman (eds) *Mediated Politics*, Cambridge: Cambridge University Press.

Dahlgren, P. and Gurevitch, M. (2005) 'Political Communication in a Changing World', in J. Curran and M. Gurevitch (2005) *Mass Media and Society*, London: Arnold.

Dahlgren, P. and Sparks, C. (eds) (1991) *Communication and Citizenship*, London: Routledge.

'Davies Committee' (1999) *The Future Funding of the BBC*, Report of the Independent Review Panel, chaired by G. Davies, London: DCMS 1999.

Davis, A. (2002) *Public Relations Democracy*, Manchester: Manchester University Press.

—— (2003) 'Whither Mass Media and Power? Evidence for a Critical Elite Theory Alternative', *Media, Culture and Society* 25 (5): 669–90.

Deacon, D. (2003) 'Holism, Communion and Conversion: Integrating Media Consumption and Production Research', *Media, Culture and Society* 25: 209–31.

De Bens, E. (2004) 'Belgium', in M. Kelly *et al.* (eds) *The Media in Europe*, London: Sage.

De Bens, E. and De Smaele, H. (2001) 'The Inflow of American Television Fiction on European Broadcasting Channels Revisited', *European Journal of Communication* 16 (1): 51–76.

De Bens, E., Kelly, M. and Bakke, M. (1992) 'Television Content: Dallasification of Culture?', in K. Siune and W. Truetzschler (eds) *Dynamics of Media Politics*, London: Sage.

d'Haenens, L. and Saeys, F. (2001) *Western Broadcasting at the Dawn of the 21st Century*, Berlin: Mouton de Gruyter.

Delli Carpini, M. and Williams, B. (2001) 'Let Us Infotain You: Politics in the New Media Environment', in W. L. Bennett and R. Entman (eds) *Mediated Politics*, Cambridge: Cambridge University Press.

de Mateo, R. (2004) 'Spain', in M. Kelly *et al.* (eds) *The Media in Europe*, London: Sage

de Moragas Spà, M. and López, B. (2000) 'Decentralization Processes and "Proximate Television"', in G. Wang, J. Servaes and A. Goonasekera (eds) *The New Communications Landscape*, London: Routledge.

de Moragas Spà, M., Garitaonandía, C. and López, B. (1999) *Television on Your Doorstep: Decentralization Experiences in the European Union*, Luton: University of Luton Press.

Department of National Heritage (1995) *Media Ownership: The Government's Proposals*, London: HMSO.

Dimock, M. and Popkin, S. (1997) 'Political Knowledge in Comparative Perspective', in S. Iyengar and R. Reeves (eds) *Do the Media Govern?* Thousand Oaks, CA: Sage.

Donoghue, B. (1987) *Prime Minister*, London: Jonathan Cape.

Donsbach, W. (1995) 'Lapdogs, Watchdogs and Junkyard Dogs', *Media Studies Journal* 9 (4): 17–30.

Downey, J. (2006) 'The Media Industries: Do Ownership, Size and Internationalisation Matter?' in D. Hesmondhalgh (ed.) *Media Production*, Maidenhead: Open University Press.

Downing, J. (1996) *Internationalizing Media Theory*, London: Sage.

—— (2001) *Radical Media*, London: Sage.

Downing, J., McQuail D., Schlesinger, P., Wartella, E. (eds) (2004) *The Sage Handbook of Media Studies*, London: Sage.

Doyle, G. (1999) 'Convergence: "A Unique Opportunity to Evolve in Previously Unthought-of-ways" or a Hoax?', in C. Marsden and S. Verhulst (eds) *Convergence in European Digital TV Regulation*, London: Blackstone Press.

—— (2002a) *Media Ownership*, London: Sage.

—— (2002b) *Understanding Media Economics*, London: Sage.

DTI/DCMS (1998) *Regulating Communications: Approaching Convergence in the Information Age*, Cmd. 4022, London: The Stationery Office.

—— (2000) *A New Future for Communications*, Cm 5010. London: The Stationery Office.

Du Gay, P. (ed.) (1997) *Production of Culture/Cultures of Production*, London: Sage.

Dyson, K. and Humphreys, P. (eds) (1990) *The Political Economy of Communications*, London: Routledge.

Dyson, K. and Humphreys, P., with Negrine, R. and Simon, J.-P. (1988) *Broadcasting and New Media Policies in Western Europe*, London: Routledge.

EBU (European Broadcasting Union) (2006) *Volume 2: EBU Members' Audience Trends*, June, Geneva: EBU.

EC (European Commission) [formally the Commission of the European Communities] (1983) *Interim report. Realities and Tendencies in European Television*, Com (83) 229 final, Brussels: European Commission.

—— (1992) *Pluralism and Media Concentration in the Internal Market. An Assessment of the Need for Community Action*, COM (92) 480 final, Brussels: European Commission.

—— (1994) *Communication from the Commission to the Council and the EP*, COM (4) 353 final, Brussels: European Commission.

—— (1997) *Protocol on Public Service Broadcasting*, Treaty of Amsterdam. Available at eur-lex.europa.eu/LexUriServ/LexUriServ.do?uri=OJ:C:2004:310:0372:0372:EN: PDF (accessed 28 August 2007).

—— (2006) *Broadband Coverage in Europe*, DG INFSO, Brussels: European Commission.

—— (2007a) *Newly Modified Commission Proposal for an Audiovisual Media Services Directive*, Brussels: European Commission.

—— (2007b) *MEMO/07/206* (24 May 2007), Brussels: European Commission.

—— (2007c) *Media pluralism in the Member States of the European Union*, SEC. Brussels: European Commission.

Edelstein, A. (1982) *Comparative Communication Research*, Beverly Hills, CA: Sage.

Eldridge, J. (1993) 'News, Truth and Power', in J. Eldridge (ed.) *Getting the Message*, London: Routledge.

Emery, M. and Emery, E. (1996) *The Press and America*, 8th edn, Boston, MA: Allyn and Bacon.

Entman, R. (1985) 'The Marketplace of Ideas Revisited: Newspaper Competition and First Amendment Ideals: Does Monopoly Matter?', *Journal of Communication* 35 (3): 147–65.

—— (1993) 'Framing: Toward Clarification of a Fractured Paradigm', *Journal of Communication* 43 (4): 51–8.

—— (2005) 'Media and Democracy without Party Competition', in J. Curran and M. Gurevitch (eds) *Mass Media and Society*, London: Hodder Arnold.

Esser, F., Reinemann, C. and Fan, D. (2001) 'Metacommunication about Media Manipulation: Spin Doctors in the United States, Great Britain, and Germany', *Harvard International Journal of Press/Politics* 6 (1): 16–45.

Eurobarometer (1999) *Public Opinion in the European Union*, Report No. 51, Brussels: European Commission.

—— (2002) *Europeans' participation in cultural activities*, Brussels: European Commission.

—— (2007) *E-Communications Household Survey*, Brussels: European Commission.

European Audiovisual Observatory (2004) *Transfrontier Television in the European Union*, Background paper for Ministerial Conference organised by the Irish Presidency, Strasbourg: European Audiovidual Observatory.

—— (2005a) *Yearbook 2005* Volume 4.

—— (2005b) *Yearbook 2005* Volume 5.

—— (2006a) *Yearbook 2007* Volume 1.

—— (2006b) *Yearbook 2007* Volume 2.

European Council (1989) *Directive 89/552/EEC, on the co-ordination of certain provisions laid down by law, regulation or administrative action in Member States concerning the pursuit of television broadcast activities*, OJ 1989 L298/23. Brussels: European Commission.

European Parliament (1996) *The Future of Public Service Television in a Multi-channel Digital Age*, A4-0243/1996, Brussels: European Parliament.

Evans, H. (1994) [1983] *Good Times, Bad Times*, London: Phoenix.

FCC (2002) *Consumer Survey on Media Usage 8*, Nielsen Media Research, Washington, DC: FCC.

Featherstone, M. (1996) 'Localism, Globalism and Cultural Identity', in R. Wilson and W. Dissanayake (eds) *Global/Local*, Durham, NC: Duke University Press.

Feintuck, M. and Varney, M. (2006) *Media Regulation, Public Interest and the Law*, Edinburgh: Edinburgh University Press.

Feldman, D. (1993) *Civil Liberties and Human Rights in England and Wales*, Oxford: Clarendon Press.

Ferguson, M. (ed.) (1990) *Public Communication*, London: Sage.

—— (1992) 'The Mythology about Globalization', *European Journal of Communication*, 7: 69–93.

Ferguson, M. and Golding, P. (eds) (1997) *Cultural Studies in Question*, London: Sage.

Ferreras, I. (2007) 'Over 4.2 million Spanish get DTT', Rapid TV News (14 November). Available at www.rapidtvnews.com.

Fiske, J. (1990) *Introduction to Communication Studies*, 2nd edn, London: Routledge.

Flew, T. (2002) 'Broadcasting and the Social Contract', in M. Raboy (ed.) *Global Media Policy*, Luton: University of Luton Press.

—— (2007) *Understanding Global Media*, Basingstoke, Hampshire: Palgrave.

Foley, C., Bryan, C. and Hardy, J. (1994) *Censored: Freedom of Expression and Human Rights*, London: Liberty.

Franklin, B. (1994) *Packaging Politics*, London: Arnold.

—— (1997) *Newszak and News Media*, London: Arnold.

Freedman, D. (2003) *Television Policies of the Labour Party 1951–2001*, London: Frank Cass.

—— (2004) 'Internet Transformations: "Old" Media Resilience in the "New Media" Revolution', in J. Curran and D. Morley (eds) *Media and Cultural Theory*, London: Routledge.

Freedom House (2006) *Freedom of the Press 2005*. Available at www.freedomhouse.org/template.cfm?page=251&year=2006 (accessed 20 April 2007).

Frith, S. (1996) 'Entertainment', in J. Curran and M. Gurevitch (eds) *Mass Media and Society*, London: Arnold.

Galperin, H. (2004) *New Television, Old Politics: The Transition to Digital Television in the United States and Britain*, Cambridge: Cambridge University Press.

Gandy, O. H. (1982) *Beyond Agenda Setting*, Norwood, NJ: Ablex.

—— (2004) 'Audiences on Demand', in A. Calabrese and C. Sparks (eds) *Towards a Political Economy of Culture*, Lanham, MD: Rowman and Littlefield.

Gans, H. (1980) *Deciding What's News*, London: Constable.

—— (2003) *Democracy and the News*, Oxford: Oxford University Press.

García Canclini, N. (1995) *Hybrid Cultures*, Minneapolis, MN: University of Minnesota Press.

Gardini, F. and Galperin, H. (2005) 'Italy: Slow Penetration, High Potential?', in A. Brown and R. Picard (eds) *Digital Terrestrial Television in Europe*, Mahwah, NJ: Lawrence Erlbaum.

Garnham, N. (1990) *Capitalism and Communications*, London: Sage.

—— (1992) 'The Media and the Public Sphere', in C. Calhoun (ed.) *Habermas and the Public Sphere*, Cambridge, MA: MIT Press.

—— (1996) 'Constraints on Multi-media Convergence', in W. Dutton (ed.), *Information and Communication Technologies*, Oxford: Oxford University Press.

Garnham, N. (2000) *Emancipation, the Media and Modernity*, Oxford: Oxford University Press.

Gibbons, T. (1992) 'Freedom of the press: ownership and editorial values', *Public Law* (Summer): 279–99.

—— (1998) *Regulating the Media*, 2nd edn, London: Sweet & Maxwell.

Giddens, A. (1999) 'Runaway World', The BBC Reith Lectures. Available at http://news.bbc.co.uk/hi/english/static/events/reith_99/ (accessed 25 October 2007).

Giles, F. (1986) *Sundry Times*, London: John Murray.

Gillespie, M. (2000) 'Transnational communications and diaspora communities', in S. Cotttle (ed.), *Ethnic Minorities and the Media*, Buckingham: Open University Press.

Gilroy, P. (1992) *The Black Atlantic*, London: Verso.

Gitlin, T (1991) 'Bites and Blips: Chunk News, Savvy Talk and the Bifurcation of American Politics', in P. Dahlgren and C. Sparks (eds) *Communication and Citizenship*, London: Routledge.

—— (2002) 'The Unification of the World under the Signs of Mickey Mouse and Bruce Willis: The Supply and Demand Sides of American Popular Culture', in J. M. Chan and B. T. McIntyre (eds) *In Search of Boundaries*, Westport, CT: Ablex.

Goldberg, D., Prosser, T. and Verhulst, S. (1998a) *Regulating the Changing Media: A Comparative Study*, Oxford: Oxford University Press.

—— (1998b) *EC Media Law and Policy*, London: Longman.

Golding, P. and Ferguson, M. (eds) (1997) *Cultural Studies in Question*, London: Sage.

Golding, P., Ferguson, M. and Murdock, G. (1996) 'Culture, Communication and Political Economy', in J. Curran and M. Gurevitch (eds) *Mass Media and Society*, London: Arnold.

Goldsmiths Media Group (2000) 'Central Issues', in J. Curran (ed.) *Media Organisations in Society*, London: Arnold.

Goodwin, P. (1998) *Television under the Tories*, London: BFI.

Gorman, L. and McLean, D. (2003) *Media and Society in the Twentieth Century*, Oxford: Blackwell.

Graham, A. and Davies, G. (1997) *Broadcasting, Society and Policy in the Multimedia Age*, Luton: John Libbey.

Graham, A. *et al.* (1999) *Public Purposes in Broadcasting*, Luton: University of Luton Press.

Greenslade, R. (2003) 'Their Master's Voice', *Guardian* (17 February).

Gunaratne, S. A. (2001) 'Prospects and Limitations of World System Theory for Media Analysis', *Gazette* 63 (2–3): 121–48.

Gunther, R. and Mughan, A. (eds) (2000) *Democracy and the Media*, Cambridge: Cambridge University Press.

Gupta, A. and Ferguson, J. (1992) 'Beyond Culture: Space, Identity, and the Politics of Difference', *Cultural Anthropology* 7: 6–23.

Gurevitch, M. and Blumler, J. (1977) 'Linkages between the Mass Media and Politics: a Model for the Analysis of Political Communication Systems', in J. Curran *et al.* (eds) *Mass Communication and Society*, London: Arnold.

—— (2004) 'State of the Art for Comparative Political Communication Research: Poised for Maturity?', in F. Esser and B. Pfetsch (eds) *Comparing Political Communication*, Cambridge: Cambridge University Press.

Gustafsson, K. E. and Weibull, L. (1997) 'European newspaper readership. Structure and development', *European Journal of Communication Research* 22: 249–74.

Habermas, Jürgen (1989) [1962] *The Structural Transformation of the Public Sphere*, (trans. T. Burger), Cambridge: Polity Press.

Hadenius, S. and Weibull, L. (1999) 'The Swedish Newspaper System in the Late 1990s', *The Nordicom Review* 20: 129–52.

Hafez, K. (2007) *The Myth of Media Globalization* (trans. A. Skinner), Cambridge: Polity Press.

Hall, S. (1991) 'The Local and the Global: Globalization and Ethnicity', in A. King (ed.) *Culture, Globalization and World-System*, Basingstoke: Macmillan.

—— (1992) 'The West and the Rest: Discourse and Power', in S. Hall and B. Gieben (eds) *Formations of Modernity*, Cambridge: Polity Press.

—— (1993) 'Encoding and Decoding in Television Discourse', in S. During (ed.) *The Cultural Studies Reader*, London: Routledge.

Hallin, D. (2000) 'Commercialism and Professionalism in the American News Media', in J. Curran and M. Gurevitch (eds) *Mass Media and Society*, London: Arnold.

Hallin, D. and Mancini, P. (2004a) *Comparing Media Systems: Three Models of Media and Politics*, Cambridge: Cambridge University Press.

—— (2004b) 'Americanization, Globalization and Secularization', in F. Esser and B. Pfetsch (eds) *Comparing Political Communication*, Cambridge: Cambridge University Press.

—— (2005) 'Comparing Media Systems', in J. Curran and M. Gurevitch (eds) *Mass Media and Society*, London: Arnold.

Hamelink, C. (2002) 'The Civil Society Challenge to Global Media Policy', in M. Raboy (ed.) *Global Media Policy in the New Millennium*, Luton: University of Luton.

Harcourt, A. (1996) 'Regulating for Media Concentration: The Emerging Policy of the European Union', *Utilities Law Review* 7 (5): 202–10.

—— (2005) *The European Union and the Regulation of Media Markets*, Manchester: Manchester University Press.

Hardy, J. (2004a) 'Convergence and Commercial Speech: A Study of the Dynamics and the Regulation of Cross-media Promotion in UK Media', unpublished PhD thesis, University of London.

Hardy, J. (2004b) 'Safe in Their Hands? New Labour and Public Service Broadcasting', *Soundings* 27: 100–14.

Hart, R. (1999) *Seducing America: How Television Charms the Modern Voter*, New York: Oxford University Press.

Hartley, J. (1996) *Popular Reality*, London: Arnold.

Harvey, S. (2002) 'Policy', in A. Briggs and P. Cobey (eds) *The Media: An Introduction*, 2nd edn, Harlow, Essex: Longman.

Head, S. W. (1985) *World Broadcasting Systems: A Comparative Analysis*, Belmont, CA: Wadsworth.

Held, D. (1996) *Models of Democracy*, 2nd edn, Cambridge: Polity Press.

Held, D. and McGrew, A. (2000) 'The Great Globalization Debate: An Introduction' *The Global Transformations Reader*, Cambridge: Polity Press.

Held, D., McGrew, A., Goldblatt, D. and Perraton, J. (1999) *Global Transformations*, Cambridge: Polity Press.

Herman, E. (1999) 'The Propaganda Model Revisited', in *The Myth of the Liberal Media*, New York: Peter Lang.

Herman, E. and Chomsky, N. (1994) [1988] *Manufacturing Consent*, New York: Pantheon.

Herman, E. and McChesney, R. (1997) *The Global Media*, London: Cassell.

Hesmondhalgh, D. (2002) *The Cultural Industries*, London: Sage.

—— (2007) *The Cultural Industries*, 2nd edn, London: Sage.

Hickethier, K. (2006) 'The Media in Germany', in T. Weymouth and B. Lamizet (eds) *Markets and Myths*, Harlow: Longman.

Hird, C. (1994) 'Reach for the Skies', *Index on Censorship* Vol. 23 (Sept/Oct): 27–37.

Hirst, P. and Thompson, G. (1996) *Globalization in Question*, Cambridge: Polity Press.

Hitchens, L. P. (1994) 'Media Ownership and Controls: A European Approach', *Modern Law Review* (57): 585–601.

Hitchens, L. P. (1995) '"Get ready, fire, take aim", The Regulation of Cross Media Ownership – an Exercise in Policy Making', *Public Law* (Winter): 620–41.

Hobsbawm, E. (1994) *Age of Extremes: The Short Twentieth Century 1914–1991*, London: Penguin.

Hobsbawm, E. and Ranger, T. (eds) (1983) *The Invention of Tradition*, Cambridge: Cambridge University Press.

Hoffmann-Riem, W. (1992) 'Protecting Vulnerable Values in the German Broadcasting Order', in J. Blumler (ed.) *Television and the Public Interest*, London: Sage.

—— (1996a) *Regulating Media: the Licencing and Supervision of Broadcasting in Six Countries*, New York: Guilford Press.

—— (1996b) 'New Challenges for European Multimedia Policy: A German Perspective', *European Journal of Communication* 11 (3): 327–46.

Horgan, J. (2001) *Irish Media*, London: Routledge.

Horsman, M. (1998) *Sky High*, London: Orion.

Horwitz, R. (1989) *The Irony of Regulatory Reform*, New York: Oxford University Press.

Hoskins, C., McFadyen, S. and Finn, A. (1997) *Global Television and Film*, Oxford: Oxford University Press.

—— (2004) *Media Economics*, Thousand Oaks, CA: Sage.

Hoynes, W. (1994) *Public Television for Sale*, Boulder, CO: Westview Press.

—— (2002) 'Why Media Mergers Matter', OpenDemocracy, www.opendemocracy.net/media-globalmediaownership/article_47.jsp (accessed September 2007)

Huang, C. (2003) 'Transitional Media vs. Normative Theories: Schramm, Altschull, and China', *Journal of Communication* 53: 444–59.

Hujanen, T. (2005) 'Implications for Public Service Broadcasters', in A. Brown and R. G. Picard (eds) *Digital Terrestrial Television in Europe*, Mahwah, NJ: Lawrence Erlbaum.

Hultén, O. (2004) 'Sweden', in M. Kelly *et al.* (eds) *The Media in Europe*, London: Sage.

Hultén, O. and Brants, K. (1992) 'Public Service Broadcasting Reactions to Competition', in K. Siune and W. Truetzscher (eds) *Dynamics of Media Politics*, London: Sage.

Humphreys, P. (1996) *Mass Media and Media Policy in Western Europe*, Manchester University Press.

—— (2000) 'Regulating for Pluralism in a Digital Age', in T. Lees, S. Ralph and J. Langham Brown (eds) *Is Regulation Still an Option in a Digital Universe?* Luton: University of Luton Press.

Hutton, W. (1996) *The State We're In*, London: Vintage.

Innis, H. (1991) *The Bias of Communication* [1951], Toronto: University of Toronto Press.

Iosifides, P. (1997) 'Methods of measuring media concentration', *Media Culture and Society* 19 (4): 643–63.

Iosifides, P., Steemers, J. and Wheeler, M. (2005) *European Television Industries*, London: BFI.

Jakubowicz, K. (2003) 'Bringing Public Service Broadcasting to Account', in G. F. Lowe and T. Hujanen (eds) *Broadcasting and Convergence: New Articulations of the Public Service Remit*, Gothenberg: Nordicom.

Jenkins, H. (2001) 'Convergence? I Diverge', *Technology Review* (June).

Karim, K. (ed.) (2003) *The Media of Diaspora*, London: Routledge.

Katz, H. (1989) 'The Future of Public Broadcasting in the US', *Media, Culture and Society* 11: 195–205.

Katzenstein, P. J. (1985) *Small States in World Markets: Industrial Policy in Europe*, Ithaca, NY: Cornell University Press.

Keane, J. (1991) *The Media and Democracy*, Cambridge: Polity Press.

—— (1998) *Civil Society*, Cambridge: Polity Press.

Kelly, M. (1983) 'Influences on Broadcasting Policies for Election Coverage', in J. Blumler (ed.) *Communicating to Voters: Television in the First European Parliamentary Elections*, London: Sage.

Kelly, M., Mazzoleni, G., McQuail, D. (eds) (2004) *The Media in Europe*, London: Sage.

King, A. (1998) 'Thatcherism and the Emergence of Sky Television', *Media, Culture and Society* 20: 277–93.

King, R. and Wood, N. (eds) (2001) *Media and Migration*, London: Routledge.

Kleinsteuber, H. (2004) 'Germany', in M. Kelly *et al.* (eds) *The Media in Europe*, London: Sage.

Kuhn, R. (1995) *The Media in France*, London: Routledge.

Kunz, W. M. (2007) *Culture Conglomerates*, Lanham, MD: Rowman and Littlefield.

Lange, A. and Van Loon, A. (1991) *Pluralism, Concentration and Competition in the Media Sector*, Strasbourg: Council of Europe.

Lee, C.-C., Chan, J., Pan, Z. and So, C. (2005) 'National Prisms of a Global "Media Event"', in J. Curran and M. Gurevitch (eds) *Mass Media and Society*, London: Arnold.

Levy, D. (1999) *Europe's Digital Revolution*, London: Routledge.

Leys, C. (2001) *Market-Driven Politics*, London: Verso.

Lichtenberg, J. (ed.) (1990) *Democracy and the Mass Media*, Cambridge: Cambridge University Press.

Lijphart, A. (1971) 'Comparative Politics and Comparative Method', *American Political Science Review* 65 (3): 682–93.

—— (1999) *Patterns of Democracy: Government Forms and Performance in Thirty-Six Countries*, New Haven, CT: Yale University Press.

Lister, M. *et al.* (2003) *New Media: A Critical Introduction*, London: Routledge

Livingstone, S. (2003) 'On the Challenges of Cross-national Comparative Research', *European Journal of Communication* 18 (4): 477–500.

Lorimer, R. and Gasher, M. (2004) *Mass Communication in Canada*, 5th edn, Oxford: Oxford University Press.

McAllister, M. (1996) *The Commercialization of American Culture*, Thousand Oaks, CA: Sage.

—— (2000) 'From Flick to Flack: The Increased Emphasis on Marketing by Media Entertainment Corporations', in R. Andersen and L. Strate (eds) *Critical Studies in Media Commercialism*, Oxford: Oxford University Press.

McChesney, R. (1993) *Telecommunications, Mass Media and Democracy*, New York: Oxford University Press.

—— (1998) 'The Political Economy of Global Communication', in R. McChesney, E. M. Wood and J. B. Foster (eds) *Capitalism and the Information Age*, New York: Monthly Review Press.

—— (1999) *Rich Media, Poor Democracy*, Urbana, IL: University of Illinois Press.

—— (2000) 'The Titanic Sails On – Why the Internet Won't Sink the Media Giants', *EXTRA!* Journal of FAIR (March–April).

—— (2002) 'The Global Restructuring of Media Ownership', in M. Raboy (ed.) *Global Media Policy in the New Millennium*, Luton: University of Luton Press.

—— (2003) 'September 11 and the Structural Limits of US Journalism', in S. Allen and B. Zelizer (eds*) Journalism after September 11*, London: Routledge.

McChesney, R. (2004) *The Problem of the Media*, New York: Monthly Review Press.

McChesney, R. and Scott, B. (2004) *Our Unfree Press*, New York: The New Press

McCombs, M. (2004) *Setting the Agenda*, Cambridge: Polity Press.

McGuigan, J. (1992) *Cultural Populism*, London: Routledge.

—— (1996) *Culture and the Public Sphere*, London: Routledge.

—— (1998) 'What Price the Public Sphere?', in D. K. Thussu (ed.) *Electronic Empires*, London: Arnold.

MacKay, H. (2000) 'The Globalization of Culture?', in D. Held (ed.) *A Globalizing World?* London: Routledge.

McKercher, C. (2001) 'Commerce versus Culture: The Print Media in Canada and Mexico', in V. Mosco and D. Schiller (eds) *Continental Order?* Lanham, MD: Rowman and Littlefield.

McKinsey and Co. (2004) *Review of Public Service Broadcasting Around the World*, London: McKinsey and Co.

MacLeod, V. (ed.) (1996) *Media Ownership and Control in the Age of Convergence*, London: International Institute of Communications.

McLeod, J. and Blumler J. (1989) 'The Macrosocial Level of Communication Science', in C. Berger and S. Chaffee (eds) *Handbook of Communication Science*, California: Sage.

McLuhan, M. (1994) [1964] *Understanding Media*, Cambridge, MA: MIT Press.

McManus, J. (1994) *Market-driven Journalism*, Thousand Oaks, CA: Sage.

McNair, B. (1998) *The Sociology of Journalism*, London: Arnold.

—— (2003) *An Introduction to Political Communication*, 3rd edn, London: Routledge.

—— (2006) *Cultural Chaos*, London: Routledge

McPhail, T. (2006) *Global Communication*, 2nd edn, London: Blackwell.

McQuail, D. (1983) *Mass Communication Theory*, London: Sage.

—— (1987) *Mass Communication Theory*, 2nd edn, London: Sage.

—— (1992) *Media Performance*, London: Sage.

—— (1994) *Mass Communication Theory*, 3rd edn, London: Sage.

—— (2005a) *Mass Communication Theory*, 5th edn, London: Sage.

—— (2005b) 'Comparing Media Systems: Three Models of Media and Politics', *European Journal of Communication* 20 (2): 266–8.

McQuail, D. and Siune, K. (1992) 'Wake up, Europe!', in K. Siune and W. Truetzschler (eds) *Dynamics of Media Politics*, London: Sage.

—— (eds) (1998) *Media Policy*, London: Sage.

Magder, T. (1993) *Canada's Hollywood*, Toronto: University of Toronto Press.

—— (1998) 'Franchising the Candy Store: Split-Run Magazines and a New International Regime for Trade in Culture', *Canadian-American Public Policy*, 34, Orono: The Canadian-American Center.

Mancini, P. (1991) 'The Public Sphere and the Use of News in a "Coalition" System of Government', in P. Dahlgren and C. Sparks (eds) *Communication and Citizenship*, London: Routledge.

—— (2000) 'Political complexity and alternative models of journalism: The Italian case' in J.Curran and M.-J. Parks (eds) *De-Westernizing Media Studies*, London: Routledge.

Mancini, P. and Swanson, D. (1996) 'Politics, Media and Modern Democracy: Introduction', in D. L. Swanson and P. Mancini (eds) *Politics, Media and Modern Democracy*, New York: Praeger.

Manning, P. (2001) *News and News Sources*, London: Sage.

Marletti, C. and Roncarolo, F. (2000) 'Media Influence in the Italian Transition from a Consensual to a Majoritarian Democracy', in R. Gunther and A. Mughan (eds) *Democracy and the Media*, Cambridge: Cambridge University Press.

Marsden, C. and Verhulst, S. (eds) (1999) *Convergence in European Digital TV Regulation*, London: Blackstone Press.

Marsden, C. and Ariño, M. (2005) 'From Analogue to Digital', in A. Brown and R. G. Picard (eds) *Digital Terrestrial Television in Europe*, Mahwah, NJ: Lawrence Erlbaum.

Martin-Barbero, J. (1993) *Communication, Culture and Hegemony*, London: Sage.

Mattelart, A. (1991) *Advertising International* (trans. M. Channan), London: Routledge.

—— (1994) *Mapping World Communication* (trans. S. Emanuel and J. A. Cohen), Minneapolis, MN: University of Minnesota Press.

—— (1996) *The Invention of Communication* (trans. S. Emanuel), Minneapolis, MN: University of Minnesota Press.

Mattelart, A., Delcourt, X. and Mattelart, M. (1984) *International Image Markets*, London: Comedia.

Mazzoleni, G. (1987) 'Media Logic and Party Logic in Campaign Coverage: The Italian General Election in 1983', *European Journal of Communication* 2 (1): 55–80.

—— (1992) 'Is there a Question of Vulnerable Values in Italy?', in J. Blumler (ed.) *Television and the Public Interest*, London: Sage.

Mazzoleni, G. and Schultz, W. (1999) 'Mediatization of Politics: A Challenge for Democracy', *Political Communication* 16: 247–61.

Meehan, E. (1999) 'Commodity, Culture, Common Sense: Media Research and Paradigm Dialogue', *Journal of Media Economics* 12 (2): 149–63.

Meier, W. and Trappel, J. (1998) 'Media Concentration and the Public Interest', in D. McQuail and K. Siune (eds) (1998) *Media Policy*, London: Sage.

Merrill, J. (1974) *The Imperatives of Freedom*, New York: Hastings House.

—— (2002) 'The Four Theories of the Press Four and a Half Decades Later: A Retrospective', *Journalism Studies* 3 (1): 133–4.

Michael, J. (1990) 'Regulating Communications Media: From the Discretion of Sound Chaps to the Arguments of Lawyers', in M. Ferguson (ed.) *Public Communication*, London: Sage.

Mill, J. S. (1998) [1859] *On Liberty*, Oxford: Oxford University Press.

Miller, D. and Dinan, W. (2000) 'The Rise of the PR Industry in Britain, 1979–98', *European Journal of Communication* 15 (1): 5–35.

Miller, T., Govil, N., McMurria, J., Maxwell, R. and Wang, T. (2005) *Global Hollywood 2*, London: BFI.

Mitchell, J., Blumler, J., Mounier, P. and Bundschuh, A. (eds) (1994) *Television and the Viewer Interest*, Luton: John Libbey.

Moog, S. and Sluyter-Beltrao, J. (2000) 'The Transformation of Political Communication?', in B. Axford and R. Huggins (eds) *New Media and Politics*, London: Sage.

Morley, D. and Robins, K. (1995a) *Spaces of Identity*, London: Routledge.

—— (1995b) 'Euroculture: Communication, Space and Time', in *Spaces of Identity*, London: Routledge.

Morris, N. and Waisbord, S. (eds) (2001) *Media and Globalization*, Lanham, MD: Rowman and Littlefield.

Morrison, D. and Tumber, H. (1988) *Journalists at War*, London: Sage.

Mortensen, F. (2004) 'Denmark', in M. Kelly *et al.* (eds) *The Media in Europe*, London: Sage.

Mosco, V. (1996) *The Political Economy of Communication*, London: Sage.

—— (2004) *The Digital Sublime*, Cambridge, MA: MIT Press.

Mosco, V. and Reddick, A. (1997) 'Political Economy, Communication and Policy', in M. Bailie, D. Winseck and S. Yoon (eds) *Democratizing Communication?*, Cresskill, NJ: Hampton Press.

Murdock, G. (1982) 'Large Corporations and the Control of the Communications Industries', in M. Gurevitch *et al.* (eds) *Culture, Society and the Media*, London: Routledge.

—— (1990) 'Redrawing the Map of the Communications Industries: Concentration and Ownership in the Era of Privatization', in M. Ferguson (ed.) *Public Communication*, London: Sage.

Murdock, G. (1992a) 'Embedded Persuasions: The Fall and Rise of Integrated Advertising', in D. Strinati and S. Wagg (eds) *Come on Down?* London: Routledge.

Murdock, G. (1992b) 'Citizens, Consumers, and Public Culture', in I. M. Skovmand and K. C. Schroder (eds) *Media Cultures: Reappraising Transnational Media*, London: Routledge.

—— (2000) 'Digital Futures: European Television in the Age of Convergence', in J. Wieten *et al.* (eds) *Television Across Europe*, London: Sage.

Murdock, G. and Golding, P. (1999) 'Common Markets: Corporate Ambitions and Communication Trends in the UK and Europe', *Journal of Media Economics* 12 (2): 117–32.

—— (2005) 'Culture, Communications and Political Economy', in J. Curran and M. Gurevitch (eds) *Mass Media and Society*, London: Hodder Arnold.

Murschetz, P. (1998) 'State Support for the Daily Press in Europe: A Critical Appraisal', *European Journal of Communication*, 13: 291–313.

Näränen, P. (2005) 'European Regulation of Digital Television', in A. Brown and R. Picard (eds) *Digital Terrestrial Television in Europe*, Mahwah, NJ: Lawrence Erlbaum.

Negrine, R. (1994) *Politics and the Mass Media in Britain*, 2nd edn, London: Routledge.

—— (1996) *The Communication of Politics*, London: Sage.

Negrine, R. and Papathanassopoulos, S. (1991) 'The Internationalization of Television', *European Journal of Communication* 6 (1): 9–32.

Negroponte, N. (1995) *Being Digital*, London: Hodder and Stoughton.

Negt, O. and Kluge, A. (1993) [1972] *Public Sphere and Experience* (trans. P. Labanyi, J. Owen Daniel and A. Oksiloff), Minneapolis, MN: University of Minnesota Press.

Negus, K. (1997) 'The Production of Culture', in P. Du Gay (ed.) *Production of Culture/Cultures of Production*, London: Sage.

—— (1999) *Music Genres and Corporate Cultures*, London: Routledge.

Neil, A. (1997) *Full Disclosure*, 2nd edn, London: Pan Books.

Nerone, J. (ed.) (1995) *Last Rights: Revisiting Four Theories of the Press*, Urbana, IL: University of Illinois Press.

—— (2002) 'The Four Theories of the Press Four and a Half Decades Later: A Retrospective', *Journalism Studies* 3 (1): 134–6.

Neveu, E. (1999) 'Politics on French Television', *European Journal of Communication* 14 (3): 379–409.

Newman, B. I. (1999) *The Mass Marketing of Politics*, Thousand Oaks, CA: Sage.

Nordenstreng, K. (2001) 'Epilogue', in N. Morris and S. Waisbord (eds) *Media and Globalization*, Lanham, MD: Rowman and Littlefield.

Nordenstreng, K. and Varis, T. (1974) *Television Traffic – A One-way Street*, Paris: UNESCO.

Nordicom (2007) *European Media Policy Newsletter*, No. 1. Available at www.nordicom.gu.se/mt/letter.php?id=76 (accessed 19 May 2007).

Norris, P. (1999) 'The Internet in Europe: A New North–South Divide?', *Harvard International Journal of Press/Politics* 5 (1): 1–12.

—— (2001) *Digital Divide*, Cambridge: Cambridge University Press.

Nowak, K. (1991) 'Television in Sweden 1986: Position and Prospects', in J. Blumler and T. Nossiter (eds) *Broadcasting Finance in Transition: A Comparative Handbook*, Oxford: Oxford University Press.

Nozick, R. (1974) *Anarchy, State and Utopia*, New York: Basic Books.

OECD [Organization for Economic Cooperation and Development] (2000) *Telecommunications Regulations*, DSTI/ICCCP/TISP (99) 15/FINAL, Paris: OECD.

Ofcom (2005) *The Ofcom Broadcasting Code*, London: Ofcom.

—— (2006a) *The Communications Market 2006 International*, London: Ofcom.

—— (2006b) *The Communications Market 2006* [UK], London: Ofcom.

—— (2007) *The Communications Market: Digital Progress Report*, London: Ofcom.

O'Malley, T. (1994) *Closedown? The BBC and Government Broadcasting Policy, 1979–92*, London: Pluto Press.

—— (1997) 'Labour and the 1947–9 Royal Commission on the Press', in M. Bromley and T. O'Malley (eds) *A Journalism Reader*, London: Routledge.

—— (1998) 'Demanding Accountability: The Press, the Royal Commissions and Pressure for Reform, 1945–77', in H. Stephenson and M. Bromley (eds) *Sex, Lies and Democracy*, London: Longman.

—— (2000) 'Part 1: The History of Self-Regulation', in T. O'Malley and C. Soley, *Regulating the Press*, London: Pluto Press.

Ó Siocrú, S., Girard, B. and Mahan, A. (2002) *Global Media Governance*, Lanham, MD: Rowman and Littlefield.

Ornebring, H. (2003) 'Televising the Public Sphere: Forty Years of Current Affairs Debate Programmes on Swedish Television', *European Journal of Communication* 18: 501–27.

OSI [Open Society Institute] and EUMAP [EU Monitoring and Advocacy Programme] (2005) *Television Across Europe*, Volume 1, Budapest: OSI.

Østbye, H. (2004) 'Norway', in M. Kelly *et al.* (eds) *The Media in Europe*, London: Sage.

Österlunnd-Karinkanta, M. (2004) 'Finland', in M. Kelly *et al.* (eds) *The Media in Europe*, London: Sage.

Ostini, J. and Fung, A. Y. H. (2002) 'Beyond the Four Theories of the Press: A New Model of National Media Systems', *Mass Communication & Society* 5 (1): 41–6.

Padioleau, J. (1985) *Le Monde et Le Washington Post: Précepteurs et Mousquetaires*, Paris: Presses Universitaires de France.

Page, B. (2003) *The Murdoch Archipelago*, London: Simon & Schuster.

Papathanassopoulos, S. (2001) 'Media Commercialization and Journalism in Greece', *European Journal of Communication* 16: 505–21.

—— (2002) *European Television in the Digital Age*, Cambridge: Polity Press.

Papatheodorou, F. and Machin, D. (2003) 'The Umbilical Cord that was Never Cut: The Post-dictatorial Intimacy Between the Political Elite and the Mass Media in Greece and Spain', *European Journal of Communication* 18 (1): 31–54.

Parnis, D. (2000) 'Tuning in the Future: Digital Technology and Commercial Radio Broadcasting in Canada', *Journal of Canadian Studies* 35 (3): 231–50.

Patelis, K. (2000) 'The Political Economy of the Internet', in J. Curran (ed.) *Media Organisations in Society*, London: Arnold.

Pauwels, C. and Loisen, J. (2003) 'The WTO and the Audiovisual Sector: Economic Free Trade vs Cultural Horse Trading?', *European Journal of Communication*, 18 (3): 291–313.

Pekic, B. (2007) '4.5 Million Italian Families Receive DTT', www.advanced-television.com/2007/july30_aug3.htm#m5 (accessed 19 Sept 2007).

Peterson, T. (1963) 'The Social Responsibility Theory', in F. S. Siebert *et al.*, *Four Theories of the Press*, Champaign, IL: University of Illinois Press.

Petley, J. and Romano, G. (1993) 'After the Deluge: Public Service Television in Western Europe', in T. Dowmunt (ed.) *Channels of Resistance*, London: BFI.

Pew Internet Project (2002) 'Getting Serious Online'. Available at www.pewinternet.org/reports.

Pfetsch, B. (2001) 'Political Communication Culture in the United States and Germany', *Harvard International Journal of Press/Politics* 6 (1): 46–67.

Pfetsch, B. and Esser, F. (2004) 'Comparing Political Communication: Reorientations in a Changing World', in F. Esser and B. Pfetsch (eds) *Comparing Political Communication*, Cambridge: Cambridge University Press.

Picard, R. (1985) *The Press and the Decline of Democracy*, Westport, CT: Greenwood Press.

Picard, R. (1989) *Media Economics*, Newburg Park, CA: Sage.

Pieterse, J. (1995) 'Globalization as Hybridization' in M. Featherstone, S. Lash and R. Robertson (eds) *Global Modernities*, London: Sage.

Pieterse, J. N. (2004) *Globalization or Empire*, New York: Routledge.

Pilkington Committee on Broadcasting (1962) *Report of the Committee on Broadcasting*, Cmnd. 1753, London: HMSO.

Pinto, M. and Sousa, H. (2004) 'Portugal', in M. Kelly *et al.* (eds) *The Media in Europe*, London: Sage.

Plasser, F. and Plasser, G. (2002) *Global Political Campaigning*, Westport, CT: Praeger.

Plasser, F., Scheucher, C. and Senft, C. (1999) 'Is there a European style of political marketing? A survey of political managers and consultants', in B. I. Newman (ed.) *Handbook of Political Marketing*, Thousand Oaks, CA: Sage Publications.

Poster, M. (1997) 'Cyberdemocracy: The Internet and the Public Sphere', in D. Holmes (ed.) *Virtual Politics*, London: Sage.

Postman, N. (1987) *Amusing Ourselves to Death*, London: Methuen.

Price, M. E. and Weinberg, J. (1996) 'United States (2)', in V. MacLeod (ed.) *Media Ownership and Control in the Age of Convergence*, London: IIC.

Raboy, M. (ed.) (2002) *Global Media Policy in the New Millennium*, Luton: University of Luton Press.

Radaelli, C. M. (1999) *Technocracy and the European Union*, London: Longman.

Raphael, C. (2001) 'The Web', in R. Maxwell (ed.) *Culture Works*, Minneapolis, MN: University of Minnesota Press.

Reith, J. (1924) *Broadcast Over Britain*, London: Hodder and Stoughton.

Remington, P. (2006) 'Comparing Media Systems: Three Models of Media and Politics', *Global Media Journal: Mediterranean Edition* 1(1): 141–4.

Report of the Committee on Financing the BBC (1986) Cmnd 9824, London: HMSO.

Rheingold, H. (1993) *The Virtual Community: Homesteading on the Electronic Frontier*, London: Secker and Warburg.

Rice, R. (1999) 'Artifacts and Paradoxes in New Media', *New Media and Society* 1 (1): 124–32.

Robertson, G. and Nicol, A. (2002) *Media Law*, 4th edn, London: Penguin.

Robins, K. (1997) 'What in the World's Going On?', in P. du Guy (ed.) *Production of Culture / Cultures of Production*, London: Sage.

Robins, K. and Aksoy, A. (2005) 'Whoever Looks Always Finds: Transnational Viewing and Knowledge-Experience', in J. K. Chalaby (ed.) *Transnational Television Worldwide*, New York: I.B. Tauris.

Roe, K. and De Meyer, G. (2000) 'Music Television: MTV-Europe', in J. Wieten *et al.* (eds) *Television Across Europe*, London: Sage.

Rollet, B. (1997) 'Television in France', in J. A. Coleman and B. Rollet (eds) *Television in Europe*, Exeter: Intellect.

Rose, R. (ed.) (1974) *Lessons from America*, London: Macmillan.

Rosengren, K., McLeod, K. and Blumler, J. (1992) 'Comparative communication research: from exploration to consolidation', in J. Blumler, J. McLeod and J. K. Rosengren (eds) (1992) *Comparatively Speaking: Communication and Culture Across Time and Space*, London: Sage.

SAGIT [Cultural Industries Sectoral Advisory Group on International Trade] (1999), *New Strategies for Culture and Trade*, Ottawa, Department of Foreign Affairs and International Trade.

Said, E. (1978) *Orientalism*, London: Penguin.

—— (1993) *Culture and Imperialism*, London: Chatto and Windus.

Sánchez-Ruiz, E. (2001) 'Globalization, Cultural Industries, and Free Trade: The Mexican Audiovisual Sector in the NAFTA Age', in V. Mosco and D. Schiller (eds) *Continental Order?* Lanham, MD: Rowman and Littlefield.

Sánchez-Tabernero, A., Denton, A., Lochon, P.-Y., Mounier, P. and Woldt, R. (1993) *Media Concentration in Europe*, Dusseldorf: European Institute for the Media.

Sánchez-Tabernero, A. and Carvajal, M. (2002) *Media Concentration in the European Market*, Universidad de Navarra.

Sarikakis, K. (2004) *Powers in Media Policy*, Bern: Peter Lang.

Sartori, G. (1966) 'European Political Parties: The Case of Polarized Pluralism', in J. La Palombara and M. Weiner (eds) *Political Parties and Political Development*, Princeton, NJ: Princeton University Press.

Scammel, M. (1998) 'The Wisdom of the War Room: US Campaigning and Americanization', *Media, Culture and Society* 20: 251–75.

Scannell, P. (1990) 'Public Service Broadcasting: the History of a Concept', in A. Goodwin and G. Whannel (eds) *Understanding Television*, London: Routledge.

Scannell, P. and D. Cardiff (1991) *A Social History of British Broadcasting: Serving the Nation, 1923–1939*, Oxford: Blackwell.

Schatz, T. (1997) 'The Return of the Hollywood Studio System', in E. Barnouw *et al.*, *Conglomerates and the Media*, New York: The New Press.

Schiller, D. (1981) *Objectivity and the News*, Philadelphia, PA: University of Pennsylvania Press.

—— (1996) *Theorising Communication*, New York: Oxford University Press.

—— (2000) *Digital Capitalism*, Cambridge, MA: MIT Press.

Schiller, H. (1992) *Mass Communications and American Empire*, 2nd edn, Boulder, CO: Westview Press [first edition 1969].

—— (1989) *Culture, Inc.* New York: Oxford University Press.

—— (1996) 'United States 1', in V. MacLeod (ed.), *Media Ownership and Control*, London: IIC.

—— (1998) 'Striving for Communication Dominance: A Half-Century Review', in D. Thussu (ed.) *Electronic Empires*, London: Arnold.

Schlesinger, P. (1991) *Media, State and Nation*, London: Sage.

—— (2001) 'Tensions in the Construction of European Media Policies', in N. Morris and S. Waisbord (eds) *Media and Globalization*, Lanham, MD: Rowman and Littlefield.

Schramm, W. (1964) *Mass Media and National Development*, Stanford, CA: Stanford University Press.

Schudson, M. (1978) *Discovering the News*, New York: Basic Books.

—— (2000) 'The Sociology of News Production Revisited (Again)', in J. Curran and M. Gurevitch (eds) *Mass Media and Society*, London: Arnold.

—— (2003) *The Sociology of News*, New York: W.W. Norton and Company.

Schulz, W., Zeh, R. and Quiring, O. (2005) 'Consequences of Media Change in Germany. Voters in a Changing Media Environment: A Data-Based Retrospective', *European Journal of Communication* 20 (1): 55–88.

Screen Digest (2007) 'Government Plans Public Broadcasting Shake-up' (15 January), www. screendigest.com (accessed 5 March 2007).

Seaton, J. (1998) 'A Fresh Look at Freedom of Speech', in J. Seaton (ed.) *Politics and the Media*, Oxford: The Political Quarterly.

—— (2003) 'Global Futures', in J, Curran and J. Seaton, *Power without Responsibility*, London: Routledge.

Seaton, J. and Pimlott, B. (1980) 'The Role of the Media in the Portuguese Revolution', in A. Smith (ed.) *Newspapers and Democracy*, Cambridge, MA: MIT Press.

Semetko, H. (1996) 'Political Balance on Television: Campaigns in the United States, Britain and Germany', *Harvard International Journal of Press/Politics* 1 (1): 51–71.

—— (2004) 'Media, Public Opinion and Political Action', in J. Downing *et al.* (eds) *The Sage Handbook of Media Studies*, London: Sage.

Semetko, H., Blumler, J., Gurevitch, M. and Weaver. D. (1991) *The Formation of Campaign Agendas: A Comparative Analysis of Party and Media Roles in Recent American and British Elections*, Hillside, NJ: Lawrence Erlbaum Associates.

Sepstrup, P. (1989) 'Implications of Current Developments in West European Broadcasting', *Media, Culture and Society* 11 (1): 29–54.

—— (1990) *Transnationalization of Television in Western Europe*, Luton: John Libbey.

Seymour-Ure, C. (1974) *The Political Impact of Mass Media*, London: Constable.

—— (1991) *The British Press and Broadcasting since 1945*, Oxford: Blackwell.

Shawcross, W. (1997) *Murdoch*, New York: Simon & Schuster.

Shoemaker, P. J. and Reese, S. D. (1996) *Mediating the Message*, New York: Longman.

Shohat, E. and Stam, R. (1994) *Unthinking Eurocentrism*, London: Routledge.

Siebert, F. S., Peterson, T. and Schramm, W. L. (1963) [1956] *Four Theories of the Press*, Urbana, IL: University of Illinois Press.

Sinclair, J., Jacka, E. and Cunningham, S. (1996) *New Patterns in Global Television*, Oxford: Oxford University Press.

Siune, K. and Hultén, O. (1998) 'Does Public Broadcasting Have a Future?', in D. McQuail and K. Siune (eds) *Media Policy*, London: Sage.

Siune, K. and Truetzschler, W. (eds) (1992) *Dynamics of Media Politics*, London: Sage.

Smith, Adam (1776) *The Wealth of Nations*. Available at www.adamsmith.org/smith/won-index.htm (accessed 20 July 2007).

Smith, A. (1979) *The Newspaper: An International History*, London: Thames & Hudson

—— (1993) *Books to Bytes*, London: BFI.

Smith, C. (1999) Speech to Royal Television Society Conference, 17 September. Available at www.digitaltelevision.gov.uk/press_notices/cdms245_99.html (accessed 23 July 2002).

Smulyan, S. (2001) *Selling Radio: The Commercialization of American Broadcasting, 1920–1934*, Washington, DC: Smithsonian Institution Press.

Snoddy, R. (1998) 'It's Our Job to Tell the Truth About the Corp', *The Times* (6 March): 45.

—— (2007) 'User Content Won't Kill Off Old Media', *Marketing* (17 January): 18.

Soley, L. (2002) *Censorship Inc.*, New York: Monthly Review Press.

Sparks, C. (1998a) *Communication, Capitalism and the Mass Media*, London: Sage.

—— (1998b) 'Is There a Global Public Sphere?', in D. Thussu (ed.) *Electronic Empires*, London: Arnold.

—— (1999) 'The Press', in J. Stokes and A. Reading (eds) *The Media in Britain*, London: Macmillan.

—— (2000a) 'The Global, the Local and the Public Sphere', in G. Wang, J. Servaes and A. Goonasekera (eds) *The New Communications Landscape*, London: Routledge.

—— (2000b) 'From Dead Trees to Live Wires: The Internet's Challenge to the Traditional Newspaper', in J. Curran and M. Gurevitch (eds) *Mass Media and Society*, London: Arnold.

—— (2000c) 'Media Theory After the Fall of European Communism: Why the Old Models from East and West Won't Do Any More', in J. Curran and M. Park (ed.) *De-Westernizing Media Theory*, London: Routledge.

—— (2001) 'The Internet and the Global Public Sphere', in W. L. Bennett and R. Entman (eds) *Mediated Politics*, Cambridge: Cambridge University Press.

—— (2004) 'The Impact of the Internet on the Existing Media', in A. Calabrese and C. Sparks (eds) *Toward a Political Economy of Culture*, Lanham, MD: Rowman and Littlefield.

Sparks, C. and Tulloch, J. (2000) (eds) *Tabloid Tales*, Lanham, MD: Rowman and Littlefield.

Squires, J. (1994) *Read All About It!* New York: Times Books.

Sreberny, A. (1997) 'The Many Cultural Faces of Imperialism', in P. Golding and P. Harris (eds) *Beyond Cultural Imperialism*, London: Sage.

Sreberny-Mohammadi, A. (1996) 'The Global and the Local in International Communication', in J. Curran and M. Gurevitch (eds) *Mass Media and Society*, London: Arnold.

Sterling, C. and Kitross, J. (2002) *Stay Tuned*, Mahwah, NJ: Lawrence Erlbaum.

Stratham, P. (1996) 'Berlusconi, the Media and the New Right in Italy', *Harvard International Journal Press/Politics* 1 (1): 87–106.

Straubhaar, J. (1997) 'Distinguishing the Global, Regional and National Levels of World Television', in A. Sreberny-Mohammadi, D. Winseck, J. McKenna and O. Boyd-Barrett (eds) *Media in Global Context*, London: Arnold.

—— (2002) '(Re)asserting National Television and National Identity Against the Global, Regional and Local Levels of World Television', in J. Chan and B. McIntyre (eds) *In Search of Boundaries*, Westport, CT: Ablex.

Steven, P. (2003) *The No-nonsense Guide to Global Media*, London: Verso.

Stevenson, N. (1999) *The Transformation of the Media*, Harlow: Longman.

Street, J. (2001) *Mass Media, Politics and Democracy*, London: Palgrave.

Streeter, T. (1996) *Selling the Air*, Chicago: University of Chicago Press.

—— (2004) 'Romanticism in Business Culture: The Internet, the 1990s, and the Origins of Irrational Exuberance', in A. Calabrese and C. Sparks (eds) *Toward a Political Economy of Culture*, Lanham, MD: Rowman and Littlefield.

Strinati, D. (1992) 'The Taste of America: Americanization and Popular Culture in Britain', in D. Strinati and S. Wagg (eds) (1992) *Come on Down?* London: Routledge.

Sturmer, C. (1993) 'MTV's Europe – An Imaginary Continent', in T. Dowunt (ed.) *Channels of Resistance*, London: BFI.

Swanson, D. L. (2004) 'Transnational Trends in Political Communication: Conventional Views and New Realities', in F. Esser and B. Pfetsch (eds) *Comparing Political Communication*, Cambridge: Cambridge University Press.

Sykes Committee (1923) *Report of the Broadcasting Committee* (Cmnd 1951), London: HMSO.

Syvertsen, T. (1991) 'Public Television in Crisis: Critiques Compared in Norway and Britain', *European Journal of Communication* 6 (1): 95–114.

Thompson, J. B. (1988) 'Mass Communication and Modern Culture: Contribution to a Critical Theory of Ideology', *Sociology* (22): 359–83.

—— (1990) *Ideology and Modern Culture*, London: Polity Press.

—— (1995) *The Media and Modernity*, Cambridge: Polity Press.

Thussu, D. (2006) *International Communication*, 2nd edn, London: Hodder Arnold.

Times, The (1985) 'The Times and the BBC: a statement' (19 June).

Tomlinson, J. (1991) *Cultural Imperialism*, London: Pinter.

—— (1999) *Globalization and Culture*, Cambridge: Polity Press.

Tongue, C. (1999) 'Culture or Monoculture – The European Audiovisual Challenge', in C. Marsden and S. Verhulst (eds) *Convergence in European Digital TV Regulation*, Blackstone Press.

Tracey, M. (1998) *The Decline and Fall of Public Service Broadcasting*, Oxford: Oxford University Press.

Trappel, J. (1992) 'Austria', in B. S. Østergaard (ed.) *The Media in Western Europe*, London: Sage.

—— (2004) 'Austria', in M. Kelly *et al.* (eds) *The Media in Europe*, London: Sage.

Trappel, J. and Meier, W. (1998) 'Media Concentration: Options for Policy', in D. McQuail and K. Siune (eds) *Media Policy*, London: Sage.

Truetzschler, W. (2004) 'Ireland', in M. Kelly, G. Mazzoleni and D. McQuail (eds) *The Media in Europe*, London: Sage.

Tunstall, J. (1977) *The Media are American*, London: Constable.

—— (1986) *Communications Deregulation*, Oxford: Blackwell.

—— (1996) *Newspaper Power*, Oxford: Oxford University Press.

—— (2008) *The Media were American*, Oxford: Oxford University Press

Tunstall, J. and Machin, D. (1999) *The Anglo-American Media Connection*, Oxford: Oxford University Press.

Tunstall, J. and Palmer, M. (1991) *Media Moguls*, London: Routledge.

Turow, J. (1997) *Breaking Up America: Advertisers and the New Media World*, Chicago, IL: University of Chicago Press.

Underwood, D. (1995) *When MBAs Rule the Newsroom*, New York: Columbia University Press.

UNESCO (1963) *Statistics on Radio and Television 1950–1960*, Paris: UNESCO.

—— (1999) *Preserving Media Independence: Regulatory Frameworks* (compiled by C. Hamelink), Paris: UNESCO.

—— (1997) *World Communication Report*, Paris: UNESCO.

—— (2003) *Institute for Statistics – Culture and Communication Sector*, Paris: UNESCO.

—— (2005a) *International fFows of Selected Cultural Goods and Services 1994–2003*, Paris: UNESCO.

—— (2005b) *Convention on the Protection and Promotion of the Diversity of Cultural Expressions*, Paris: UNESCO.

United States (2000) *Communication from the United States: Audiovisual and Related Services*, 18 December, S/CSS/W/21. Available at: http://docsonline.wto.org.

Usherwood, B. (1997) 'Transnational Publishing: The Case of Elle Decoration', in M. Nava, *et al.* (eds) *Buy This Book*, London: Routledge.

Van Cuilenburg, J. and McQuail, D. (2000) 'Media Policy Paradigm Shifts: In Search of a New Communications Policy Paradigm', in B. Cammerts and J.-C. Burgelman (eds) *Beyond Competition*, Brussels: VUB University Press.

Van Dijk, J. (2005) *The Deepening Divide*, London: Sage.

Van Miert, K. (1997) 'The Impact of Digital Technologies on the Telecommunications and Television Sectors', speech in Rome (12 June).

Varis, T. (1985) *International Flow of TV Programmes*, Paris: UNESCO.

Veronis Suhler Stevenson (2005) *Communications Industry Forecast Highlights* www.vss.com/pubs/pubs_cif_highlights.html (accessed 10 May 2007).

Voices 21 (2002) 'A Global Movement for People's Voices in Media and Communication in the 21st Century', in M. Raboy (ed.) *Global Media Policy in the New Millennium*, Luton: University of Luton Press.

Voorhoof, D. (1995) *Critical Perspectives on the Scope and Interpretation of Article 10 of the European Convention on Human Rights*, Mass media files No. 10, Strasbourg: Council of Europe.

Wallerstein, I. (1974, 1980, 1989) *The Modern World-System* (3 vols), New York: Academic Press.

—— (2006) *World-Systems Analysis*, Durham, NC: Duke University Press.

Wang, G. and Servaes, J. (2000) 'Introduction', in G. Wang, J. Servaes and A. Goonasekera (eds) *The New Communications Landscape*, London: Routledge.

WARC (World Advertising Research Center) (2006) *Media Report Global Newspaper Trends*, Henley on Thames: WARC.

Ward, D. with Carsten Fueg, O. and D'Armo, A. (2004) *A Mapping Study of Media Concentration and Ownership in Ten European Countries*, Hilversum, Netherlands: Commissariaat Voor De Media.

Ward, K. (1989) *Mass Communication and the Modern World*, Basingstoke: Macmillan.

Wasko, J. (1994) *Hollywood in the Information Age*, Cambridge: Polity Press.

Waterman, D. (1988) 'World Television Trade: The Economic Effects of Privatization and New Technology', *Telecommunications Review*, 12 (2): 141–51.

Waters, M. (1995) *Globalization*, London: Routledge.

Webster, F. (2002) *Theories of the Information Society*, 2nd edn, London: Routledge.

Weiss, L. (1998) *The Myth of the Powerless State*, Cambridge: Polity Press.

Weymouth, A. (1996) 'Introduction: The Role of the Media in Western Europe', in A. Weymouth and B. Lamizet (eds) *Markets and Myths*, London: Longman.

Whish, R. (1989) *Competition Law*, London: Butterworths.

Whitehead, P. (1997) *The Protection of Minors and Human Dignity*, Brussels: EP.

Wieten, J., Murdock, G. and Dahlgren, P. (eds) (2000) *Television Across Europe: A Comparative Introduction*, London: Sage.

Williams, G. (1996) *Britain's Media: How They Are Related*, London: Campaign for Press and Broadcasting Freedom.

—— (2007) 'From Isolation to Consensus: The UK's Role in the Revision Process of the Television Without Frontiers Directive', *Westminster Papers in Communication and Culture* 4 (3): 26–45.

Williams, K. (1998) *Get Me a Murder a Day!* London: Arnold.

—— (2005) *European Media Studies*, London: Hodder Arnold.

Williams, R. (1974) *Television: Technology and Cultural Form*, London: Fontana.

—— (1976) *Communications*, 3rd edn, London: Penguin.

—— (1977) *Marxism and Literature*, Oxford: Oxford University Press.

—— (1980) 'Base and Superstructure in Marxist Cultural Theory', in R. Williams, *Problems in Materialism and Culture: Selected Essays*, London: Verso.

—— (1983) [1976] *Keywords*, London: Fontana.

—— (1989) *Resources of Hope*, London: Verso.

Wilson, H. H. (1961) *Pressure Group*, London: Secker & Warburg.

Winseck, D. (1998) 'Pursuing the Holy Grail: Information Highways and Media Reconvergence in Britain and Canada', *European Journal of Communication* 13 (3): 337–74.

Wolf, M. (1999) *The Entertainment Economy*, London: Penguin.

World Association of Newspapers [WAN], *World Press Trends 2005*, Paris: WAN.

Zenith Optimedia (2007) 'Rocketing Internet Advertising to Overtake Radio a Year Early' (Press Release, 20 March), London: Zenith Optimedia.

Index

Related titles from Routledge

Television Entertainment

Jonathan Gray

Television entertainment rules supreme, one of the world's most important disseminators of information, ideas, and amusement. More than a parade of little figures in a box, it is deeply embedded in everyday life, in how we think, what we think and care about, and who we think and care about it with.

But is television entertainment art? Why do so many love it and so many hate or fear it? Does it offer a window to the world, or images of a fake world? How is it political and how does it address us as citizens? What powers does it hold, and what powers do we have over it? Or, for that matter, what is television these days, in an era of rapidly developing technologies, media platforms, and globalization?

Television Entertainment addresses these and other key questions that we regularly ask, or should ask, offering a lively and dynamic, thematically based overview that offers examples from recent and current television, including *Lost*, reality television, *The Sopranos*, *The Simpsons*, political satire, *Grey's Anatomy*, *The West Wing*, soaps, and *24*.

Communication and Society
Series Editor: James Curran

ISBN13: 978-0-415-77223-5 (hbk)
ISBN13: 978-0-415-77224-2 (pbk)

Available at all good bookshops
For ordering and further information please visit:
www.routledge.com

Related titles from Routledge
The Mediation of Power
A Critical Introduction
Aeron Davis

The Mediation of Power investigates how those in positions of power use and are influenced by media in their everyday activities. Each chapter examines this theme through an exploration of some of the key topic areas and debates in the field. The topics covered are:

* theories of media and power
* media policy and the economics of information
* news production and journalistic practice
* public relations and media management
* culture and power
* political communication and mediated politics
* new and alternative media
* interest group communications
* media audiences and effects.

In addition, the book presents a series of critical dialogues with the traditional paradigms in the field. These are rethought, supplemented or discarded altogether. The discussions are illustrated with original research material from a range of communication environments and case study examples. These document stock market crashes, e-democracy, the subcultures of the London Stock Exchange and Westminster Parliament, the strategies of corporate and political spin doctors, mass media influences on politicians and the Make Poverty History campaign.

The debates are enlivened by first-hand accounts taken from over 200 high-profile interviews with politicians, journalists, public officials, spin doctors, campaigners and captains of industry. Tim Bell, David Blunkett, Iain Duncan Smith, Simon Heffer, David Hill, Simon Hughes, Trevor Kavanagh, Neil Kinnock, Peter Riddell, Polly Toynbee, Michael White and Ann Widdecombe are some of those cited.

Communication and Society
Series Editor: James Curran

ISBN13: 978-0-415-40490-7 (hbk)
ISBN13: 978-0-415-40491-4 (pbk)

Available at all good bookshops
For ordering and further information please visit:
www.routledge.com